Fool's Gold

By the same author

*The Lights of Liberalism: University Liberals and the
Challenge of Democracy*

Scotland and Nationalism: Politics and Culture

No Gods and Precious Few Heroes: Scotland since 1914

*The Centre of Things: Political Fiction in Britain from
Disraeli to the Present*

Cultural Weapons: Scotland and Survival in a New Europe

The Rise of Regional Europe

Fool's Gold
The Story of North Sea Oil

CHRISTOPHER HARVIE

Gluck. Was war das?
Wenn kommt es wieder?

Erich Fried

HAMISH HAMILTON · LONDON

HAMISH HAMILTON LTD
Published by the Penguin Group
Penguin Books Ltd, 27 Wrights Lane, London w8 5tz, England
Penguin Books USA Inc., 375 Hudson Street, New York, New York 10014, USA
Penguin Books Australia Ltd, Ringwood, Victoria, Australia
Penguin Books Canada Ltd, 10 Alcorn Avenue, Toronto, Ontario, Canada m4v 3b2
Penguin Books (NZ) Ltd, 182–190 Wairau Road, Auckland 10, New Zealand

Penguin Books Ltd, Registered Offices: Harmondsworth, Middlesex, England

First published 1994
1 3 5 7 9 10 8 6 4 2

Typeset by Datix International Limited, Bungay, Suffolk
Set in 11.5/14 pt Monophoto Bembo
Printed in Great Britain by Clays Ltd, St Ives plc

A CIP catalogue record for this book is available from the British Library

ISBN 0–241–13352–1

Contents

Preface and Acknowledgements

Christopher Smout, then Professor of Scottish history at St Andrews, set me off on this trail, when he asked in 1988 for a paper connected with 'Scotland and the Sea'. With Stephen Maxwell, publicity chief of the Scottish National Party in the 1970s, I sketched an essay in contemporary history which proved almost alarmingly interdisciplinary in scope. The idea of a piece of 'contemporary economic history' impressed Kate Jones of Hamish Hamilton, and then impelled Denys Blakeway, fresh from *Thatcher: The Downing Street Years*, into a linked project, for a documentary film series. This altered the direction of the book. Feeding Denys and Leonie Jameson with chapters, against a strict time-schedule, seemed the irritant necessary to open the project out into a cultural and political account of the central fact of British history in the 1970s and 1980s.

In this process, George Dangerfield's *The Strange Death of Liberal England*, of 1934, kept recurring to mind. Though I couldn't hope to match his narrative skills, I had to keep the reader's mind on the story, a demanding task when so little had been written about the history – as opposed to the economics or technology – of North Sea Oil. The coverage of it in the biographies of politicians reads like Louis XVI's diary entry for 14 July 1789: 'rien'. Only Tony Benn, Nigel Lawson and Edmund Dell had troubled even to record their own part, although Gerry Corti's and Frank Frazer's 1983 account, *The Nation's Oil*, was of great value. My main resource was the *Economist*, the *Financial Times*, the *Scotsman* and the statistical series and learned journals that were accessible in the British Library of Political and Economic Science, the City Business Library, Tübingen University or

vi

at the National Library of Wales. From these came the framework of this account.

W. G. Carson characterized the North Sea Oil business as 'the political economy of speed'. The relevance of this was dramatized when Tony Benn MP, Energy Minister, 1975–9, offered me the run of his huge archive, only a small section of which did I have time to tackle. Utilization of this sort of resource will inevitably affect the definitive accounts of detailed policies which remain to be written. But, the more material opened up before me, the more I became convinced that a story had formed which it was essential to put across, with what abilities I had, as soon as possible. The winning of the oil required technical changes amounting to an industrial revolution, but half-way through it another revolution of information technology and instantaneous communication, coupled with the political revolution of 1989–90, had altered the landscape overwhelmingly.

By bankrolling the dynamism of Mrs Thatcher, Britain's oil played a part in funding the ideology of such changes – just as the gold of the Andes sustained imperial Spain and the Counter-Reformation. As, in the mid-1990s, we try to cope with the consequences both of a 'wasted windfall' and of butchered political conventions, its history has become a necessity.

North Sea Oil was something which, in the 1970s, I saw close-up, recording impressions and interviews; but I owe much to my colleague Professor Roland Sturm in making available material on regional economics and policy which he had collected at that time. This was to be supplemented by interviews in 1993 and 1994, and I must also thank Sir Iain Noble, Hamish Morrison of the Scottish Council, Christopher Roundell, George Rosie and Tom Nairn, Professor Gavin McCrone, late of the Scottish Office, and Professor John Foster of Paisley University, Bob Campbell, Magnus Linklater and Frank Frazer of the *Scotsman* – and, of course, Alastair Dunnett. Alan Campbell of Grampian Regional Council sent much useful material. On the cultural side I am much indebted to the Revd Andrew Ross, Isobel and Bob Tait, Angus Calder, Professor Douglas Dunn, John McGrath, and

George Bruce. Dr Gordon Wilson, Jim Sillars, Billy Wolfe, Stephen Maxwell and Alex Salmond gave much information on the connections between oil and Scottish nationalism. Professor Bernard Crick and Principal Kenneth Morgan, biographer of James Callaghan, were similarly helpful from the Labour party side, as was Dr Iain MacLean of Nuffield College, Oxford. The Scottish political background was illuminated by Douglas MacLeod and John Milne of the BBC. I am particularly grateful to the Hon. Richard Funkhouser, United States Consul General in Edinburgh for his memories of oil affairs and Scottish politics in the mid-1970s. Besides many illuminating comments, Neal Ascherson also contributed the epigraph on the title page – 'Good fortune. What was that? When will it come again?' – from Erich Fried.

As far as the process of writing and publishing is concerned, I am much indebted to Kate Jones, Katharina Bielenberg, Charles Drazin and Keith Taylor of Hamish Hamilton, to Denys Blakeway and Leonie Jameson of Fine Art Films, to the staff of *Planet* magazine in Aberystwyth, and, as ever, to the sagacity of Tony Peake. At Tübingen my assistant Carola Ehrlich keyed in early drafts and kept my files in a state which made redrafting and cross-referencing easy. Paddy Bort collected much material from the German press, and Thomas Rommel and J. P. Schnierer intervened at crucial moments when academic life and computer seemed about to emulate John Stuart Mill's maid incinerating Carlyle's *French Revolution*. My wife Virginia read and commented on the manuscript, offering encouragement at moments of indecisiveness; and my daughter Alison was very tolerant of paternal preoccupation and irritation; as ever, my family in Scotland was endlessly hospitable.

While writing, I have found myself continually in the debt of three ladies, respectively from Scotland, England and Wales, children during the years covered by Dangerfield and veterans of a pre-oil society. Their kindness, support and effervescent interest in past, present and future have been a marvellous bonus for my family. This book is for Jessie Harvie, Lydia Roundell and Sophia Thomas.

Introduction

Discovery

'I think we have something special. You will find it different
from what you expect.'

The drilling-rig *Sea Quest* was unusual. Of the fifty or so working
in the North Sea in the summer of 1969, she was one of the
handful built in Britain, or at least in a Northern Ireland undis-
turbed in 1967 by bomb and bullet. The Protestant workers who
had welded her strange but striking shape – an equilateral triangle
of deck, supported by three huge columns resting on submersible
pontoons – were the sons of the men who had built the *Titanic*.

Sea Quest, owned by British Petroleum, was under charter to
the American Oil Company (Amoco), a company with years of
gas-drilling behind it, and a couple of billion barrels of reserves,
world-wide. Its crew was as secretive in its transmissions as a
Lowestoft trawler out after haddock. They used a code in which
numbers were represented by the names of American universities –
Texas, Notre Dame, Rice – and these numbers were changed
each day. In September, *Sea Quest* was drilling in block 22/17,
about 150 miles east of Aberdeen, for which Amoco had the
exploration rights in partnership with British Gas, Texas Eastern
and Amerada. Brendon MacKeown, a geologist, was flying
reports by helicopter to Mitch Watt at the exploration headquarters in Great Yarmouth, 400 miles south. One had obviously
hit the button:

I suspected from the information that was available on the logs that we
would see good oil. The most significant thing was to see if the pressure

I

and the flow would stabilize over a period of time. As soon as the valves opened we knew we had a winner . . .

None of us were prepared for oil. We thought we might find some gas or at the most watery oil traces, so I didn't have any stainless-steel containers. I had to clean out an empty pickle jar from the mess hall to collect the sample.

It was what we call sweet oil with not a trace of hydrogen sulphide. Mitch then poured it into an ashtray on his desk and set it alight and it burned well. But unfortunately the heat caused the ashtray to crack and the bloody stuff spilled all over the floor.[1]

Interrogation

Twenty-five years have passed since *Sea Quest* found the Montrose field. After a search of five years, several false leads and a couple of disasters, commercially exploitable oilfields had been detected beneath the North Sea. In 1977, the Prime Minister, James Callaghan, said, 'God has given Britain her best opportunity for one hundred years in the shape of North Sea oil.'[2] In 1994, dissension exists about what actually remains. Annual production, rising to a second peak in the mid-1990s at around 110 million tons (one ton of oil equals 7.5 barrels), will eat into about 1,900 million tons in reserves; this would give around seventeen years' life to the North Sea, with supply dwindling away in the second decade of the new millennium.[3] But the upper projections reach as high as 7,000 million tons, accessible through new technology and a higher price of oil. There could be new fields in the North Atlantic, Celtic Sea, Cardigan Bay and Purbeck; 'second genera-tion' discoveries in the strata of existing fields; more efficient extraction methods lowering overheads. Oil was a bright spot in the 1994 economy, with a 37 per cent increase in output up to June. But the North Sea, after bringing in £100 billion between 1977 and 1985, had done little to solve Britain's balance of payments problem.[4] Indeed, as the oil price fell – only £42 billions' worth was sold between 1986 and 1990 – the oil industry itself retreated mysteriously into the background, overshadowed by the battle of Thatcherism: for and against, even though such economic success as the Conservatives enjoyed largely depended on oil's ability to turn Britain's perennial balance of payments deficit into a glittering surplus. Ministers themselves admitted as much:

The direct contribution of North Sea oil output to the balance of payments, taking into account both the reduction in oil imports and the current level of net oil exports, can be gauged from the total value of continental shelf oil sales, which in 1983 amounted to £17 billion.[5]

The rise and fall of Britain's 'third industrial revolution' has never been adequately dealt with *as history*. This seems incredible when one contrasts it with the other great – and tragic – upheaval which began in 1968, only a year before *Sea Quest's* discovery. There are scores of books about Northern Ireland, and a like number dealing with the career of Margaret Thatcher, in reverence or execration. Britain in the 1980s may have undergone a renaissance of sorts; friend and foe alike had to admit that Thatcher made a world impact, for good or ill.[6] Yet the pathological, not the exemplary, preoccupied writers about the country. Monarchy as 'the glamour of backwardness', national and class conflict, the fossilizing of history into heritage, the retreat from industry: all these preoccupied social critics from right and left – Tom Nairn, Hugh Thomas, Norman Stone, David Cannadine. What had once bound together now seemed to throttle. Yet the huge North Sea achievement (and it was an achievement, whatever the uses to which the wealth was put) somehow failed to figure. Perhaps this was because, with it, commentators had to deal with an issue which in its complexity went beyond the conventional categories of politics, economics and history, and so was difficult to handle; particularly by a society which was no longer speaking a common political language.

Hence the secondary concern of this book. In Chapter 1 I use a quotation from Tennyson as a prologue, for two reasons. First, the Arthurian epic was always a symbol of 'British' rebirth, a

Welsh legend tailored to emphasize the collaborative power of the nationalities of 'the island of the mighty'. Second, because Tennyson, looking out from Somersby in Lincolnshire on the very seas under which the rigs would find enough natural gas to heat and cook for the country for several decades, would have appreciated – if not commended – the sort of science necessary to set up the machinery for extracting oil from one of the world's most difficult terrains.

Much the same qualifications applied to oil as those which informed Merlin's solemn advice to Arthur on Excalibur: choose the right time and then use it decisively. But the oil did not come as a gift. It also consumed up to a quarter of British industrial investment in the 1970s and 1980s. The money had to come from somewhere; and the profit from the venture also depended on external factors. The oil issue was in no way crude, but complex. It required that grasp of the totality of their society and its culture which – despite its headlong transformation – the Victorians possessed. Matthew Arnold called it 'insight'. In the 1860s Tennyson and Gladstone had agonized over the coal question: the economist Stanley Jevons's calculation that Britain's coal reserves might run out. Arnold himself used this *angst* in *Culture and Anarchy* (1868) as a stick with which to beat his 'philistines'.[7] Yet the far greater incident of the oil discoveries inspired no equivalent curiosity or pride among the élite or the masses of 1970s Britain. Why?

North Sea oil meant engineering which rivalled in scale some of the greatest schemes of the nineteenth or twentieth centuries – production platforms the height of the Post Office Tower; ports and oil terminals which dwarfed the Mulberry Harbours of D-Day; gas-turbine generators which could light a city the size of Aberdeen. It also involved considerable risks to those employed in it – something made tragically apparent in the Piper Alpha disaster of July 1988. Yet despite Britain's, and in particular Scotland's, expertise in engineering, the bulk of orders for equipment went overseas, particularly to the United States, Norway, Japan and the Netherlands. Was this because of the speed of development demanded by government policy in 1973? Or because oil was discovered on the 'wrong side' of Scotland? Had Britain come too late to a technology which was already highly sophisticated? Or had 'de-industrialization' already gone too far?

British offshore technology might be limited, but the finance and organization necessary to fund exploration and production caused vast changes in banking and created new financial networks. The Scots regarded themselves as particularly good at this, and for the first time many became aware of the huge, globally sensitive complex of financial services and fund management centred on Edinburgh's Charlotte Square. But doubts remained. Did this cousinhood of lawyers, accountants and bankers create the sort of international co-operation required (of which the Thompson Organisation's partnership with Armand Hammer's Occidental Petroleum in the Piper field was exemplary), or were the oil operations incidental to a business which was increasingly multinational and heedless of local élites, let alone local social problems? Were the real beneficiaries not the industrialists but the speculators?

The finance and control of the oil business were deeply affected after 1974 by the election of a Labour government with a tiny majority and formidable problems. It created a 'national interest' in the shape of the British National Oil Corporation, and this was defended by the radical Energy minister Tony Benn in a battle with the Common Market, the American majors and, not least, the two 'British-based' multinationals, Shell and BP. In Benn's campaign there could be seen one *étatiste* prescription for the reconstruction of the British economy. Did it have any chance of success?

But the 'oil factor' had its drawbacks, even if the sea yielded its bounty efficiently and the price per barrel kept up. Would a high pound penalize traditional export areas? Was it a better strategy, as some Conservatives argued – and after 1979 put into practice – to reverse much of Labour's industry-sensitive approach, and encourage tax reductions and overseas investment instead? Or would this tend to benefit the other industrial powers, notably the Federal Republic of Germany, which was both the principal purchaser of the oil and the main recipient of British investment? Indeed, by the mid-1990s was anything left of the oil windfall, in a country characterized by manufacturing decline, a large balance of payments deficit, continuing low productivity, and burgeoning social problems?

How much autonomy, finally, did any British government have? Was the price of oil not decided as much by politics as economics, with the North Sea temporarily important because Middle Eastern affairs had moved it from being a marginal production area to one of tactical significance? Were its creators not the British, or even the majors, but the Arabs who dominated the Organization of Petroleum Exporting Countries (OPEC), whose 'oil muscle' increased the price of crude sixfold in 1973–4 in the master-stroke of energy politics, and whose grasp of their cartel fatally loosened a decade later, letting oil prices fall again and bringing the windfall to an end?

The Arabs were not the only nationalists around. Exploiting this hazardous sea was difficult enough for British governments distracted by labour unrest, civil war in Ulster and the Rhodesian rebellion, all of which impacted on the energy issue. Was the necessary co-ordination frustrated by the political implications of energy policy in a centralized state made up of mutinous nations – particularly Scotland, where the Scottish National Party, with almost a third of the popular vote in 1974, threatened secession from the United Kingdom? This quickly supplemented an energy crisis with a constitutional one. Did this divert politics from industrial issues? Or even if the devolution exercise was negated by the result of the referendum of 1 March 1979, did it buy time for the British establishment to get its hands on the oil?

During the 1980s Anglo-Scottish relationships continued to change, and with them the political complexion of a country which already enjoyed a substantial degree of administrative devolution. More fundamental nationalist impulses were being released whose impact has yet to be understood, let alone resolved. An energetic and unapologetic international capitalism, rooted in two less-than-stable regions – Texas and the Middle East – had taken on an ageing centralized state. A Scotland whose political culture was both semi-collectivist (Neal Ascherson thought it closer to Poland than to London) and post-imperial found itself being 'colonized'. What was the upshot of this for the people involved, and their attempt to control their lives? Where did the image of a new Klondyke, on the rigs, platforms and onshore installations, give way to a reality of unpredictable, primitive conditions, exploitation and often desperate isolation? Could there even be any countervailing solidarity in a dispersed work-force which only came together for a fortnight of punishing twelve-hour shifts?

Oil had ramifying cultural and human consequences in a country jolted by the decline of traditional heavy industries. These were filtered by a complicated civil society, by a trade-union movement which shifted from being a labour organization to becoming a 'national forum', by observation of another small country, Norway, coping with the oil challenge, and by a remarkable Scottish cultural renaissance in the 1970s and 1980s. Evident in productions such as John McGrath's *The Cheviot, the Stag, and the Black, Black Oil* and Bill Forsyth's *Local Hero*, and in a more allegorical way in the novels of Alasdair Gray, what did 'oil culture' do to Scottish – and to English – *mentalités*? Did such a transformation lie behind the rapid decline of British loyalties, and the popularity of appeals for 'an independent Scotland in a united Europe' which threatened by the mid-1990s to wipe Conservatism off the Scots political map?

The oil story is not over, but has the time for British economic and industrial reconstruction now passed? Or perhaps, to use the language of the oilfields, this 'weather-window' had never really existed, circumstances being far more complex than many made out? Was the oil even a political and ecological disadvantage? Other countries had after 1974 an enforced and salutary education in energy policy, conservation and transport reforms – insulation, wave power, railway modernization. In Britain these were shelved by a government which was either dogmatic or lazy, while conventional energy resources were easily available. Is the continuing deterioration of the land and sea environment, as much as Anglo-Scottish relations, a reflection both of the uncertain future of the Union, and of the failure of 'Britain' to function as a political or moral community which treats such questions seriously?

An introduction is not the place for explanations. But the more questions one tackles, the more they seem to multiply; despite the wealth of writing on the subject, it remains oddly disarticulated. Treatments of oil in its various aspects – technology, economics, entrepreneurship, policy-making, social impact – seem to stand by themselves, failing to communicate. How much is this the product of the subdivided nature of modern research, where the specialized treatise has by definition to be self-limiting? Or of the vastness of the topic? Or is it something to do with the nature of the political community which found itself under stress?

Which takes us back to Tennyson. The public morality of his age was important to him, but by the 1960s a dissociation of sensibility seemed to have gripped his successors. Discussion of oil, its use and abuse, seemed to vanish into a morass of specialism and shop-talk. Which fact was the more bizarre: that three lengthy biographies published in 1992 and 1993 of Harold Wilson, Prime Minister when gas from the North Sea revolutionized one part of the country's energy supply, when oil was first discovered, and when the essential interventionist legislation was passed, mentioned the subject not once?[8] Or that, while in the 1980s oil guaranteed the country's income and bankrolled the messianic style of Mrs Thatcher, it vanished almost completely from her version of British history?[9] In its turn the Thatcher 'miracle' became of fateful significance in formulating the 'shock therapy' of new economic policies in a fast-changing Eastern Europe after 1989. The jury is still out on that one.

Oil could have been used by the British establishment as an experiment in 'designing change' and securing industrial modernization through conscious social planning, but by the late 1980s this establishment, what Lord Annan called *Our Age*,[10] seemed fatally weakened. Did the multinational origins of its successor's wealth – in City speculation, property, tax havens – mould the image of a self-serving plutocracy, calculating only with reference to its own cash outcomes? Had the people who mocked the crassness of the Texan Bunker Hunts and high-rolling oil sheikhs not ended up behaving rather like them? At issue was the competence of the British state. It had been given a mighty opportunity to rebuild itself. What had it done with it? The answer to this lay not just in economic policy but in the facility with which the national culture – the principles inherent in British social arrangements – could make the necessary connections between technology, economics and politics. Was it still capable of doing so? And if it was not, who carries the blame?

Our Age?

Finally, I have to interrogate my own motives for writing this: not out of self-advertisement, but because the historian is part of the history he or she writes. Guy Arnold's *Britain's Oil* (1977) was an important source of material in its time; my own book, *Scotland and Nationalism*, figured therein and the picture given in it of the development and the programme of a Scottish national movement which extended beyond the Scottish National Party.[11] In 1977 I was a critic of the SNP. Since 1989 I have been a member. One has to come clean. It is not the business of an historian to project a political interpretation, yet the selection of evidence is inevitably affected by the direction which he or she sees affairs taking. Carlyle wouldn't have written on the French Revolution had he not regarded it as a *Zeitbruch*, after which the nature of history was quite different. The global events of the two decades since 1973 have made the Britain which, in a reformed, federalized form, was worth the struggle in 1977 seem much less of a cause today. It has been overtaken by the need to safeguard communities from an insensate international commerce, and the need for environmental and economic co-operation. The oil episode seemed to me to demonstrate that the nation-state had had its day, and Europe – and Scotland – were worth the commitment.

Politics apart, I have tried to tell a story and to fit it into a broader historical context. The author's experience matters in so far as it illuminates a particular political and interpretive *milieu*, even if at times one feels like Stendhal's Fabrizio, galloping round the battlefield and trying to find out what is going on at its centre. Yet Scotland was anything but marginal in the 1970s; not just because the oil business was tangibly close, but because it reacted on an argumentative, practical society moulded by technology and ideology. Someone from a Scottish middle-class background, from a family of engineers, attending the High School of Edinburgh, and the university in the 1960s, involved in the Labour Party in Edinburgh, inevitably felt, like J.M. Barrie describing the onset of the factory age in Angus, that 'a giant had entered our native place in the night'; like most of my contemporaries, I tried to make something of it.

In contrast with the political amnesia of the Wilson biographers and Thatcher – and they can be taken as broadly representative of the metropolitan élite, left and right – the Scots in the 1970s, the people who ran the parties, argued in pubs, phoned up about articles or broadcasts, could not avoid the offshore issue. David Steel, Gordon Brown, John Smith and Robin Cook influenced and were influenced by 'oil politics', in its widest sense, on the Liberal and Labour side. Stephen Maxwell and Billy Wolfe in part created the Nationalist policy. Malcolm Rifkind, James Mackay and Andrew Neil wriggled their way into the metropolitan establishment with the help that oil gave Scottish career prospects. Bob Tait, Jonathan Wills and George Rosie, Neal Ascherson and Tom Nairn, were among those – whom the Germans would call *Publizists* rather than journalists – who created a climate of opinion about it. More academic interpretations – by John Kay, Iain MacLean, William Miller – of aspects of the oil and nationalism issue, analysing its financial and political impact, emanated from school-friends and contemporaries.

The result has given the British political class in the 1980s and 1990s a marked Scottish element. At the same time it has done little for the Union. Few people seemed to know more about oil, without making money out of it, than the Anglo-Scots. But élite they were not; success is the essential qualification of an élite. And what remains of that centralized and centrist élitism, of the statistics of W.L. Guttsmann,[12] or Noel Annan's mandarinate in *Our Age*, with its 'effortless superiority'? Cook, Smith and so on aimed at the commanding heights of British politics. But were the heights commanding enough, particularly after the upheavals of 1989–92?

Was this generation business sheer coincidence? It could be, but Scotland at this juncture was peculiarly sensitive. Ian Jack, in *Before the Oil Ran Out*, has shown, out of his own experience, how 'his age' found itself in a second historical transition: between empire and civic identity. Our parents had experienced the war; we grew up in a community in which heavy industry still dominated, where the kirk or left-wing politics still prescribed – with quasi-utopian goals in mind – most of the activities of the week. Scottish nationalism did not fit easily into this, as a glance at *Scotland and Nationalism* will show; but Scottish ways of thinking did. The sense of deducing social action from an interpretive philosophy, a legacy of the Enlightenment, if not of Calvinism, intervened when one tried to fathom a new and dramatic situation.

The impact of a technology as elaborate and apparently alien as that of oil extraction meant that a lot of learning went on in those two decades. Partly grasping what it meant and where it was likely to go; chiefly, perhaps, realizing that we were no longer, however guiltily, the exploiters, but the exploited. The American sociologist Michael Hechter's 'internal colonization' theory, unhelpful where he placed it – in Scottish history – seemed to fit the Scottish present. Were we just there to spectate knowingly on the barbarians – whether Texan oilmen or City dealers – just as, two hundred years ago, the Brahmins had regarded the Scots soldiers and civilians who took over India? Or could we get out of this experience some bitter wisdom which would enlighten others, faced with cognate problems?

A lot of mistakes were made, but the Scots knew that 'the oil' had happened, that nothing would be the same again. Did this register on Britain?

I

Prelude on the Red Clyde

'There likewise I beheld Excalibur
Before him at his crowning borne, the sword
That rose from out the bosom of the lake,
And Arthur row'd across and took it – rich
With jewels, elfin Urim, on the hilt,
Bewildering heart and eye – the blade so bright
That men are blinded by it – on one side,
Graven in the oldest tongue of all this world,
"Take me," but turn the blade and ye shall see,
And written in the speech ye speak yourself,
"Cast me away!" And sad was Arthur's face
Taking it, but old Merlin counsell'd him,
"Take thou and strike! The time to cast away
Is yet far-off." So this great brand the King
Took, and by this will beat his foemen down.'

Alfred Tennyson, 'The Coming of Arthur'

Oil Country: 1911, 1962 and 1993

In 1911 Winston Churchill, recently appointed First Lord of the
Admiralty, visited the Prime Minister, H. H. Asquith, at Archer-
field, the house which the latter had rented near North Berwick.
As the pair walked the links and discussed the naval race with
Germany and the looming threat of war, Churchill observed, out
in the Firth of Forth, great grey Dreadnoughts steaming past the
Bass Rock. He was never one to throw away a scene like this,
radiating destiny, and commemorated it in sonorous prose.
Three years later, convinced that the Grand Fleet would be able

to stay at sea longer if its boilers were oil- instead of coal-fired, he took out a government share in the recently founded Anglo-Persian Oil Company, exploiting a 'gusher' detected in the southern part of Persia which, thanks to the Entente of 1908, had passed into the British sphere of influence. In due course this became the British Petroleum Company, in which 47 per cent of the shares were, in 1962, held by the British government.

In 1962 Churchill was in his dotage, and in Scotland a small part of the BP empire was dying. Twenty-five miles further up the Firth from the now derelict Archerfield, rusting narrow-gauge tracks led straight downhill towards bright-red spoil-heaps. Above them the overhead electric wire sagged; in some places stretches of it were already missing. In the works weeds were advancing on the retorts; the dwarfish green electric locomotives stood motionless, soon to be claimed by the demolition contractors. This was the Winchburgh refinery of Scottish Oils Ltd, in the year that the cheap crude coming by supertanker from the Gulf undermined the subsidy for domestically produced oil. The subsidy went, and the Scottish oil-shale industry ceased to exist. The refinery had been built in the 1890s by the company founded by Dr James Young, who a couple of decades earlier had perfected a means of roasting the oil-shales of West Lothian to yield paraffin. As an innovation, it had been connected up to its mines by a narrow-gauge electric tramway, the second to be built in Scotland. Although the Scots had been, in 1846, the first to put an electric locomotive on the rails, the equipment had come from America, from Baldwin's of Philadelphia.

Industrial archaeology, we were starting to call it, before 'heritage' came to employ more people than the shipyards. The Scottish Railway Preservation Society was trying to rescue one of the little engines. I reckoned we could scrape together £45 for it – about the last believable sum of money you will read about in this book – but it was eventually taken over by the Royal Scottish Museum in Edinburgh. Politics, too, mattered to me, especially the by-election at the time preoccupying the West Lothian constituency, with the young Labour candidate Tam

Dalyell, laird of the Binns, which lay only a mile from one of the Winchburgh mines. The election didn't turn out quite as the university Labour Club had anticipated. Dalyell got in, but was pursued by the Scottish National Party candidate, Billy Wolfe, whose near-success announced the début of a new actor on the Scottish political scene. One substantial plank of the SNP platform was the neglect of Scottish interests by the Macmillan government, demonstrated by the removal of the oil subsidy.[1]

The symbolism wasn't as heavy as that of Churchill and his battleships, but several of the factors which were collectively to transform the politics and economy of late twentieth-century Scotland, and Britain, had coincided in time and place. The issue of oil, and its dependence on international politics; the industrial decline of the country, foreshadowed by that electric tramway – even in the 1900s the exploitation of at least one of Scotland's resources needed American equipment; the challenge of political nationalism. Not to speak of the emergence, in Tam Dalyell, of an idiosyncratic but determined opponent of constitutional change; and one of the very few MPs who knew anything about science . . .

In 1994, if you were to climb the 'West Lothian Alps' above Winchburgh, a 150-foot table-mountain of burnt shale, you would see to the north-east a similar range of red, man-made hills; beyond this the Forth road and rail bridges, and then a series of metal islands in the river, off the shore of the Dalmeny estate, from which the Earl of Rosebery had, exactly a century earlier, ruled the British Empire. The bings above South Queensferry still contained oil, but this now took the form of a huge tank-farm with a pipeline running downhill to the mooring platforms, the most important port installations in the Firth. Around 7 million tons of oil each year were piped from the Forties field to Grangemouth, there refined, and dispatched from Hound Point. Perhaps six men were needed to handle the 375,000-ton supertankers which edged in from Rotterdam and Antwerp.[2]

Around Hound Point not much had changed since 1962, or

even since Rosebery's day: a few miles of new roads had been built; Edinburgh Airport had been modernized; the railway remained unelectrified; some new factories, American- or Japanese-owned, had been set up; more, Scottish or state-owned, had been closed. The yachts and sailing dinghies of the Edinburgh middle class skittered around the Firth, easily and tantalizingly visible from the Pilton housing estate, whose people suffered perhaps the most concentrated Aids and drugs problem in Europe. Deprived of contracts for refitting Trident missile-carrying submarines, the great naval base at Rosyth, at the other end of the two bridges, was being run down. Of the complex onshore construction centres which marked the littoral of Holland and Norway there was not much sign; no shipyard remained on the Firth. Burntisland had gone over to oil work, but Robbs had vanished from Leith, and my great-uncle's Grangemouth Dockyard, which in 1802 had built the first steamer in the world, William Symington's *Charlotte Dundas*, closed in the 1970s. The Scottish National Party was getting 25 per cent in the polls, and Labour (as ever?) 50 per cent, but separation was regularly level-pegging with devolution, while support for the Conservatives and the *status quo* rarely rose above 15 per cent. Most Scots, if pressed, would opt for a republic rather than a monarchy.

This book is about the sea, human ingenuity, and the travails of a political community. By any standards North Sea oil was the greatest civilian project in Britain since, between 1845 and 1850, navvies using spades and pickaxes and gunpowder built 5,000 miles of railway, a network stretching from Aberdeen to Plymouth. In 1983, only a decade after construction started and two decades after the first exploration for gas, twenty-five oilfields were in production, the oil being pumped from scores of wells and regulated and dispatched by immense metal and concrete towers. The latest, the Magnus, was taller than the Post Office Tower. Pipeline networks connected these to satellite wells and to the mainland. On the platforms were communities of hundreds of men and concentrations of elaborate machinery, served by dense helicopter traffic: communities almost beyond the imagination of H.G. Wells or Jules Verne. Even within that first decade the technology of oil extraction had undergone a revolution, from the skill and brawn of the Texan oilmen – the bears and roughnecks – who had got things going, to a high-technology business involving satellites and fibre-optic cable, supercomputers and revolutionary diving techniques: innovations unthinkable when the first primitive drilling-rig, *Sea Gem*, struck a field of natural gas off Norfolk at the end of 1965.

By 1994 North Sea oil and gas might have earned the country £220 billion, but the costs involved were equally spectacular: about £60 billion had been invested in drilling, platforms, pipelines and refineries; over £70 billion had passed to the British government in royalties and tax. Without it, life in Britain in the 1980s would have been vastly different.

But despite the aggressive marketing of petrol products on every filling-station forecourt, this was a reticent revolution. It didn't advertise itself. There was a dense – in every sense of that word – trade technology press; shop-talk made absolute; complex economic models crunched through computers. But there were almost no paperback books about the oil, no popular magazines or partworks, or the sort of hard sell which drew kids to Nintendo or dinosaurs or airliners. An oil rig was a Meccano construction; but Meccano had gone out of business, or at least emigrated to Germany. (It now lives thirty miles up the railway from me, and is called Märklin Technik.) There were no models of rigs or platforms, supply boats or pipelaying barges to be found in British toyshops.[3]

This was interesting, because no sooner had the Victorians built their railways and launched their steamships than their publicity machine moved in. A huge 'railway press' urged investors to sink their money in railway shares; Samuel Smiles and his ilk commemorated the engineers; encyclopedias covering equipment, organization and management were churned out; there were railway card games and board games of a proto-Monopoly type; railway fashions and railway polkas. But the mighty technology of North Sea oil evoked only a limited resonance. A handful of mentions in the autobiographies of the responsible politicians, and silence from that of the politician who benefited most from it: Mrs Thatcher. At most a page of treatment in the standard histories; and save for a brief moment of conscious-ness in the mid-1970s, almost complete public indifference.

In 1994 there was some controversy about what remained in the North Sea, but none about the key factor: the price. And what determined this was by no means straightforward: a combi-nation of demand, and combinations among suppliers, whether multinational oil majors or OPEC governments. If the price stayed low, at under $15 a barrel for Brent crude, it had fallen in real terms to below that of the early 1970s, when the field had first been exploited. If it fell to single figures, then Britain's oil age would truly have come to an end, leaving the country in a chronic balance of payments deficit; a net importer of manufac-tured goods since 1985, with foreign companies – Swedish, German, Norwegian – already owning what was left of the British railway equipment, car and shipbuilding industries.

At South Queensferry, a tattered SNP poster from years back, 'It's your oil she's after!', on a bus shelter: a vampiric Thatcher dripping black blood. The recollection of Tony Benn recording in his diaries a 1978 session of *The Frost Programme* at Leeds:

The thing was wildly unbalanced, tremendously anti-government, and this man from Chevron attacked the British government . . . Milton Friedman just sat there giggling and said sell it all off, and denationalize everything. Give the money away, and let every man be a capitalist. It wasn't a serious contribution at all but Friedman is the arch-priest of Monetarism.[4]

It's not a serious contribution either to point out that the main point of entry for the oil was Cruden Bay, where Bram Stoker himself used to spend his holidays, but the metaphor seems apt. Manufacturing was cut by a fifth; the oil income dwindled, but Lady Thatcher ended the 1980s as a missionary of the market. Ejected from British politics in an unprecedented party *coup d'état*, she was ideologically re-animated by the collapse of the

East European command economies. She circled the world, preaching her, or Friedman's, doctrines to admiring audiences of millionaires – notably in Texas – and/or young hopefuls who believed that unchecked *laisser-faire* would restore their lost civil societies. The bounty of the Forties, which had permitted her experiment, was never alluded to – although 'Brent crude' became part of the speculators' shorthand of this brave new world of trading in currencies, commodities and derivatives whose growth far outpaced manufacturing in the West.

In 1994 such 'lessons' – administered without the anaesthetic of oil – had lost some of their persuasiveness. Thatcherism had tested the patience of British society, but 'shock therapy' caused mounting chaos in the East, leading to a situation in which Western governments seemed quietly relieved at the return of former Communists at the ballot box, as infinitely preferable to the populist and nationalist monsters, mafias and military, waiting in the wings.

Between fact and ideology, where did the reality lie? North Sea oil was neither a panacea nor a sideshow, but a potential national benefit which demanded huge investment, a complex process of adaptation and a willingness to take risks. The risk factor was given additional salience by events beyond the control of any government. The chances of mastering the situation were complicated by the travails of British politics in the 1970s, and challenges which distracted the élite from coping with the oil factor, *and* from assessing its own performance. In a detailed and judicious overview, a young *Economist* journalist concluded in 1975 that chances of effective control had been thrown away by the Tories, but

The present Labour government has been involved in a catching-up exercise to close the gaps in British North Sea oil policy. Despite some stupid threats it appears to be working out fairly well.[5]

A decade later the exercise had been abandoned, the market ruled, and Mrs Thatcher had no more unqualified admirer than Andrew Neil, editor of the *Sunday Times*.

Neil was lieutenant to Rupert Murdoch, the media imperialist whose aggressive individualism contrasted with the anonymity of oil multinationals. Yet Murdoch calculated as deftly as these effective sovereign states, and in Scotland his populist tabloid, the *Sun*, supported independence. Which raises a contentious sub-theme. In 1981 William Miller, Professor of Politics at Glasgow University – a political colleague of Winchburgh and West Lothian days – wrote *The End of British Politics*. The title seemed to smack of *chutzpah* after the result of the devolution referendum of 1 March 1979, in which, after ranting about the subject for half a decade, the Scots decided so narrowly in its favour that the bill toilsomely carried by James Callaghan fell, bringing the government down with it. Yet, Miller argued, to defeat devolution – which the Conservative Party, pledged to it in 1975, had successfully done – meant admitting that Scottish politics were run on rules quite different from those of England. The two-party settlement on which Westminster constitutionalism depended had been breached beyond recall.[6]

In 1974 and 1975 Scottish nationalism was the most salient threat to Britain's unity, and oil-driven at that. But this was merely the most 'political' challenge released by the oil. The relationship of national to global industries, the implications of entry into Europe, the conservation of energy supplies, the recrudescence of fundamentalist politics: all of these assaulted not just the economy but a political culture wedded to 'the orderly management of decline'. Between 1964 and 1979 one type of politics – centre-left social democracy – attempted to resolve the issue of modernization and failed. From 1979 to 1994 it was the turn of a highly ideological right. It evolved a politics which were not national in the least, but it was given scope by the oil surplus.

'A lump of coal, surrounded by fish' was how Aneurin Bevan had described the natural resources whose early exploitation had made Britain the first industrial nation. Substitute oil for fish, and the country's natural advantages seemed enviable in a period of population growth pressing on scarce resources. Yet it proved difficult even to discuss in any sort of consensual way the utilization of this resource, given Britain's deficiencies in technology, the divisions within its industrial structure, and the damage to its political habits incidental on entering the Common Market in 1973. At one level the winning of the oil was a remarkable triumph for a country written off as an industrial state; at another it subjected it to violent political, economic and cultural stresses from which it never really recovered.

Prelude on the Red Clyde

The River Clyde was, and always had been, quite different from the Forth. When Scottish Oils Winchburgh was being closed down there were still twenty-odd functioning shipyards in Auden's 'glade of cranes'; the contract had just gone to John Brown's at Clydebank for the successor to the *Queen Mary* and *Queen Elizabeth*. This had never been a Scotland that the Earl of Rosebery and his like had been comfortable in: industrial, clangorous, confrontational. Never more so than nine years later, in the autumn of 1971, when thousands of shipyard and engineering workers, local politicians, and church and civic leaders paraded through Glasgow to support the Upper Clyde Shipbuilders' work-in. I was in a minibus with a group of students from the newly formed Open University, going round various of the monuments of industrial Glasgow before the developers set their bulldozers on them, when down Jamaica Street came the magnificence of the Shotts and Dykehead Miners' Pipe Band, followed by the heroes of the hour: Jimmie Reid and Jimmie Airlie, the Communist leaders of the work-in, Tony Benn, the former Labour Minister of Technology, and even Billy Wolfe, who had given Labour such a shock in West Lothian nine years earlier. As an image of solidarity, it lodged itself as vividly as the red flag carried by strikers in George Square half a century earlier.

Industrial relations along the Clyde had always been sulphurous. Shipyards organized as family partnerships confronted proud skilled men who feared that at the end of every contract, when the tugs ushered the new liner or freighter 'doon the watter' to run its trials over the measured mile off Arran, they would be down the road. The owners – Stephens and Lithgows, Yarrows and Dennys – would combine defensively from time to time against their union opponents; they were less successful at any form of corporate planning for the modernization of their industry. In the early 1950s, 9 engineering works served 16 shipyards; the equivalent figures for Japan were 5 and 18.[7] The Clyde specialized in freighters of up to 6,000 tons, the sort of ship which, steaming in convoy, had provided Britain's lifeline in the Second World War. It was less adept in constructing the tankers of around 30,000 tons which passed through the Suez Canal to the oilfields of Bahrein and Kuwait.

Then in 1956 everything changed. In Egypt, Colonel Nasser nationalized the Suez Canal; the British and French intervened and then retreated; the canal was closed for three years. This was just long enough for a quantum change in the nature of oil transport. Vessels now had to be big and cheap enough to tackle the Cape of Good Hope; there was no restriction on size, and within a few years the size of tankers had increased more than tenfold. Not only were the working practices and technology of the Clyde yards archaic – in the 1950s annual depreciation was £9 million, new investment half that, research and development scarcely £250,000 – the river itself was simply too small. Scott Lithgow at Greenock could manage a supertanker, but only if built in two sections.[8] Sir William Lithgow found it more profitable to advise the Korean Hyundai Corporation on how to build these monsters on 'green field' sites.[9]

The result was a series of crises of mounting intensity, and the closure of over two-thirds of the river's shipyards and engineering works, which fell from 28 to 7 between 1950 and 1968.[10] Tony Benn was already familiar here; in 1968, while Minister of Technology, he had played midwife to the amalgamation of all the yards in the dredged section of the river, from Clydebank to Glasgow, into a consortium called Upper Clyde Shipbuilders. This was looted blind by both sides: by the old family dynasties, retreating in good order to their country estates; by the unions, evacuating messily a series of last ditches. In 1971 there came a crisis. Edward Heath's government, formally committed to the Selsdon Park programme of economic retrenchment and the slaughter of 'lame ducks', evolved a confidential programme of running down the shipbuilding industry, and placed it in the eager hands of Nicholas Ridley. When this was – expertly – publicized by Reid and comrades as meaning that John Brown's, the flagship of the Scottish shipbuilding industry, was doomed, the balloon went up.[11]

The work-in was never really an employee takeover, although most of its supporters liked to think that it was. It was an inspired piece of public relations, which drew on the pugnacity of a country which in the preceding decade had come, through the rise of the SNP, to regard itself as being somewhere special. And it had the desired effect, not least on a Labour Party unsure of its position north of the border. The government backed off, Ridley resigned (although he lived to take his revenge on organized labour). UCS was modified into Govan Shipbuilders, under the chairmanship of an oil man, Billy Fraser, Lord Strathalmond, brought in from BP.[12] And a purchaser was found for the threatened Clydebank yard in the form of the Marathon Manufacturing Co. of Houston, Texas, which specialized in the construction of drilling-rigs and exploration vessels for the exploitation of offshore oil reserves. Danny McGarvey, the president of the Boilermakers Union, flew twice to Texas to sell the scheme, and Christopher Chataway, the new Industry minister (and a confirmed interventionist) handed out £12 million in subsidy.[13] In January 1972 most Scots took on board, for the first time, the consequences of the oil off their coasts.

In June 1974 the *Penrod 64* took to the water at Clydebank. It didn't slip into the Clyde, champagne dripping from its bows, as only ten years earlier the *Queen Elizabeth II* had done. It splashed sideways into the river, like something wrenched loose from some complex industrial process, or a gigantic upside-down table. From the corners of 3,000 square metres of platform rose four trellis-like legs, 300 feet above the water. The legs themselves were controlled by huge hydraulic jacks, and dwarfed the 100 feet of derrick at the centre of the platform, a mighty crane for dropping thirty-foot sections of drilling pipe into a hole which might travel 10,000 feet into the earth's crust.

A powerful diesel generator was tethered to the deck. Its current passed to a hydraulic ram, and to an engine house whose electric motor rotated a drilling plate. Another motor pumped a mixture of heavy barytes into the shaft to drop to its foot, lubricating the drill pipe as it did so, and extracting samples of strata to be examined on the platform. This was done by geologists and chemists among an overall crew of sixty, housed in shack-like living quarters. Opposite these, on the other side of the generator house, was a helicopter landing pad. The Clyde had seen nothing odder since Admiral Popov's circular battleship eighty years earlier, save perhaps for the components of the Mulberry Harbour being assembled for the Normandy landings. And for Marathon, with yards in Texas and Louisiana and Singapore, the Clyde was nowhere special. Nor was *Penrod 64*. But the Clyde wanted to see more, many more, of her kind.

The End of an Old Song

When his time was served he became a Union man, and thought all the world of his District Delegate. He is a very good workman, who could turn his hand to many things, and 'make a job o' them a''. He is intelligent, and has a clear perception of injustice. But according to his lights he is a reasonable man. He stands up for himself not only against the common enemy, his employer, but also against his comrades in allied trades if they invade his frontiers. He is gruff, intractable and independent, and his latent irritability takes fire if his rights are infringed. Of servility he has not a trace.

Thus wrote the brothers Bone about the Clydeside worker in 1901.[14]

The Clyde was typical of British industrial regionalism in being specialized, and distinctive on account of this specialism: a fortress of the skills and class-consciousness which had secured British social and political stability, albeit as part of a baleful stand-off with capital. Men in caps, mufflers and old 'best suits' who, with a micrometer, a spanner and a file, could convert a heap of rust back into a working engine, were more Atlanticist than nationalist. With perhaps a third of their folk in the States, multinational capitalism was nothing new. But responses were qualified by the hierarchies of skills and religion. As recently as 1955 the Tories had polled a majority of seats and votes in Scotland; 'red' Glasgow had a majority of right-wing MPs.

An image of patriotic collaboration – real enough at the time – was given by one wartime film, John Baxter's *The Shipbuilders* (1943). In this, the devotion to his job of the tough little Glasgow riveter Danny Shields makes his boss, played by that great celluloid proconsul Clive Brook, campaign for the re-equipment of the slump-struck yards. The original novel by George Blake had seen the Brook character scuttling off to a southern mansion – like many of his actual contemporaries – and the resilience of the work-force had its limits.[15] Its patriotism, cheering royalty as it launched another ship, was qualified by the prospect of unemployment; just as the skirls of the Braemar Gathering didn't quite mask the 'gloomy memories' of evicted crofters. With the dislodging of Scottish heavy industries, patriotism was tested to destruction.

By 1970 only two Tories remained in Glasgow. The working class was dominant in Scottish politics, but its old hierarchies had weakened. It was more and more unskilled.[16] This had first become apparent in 1961 with the removal of the North British Locomotive Co.; a couple of years later the Pressed Steel wagon plant at Linwood made way for a car plant – remember the Hillman Imp? – which almost wiped out one of Europe's largest railway equipment industries. Scotland then attempted to move into the automotive age, with government-subsidized vehicle-building plants at Bathgate as well as Linwood, backed up by a subsidized strip mill at Ravenscraig, near Motherwell. These created mainly semi-skilled jobs, but secured some continuing employment for engineers.

At a price. Since the economic downturn of the mid-1960s none of the new factories had functioned at anything near capacity. Nor had they renewed the industrial élite of the locally owned heavy industries, since most were branch plants controlled from London or the United States. Some American plants had made it to Scotland during the heavy-industry epoch: Babcock and Wilcox, the huge Singer sewing-machine works at Clydebank, the North British Rubber Co. in Edinburgh. But after 1945 the inflow intensified until in the 1970s over 14 per cent of Scottish manufacturing came from such factories, ranging from Caterpillar Trucks to IBM. In embryo, Scotland awkwardly combined both the 'rustbelt' and the 'sunbelt' of the contemporary United States.[17]

As in the United States under the New Deal, the hand of the central state was visible in elaborate schemes of social engineering. Many argued these were breaking up the traditional character of the country, assimilating it more and more into the rest of Britain. Belated efforts were made to replace the appallingly cramped housing of the old city centres in which the skilled working men had lived. Tens of thousands of families were moved to new towns, peripheral estates, or (the new solution) high-rise point-blocks. The power of religious fanaticism was waning; despite the reputation of the 'Old Firm' in Glasgow, events in Belfast were to have few Scottish parallels. With the end of Britain's empire in the 1960s, overseas administration and trade, militarism and settlement mattered less. The last troops were coming back from the last colonies; former district officers were fitting in – or not fitting in – as academic administrators or civil servants. Emigration was continuing, but southwards rather than to the United States, the traditional destination. Europe was beckoning and challenging, for holidays, for ideas about modernity, for industrial markets.[18] Traditional constraints were proving difficult to apply.

Penrod 64 was towed west into the Atlantic and then, weeks later, to the Caribbean. We will not encounter it again, but plenty like it. The Clyde had always been oriented westwards; for 250 years it had channelled the ambitions of the Scots, typified by Bailie Nicol Jarvie in Scott's *Rob Roy*:

'. . . Now, since St Mungo catched herrings in the Clyde, what was ever like to gar us flourish like the sugar and tobacco trade? Will anybody tell me that, and grumble at a treaty that opened us a road west-awa' yonder?'[19]

It had been Jarvie's grandchildren who had helped set up the oil industry in the United States. But now the Scots realized uneasily that the Atlantic's time was passing. The road now lay east-awa', if it led anywhere.

When Dinosaurs Roamed North Berwick

What happens to us
Is irrelevant to the world's geology
But what happens to the world's geology
Is not irrelevant to us.
We must reconcile ourselves to the stones,
Not the stones to us.
Here a man must shed the encumbrances that muffle
Contact with elemental things, the subtleties
That seem inseparable from a humane life, and go apart
Into a simple and sterner, more beautiful and more oppressive world,
Austerely intoxicating; the first draught is overpowering;
Few survive it.[20]

Supply boats bound for Sullom Voe from the south would, by 1978, slip past the coast of Whalsay. In the 1930s Hugh MacDiarmid, founder of modern Scottish nationalism, ferocious autodidact and political radical, found exile here. 'On a Raised Beach' turned its bleak geology into a sort of materialist mysticism. Rocks were truth.

27

Particularly in the country which had invented geology, whose pioneers would be commemorated in oilfield names: William Hutton, Roderick Murchison, Hugh Miller. Two centuries before, the Scots had loosed themselves on their remarkable terrain. No one, even on Clydeside, can be unaware of the crags and heaving moors which threaten to sweep over the bungalows and point-blocks. Only a few miles away from the housing schemes, real Munros surge from sea-level to over 3,000 feet. The Scottish landscape harbours some of the world's most ancient rocks, relics of the crunching together of the tectonic plates which make up the globe – 'an assemblage of bits of the world's crust separated by more than 2,500 million years of time'. Compared with this ancestry the Alps were jerry-built, run up with breeze-blocks.

In the beginning . . . volcanic crystals and sands were melted, fused, blown apart, overlaid, until they were smoothed down into a plain of hard schists, granitic rocks ten kilometres thick. On top of this were deposited further kilometres of what would become ancient sandstones, followed by compressed layers of schists and quartzes. But the 'frontier' situation of the area, on the edge of two plate systems, meant that there could be no smooth evolution of the landscape. Scotland, then on the south-eastern rim of one continent, was forced together with what are now England and Wales, when the globe rotated on a different axis and the ensemble was in the southern hemisphere. Four hundred million years ago, a tropical Scotland founded on a raft of old red sandstone had mountains and volcanoes. The region looked rather like the present Andes, but was riven by earth movements of enormous power which forced volcanic shafts to the surface. Over its lower limits, about 370 million years ago, a warm, shallow sea spread; the creatures and plants which throve in it decayed into limestones and the oil shales that the miners of Winchburgh would later quarry.

The jungles of the carboniferous period rotted and were com-pressed to form the coalfields; then a further tectonic upheaval thrust more volcanic cores and spines into the sedimentary sand-stones which heat, aridity and erosion had laid over the organic material. They left behind them the Castle Rock at Stirling, and North Berwick Law. Two hundred million years ago, and for another 150 million years, dinosaurs roamed what geologists call the Variscan mountains and their surrounding shallow seas and lake systems. The vegetation and plankton of these, overlaid by drifts of sand, became an organic mud which in turn decayed into oil and gas which were stored beneath the 'domes' of the Jurassic sandstones. Further volcanic activity canted the western rim of Scotland upwards, while waters flowed into what would become the North Sea. About 58 million years ago a last outbreak of volcanic activity forced more new mountain ranges to the surface, only to be worn down by inundation and glaciation, followed by further erosion as the changing axis of the earth bore the future Britain further and further to the north. The organic sediments of the North Sea were gradually covered with thousands of feet of sandstone strata, mud, and ultimately salt water.[21]

The sea yielded up food and heat and light; fish, salt to preserve the fish and meat from the autumn slaughter, fish-oil and whale-oil for the lamps, sea-coal picked from the beaches. In the Middle Ages salt was dried off from the sea-water in great metal pans, heated by burning the coal raised from local coal measures. Originally this business was carried on by monks, and it proved difficult to adjust to the secular order which followed the Reformation in 1560. So important was the trade that in the 1690s the Scottish parliament placed the miners and salt-workers and their families in perpetual servitude. This was only lifted in 1800. An ominous precedent for the relationship between energy production and civil rights![22]

What concerned the petroleum geologists lay 9,000 feet below the sea-bed, about 7,000 feet deeper than the deepest coalmine of the Durham or Fife fields, in search of whose measures the first sub-sea drilling had been undertaken. Oil and natural gas occurred, not in lakes or chambers, but under immense pressure in the crevices of sedimentary limestones and sandstones, a stone sponge squashed under 'caps' of denser rock.[23] But first the geologists had to reach it, which meant facing the tormented waters above. The North Sea was shallow. A sub-sea plateau, mostly no more than 300 feet deep, extended northwards from the Dogger Bank eighty miles east of Scarborough, where there was scarcely seventy feet, to terminate on a ridge running 200 miles east of Buchan. But between Norway and the eastern part of the ridge, the Great Fisher Bank, across which the UK–Norwegian boundary ran, was a trench 1,200 feet deep, dropping in parts to over 2,400 feet. Neither shallowness nor depth made for tranquillity. On the plateau, storms had been known to shift telegraph cables by half a mile. The great swells of the Atlantic and the Gulf Stream, funnelling into the area around the Shetlands, encountered a flow from the Baltic. The result caused powerful currents and violent storms. The North Sea was 'unique', as Peter Baxendell of Shell put it, 'in its sustained nastiness. It is not just the wind or wave height or the water depth, but a combination of all three factors (and others).'[24]

On 6 March 1968 the semi-submersible *Ocean Prince*, 10,000 tons and insured for £7 million, drilling for Burmah 125 miles east of Scarborough, was destroyed by fifty-foot waves driven by a ninety-mile-an-hour gale. Against the odds, the twenty-six-man crew was rescued by helicopter. A year later, on 18 March 1969, the *Irene*, a clapped-out Liberian freighter which I had sketched while it was unloading esparto grass at Granton, ran out of fuel while steaming in ballast to Kristiansand. The lifeboat from Longhope, on the southern tip of Hoy in the Orkneys, opposite Flotta where Occidental would start building the terminal for its Piper Field three years later, went to her aid and was overwhelmed. The father of a friend, who had just gone as minister to South Walls, had as almost his first task the burial of eight men – a third of the working population of the village.

The Sea

For one of the world's greatest mythmakers, the North Sea was central. At the Hawes Inn, near Dalmeny and westward from

Hound Point, David Balfour, the hero of *Kidnapped*, met Captain Hoseason and was shanghaied aboard the *Covenant*. Concealed in an apple-barrel on the deck of a lighthouse yacht, Thomas Stevenson heard his father's trusted mate, John Soutar, brag about his rascality. His son gave him immortality, plus a parrot and minus a leg, in *Treasure Island*. After centuries when only a fire-basket on the Island of Mey had directed the shipmasters, Robert Louis Stevenson's engineer father and grandfather had built the great stone lighthouses which made safe the northern approaches and the entries to the Firths of Forth and Tay, their workmen clinging to tidal rocks while fitting together the giant jigsaw-puzzle blocks, waist-deep in icy surf.

The younger, velvet-coated Stevenson, almost a prototype 1960s rebel, wrote of his forebears' fascination with this fierce sea. To his grandfather Robert,

it was great gain to be eight nights and seven days in the savage bay of Levenswick – to read a book in the much-agitated cabin – to go on deck and hear the gale scream in his ears, and see the landscape dark with rain, and the ship plunge at her two anchors – and to turn in at night and wake again at morning, in his narrow berth, to the clamorous and continued voices of the gale.[25]

The works of the Stevensons were indispensable to the oilmen, but the Scots, and for that matter the English, had regarded the North Sea with only restrained interest for almost two centuries. Trade with the Americas and the Empire lay to the west; the Atlantic had borne the prosperity of fictional Jarvies – and real Finlays and Glassfords – out of the Clyde; the slavers of Bristol and Liverpool, the cotton merchants, the collier-owners of the South Wales ports, all looked to the west. The medieval dominance of the trading Norsemen had long ago declined – those past years which saw the same masons at work on the cathedrals of Durham, Kirkwall and Trondheim, the era when, failing to give an adequate tocher of 60,000 florins, along with the Princess Margaret, King Christian had to hand over the Northern Isles – Orkney and Shetland – to the Scottish king in 1469.[26]

The Baltic trade slumped as steel and steam replaced the wood, pitch and hemp which had once come from the Russian provinces. The herring fishery passed from Dutch to Scottish control and prospered in the late nineteenth century, with steam drifters and fast cargo boats ousting the great square-sailed Fifies, Scaffies and Zulus which had once moved in their hundreds from the Minch to the Dogger Bank, with the Dutch 'busses' which conveyed their catch to the European ports. But the trade with Russia ended with the First World War, and was never resumed. The herring fishing dwindled, and the deep-sea fishery followed it, the new Iceland fishing limits writing an end to it in 1975.

Energy had been shipped from here, too. In the two decades before 1914 coal export had replaced manufacture as the major trade of the Scottish east-coast ports, something that worried contemporary economists. Coal for Scandinavia roared down the chutes into the holds of the tramp steamers at Methil and Grangemouth, while German steel plate was 'dumped' on the quay at Leith. But the First World War struck at the trade, and the Second World War practically finished it: the many loading installations in Fife and Northumbria were derelict after the 1950s. When crude oil reached the refinery at Grangemouth after 1947, it came by pipeline from a deep-water terminal at Finnart on Loch Long, a long, deep inlet of the Firth of Clyde. The roadsteads off Antwerp and Rotterdam might be the busiest in the world, but the northern approaches were for small ships, dwindling into large, empty docks. The first vehicle ferries, built in Swedish or German yards, were a portent of a new, dense, short-sea traffic, but this happened a long way south of the quays of Dundee and Leith.

The gust of 136 mph which hit Kirkwall on 7 February 1969 – a month before the Longhope tragedy – was a record, but weather in the North Sea was overall windy: bracing, as the holiday posters would put it. Even on a blazing summer day in 1991, when it was painful to walk on the sand, the water off Spittal, south of Berwick upon Tweed, seemed oblivious to any notion of global warming. Charles Forte was said to have started his career in the Beach Pavilion there, but the bracing climate could not compete with charter jets and guaranteed Mediterranean sun. Along those great arcs of sand and low mud-coloured cliffs, private hotels and fairgrounds gave up the ghost, piers decayed, and the branch lines which had borne Wakes Week families to them rusted and were ripped up. Britain had turned her back on the North Sea – but, as it turned out, only temporarily. In the 1960s the tiny port of Felixstowe started its unstoppable rise as a container terminal, boosted by containerization. The prospect of the European Community and the re-orientation of British patterns of trade, away from America and the Commonwealth and in favour of the Continent, raised the business of the Humber by 38 per cent in 1970–72, after a decade of decline.[27]

Twenty-four hours' steaming time from the Tyne Commission Quay at Newcastle was Stavanger, whence the Bergen Line ferry turned north to proceed through the islands to Bergen. The nation whose claim on the sea-bed of the North Sea was exceeded only by that of Britain had in 1970 a population of just 4.2 millions. An elderly Norwegian like King Olaf would remember when the country belonged to the King of Sweden; after a long and tiresome battle for its own identity, a Danish prince had mounted the throne – although he had not, in that radical land, been crowned – in 1905. The connections with Scotland, 400 miles to the south-west, were many. The semi-autonomous constitution of 1812 was drafted by a Bergen merchant called William Christie. The composer Grieg was the descendant of a Jacobite refugee from Leith. The great Ibsen himself believed he was of Scots ancestry, and was translated by the Scoto-Norwegian William Archer. In 1939–45 the Norwegian resistance had harassed the German invaders from Scottish ports and airfields.

But as the ferry steamed through the Haugesund, the country showed that it lived by the sea, from the great tankers being fitted out in the shipyards to the little motorships carrying freight around the islands like so many lorries. Outside every wooden house stood its white flagstaff with the national colours: the mark of a democratic, collective patriotism. Here the sea mattered; mastering it had enabled a small and poorly endowed population to create a respectable welfare state and high level of education; but this was the result of conscious planning and a careful social-democratic bureaucracy. The state was something to count on, to be proud of.[28]

Perhaps there were other reasons for the British to avert their eyes from the North Sea. The North Sea made up only 0.002 per cent of the world's water surface, but it provided 4.3 per cent of its fish catch, and 30 per cent of the world's sea freight used it.[29] Bracingness and an offshore wind masked the fact that in the 1970s and the 1980s it was becoming a vast open sewer:

Over a million tons of nitrates flow from the rivers of its neighbouring states into the North Sea, 76,500 tons of phosphates, 50 tons of cadmium, 20 tons of mercury, 1,300 tons of copper, 1,000 tons of lead, 7,300 tons of zinc, 360 tons of arsenic, 29,000 tons of oil from the offshore oil and gas plants alone, 85 million tons of industrial waste, treated sludge and rubble, to a greater or lesser extent containing oil.[30]

Britain and Ireland were the only European states dumping sewage sludge (and worse) in the sea – and defending it.[31] In 1965, at the beginning of the campaign to extract gas from the North Sea, British farmers were spreading 500,000 tons of nitrate fertilizer on their fields. Twenty years later this had risen three-fold, and most of the discharge made its way into a sea in peril of biological death.[32]

'Something seems to be wrong with our bloody ships'

'In my diary,' wrote the Rt Hon. Edmund Dell, the minister to whom Harold Wilson had in 1974 delegated the business of creating an oil taxation regime,

I noted that, like Jellicoe at the Battle of Jutland, I sometimes felt that I was the only minister who could sink the British economy in an afternoon, by miscalculating the new tax and thus irrevocably alienating the oil companies and consequently the market, from the government. This merely illustrates the self-importance to which ministers are susceptible.[33]

It also illustrates the ambiguous role which the North Sea played in the British memory. The North Sea was important, but it was not a *world*, like Fernand Braudel's Mediterranean. There had once been the community of the Hanseatic towns, but their power had declined in the sixteenth century and the most important of their élites had migrated, first to Amsterdam and then to London, where they had become the great merchant-banking families of Baring and Schröder, Brandt, Kleinwort and Huth. Their fortunes, based on loans to foreign governments, had dwindled since the 1930s, although they were to undergo a renaissance, in part oil-based, in the 1970s.[34]

But as far as the British were concerned, the North Sea was marked by their conflict with the two great powers to which it gave access. In 1904 the Russian fleet, steaming towards its defeat at Tsu-shima on the other side of the world, shelled the herring drifters fishing the Dogger Bank, thinking them to be Japanese torpedo-boats. In 1916 the British and German battle-fleets clashed off the Danish coast in the Battle of Jutland.

The Germans lost, in the sense that the High Seas Fleet only left port again to surrender (and subsequently to be scuttled in Scapa Flow), but the exclamation of Admiral Jellicoe's lieutenant, Admiral Beatty, as he saw the inadequately protected *Indefatigable*, *Invincible* and *Queen Mary* explode – 'Something seems to be wrong with our bloody ships!' – seemed to dog subsequent British technology. In the next war the *Prince of Wales* and the *Repulse* were lost in the Far East, sunk by an air power of which British admirals seemed only half aware. The misconceived carpet bombing campaign over Germany after 1942, which wiped much of the Hanseatic inheritance off the map, seemed to many a war crime in killing hundreds of thousands of civilians; it also claimed the lives of 50,000 aircrew: part of a new generation of potential technologists and managers. By 1961, when the airborne oil reconnaissance was under way and the word 'province' was beginning to be applied to it, the North Sea was again becoming a link instead of a 'moat defensive', and Britain's own history was coming under interrogation.

One cause of this was the comparatively archaic nature of Britain's industrial base. The country had survived the war and managed a remarkable export performance in the late 1940s, but this had been achieved on an ageing infrastructure and low investment, poor research and development and inadequate training. The country still had advantages – Alan Milward has shown how, until the mid-1960s, it was keeping up with Germany in the car industry – but its growth had slowed, and with it the transition to modern consumer-goods manufacturing.[35] Britain spent too much on defence (even in 1980, on the plans formulated by a Labour government, it was 5.7 per cent of GNP compared with West Germany's 2.7 per cent), and this in turn consumed too much of the research budget. Management was simultaneously overprivileged, underqualified and underpaid; Sir Llewellyn Woodward, a British historian of Harold Macmillan's generation who was not known for his radicalism, remembered that in his London day school, Merchant Taylors', 'The stupider boys, including most of the boors and the bullies, left at sixteen or seventeen to "go into business"; the boys who stayed on were those aiming at the professions.'[36]

The trade unions with which this generation had to deal in the 1950s and 1960s – and there were over a hundred of these, compared with seventeen in Germany – enjoyed no *Mitbestimmung* of the German sort, with seats on advisory boards; as a result they were ill-informed about the industries in which they operated, suspicious of one another, disorganized in terms of works representation, and often incompetently, sometimes corruptly, led. In this situation the slump of 1957, triggered by Suez and the subsequent fuel crisis, induced a period of profound upheaval in British industry; in some capital-goods industries, notably in Scotland and the north of England, the outcome was near-total collapse. In 1961 British production still led Europe. By 1964 Germany had pulled level; by 1973 German *per capita* output was almost 30 per cent ahead. On the eve of its mistrustful entry into the EEC, Britain had the longest working hours *and* the highest strike-level in Europe, the highest rate of inflation and the lowest holiday entitlement.[37] Even its traditional strengths did not seem capable of helping it to cope with challenges such as that of oil exploitation.

Two examples: Britain was still in the late 1940s the premier export shipbuilder, with 38 per cent of world tonnage, and a particular dominance in general cargo ships of around 10,000 tons and 'hotel' ships, the large passenger liners which still ruled the Atlantic. Within a decade both types would be obsolete, thrust aside by the bulk-carrier, the container ship and the airliner. In 1977 tonnage was down to only 4 per cent of world output. Adaptation had been, as on the Clyde, too slow in coming. German, Japanese and Swedish yards captured orders for new types of vessels, such as car ferries – and oil rigs and their tenders.[38]

This was not just because of the internal failings of the industry. Shipbuilding, like other areas of manufacturing, suffered from the dissociation of ownership and investment. The British merchant marine was dwindling, as the new post-Suez generation of tankers and bulk-carriers were out-flagged to Greece, Liberia or Panama. Shipowners out to cut costs to a minimum would not use British yards, however well run. If the yards managed to compete, they could only do so by sacrificing the research and development investment on which innovative and profit-yielding manufacture depended.[39]

Another problem had already been highlighted by the Scottish experience: the banks which in the eighteenth and nineteenth centuries had assisted industrialization remained based in Scotland. But their investment policies were aimed at the areas of highest return: in the booming south-east of England, in property, and abroad. Their investment was one contributory factor to the situation in which Britain still had six of the twenty biggest European firms, but a declining rate of domestic investment. To bring productivity abreast of the rest of Europe, it was estimated that £20 billion would be required by 1980. But investment had fallen by 7.6 per cent in 1971, and by 12 per cent in 1972. True, in the next year it had risen, but £200 million of the cash then invested had gone to the EEC, while £6 billion was estimated to have been swallowed up in a highly speculative property boom.[40]

More seriously, attempts to rationalize British industry were partial, secretive, and almost wholly lacking in any sense of long-term appraisal. Beeching and Buchanan have been mentioned. In the headlines for a time, they represented the policies of deter-mined pressure groups − notably the road and construction lobbies − and made a bad transport system worse. Other lobbies got their way in defence research, Concorde or the nuclear power programme; the latter in particular swallowed billions and, worse still, the services of thousands of young scientists whose abilities could have been used on more modest, more perceptive programmes of technological improvement. When a correction came, as come it did with the report of Sir Burke Trend in 1963 and Lord Rothschild's report of 1971, it swung too far in the opposite direction. Research was increasingly tied to direct industrial demand, and so tended to reflect the patchiness of a failing manufacturing base.[41] A fraction of the funds invested in any of the research-guzzlers of the 1960s would have set up at least the means of appraising the industrial implications of the North Sea's bounty, but it was not done, and for its first decade foreign technologies would have the province to themselves.

Struthonians and Hungarians

Exploration for gas and oil in the North Sea started to get under way only five years after the collapse of Britain's direct role in the Middle Eastern oil province, as a result of the Suez fiasco. The subsequent national navel-gazing, increasingly obsessive as the EEC nations began to forge ahead, uncovered cognate sequences of technological mishaps. The wartime bombing campaign came under scrutiny when the novelist and scientist C.P. Snow castigated successive British governments, and the whole caste system of the British upper-class literary intelligentsia – from T.S. Eliot to W.B. Yeats – for its pathological neglect of the sciences. Snow had observed the conflict between scientists engaged in researching the actual effectiveness of weapons (headed by his friend Lord Blackett, a Jutland veteran) and Churchill's advisers, who had insisted for ideological reasons, and because of the RAF's *amour propre*, on the bombing offensive. He did not find the decision-making structure reassuring and did not believe it had changed.[42]

A more optimistic assessment had come from a younger man, the Labour MP Anthony Crosland, who represented a gas-involved constituency at Grimsby and Immingham. To Crosland, the lazy, charming Keynesian economist, there had been

. . . a peaceful revolution. One cannot imagine today a deliberate offensive alliance between Government and the Unions . . . on the 1921, 1925–6 or 1927 models . . . Instead the atmosphere in Whitehall is almost deferential, the desire not to give offence positively ostentatious . . .[43]

This assumption of consensus seemed less attractive as British productivity bumped along the bottom in the early 1960s and C.P. Snow's *Two Cultures* was not the only text to be hurled at the establishment in the early 1960s. *Suicide of a Nation* was another, edited by the former Communist Arthur Koestler and sponsored by the magazine *Encounter* (and thus indirectly by the American CIA). Koestler threw out the Marxian notion of 'scientific materialism' and class struggle in favour of the determination of economic change by ideas. He and his centre-left Labour Party contributors saw Britain as run by 'Old Struthonians', a warped élite of ostriches who stuck their heads in the sand rather than attempt to come to terms with the social, educational and scientific demands of modernization.

Yet another symposium, edited by the Labour academic Hugh Thomas, tackled the establishment head-on – in the forces, the City, politics and academia. Its most aggressive and enduring piece was an attack on the civil service by an Oxford economics don, who might have come out of one of Snow's *Strangers and Brothers* novels:

The unsuitability of the present organization of the British administration at the higher policy-making level is the principal explanation of the drift toward *laisser-faire*. In a planned economy, the crossword puzzle mind, reared on mathematics at Cambridge or Greats at Oxford, has only a limited outlook. They must define themselves against a system in which positive action is in order because they can only express themselves by transferring decisions from the realm of economic reality into the sphere of pseudo-moral philosophy. This is only possible in a 'free' economy where the state has no, or at most very limited functions. Complicated problems are then cheerfully solved by the application of so-called 'general principles'.[44]

An immigrant (like Koestler and his friend Nicholas Kaldor) from Admiral Horthy's Hungary in the 1920s, promoted through the patronage of J.M. Keynes, Thomas Balogh had been a leading left-wing economist in the 1950s and was coming to the fore as an adviser to the Labour Party. His indictment of the Whitehall mandarinate was damning: it was selected from the 'liberal arts' monopolized by the English public schools and the Universities of Oxford and Cambridge; it cultivated a myth of 'generalism' whereby 'effortless superiority' (demonstrated, ironically, by Balogh's own Balliol) was supposed to compensate for professional inadequacies; it shuffled people from ministry to ministry, just at the point when they were in danger of mastering their subjects. Its orders and knighthoods upheld an *ancien régime* of privilege and inequality, when expertise and democratic accountability, in exchange for proper pay, were required.[45]

Keynes had been urbane; Balogh was effervescent to the point of incoherence. He got some distance under the Wilson government, to which he acted as an adviser, presuming on the tolerance of Wilson's secretary, Marcia Williams:

Invaluable though it was, his frequent telephone calls irritated my colleagues, who did not hesitate to show it. Usually, therefore, it fell to me to speak to him when Harold Wilson was busy, and I had the task of simplifying his messages for transmission to the leader and bringing the call to an end as quickly as possible when urgent matters demanded attention elsewhere.[46]

'He talks too much' was ever the response of the Westminster professional. A Royal Commission on the Civil Service was set up under the Scottish academic Lord Fulton. The mandarinate made some concessions, but held its main position: that professionals could not compete at all levels of the service. Wilsonian economic policy – determined until 1967 by the American insistence that sterling remain a reserve currency – was no more encouraging to those who wanted devaluation and cheap money for industrial investment. Balogh and his criticisms figure nowhere in the *Personal Record* of the Prime Minister he was supposed to advise.[47]

Balogh was patriotic, and interventionist where Crosland had seen a corporatism achieved through inertia. Balogh's Britain would be centralized under a Weberian élite of expert bureaucrats who would control the unions as much as it would plan the economy. In the late 1960s oil seemed to him, frustrated as an adviser to Wilson, a classic case of a tradition-bound, inept British élite selling out to the multinationals. *Private Eye*'s Sheikh Baloghi had already started to fret in the wings, and as the American energy crisis began to define itself in 1972, he got his chance. He launched himself, in a remarkable *Sunday Times* article in February 1972, on the oil majors, the British Department of Trade and Industry, and the old political élite, accusing them of letting an unparalleled opportunity for national reconstruction slip through their fingers.

To be a Hungarian radical in the inter-war years was to experience a sclerotic, semi-fascist regime, brooding over its Habsburg past. Against this, the experimentation, the five-year plans, the almost instant industrialization of Russia were fascinating, while the crab-like approach to the modern industrial world

of the Macmillanite Conservative Party seemed a sort of home-
grown Horthyism. Oil would change this, Balogh argued, and
enable the Labour Party to develop a much more efficient
collective *étatisme* to underpin the welfare state. It was a material
impulse Britain had lacked, since coal production had reached a
peak in 1914. Others looked at the oil, at the greatest oil power,
the United States, and at the way its politics were tending, and
saw development going in quite a different direction.[48]

Gas and GUMBP

In the 1930s Alastair Dunnett, doubtless inspired by Stevenson's
Inland Voyage, took a canoe round the coast of Scotland. He
recollected years later a conversation about this risky venture
with his brother and a geologist called Armour, in which the
latter had drawn his attention to the possibility of sea-bed oil and
minerals in the rock strata of the Scottish coast.[49] In fact, in 1937 a
small gas field had been discovered near Whitby in Yorkshire.
Other issues supervened, but this began in the later 1950s to
achieve significance. On 29 July 1959, after sixteen years' fruitless
drilling, a land-based rig of the Nederlandse Aardolie Maatschapp-
pij struck gas at Schlochteren near Groningen in Friesland. This
turned out to be the second largest field in the world, and geologists
could see that the strata of Yorkshire re-emerged in Holland.[50]

Almost immediately, Shell, BP and Esso began to survey the
southern sector of the sea, initially with an airborne magnetometer
which probed for areas of sedimentary rock. In operations 'Sea-
shell' and a joint venture of Gulf, Union Oil, Mobil and BP with
the charming acronym of GUMBP, they discovered several
large sedimentary basins of the sort which contained gas and
possibly oil. BP followed this up in 1964 with the jack-up
drilling rig *Sea Gem*, converted rather perilously from a barge in
France, which began in that year to detect natural gas in commercial quantities in shallow water (about fifty to seventy feet) off

the Norfolk and Lincolnshire coasts. In November 1965 *Sea Gem* discovered what was to become the West Sole gas field. Only six days later it capsized and sank with the loss of thirteen lives.

One cubic metre of gas contains as much energy as three-quarters of a kilo of crude oil. It also has the advantage that it can stream straight from its harbouring strata, without much treatment, into a cooker, a heating boiler, or a power station. Provided a pipe system exists, it causes a third less environmental damage than oil, as tankers, refineries and road space are redundant. So Britain's gas fields – Shell's Leman, Indefatigable and Hewett were discovered between 1966 and 1969 – were soon in full commercial exploitation, and the state-owned Gas Council, monopoly buyer of the stuff at its own (low) valuation, had adapted its system to cope with the new supply between then and 1975. Gas had always – much as the tortoise – been the symbol of the British Fabian socialists, their practical answer to the revolutionary rhetoric of the continentals. Now, translated from a municipal to a national level, it proved to be a success of the Wilson government; but it was one which was little publicized, and whose lessons were even less instructive. In 1966 a young lecturer at the London School of Economics argued for a major planning scheme for a linear development of gas-related industry and settlement along the east coast, supervised by a body modelled on the new Highlands and Islands Development Board. The scheme vanished without trace, but more was to be heard of Dr Peter Odell, and the quest for oil and gas would shortly alight on the HIDB's doorstep.[51]

The explorers shifted to the north, and went in search of oil. Would this be of more than marginal interest? Oil prices had actually *fallen* during the 1960s and oil cost less than £2 a ton in 1969. Yet by that date one in eight of the drillings in the Scottish sector was locating oil, among them the rigs at work on the Montrose field.[52] While the Upper Clyde crisis was going on, rumours alleged that BP was sitting on the fact that its rigs had discovered in late 1970 a field scarcely smaller than Norway's oil-and-gas Ekofisk, detected in 1969. The Forties field prompted guesses that 12 million tons a year (one-eighth of UK demand) might be possible. Within a year complacency had given way to a scramble for exploration rights and for sites at which production platforms (much larger than the drilling-rigs Marathon was building at Clydebank) could be constructed.[53] Nevertheless, for the Scottish National Party to claim in September 1972 that oil production could be worth £2,200 million per annum – £14.60 a ton – by 1980 still appeared astonishing. The grounds for this development lay elsewhere, beyond the North Sea's horizon.

2

The High-Energy Society

'"Glorious stirring sight!" murmured Toad, never offering to move. "The poetry of motion! The *real* way to travel! The *only* way to travel! Here today – in next week tomorrow! Villages skipped, towns and cities jumped – always somebody else's horizon! O bliss! O poop-poop! O my! O my!"
'"O *stop* being an ass, Toad," cried the Mole despairingly.'

Kenneth Grahame, *The Wind in the Willows*

Motorway City

Three miles up-river from Clydebank, the concrete span of the Kingston Bridge arched over the Clyde, with ample clearance for the tallest of masts. Even in its details, the bridge was a folly; no ships of any size steamed as far as the Broomielaw. It carried the first stage of the urban motorway which Glasgow Corporation was building; one of Europe's most ambitious schemes in a city which in 1966 had only one car per eleven inhabitants – Surrey had one car to every four.[1] But few places in Britain had more enthusiastically adopted the doctrine, derived from the United States, that mobility was a positive benefit. Even in the 1990s, when the horrendous consequences for society and the environment of mass-motorization were glaringly apparent, the Corporation's successor, Strathclyde Region, could still give priority to doubling the traffic lanes over the bridge, and the Scottish Office minister responsible for transport, Lord James Douglas-Hamilton, could commend the car as an unqualified blessing while praising the project – on Scotland's other sea coast – of building a second Forth Road Bridge.[2]

By this time there were four people per car in Glasgow, compared with one and a half in Surrey. Motorization had become a fact, and the conventional account – reflected by the minister's view – assumed that the yen for mobility was some sort of substantive human quality. It was not. In 1956, the year of the Suez crisis, there were not many more cars than there had been in 1939. After 1956, car journeys in European countries quickly rose by a factor of four, double the growth in national product. Americans were travelling 5,000 kilometres annually in 1950, against scarcely 1,500 kilometres in Europe. By 1970 the equivalent figures were 8,000 and 6,000 kilometres respectively; and about 90 per cent of these extra kilometres were by car.[3]

The car was far more than a means of transport. In the 1960s and 1970s it disrupted Western Europe more than the bombers which had obliterated whole city centres in the Second World War. But it was a peaceful and ostensibly progressive disruption, supposedly creating new freedoms for a society which had been at peace for a quarter-century. This was vividly evident on Clydeside where in 1950 the word 'car' didn't even mean a motor-car but one of Glasgow's trams. The Glasgow of 1950 had run on steam and steel, the two connected by an electricity supply which had until 1947 belonged to the Corporation. People lived in large families in small flats heated by coal fires; they travelled to work by tram, bus or steam train; they went on their holidays by steamer to Rothesay or Dunoon. But they also went, up to three times a week, to the cinema, where they saw a wondrous world of freeways and huge Buicks, blondes and tough-guy gangsters or gumshoes. Los Angeles existed in Glasgow's imagination, and the city was trying to get there; as were, in various ways, most of Europe's cities. The television advertisements of the 1950s stressed a brave new world of consumer goods, nearly all of which were, or were accessible through, derivatives of petroleum: from the plastics used in fridges or washing-machines, televisions or record players, to nylon stockings, terylene trousers and drip-dry shirts, the paints and veneers of the do-it-yourself enthusiasts, the carpets and shelves and three-piece suites of the new house in 'one of the better schemes'. The car might not yet have arrived in the garage, but the holiday on the Costa del Sol was assumed, by plane from Turnhouse or Renfrew. And it was paid for by new sorts of work, in light-engineering factories making computers (at Greenock), or vacuum cleaners (at Cambuslang) or the Playtex Living Bra (at Hillington), for which Clydeside Man's wife or daughter were better fitted than old rivet-chewing MacHismo himself.

By 1970 this new world had burst the bonds of the old; but that didn't mean that it was in any sense predictable: rather the reverse. In technological terms man had never advanced along a smooth evolutionary line. The earliest theorists of social change – the French sociologist Henri de Saint-Simon, and following him Auguste Comte and Karl Marx – had seen long 'organic' periods of technical and social co-ordination being followed by short and chaotic episodes in which change tended to come all at once and from all directions. The Clyde had gone through one such period in the mid-nineteenth century, with the steamship, the railway, electricity. Indeed, it had largely started it. But things had been much more complex in the twentieth century. The Clyde had missed out on the automotive age – the huge, empty factory of the failed Argyll Car Co. can still be seen at Alexandria – until 1964, and the disruptions caused by two world wars, which had distorted technical evolution in favour of military goals, had preserved it in a retarded condition. The Europe of the Treaty of Rome in 1957 was closer to that of the Kaiser and the Tsar than to the Europe of 1973, but some areas were more Edwardian than others.

In the 1960s technology and economics *seemed* to have taken the lead once again and forced open the future. Motorization, contraception, television, home and business electronics, air travel, multi-storey buildings, supermarkets: oil was merely a membrane connecting these revolutions, which all too soon became mundane. 'Stroked nylon hisses over groin and bum,' wrote Brian Patten from Liverpool, 'like granny's wireless caught on Hilversum': life's oldest struggle, going on in the car parks of the West after Saturday discos, was fought over, and by, petroleum derivatives: Revlon, Crimplene, Nylon, Lycra.

And where technology and society were going was no more rational or predictable than sex.

Petrol Politics

Dallas, the quintessence of Scoto-American oil hedonism, couldn't have happened in Britain. Oil in America was different from most other places in the world in being privately owned. While most European states had taken subsoil minerals into public ownership (Britain in 1934, under a Conservative-dominated government), American landowners owned the bounty beneath their fields and forests. But the oil business was more dynamic in America than anywhere else, because oil had propelled the expansion of the country from rough parity with the major European powers in 1914 to world dominance. The roots of American motorization – an export far more durable than republicanism or democracy – did not just lie with the early technological triumphs of Henry Ford, or with the beneficial aspects of free-market competition. In the year in which North Sea surveys started, the last line of the Pacific Electric Railway closed down in Los Angeles. This suburban network, built in the 1900s, had once operated some two hundred miles of commuter line, but from the 1930s on it had been bought out by oil interests, notably Standard Oil itself, and throttled of investment, while federal and California State funds were funnelled into a vast highway system which by 1990 was sustaining 8 million cars. Such situations were repeated in countless American cities, with public transport gradually being run down until it became a residual service (in Los Angeles it was used in 1990 by only 6 per cent of travellers) cheaply provided by battered, ancient buses, for the marginal classes in American society. If only 30 per cent of the buses kept to an acceptable schedule, then on only 30 per cent of the days of the Los Angeles year did the city's smog fall to a tolerable level.[4]

Thanks to air competition, the same decline afflicted American railroad passenger services, which fell by three-quarters after the 1960s. The trains that remained in the 1970s, run by the state-owned Amtrak Corporation, were fewer than those of any British Rail region. In continental Europe the branch-lines might have withered, but states were accepting responsibility for deficits and adapting their networks to a predominantly urban society – electrifying lines, installing metros – otherwise Paris or London or Madrid would simply have seized up. But in America cheap energy, and in particular cheap petrol, enabled a new, 'green field' industrialization. The sweltering springs and summers of the south and west had hitherto deterred high-value industry and made public transport purgatorial; now the creation of low-density suburbia and air-conditioning – in home, car, office and factory – enabled the industrial migration which was the up-side to the Vietnam War. But aircraft, trucks, Mississippi barge-tows, the railroads themselves: all ran on oil.

America's fixation with the car and the plane, due above all to the cheapness of fuel, showed that oil didn't follow the dictates of the market, which would register the resulting industrial and social diseconomies. Indeed it was difficult in any sense to talk about an 'energy market'.[5] Cheap petrol was provided to the American market by a combination of private companies operating in conjunction with one another, state subsidies for roads and bridges, and international measures by the United States to secure world-wide supplies of oil. Its spin-offs were present in the 'embedded energy' which was part of the plastics, automobile, artificial fibre and tourist industries. A glance at any university library shelf of books dealing with energy questions would show that those on 'oil diplomacy' far outnumbered those on energy policy. Oil – as much as the US navy or the nuclear deterrent – was the basis of the *Pax Americana*, both at home and abroad. It kept the American blue-collar worker content in the Eisenhower years, with his gas-guzzler connecting him to a whole range of facilities otherwise inaccessible: airports, supermarkets, drive-in cinemas, national parks. It also bankrolled the industrialization of the old enemies Germany and Japan, and their harmless confinement to producing cheap consumer goods. Oil was in fact what American loans – the Dawes Plan, the Young Plan – had been in the 1920s: the necessary subsidy. But it was a more secure one than cash deposits which might be swept away if there was a domestic finance crisis in the States. Hence the fact that although the USA had until the 1960s only a limited need for Middle East oil, since 1945 it had taken a great interest in what was going on there. Franklin Roosevelt's meeting with King Ibn Saud in 1945 was almost as fateful as the meeting which had just preceded it, with Stalin and Churchill at Yalta, which parcelled the world out in spheres of influence.[6]

Can one overstate the case for a motor-propelled crisis? Perhaps. Europe's demand for oil, which had been growing through the 1960s at a steady 5 per cent per annum, was mainly for *fuel* oil (40–45 per cent), not for petrol (13–15 per cent). America actually used natural gas and coal for more than half its energy needs, although it was also the great petrol market, at 40 per cent of consumption. But America was the prototype for a motorized Europe; the motor-car assembly line had been the major prop of post-war industrialization – the equivalent of the cotton factory in the nineteenth century – and the new industrialization was firmly based on oil. This interlinking meant that as the number of cars increased in the 1960s, the cost of keeping them on the road fell. Oil was cheap and in real terms getting cheaper; $1.75 a barrel in 1949, $1.50 in 1960, $1.25 in 1969.[7]

Two oil-age symbols were immediately apparent from the vantage-point of the Clyde. The first was embodied in the great petro-chemical complex at Grangemouth, in which crude oil was not simply refined but acted as the feedstock for a wide range of chemical production, including fertilizers, polymers, paints and pharmaceuticals:

Breaking down thousands of millions of barrels of crude oil to quench the insatiable thirst of the car made other fractions abundant and cheap, like heating oil and heavy residuals.[8]

The saleability of such products continually acted to hold the price of petrol, and fuel oil in general, down in real terms. Even in a Britain given to upholding the 'healthiness' of unheated, draughty houses, central heating was becoming commonplace, often by oil because of the remoteness of houses from the gas grid.

The second factor was the supertankers which had come in after the Suez Canal was closed in 1956. After a momentary panic, shipowners realized they were no longer constrained by the dimensions of the Canal; that taking a very big ship from the Gulf round the Cape of Good Hope worked out much cheaper than sending lots of small ships through Suez. The growth in tanker size, from 30,000 tons to the very large crude carrier (VLCC) of 150,000 tons or more, became a fact in the early 1960s, and finished many of the Clyde shipyards. An object lesson was provided by a figure who came to exercise an influential but shadowy role on North Sea affairs. Daniel K. Ludwig's forebears came from Germany and settled in Michigan, but DKL (as he was known to friend and foe) made his money, lots of it, as a war contractor. He went on to expand his business by using 'saleable contracts', borrowing cash on the collateral of contracts to build ships. His firm, National Bulk Carriers, pioneered welded hulls, then patronized the growth of Japanese shipyards in the early 1950s, where he realized that a 200,000-ton ship cost only 20 per cent more to build and run than a 100,000-ton ship. By 1976 DKL had a fleet of fifty supertankers – the biggest concentration of tonnage in the world – and political connections with the Hollywood born-again right, with Ronald Reagan, with Howard Hughes, and with the chief oil spokesman of the conservative wing of the Democrats, Senator Henry 'Scoop' Jackson.[9]

DKL was in fact an expression of an alarming instability in American socio-economic life: the extent to which 'cheap energy' interest groups, as much as the 'military-industrial complex', were dominating American policy – particularly in the two conservative decades after the fall of Lyndon Johnson in 1968. Such groups saw America's interests as world-wide, yet through the narrow focus of the 'sunbelt' states, their great fuel firms and contractors. In 1953 a young diplomat, trained as a petroleum geologist and studying the oil companies, had written of their dinosaur-like tendencies:

Their global outlook is severely limited, not only by their shareholders, but by the narrowness of their board, and their ultimate sense of dependence on the US government.[10]

The diplomat's name was Richard Funkhouser. Two decades later he served on the State Department's committee which reported to President Nixon on the fuel emergency, in March 1972. In 1974 he became United States Consul in Edinburgh.[11]

The Powerlessness of Power

American oil diplomacy knew, in a rough-and-ready sort of way, what it was doing. It was less adept at comprehending its instruments. Technology and society have their own laws. The sociologist Sir Patrick Geddes, who died in 1931 but was still a force in Scottish social planning and among more worried Americans such as Lewis Mumford, had talked of *paleotechnic* and *neotechnic* societies. A paleotechnic society had the equipment of modern industrialization, but had not yet learned how to organize it logically. A neotechnic society could 'objectify' this problem. In the 1960s energy was in this sort of situation. Inefficiencies in its use were remedied by the tapping of new and supposedly cheap sources, not by more sophisticated technology or organization.

The spectacle of a Scottish Victorian house adapted to central heating was chilling in every sense. Heat struggled out of ancient radiators and flung itself exhilaratingly through the nominal barrier of huge sash windows. In snow, the purple slate roofs of Scots villages stood out starkly to show where lofts had not been insulated. Late paleotechnic attempts at energy forecasting were no more sophisticated. The concept of establishing statistics for national economic growth was itself new, only attempted in Britain during, and in Scotland after, the Second World War:

no attempt had yet been made to correlate this with fuel needs.[12] Energy policy, such as it was, took place as a result of the Whitehall politicking of various state lobbies: the coal, oil, and in Britain in particular, nuclear interests. These all ensured that the last thing that was ever going to be reflected was market forces; and the situation was no more straightforward when it came to the international trading of energy.

The British ministry responsible for energy was itself a baffling body, whose power appeared to wax and wane like the moon. Sometimes it seemed irrelevant, no more than a specialized annexe of the Board of Trade; sometimes it appeared to represent the country in microcosm. In 1947, when coal froze in the sidings and power-stations broke down, the Glasgow socialist Emmanuel Shinwell became (unhappily for himself) the most prominent member of the Attlee Cabinet. In the 1950s the lobbies made the Ministry of Power their own, rather as the National Farmers' Union had colonized Agriculture, supervised in a vague way by Tories of the old school. In the 1960s, for specific reasons, the Foreign Office had the say.

In 1955, in the last months of Churchill's government, the nuclear lobby, lately delivered of Britain's hydrogen bomb, gained the initiative with its White Paper, 'A Programme of Nuclear Power'. The head of the Atomic Energy Authority, Sir Christopher Hinton, visited a bleak headland in Caithness and inaugurated at Dounreay Britain's first (and, as it turned out, only) Fast Breeder Reactor Programme. Government funds committed to nuclear power tripled after Suez, which demonstrated both the risks of oil and the unreliability of Americans. The manpower strength of the Atomic Energy Authority rose from 17,000 in 1954 to 41,000 in 1961 – over half the manpower of the North Sea oil industry at its peak.[13] How much did this divert – ultimately into a *cul-de-sac* – the sort of research and organization people needed to cope with oil?

Quite a lot. But thereafter even the government's nuclear determination was skewed by an expensive and economically dubious programme of coal modernization competing with cheap oil. Coal had won on points in 1961 when the government levied a tax on heavy fuel oil, which had risen to 40 per cent by 1967. It then almost fell out of the ring in the fierce winter of 1962–3, which replicated many of the horrors of 1946–7, and did a good turn to the nuclear programme. The scientists stepped forward with their latest elephantine wonder, the Advanced Gas-Cooled Reactor (AGR), a sophisticated product with, they stressed, world markets before it.

The Conservatives put off a decision in 1964; they would probably have opted for the cheaper American Pressurized Water Reactor, but you didn't do this sort of thing before an election. Labour, patriotically – and to hold its CND left to the compromise formula of 'the peaceful uses of nuclear energy' went for the AGR. By 1968–9 this was patently a step too far; an inquiry into nuclear programme delays showed that:

The British AGR programme was an early demonstration that forecasting and planning for nuclear power could reach extremes of wild inaccuracy far beyond those encountered in other energy forecasting. Nuclear programmes elsewhere soon corroborated this.[14]

The AGR reactors went 100 per cent over cost and took decades to commission. But the nuclear brouhaha had profile, and no one noticed that next to nothing was done about oil resources, beyond throwing exploration licences to the majors.

There were reasons for the Ministry of Power's shadowy profile, rather sinister ones, which had nothing to do with energy policy. The oil department of the ministry was supposed to be in the front line of the campaign to bring down Ian Smith's white supremacist regime in Southern Rhodesia, which had declared UDI in November 1965. Oil sanctions were the chosen weapon, military intervention against something resembling a rebellious Conservative Association being ruled out by the possibility of a repetition of the Curragh Mutiny of 1914. (Such qualms were rarely in evidence when the chosen targets were workers or Irish.) A few Royal Navy frigates steamed up and down the Madagascar channel interdicting oil tankers from reaching Beira, where the pipeline to Rhodesia started. But BP and Shell continued to supply Rhodesia, initially directly and then, after intervention by the Commonwealth Office and the Ministry of Power, via South Africa and the French company Total, through a secret 'swap' operation whereby Total's South African plants were supplied by Shell and BP. In the latter company, the government had, of course, a majority shareholding. The British government was therefore collusive with the oil companies in a 'presentational' policy which was intended to, and did, deceive international opinion.[15]

This charade was not exposed until 1978 when, with the collapse of the Portuguese empire, UDI was being throttled; and when BP's Forties field was pouring forth hundreds of thousands of barrels of oil. There had therefore been good reason for the government to downplay the oil business, and its powers to control it, in the 1960s. When we ask, as D.C. Watt did in the mid-1970s, why British official policy towards appraising the future of the offshore oil industry was so supine for so long, the answer may well lie in a small department with rapidly changing but overall uninspiring political leadership – four forgettable ministers (Fred Lee, Richard Marsh, Ray Gunter, Roy Mason) and a civil service rather too close to the majors. It disappeared completely, swallowed by the Board of Trade, on 6 October 1969.[16]

The Faulty Clock

The career of the Ministry of Power was unimpressive, but not very instructive either. If it had been run intelligently and circumspectly it would still have encountered an international energy situation which consisted of incompatibilities between long-range planning and political and market movements. The result resembled a huge dysfunctional astronomical clock, with some of its movements set in ponderous rotations, and others whirling away, meeting short-range changes, and interrupting the graver motions.

The political background to energy planning did not get any

simpler with the onset of apparent energy scarcity in the 1970s. The symptoms of competing pressure groups were similar to what the British had encountered, but were demonstrated on a world scale. It is necessary to leap ahead of the narrative at this point, and explain what these were.

In terms of long-range projects, nuclear power still commanded attention, particularly in France, Britain and America. Early in 1974 Richard Nixon's advisers – 'Scoop' Jackson and Governor John Connaly prominent among them – bankrolled 'Project Independence', which put a 4,000-page report into the White House in November, after Nixon's resignation in August. 'Project Independence' reflected a nuclear bandwagon active in Europe and in the United States after 1973, but also moves to cut fuel consumption altogether through insulation, more efficient generation, and speed limits. On the other hand, the desire to strengthen the exploitation of 'native' fields was accelerated, and indeed greatly aided by the technological experiments in the North Sea; this would underlie the boom in the 'sunbelt' states in the first half of the 1980s.[17] The nuclear industry, running into technical problems – Three Mile Island was in 1979 – and accosted by an even stronger green lobby, soon peaked; manufacturers suffered huge losses. The exploitation of the North Sea would proceed against this background.

As would the use to which Arab oil profits were put. Coping with the post-Yom Kippur, oil-induced slump, it was easier to use the resources on hand to combat the sort of problems which would cause electoral trouble, than for long-term research and new technological initiatives. Britain and the United States had elaborate banking systems anxious to take over the management of the oil balances of the conservative Arab states; they had also a military-industrial complex eager for orders. Especially America, all dressed up for Vietnam and with nowhere much to go after that had fallen through. What better, then, to combat domestic unemployment and stimulate investment, than to give Arabs (whose capacity for consumer goods was limited) what they wanted? As a result, in Groucho Marx's words, 'All God's chillun got guns'; Allah's not least. America's arms exports would go up fourfold in the four years after the Yom Kippur war.[18]

And how better to use the financial services capacity which lay, on Wall Street and the City of London, near to ruin (not just because of the oil) than by recirculating the $50 billion of surpluses available to the Arabs, particularly to those 'developing' countries further impoverished by the rise in the oil price? Financial expertise in Riyadh or Qatar was strictly limited, so London and New York would do this for them.[19] Accordingly, 'recycled' Arab money surged into the bonds of South American and sub-Saharan African countries – and even a few bits of COMECON – where it subsequently vanished without trace. 'Don't think about the Bomb, think about debt repayment,' said a chirpy American postgrad at a seminar in Oxford in 1983 (her husband was a banker and she was staying at the London Hilton). By the early 1980s a combination of endemic military conflict in the Middle East, the weakness of international finance and the collapse of demand from the wretched 'developing' countries – or LDCS, 'less developed countries', as they were now more honestly christened – would induce a situation of permanent instability in the supply and pricing of oil.

The European nuclear interest was resilient. It was domestically strong, and made the external instability of oil supplies a text which would demonstrate its utility. In November 1974 the Organization for Economic Co-operation and Development published *Energy Prospects to 1985*, updated in 1977 as *World Energy Outlook*. In this, various interest groups – headed by the French and the power engineers – argued for more expansion. In 1975 the World Energy Conference established a Conservation Commission, whose reports, presented to its Istanbul conference in 1977, promised 'full speed ahead in all directions', a line partially endorsed by a Massachusetts Institute of Technology 'Workshop on Alternative Energy Strategies' in the same year, which forecast the levelling-off of oil production around 1985. In 1979 this threat of rigidity in supply seemed to be given an objective reality by the radical Islamic revolution in Iran, and the further doubling of oil prices.

In fact, the experts managed to get just about everything wrong.[20] In the 1980s it was demand, not supply, which was rigid. The oil price went up to $40 a barrel for a few years, but it did not stay up. The radicalization of the Arab world might mean higher prices in the short term, but because of ideological divisions no long-term unity was possible. The best that advocates of higher prices could expect was that internal Middle Eastern conflicts, like the Iran–Iraq war, would inhibit their exports. Secondly, although economic growth resumed in the late 1970s and 1980s, it would be much less spendthrift of energy, and was in fact to some extent derived from energy-conserving measures. In West Germany the economy would grow by 19 per cent from 1979 to 1989, while fuel consumption stagnated. In the United States the gas-guzzling Chevvy or Buick died the death of the dinosaur in the 1980s. By 1990 the average American car was subject to a 60 mph speed limit, and was smaller, slower and less energy-intensive than most of the brutes which roared along German *Autobahnen*.

Not least because the alternative energy scenarios of such as E.F. Schumacher, first postulated in the 1950s and 1960s, had been borne out. Conserving energy – through insulation programmes, more efficient combustion (combined-cycle generators which were 70 per cent rather than 30 per cent efficient, because the exhaust of a steam turbine was used to drive a gas turbine) and the steady shift of industrial activity to 'intelligent' production, which was low in energy demand, or to the service industries, whose needs were lower still – became an important part of the energy equation.

The boost that the oil price increase brought indirectly to the most socially reactionary sections of Western capitalism – armaments and finance – would be politically registered after 1980 by the rhetoric of Reagan and Thatcher. They got their chance through the Soviet invasion of Afghanistan in 1979. This reflected Russian apprehension at its swelling Moslem population, but also the fact that the oil scarcity of 1974–81 aided the Soviet Union to exploit its huge reserves, and stave off the economic nemesis which seemed to be awaiting it through its archaic and inefficient manufacturing and agricultural sectors. It was against this seemingly powerful 'Evil Empire' that the Americans directed their rearmament and technological blockade in the early 1980s.

But what would happen to Russia after the oil price collapse in 1985–6? And what would happen to the North Sea?

The World of the Seven Sisters

Oil prospects were by the early 1970s already linked with the issue of global ecology, Middle Eastern politics, and the debatable future of a high-energy economy. But they also had a diplomatic prehistory, represented by the fact that among the 'Seven Sisters' two of the major players were the British Petroleum Co. and Shell Transport and Trading. These testified to the global influence that Britain had exerted on oil affairs since Churchill had been at the Admiralty, particularly in the Middle East but also in the Indian subcontinent and Indonesia, a directly political influence which had only recently ended. The Suez invasion took place only eight years before the first licences were granted in the North Sea, and only eight years after the independence of India; it demonstrated the American foreclosure on that British involvement in the Levant established by Disraeli's purchase of Suez shares in 1876. The slyness and opportunism this had involved gave way to a more visceral if not altogether consistent American policy: a Jewish lobby committed to Israel, and an oil lobby devoted to simultaneously massaging the Arab powers and fleecing them.

Britain remained, however, greatly dependent on the power exerted by two multinationals which, although one was a semi-state concern and the other private, acted more closely with the other international oil cartel giants than with other British firms or with the British government. Together with the American majors – Standard, Gulf, Texaco, Mobil, Exxon, and Socal –

	world-wide prod. (mB)	% of world prod.
Exxon	6145	14.7
Texaco	4021	9.6
Socal	3323	7.9
Gulf	3404	8.1
Mobil	2399	5.7
BP	4659	11.1
Shell	5416	12.9

they controlled 70 per cent of world oil production in 1970.[21]

The classic problem of the oil multinationals was this. They had prospered since the 1930s by making the world oil-dominated. But they were threatened by the problem of the cash-crop farmer over the centuries: if they produced too much of the stuff, the international price would sink. So they created in the 1920s, and expanded in the following decade, a cartel which was far more cast-iron than anything inside the United States, but echoing the 'trustification' of oil, steel and railroads in the Golden Age of the 1890s. The Deterding–Teagle agreement of 1928, between the chiefs of Shell and Exxon, was the critical precedent, Henri Deterding being an enthusiastic cartel-constructor who ultimately followed his policies into the Nazi party; it was followed by the Achnacarry Compact of 1934, concluded on the Inverness-shire estate of Cameron of Locheil, which tightened up the system. As Anthony Sampson wrote, 'It may have been a cartel, but it was a cartel on the side of the consumers. Its principal purpose, in other words, was to screw the producers.'[22]

The problem was one of adaptation, escaping from the technological obsolescence of the 1960s 'rustbelt' – the automotive and steel industries of Detroit and Pittsburgh, unionized, undercapitalized and technically archaic – and going westward with smart money towards the seductive sunrise industries of the 'sunbelt'. Information technology, the media, and indeed Texan oil, speculative investments in real estate and the trackless jungle of the service industries which could stretch from computer software to junk food: these were the new order.

The motor-car was not just the physical means of this adaptation. It was the perfect implement of demand-management policies as well as the expression of the values of middle America. Its purchase could be encouraged by lowering hire-purchase controls, discouraged by restricting them. It demanded highway programmes which were flexible, in that they didn't imply, as railways did, a need for a total revolution in transportation resources to be accomplished. They enabled workers in a doomed industrial area to commute daily to a developing one, even if this involved thousands of extra miles a week. They enabled lean production, dispensing with expensive warehousing in favour of 'just-in-time' deliveries. Cars and road improvements were incremental, controllable projects which could be switched on or off at will.

But all this was predicated on the oil company as the supplier of cheap petrol at someone else's expense; cartelization had been exported. And the generation of young Arabs whose merchant families had educated them abroad and in technological subjects found that they could turn these lessons against their Western masters. Objectively, the Communist guerrilla with his Kalashnikov was much less of a menace than the youngster from a Jiddah family with an MIT degree.

In 1960 Beirut was the quiet Lausanne of the Levant, engaged in the business of getting and spending large sums of money. The *Observer*'s man in the place, Kim Philby, was still drinking the day away in the bar of the Normandy Hotel, reporting the second Arab Petrol Congress. George Stocking was a visiting professor at the American University. He attended the Congress, and thereafter was in shock:

My familiarity with the oil industry covers a span of more than half a century as an employee, student, author and government regulator. But I was unprepared for the hostility, bitterness and suspicion manifested by the congress spokesmen from the host countries, or the feeling of insecurity, uncertainty and resentment manifested by representatives of the oil industry.[23]

Relations with the latter had been complicated since the rise of Arab nationalism under Nasser and Kassem. They were further aggravated by the economic depression, which had caused a world-wide oil glut in 1960. At Beirut, the Organization of Petroleum Exporting Countries, OPEC, was founded. Originally called into being by the Venezuelans, this picked up force with the appointment of Zaki Yamani, a typical second-generation man, as Saudi oil minister in 1962. It became a cartel of the nations, pitted against the producers' cartel of the Seven Sisters, and raised the possibility that oil might be used as a political weapon, even by the more conservative Middle Eastern states.[24]

As a result of this uncertain economic outlook, two distinct and contrary movements occurred. After 1964 something like a state of war existed between the Seven Sisters and the OPEC countries; the policy of the former was co-ordinated by John J. McCloy, Assistant Secretary of War under Roosevelt, Allied High Commissioner for Germany, president of the World Bank and chairman of Chase Manhattan, who was chief of the oil companies' anti-trust department. Under McCloy the Seven Sisters moved their future policy away from the Middle East, in search of supplies from more stable regions – notably Alaska and the North Sea; while independent producers tried to muscle in on a Middle-Eastern scene in which countries were trying to establish their own technologies independent of the Western oil giants, and experimenting with increasing production as a means of undermining the Western producers' cartel. At the same time, the Nixon regime was striving to increase the price of oil, both as a means of curbing domestic consumption and of keeping the more conservative Arab states sympathetic, and detached from the nationalism (and Soviet patronage) represented by Iraq, Egypt and Syria. This became progressively more difficult to achieve. By effectively devaluing between 1971 and 1973, Nixon reduced the existing value of oil stocks, and moved Middle Eastern producers in the direction of higher prices.[25]

The immediate interest of the Seven Sisters was not in the North Sea but in Alaska, where in June 1968 a consortium in which BP had a 52 per cent stake struck oil at Prudhoe Bay, and found itself on top of one of the world's biggest reserves: equivalent to the Texas oilfield. However, because of pressure from environmental interests (which Sampson suggests was bankrolled by Exxon), production was delayed for four years. The Alaska pipeline didn't come on stream until 1972. Alternatives were necessary. Ekofisk, Montrose and Forties suggested that they existed. Where the British had done – so they insisted – the back-breaking work (or at least paid Americans to do it for them), the American majors now arrived to clean up.

Oil Diplomacy

Kissinger ... turned out to be a rather fat, oily, pompous but nice American Jew and so traitorous and anti-American that he even put me in the shade in the horrible things he said about his own country. There was no point, however extreme, in our diagnosis with which he did not agree, whether it was the futility of the nuclear obsession or the stupidity from the British point of view of British nuclear weapons, or the reckless irresponsibility of the Baghdad Pact and the American guarantee of Iran.[26]

Richard Crossman met a soulmate in Henry Kissinger in 1959. Ten years later Kissinger had become the moving force of American foreign policy, instrumental in shifting it from the world policeman role, so painful in Vietnam, to a conscious attention to national interests and, within America, favourable social groups. In the 1970s this involved serving the individualist values of a suburbanized society. Vietnam – the huge commitment and long-drawn-out failure – both increased the production statistics of Texas and California, and fostered its own conservative regionalism. The defensiveness of US foreign policy wasn't just Kissinger playing Metternich; it also reflected a profiling of direct business interests – in the securing of energy supplies and in the interdicting of the supply of high technology to Eastern Europe.

America in the early 1970s distrusted Europe. The East European repression of reform movements implied a return to Stalinism, while the Western outburst of 1968 left scars. Italy was unstable: the possibility of some sort of Communist participation in government very close. Spain and Portugal had ageing right-wing autocracies and an unsure future. France, even without De Gaulle, was suspect. Washington feared the possibility of a German reconciliation implicit in the *Östpolitik* of Willy Brandt, and therefore set particular store by the securing of adequate energy reserves in the Middle East and the cultivation of a 'special relationship' with Britain, which could also make for closer relationships with the Common Market. Energy politics belonged here. America derived only a small proportion of its energy needs from the Middle East, but through the Seven Sisters and their operation in the Gulf it could control roughly 80 per cent of fuel input into European and Japanese industry.

In an analysis briefly fashionable at the end of the 1980s the diplomatic historian Paul Kennedy argued that great powers went through a systemic process of expansion and decline, in which economic power was first stretched and then weakened by political commitment. After the periods of dominance and decline of Britain and Germany, the United States' time had now come.[27] This thesis was promptly followed by the collapse of the Soviet Union. Perhaps the paranoid style always appealed in American politics; it certainly concealed the fact of an elaborate structure of American control over the two pillars of modern economic development – energy supplies and information – which the challenges of the 1970s destabilized but did not dislodge.

Energy was something that was both limited in Europe and deeply resistant to integrationist moves. The coal supplies of all the major European economies were dwindling, and oil had in the period 1950–65 advanced from 10 per cent to 45 per cent of European energy supply. And – with the exception of the 60 per cent of Royal Dutch Shell – oil was firmly under US or British control.[28]

On the face of it this was ironic. The Soviet Union had huge fuel reserves and a low domestic demand. It should therefore have had an advantage. But in the distribution and utilization of its oil and gas it was always dependent on Western associates who were ultimately under American control, in what one commentator, Simon Bromley, has called an 'historic bloc'.[29] In the 1980s the USSR's major gas customer was West Germany, but the Soviet Union derived nothing from this but the money. American controls over the export of technology remained rigid, with the result that the most advanced part of the Comecon economy, East Germany, was never able to modernize itself to meet the challenge of the 'Pacific rim' countries who (with the application of information technology to mechanical engineering) destroyed its business in areas such as machine tools.

Bromley argues that, in themselves, the Seven Sisters had no specific reason to want to be dominant in the Middle East, from which the United States derived only a small proportion of its energy supplies; but the Sisters represented the 'great power' institutions which followed the collapse of British power after Suez. Low-price oil had been used in the 1960s by the United States to subsidize the economic growth of Germany and Japan, whose military challenge to the USA was constrained by treaty and occupation troops. Now America felt itself threatened by the very success of these former allies, aware of the debatable nature of its *point d'appui*.

The United Kingdom was not just an ally, but a particularly special relation, notably under the Labour governments which controlled the country for most of the 1970s and 1980s. Devoted, like Harold Wilson, to the Bretton Woods system of managed exchange rates, Lyndon Johnson had in the 1960s intervened on several occasions to take pressure off the pound. In return, Wilson had supported him in the Vietnam imbroglio, and thus choked the protests of his own left. The United Kingdom continued as a nuclear power, now armed with American Polaris submarines, and also acted as a safe base for American bombers and missiles. And on top of this came the oil, reserves of between perhaps 2,500 and 5,000 million tons, in a sea dominated by a heavily armed, friendly power. The great vulgar façade of the embassy in Grosvenor Square might have looked overblown when it was opened in 1960, but in the following decades it certainly paid for its existence.

3

The Capture of the Province

But the province of formulas and constraints is restricted. Even the mechanical engineer comes at last to an end of his figures, and must stand up, a practical man, face to face with the discrepancies of nature and the hiatuses of theory. After the machine is finished, and the steam turned on, the next is to drive it; and experience and an exquisite sympathy must teach him where a weight should be supplied or a nut loosened. With the civil engineer . . . the obligation starts with the beginning. He is always the practical man. The rains, the winds and the waves, the complexity and fitfulness of nature, are always before him. He has to deal with the unpredictable, with those forces (in Smeaton's phrase 'that are subject to no calculation'); and still he must predict, still calculate them, at his peril.

Robert Louis Stevenson[1]

'An Asshole of a Field'

In the seventeenth and eighteenth centuries perhaps thousands of Scots surfaced in one place or another in central Europe, usually fighting. One of them murdered Wallenstein, the greatest commander of the Imperial troops in the Thirty Years War; another became, as the Marquis of Keith, a hero-figure of Prussia. In the early 1970s the boot seemed to be on the other foot. Tough-looking Americans turned up from the Gulf and the Caribbean, as expert in their strange profession as they were cheerfully ignorant about their present whereabouts – 'Aberdeen – so that's where we are?' – and sporting political views closer to John

Wayne than *Encounter*. Roustabouts, roughnecks, bears, employed by wildcatters: their titles seemed to cast back to Wayne's heroic West, as indeed many of them did, the first exploitation of oil following not long after the great cattle drives had ended. 'An asshole of a field. Worse than the Canadian East Coast, worse even than fuckin' Alaska.' The English on the gas fields off Norfolk had already found their legendary command of obscenity trumped. Robert Orrell recorded an American engineer in negotiation with an English supplier in the mid-1960s:

Listen here, you Limey sonofabitch. Ma name's Vernon Andrews and ah'm the toolpusher on this motherfucking rig, and I ain't gonna sit around with ma finger up ma ass while you take a vacation. You get that equipment on the chopper tomorrow or you ain't got no contract.[2]

This combustible style seemed appropriate: the conditions a hundred miles east of Shetland *were* the worst in the offshore world; their awfulness was only becoming fully apparent with the extended stay of the drilling-rigs. In 1964 the highest wave-heights in the 'middle' North Sea had been reckoned at 40 feet, but the real ones came in at between 50 and 60 feet; wind-speeds were upgraded from 53 to 63 miles an hour. In the northern sectors, expected wave-heights were pushed up from 65 to 100 feet and wind-speeds from 63 to 69 mph.[3]

Men like 'Baytown Arthur', who demolished bottles of malt while regaling George Rosie with stories of Daniel K. Ludwig, were mainly from the rigs. The seismic survey people were of the more cerebral Bill Gates sort, crunching vast amounts of data into as many computers as they could lay their hands on; and doing this sort of thing more easily as the chips got bigger and bigger. Processed by conventional mathematical means, the data extracted by a seismic survey boat would take forty years to work its way through. A propensity to seasickness and a high-carbohydrate diet was just about all the two groups had in common, as the bear's business consisted in swinging thirty-foot lengths of drill-pipe in and out of the drilling hole, and heaving mud samples out of it.

Mud. There was nothing quite like it, and it provided much of the *raison d'être* for the tenders – 156 in 1974, 249 in 1975 – which were butting their way to the rigs, out of Peterhead and Aberdeen, Lerwick and Sandwick. In 1978 the supply boat *Mercia Shore* took 38,223 ton of cargo (average 466 tons a sailing) from Lerwick to the Shell/Esso rigs on the Brent field, ninety-five miles away (from Aberdeen, it could have carried an average of only 421 tons in forty-four sailings). *Mercia Shore* made eighty-two sailings and shifted *in toto* 5,819 tons of fuel for the motors and generators, 7,177 tons of drinking water and – containerized or loose on the broad deck – 5,735 tons of general stores and 3,615 tons of pipes and tubes for the drills. But roughly half its cargo was mud: 7,243 tons of mud *to* the rigs, and 7,634 tons of brine-and-mud *from* them.[4]

'Mud' was shop-talk. It meant a heavy, barytes-based substance – like a giant barium meal – which was dropped into the drill-pipe to lubricate the drill-head and then to bear to the surface the fragments of strata which the geologists, either on board or at Lerwick, would analyse. It was a boat like the *Mercia Shore* which bore the samples which showed that exploitable quantities of oil had been found at Phillips's concession in the Norwegian Ekofisk field in the summer of 1969.

The tenders were odd-looking craft, really a North Sea speciality. The Americans had brought some of their own across from the Caribbean, but they proved underpowered against the sea's winds and currents. Norwegian shipyards – Olsen, Wilhelmsen, Skaugen – fused their design to the tough sea-lorries of the fjords, horsepower went up from 2,000 to 3,000 in 1970, and by 1975 to 9,500. The type was by then spread around the globe. It had crew cabins, bridge and diesel engines, exhausting through twin funnels, bunched up forrard, and then a broad flat deck aft. Below were tanks for fresh water, cement, mud, and for trimming the vessel. But the essential innovation – and in some ways the clue to innovation in the province – was the bow-thruster propellor.[5]

In 1970 marine enthusiasts were recovering Isambard Kingdom

Brunel's *Great Britain*, then a wreck in the Falkland Islands, a faraway colony about which the public knew little and cared less. The *Great Britain* was the first commercial screw steamer, and since it was launched in 1842 propellor ships had been driven forward or in reverse by a stern-mounted screw, its thrust directed by a conventional rudder. But, not long before 1970, forms of electrical transmission were developed by which a craft's diesel motors could power further propellors mounted transversely in the bows and, later on, at any point on the hull. By enabling the craft literally to move in any direction, these allowed a much tighter manoeuvrability. In due course these propellors were able, when coupled to computers and satellites which could 'read' the winds, waves and currents, to revolutionize offshore technology, as the helicopter had revolutionized flight by being able to hover. 'Dynamic positioning' – the ability to keep station to within a few square metres – was perhaps the biggest innovation at sea since the steam engine.

The supply boat was the workhorse of the province, what the black-funnelled collier tramps, steaming out of Leith and Immingham, with their dour skippers and choleric Calvinist engineers, had been to Masefield and Kipling in the early 1900s. Life in the age of diesels and radar was every bit as hazardous: keeping station beneath the legs of a rig in a force six gale, with green seas sloshing waist-high over the payload deck as the crew made fast containers to the hooks of the rig's cranes, was as severe a test of seamanship as anything in Conrad or Stevenson. Did anyone notice?

Drilling Hole

Any oilfield will go through three phases in which different kinds of operation predominate: exploration, development, and finally production. In 1972 Shell made notional calculations about what it cost to develop a field of medium size, yielding 250,000 barrels a day. The total came to a symmetrical £250 million. £70 million would go on drilling; £100 million on platforms and production structures; £65 million on pipelines and £15 million on shore-base facilities.[6] The sums would go up with inflation, but the proportions remained roughly the same.

Exploration by airborne electromagnetic detectors could only register the slight magnetic deflections caused by different types of rock and show up those sub-sea areas which were composed of sedimentary rocks, the only possible sites of oil-bearing strata. The bulk of exploration, on which around a third of a billion pounds was being spent by 1975, essentially involved seismic surveys by research vessels, followed up by exploration drilling by rigs. A seismic survey vessel, bearing a sophisticated version of something long known to mining engineers, would explode a charge on the surface, and its shock waves, bouncing back from the strata, would register variably on its screens and print-outs. Soundings from the vessels could build up a picture of the sub-sea geology and indicate the caps of the oil-bearing strata, drawing the oilmen towards the 'dome' formations which might – or might not – indicate a field. Initially the operations of the vessels were constrained by the impossibility of fully processing the mass of data they encountered. This would be overcome in the 1980s by the use of powerful new computers. However, the microprocessor had only been invented in 1971 and the early stages were heavily dependent on the drilling rig.

The drilling technologies applied offshore had been pioneered in the Gulf of Mexico, in which twenty-three fields had been found by 1953. When the Louisiana oilfield was developed in the 1920s and 1930s the first drilling was done from piled-wood platforms, then in 1930 from barges, and in 1949 from the first purpose-built floating rig, drilling in twenty feet of water. Most exploration units, however, were submersible rigs, rigid structures which could either be shipped out to the site in bits and assembled there, from the sea-bed up, or floating gantries which could be sunk up to 200 feet into calm water. A conference in Mexico City in 1956 reviewed this increasingly important technology, which was soon using 'jack-up' rigs capable of reaching 300 feet. Clydebank's *Penrod 64* was typical of these rigs. By 1958 the semi-submersible of the *Sea Quest* type had made its appearance, just in time for the Geneva Conference, from which stemmed six years later the Continental Shelf Agreement.[7] The jack-up was the workhorse of the search for gas; the semi-submersible was for the more dangerous northern waters. For depths of around 1,000 feet there was the drill ship which kept itself on station by 'dynamic positioning', computers and side-thruster propellors. In the infancy of seismic surveys, many more borings were required than was later the case, although the province had a good record for successful strikes: one in thirteen in the southern sector, and one in eight in the north. In due course this would rise to one in every four.[8]

Drilling was expensive and complex at the best of times, since the bits had to reach the oil-bearing strata at about 9,000 feet below sea-bed level. From the 'moon-pool' on the rig, below the derrick and fifty feet or so above the seething waters, the first 250 feet would be driven down to accommodate a 30-inch diameter steel cylinder called a conductor pipe. Thence, down to about 750 feet, the drill was 23 inches. A 17.5-inch drill went down to 3,500 feet, a 12.5-inch bit to 8,500 feet, and finally an 8.5-inch bit reached the productive strata. During this process, which involved the dismantling of the drills into 90-foot lengths every time the bit had to be changed, the process was lubricated and the rock samples retrieved by the drilling mud.[9] Robert Orrell, watching the tool-pushers on the Hewett gas field off Yarmouth in the 1960s, found them a besotted race:

Their one consuming passion in life was drilling holes in the ground, whether it was dry land or the sea bed. What little conversation they had was about drill-pipes, casing, rotary bits, joints, tongs, kellys and mud. They might curse or rave about the company they worked for or the conditions they had to work in, but after only a few hours ashore they longed to be back on the rig. For a driller, happiness was the whirling rotary table controlling the drill bit that cut into rock thousands of feet below ground. 'Drillin' hole' was a disease with no known cure.[10]

The drilling-rigs had to handle stores of 500 tons, enough material for several weeks' work, in case deliveries were interrupted – which was often. Conditions were much worse than anyone had guessed they would be. Tenders could wait for weeks for a break in foul weather long enough to enable the rig's cranes to snatch up supplies from their decks. In the Caribbean, and again in the southern North Sea, the ungainly jack-up barges, dwarfed by their three to six spindly legs, had been towed into their drilling positions. The crew then dropped the legs to the sea-bed, and hydraulically raised the barge on them until its hull stood about twenty metres above the surface. The result was, effectively, an artificial island, requiring no anchoring. But could this survive waves three or four times greater than under normal conditions in the Caribbean? BP's *Sea Gem*, which had made the first successful strikes of gas off the Humber, ended as an early victim. Its legs had been overstressed when they were driven into the sea-bed, and its limited breadth gave it insufficient stability. On a relatively calm day, the legs, metal-fatigued, had buckled, and the platform canted over and sank.

The semi-submersible could theoretically cope with such conditions. Its platform, resting on its buoyant legs and pontoons, was positioned by these being partly filled with water. The whole ensemble could be self-propelled, but was usually towed to its station and there secured by up to half-a-dozen fifteen-ton anchors: a demanding task for a specially built, or adapted, tender or tug *at a price*, although one obviated in the later 1970s by 'dynamic positioning'. Even so, the North Sea could shift a 15,000-ton semi-submersible like BP's *Sea Quest* more than eight metres, anchors and all. Drilling would usually have to be called off when movement was only half as much, or the drills would snap, while the stresses generated over time by the anchor cables on the complex structure of the rig were another risk factor.[11]

Sea Gem was not the only casualty. The ambitious British independent, Burmah, took the North Sea seriously and went into partnership with Murphy Oil of America. After geophysical mapping surveys in February 1963 they got five licences and thirty-four blocks, and had a semi-submersible, *Ocean Prince*, built by Smith's dock, Middlesbrough, along with a supply ship, the *Lady Alison*. In October 1966 they struck oil off Cromer, the first in the North Sea. But the rate of flow was only 400 barrels per day, too slight to be commercial.[12] *Ocean Prince* was towed to the Dogger Bank. There, on 5 March 1968, it was hit by force eleven winds. The gale sank a Danish supply ship, and it battered the *Ocean Prince*, tethered like a baited bull to its anchors, until 10,000 tons of decking, metal columns and pontoons were wrenched apart. Only the heroism of the helicopter rescuers, headed by Captain Bob Balls, who flew twice to the disintegrating rig, saved the 26-man crew.[13]

Such experiences taught the lesson that the further north they operated, the stronger and more stable the rigs had to be. Perhaps the *Ocean Prince* lesson was too severe and discouraging, providing one reason for the reluctance of British shipyards in the 1970s to invest in rig production. Like the *Princess Victoria* car ferry and the Comet airliner, the pioneer British rigs were ambitious and innovative, but inadequately tested. An advance turned into a retreat, once the prototypes ran into trouble. Of a total of about 500 rigs world-wide – of which fewer than 100 were non-US owned – over 60 were expected to be in action in the northern North Sea by 1973.[14] Yet of the 119 rigs under construction in 1974 only 3 were being built in the UK – at Marathon on the Clyde. Norway built 12, Finland 9, France 5. But Singapore had 20 under construction, and the United States 46.[15] In this business, and at this early stage, Britain, once innovative, was now marginal. Matters did not improve.

By the middle of the 1970s the British regarded anything metal that stuck up in the middle of the sea with a derrick on it as a rig. This was wrong; or was it? A rig was fundamentally mobile or at least portable, and used for exploration; a platform was built on the sea-bed and used for production. Rigs drilled single exploration wells; a platform drilled (rather more cheaply) multiple production wells. The platform on Denmark's single field, the Dan, had only 4 wells; Shell's Auk had one platform with 6 producing wells. By contrast, the first two platforms of the Forties field each had a capacity to drill 23 'deviated' wells, tapping fields up to fifteen kilometres away; while Brent had a capacity of four platforms with 12 to 25 wells each.[16]

To complicate matters, a rig could become a platform, if firmly attached to the sea-bed and used for production; the small Buchan field would be handled by the former *Drillmaster* semi-submersible rig. Or a ship could become a production unit: by the early 1990s Norwegian technology had even perfected floating production units which looked like a combination between a tanker and a drill ship and used multiple propellors to keep perfect station.[17] Over time, in fact, there would be a convergence of the possible technologies, thanks to the development of positioning and, above all, computers. The tension-leg platforms used these to keep station 3,000 or more feet above their bases.

Rigs did not come cheap. In 1970 it cost between £3.5 and £10 million to build a semi-submersible, and an average price of £10,000 to hire a rig with a sixty-man crew for a day – plus helicopters, supply boats, and sustenance – though this could more than treble if the demand for drilling rose. By 1974, with inflation and the pressure for more exploration increasing, the price of a jack-up had risen to £13 million, of a semi-submersible to £19 million, and of a drill ship to £21 million. Drilling for ninety days in 400 feet of water – a rough average of the needs of a North Sea exploration well – worked out at £2.5 million.[18] The bills piled up. A rig would consume up to 1,000 tons of material a month – casing, fuel, mud, cement; it would need two 1,200-ton supply ships at £2 million each; onshore depots, quays and warehouses, coastal steamers, heavy lorries, onshore offices; helicopters at £550–650 an hour, running 1,250 hours per annum.[19] By 1975 a quarter of BP's capital had been invested in the Forties project; the £800 million that Shell and Exxon had by then invested in Brent equalled 8 per cent of their issued capital and reserves. Several of the smaller companies had staked anything up to ten times their reserves.[20] Although it scarcely represented 5 per cent of reserves, the North Sea accounted in 1974 for about 10 per cent (£35 billion) of world investment in oil extraction, which totalled £334 million. This was an underguesstimate, and not just because £100 in 1970 was worth £25 in 1981. All the early North Sea projects went heavily over budget.

After Ekofisk

By 1971 the sea between Thames and Tees had become 'the most minutely explored area in the world'.[21] The government had been generous with licences; in its first four rounds of 1964, 1965, 1970 and 1971–2, 2,655 blocks of 100 square miles each were offered – something which subsequently became a matter of contention – though the exploring companies were, because of the costs involved, reluctant to exercise their options.[22] But in the later sixties the first rigs began to move north from the relatively shallow waters off East Anglia and the Humber to the northern North Sea off Aberdeen, and started serious exploration off the Shetlands. By 1971, 64 groups had been granted 246 licences covering 863 blocks; 224 wells were likely to be sunk, at an overall cost of £200 million.[23]

The rigs were towed offshore, anchored, and started work. From wherever they could get quays and warehouses, the companies supplied them with water, fuel, pipes and mud. Ribald scepticism by the locals in the bars of Lerwick was, Jonathan Wills recorded, the customary reaction to all this effort. For a time,

Little did the Pierhead skippers know that within five years they would be jostling for space at their favourite bars, or that in the first decade of oil they would be elbowed out altogether by the boisterous crowds of rousta-bouts, scaffolder 'bears', drifters and swaggering buckos of all descriptions, all lured by the black gold and spending their share of it in what were to become some of the most unpleasant bars in the northern hemisphere.[24]

There were good grounds for these early doubts. Between 1963 and 1974 over 500 wells were sunk, 380 in the British sector, with distinctly variable results.[25] The Germans drilled more oil-wells in their sector than the Norwegians did in theirs, but without any success.[26] Overall, the number of wells drilled ran at 49 per annum from 1967 to 1969, then fell to 24 in 1970, and 28 in 1971.

The Dutch, who had taken thirteen years' hard drilling to find the Groningen field, provided some reassurance; by 1977 gas would be supplying 50 per cent of the country's energy needs.[27] So too did the British Gas Corporation's campaign to replace town gas with North Sea gas, under way since the mid-1960s. This cost about £1 billion for appliance adaptation, and involved some very hard bargaining with the petrol companies who actually extracted the stuff, but gave Britain the lowest domestic gas prices in Europe. Oil, on the other hand, was as complex and variable a substance as stone or wood, and its exploitation was affected by composition, situation, and the availability of refining processes.

When in December 1969 rigs under contract to Phillips Petro-leum detected the Ekofisk field, with 1.7 billion barrels in reserves, in – but only just in – the Norwegian sector 250 miles east of Dundee, only 8 of a total of 42 wells had been drilled off eastern Scotland. Thereafter drillings rose until they peaked in 1975, when 49 out of 79 were drilled off eastern Scotland and 23 in the East Shetland sector. Ultimately this region, in deep water and with the roughest weather, would account for more than 60 per cent of British North Sea output.

Things went fast on Ekofisk, which was largely licensed to private concerns. These soon installed five steel platforms and started up production in July 1971. The Norwegian trench inhibited any connection with the mainland at Stavanger and, pending construction of a pipeline to Teesside, Phillips sank a huge concrete oil tank – the first major concrete construction in the province – on to the bed of the sea; from a manned platform above this, oil could be pumped into tankers. As early as November 1971 the field was yielding 35,000 barrels per month, but 45,000 barrels per day would be possible when the tank was completed in 1973, and even more when the Teesside pipeline, costing £750,000 per mile, was ready.[28]

In November 1971 the Ekofisk success was accompanied by rumours of a BP find of similar size – 300,000 barrels per day – a hundred miles to the north-west: the Forties.[29] BP had actually detected the giant field in 1970. Initially it kept quiet about it, while discreetly negotiating with landowners and farmers for an overland pipeline from Buchan to Grangemouth; its chairman, Sir Eric Drake, was deeply sceptical about the figures. But in December 1971 the word got out at a meeting in London. Convener Maitland Mackie, in London on behalf of the County of Aberdeen, recollected that when McCleod Matthews of BP announced the size of the field, the stunned silence that followed lasted for minutes. No less dramatic was the calculation that it would cost £370 million to develop it.[30]

The Forties discovery soon led BP to announce two orders for platforms worth £20 million each, plus a pipeline to Grangemouth, and a £10 million terminal for tankers loading refined products at Hound Point.[31] By 1978 the global costs of production would have risen to £850 million. But this ambitious development was not unique. Amoco had found Montrose in September 1969 (although appraisal took nearly four years); Shell-Esso found Auk in February 1971, Hamilton's found Argyll in October. Thereafter there was little stopping the other companies. Shell and Esso detected the giant Brent field, 150 miles east of the Shetlands, in July 1971, but did not announce it until September 1972. Such delays were inevitable; small fields meant only limited amounts of equipment, but a large field had to be surveyed thoroughly to determine how many platforms were necessary, how big the pipeline ought to be, and what facilities had to be provided at the landfall site. Auk was only reckoned to have 7.3 million tons of reserves, and Montrose 20 million; in 1977 Forties and Brent were assessed at 220 million and 240 million respectively.

After a period when discoveries were played down, out came the statements that Forties was an average rather than a very big field. And following this, in 1972, the American majors moved in *en masse*, buying or leasing sheds and warehouses and stretches of quay, from Dundee north to the Shetlands. BP serviced the Forties field from Aberdeen and later, because of congestion there, from Dundee. P & O was in Montrose, Amoco and Chevron in Aberdeen, Occidental, Phillips and – later on – BNOC in Peterhead. But Aberdeen was above all 'the dour Houston of the North': 15 out of 26 fields were serviced from its docks, with 70 of the 250 companies active in the industry either there or moving there. At the end of 1971 there had been 1,000 new jobs in oil; four years later there were 19,000 new North Sea-related jobs *in toto* in Scotland, and over 7,000 of these were in the north-east. Only 5,000 had gone to unemployment-hit Strathclyde.[32]

Platforms

The size of any field could, very roughly, be estimated by the intensity of the pressure of the oil, propelled by the water below it, or by accumulated gas. As the field was depleted, the pressure dropped, although gas could be 're-injected' instead of being flared or piped off, to keep the pressure up.[33] Weather conditions imposed other limitations, notably on the supply to the rigs, which became difficult with waves of over eight feet. This hit scheduling, a factor which increased as permanent structures were considered. Because of the prevailing bad weather, the only time that a major installation – a platform or a pipeline – could be installed was in a 'weather window', usually in the early summer. A platform window was even narrower than that for pipelaying, in which waves had to be lower than 3–5 feet, or a maximum of 180 days in the year.[34] To miss this, for whatever reason, imposed a year's delay.

This factor started to exert an influence as soon as orders began to be placed for production equipment early in 1972, for a total of sixteen oil and gas fields. Platforms had to be erected and means of dispatching the oil provided (in most cases, though not all, by pipeline). Platforms consisted of three main components: first, the 'jacket': a metal or concrete tower with its feet on the sea-bed and its top fifty feet or more clear of the surface; second, the deck; and third, the 'modules', which were usually pre-assembled on land and which were dedicated to the platforms' specialized functions: drilling the production wells, separating oil from gas and water, pumping the oil, and accommodating a crew of anything up to 300. Most metal jackets weighed between 20,000 and 30,000 tons, the weight of a cruise liner, topped by the deck and modules, which weighed a further 10,000 to 15,000 tons. Special barges and buoyancy tanks had to be used to sink the jacket accurately on to the piles which had been driven to receive it in the sea-bed – a process which could go horribly and expensively wrong. These ensembles were expensive and they had to be built fast.

Despite nearly five years of North Sea gas, UK firms had little experience of platform production. The platforms used for gas exploitation in the southern North Sea were nearly all built in Holland by de Groot Zwijndrecht and IHC, to American designs. These were, anyhow, quite small and simple, requiring crews of only seven or eight men.[35] De Groot set up in Scotland, at Methil in Fife, developing a yard jointly with Redpath Dorman Long on the site of the Wellesley colliery, once one of Scotland's great coal exporters. Behind the council houses of the grim little mining town the outlandish structure of the platform for the Auk field started to rise, looking as it grew more and more like a huge spaceship with its nose buried in Fife. It stayed there longer than it ought to have done, as design changes and labour disputes meant that it was delivered badly behind schedule in July 1974.

Four platforms were needed for the Forties field: two would be built at Graythorpe on Teesside by Laing's, and two by Highland Fabricators at Nigg. Two platform orders went out from Shell-Esso at Brent, one to Methil and another, for a concrete type, to Stavanger. Hamilton Brothers at their small Argyll field used a converted semi-submersible drilling-rig, Trans-world 58, to deplete its 7.3 million tons.

The problem was that, since all of these were on the absolute frontier of technology – nothing as big had been required in the Gulf or in the Caribbean – and were aimed at a particular date, they had to be designed almost on the hoof. The first of the Forties platforms for BP had to incorporate a thousand design changes, major and minor. Later platforms were built faster and cost less.[36] But on the British side, these all tended to be one-offs. It was left to the Norwegians to develop standardized designs. More seriously, the companies learned on the job (1) that the platforms were far more expensive than they had first thought, and (2) if they planned logically they could make them do more tasks over a wider area, and that they would ultimately need fewer of them. At a time when both the UK and Norwegian governments were trying to second-guess the companies' strategies and provide platform construction facilities, this was to have unhappy consequences.

Further, in 1972 there was a technological challenge. Concrete was now much cheaper than steel because it required less energy to construct; it was corrosion-resistant; the sheer weight of the platforms (up to 500,000 tons) could settle them on the sea-bed without the need for pile-driving, and oil could be stored in a cluster of tanks around the base of the platforms. Brent Beta, built to a Norwegian design in Stavanger, had sixteen such tanks, holding a million barrels. Fearing that platform construction would emigrate, the UK government first tried to intervene to secure sites, and then got pinned down in public inquiries:

The Scottish Development Department did not introduce its *Coastal Planning Guideline* until 1974 and many controversial planning decisions had already been taken prior to the publication of this informative document. As a result of this delay in the provision of an overall planning strategy the early orders for concrete platforms in the UK sector went to Norwegian yards.[37]

No less complicated was the laying of the pipelines. In British eyes, this was overshadowed from the first by the fact that none of the underwater pipe could come from British steelworks: the plant did not exist to supply 36-inch diameter pipe. Not only had the Japanese a monopoly of this, but the economic downturn after 1973 actually made their product cheaper. Nor was British technology any better placed as regards pipelaying: the Dutch and even the Italians had, thanks to the Sicilian oilfield and the Tunis–Italy pipeline, far more experience. As with the supply tenders, the available technology evolved with awesome rapidity. The Italian pipelayers had welded the pipe together, and then slewed it over the side of their barges by davits. But in 1969 the Dutch firm Giessen and Zonen built the *Chocktaw* for Santa Fe, a catamaran barge which laid the pipe through the central well. The catamaran construction created an artificial calm in the well, and enabled laying to take place even in nine-foot waves. A second *Chocktaw* followed from Blohm and Voss, Hamburg, in 1974, and both were involved in laying the Ekofisk pipelines: one for oil to Teesside, one for gas to Emden, in German Friesland, where *Chocktaw II* could lay 1,700 metres of pipe a day.[38]

The Teesside oil pipe was 350 kilometres long and weighed 150,000 tons; the 430 kilometres of gas pipe to Emden weighed 200,000: in other words equivalent to the weight of six *QE 2*s. So a support fleet was necessary of warehouse ships, big enough to carry about 20,000 tons of pipe, and smaller pipe-delivery ships – 'stretched' versions of the familiar tenders. Even so, the northern North Sea, east of the Shetlands, required something tougher still. By 1975 the state of the art was represented by the *Viking Piper*, 66,000 tons of it and, for once, British-financed: a huge floating factory in which twelve-metre lengths of 36-inch pipe, hoisted on to the deck by 140-ton cranes, were first welded together into double that length, then transferred on to a tension-ing mechanism which delivered a continuous pipe down a curved gantry dipping into the sea. Then, 1,200 metres aft, the pipe settled in a trench on the sea-bed. Because of this curved, wasp-like protrusion, *Viking Piper* was known as a 'stinger'.[39]

With 'a marvellous crop of discoveries' in the spring and summer of 1972 it was evident that the province was a success. The oil minister at the Department of Trade and Industry, Sir John Eden, son of the victim of Suez, thought that there might be a yield of 25 million tons from the province in 1975. Other experts guessed at 50 million tons by 1980, perhaps even 150 million, with a prospect of 250 million by 1985. 'So what exactly is the Government's motive in playing down the best economic news it has had in years?' asked the *Economist*. 'It is difficult to see Mr Harold Wilson playing such a card this way.'[40] Improbable though this seemed, Wilson did just that.

It was also emerging that, globally, the future would lie with offshore oil, with such operations – in the Gulf, in the Caribbean, off the coast of China – rising world-wide from 17 per cent to 70 per cent of total production by the year 2000. To get in on North Sea technology might mean an unending succession of orders for equipment and expertise.

At Nigg Bay, north of the Cromarty Firth, the giant structure of Forties Alpha had started to rise in early 1973. This was a 450-foot metal jacket, weighing 30,000 tons, built on its side. BP thoughtfully supplied an artist's impression of what it would look like if erected on Princes Street, Edinburgh, with two feet on the street and the other two on St Andrew's Square, dwarfing the Scott Monument and the North British Hotel, its crew peering down on the Castle and the Calton Hill. It was due to be towed out in August, but was behind schedule because of technical problems and labour disputes.

Such construction was, in fact, heavily subsidized by the govern-ment, thanks to local employment legislation – even though, as far as sites were concerned, the government ought to have been in a seller's market. At the same time British industry in general was failing to make much impression on the oil business. Japan's capture of the Forties pipe was not unique, and companies and locals alike remained baffled by the government's passivity. In the fourth round, announced on 22 June 1971, 371 exploration licences still had to be allocated: 'Why do so few people in London want to know?' asked the *Economist* in January 1972.[41] It was only in May of that year that the DTI commissioned a report on the industrial implications of the oil for Britain, from the consultants International Management and Engineering Group (IMEG) of Britain.

In December 1972 the IMEG report, *Potential Benefits to British Industry from Offshore Oil and Gas Developments*, was published. 'British industry,' it said, 'generally remains extremely unsure of the facts about offshore requirements.'[42] Considering that oil-related investment would, within two years, be running at nearly 25 per cent of annual manufacturing investment, IMEG's level of accuracy wasn't much better. According to them the annual rate of expenditure in the UK sector would be £300 million; it was in fact closer to £900 million. Even allowing for inflation, IMEG's figures, as Donald Mackay and Tony Mackay reported in 1975, made up only 40 per cent of expenditure in the years 1973 and 1974.[43] IMEG's heart may have been in the right place in exhorting British manufacturers to gain a greater proportion of North Sea orders, and their report certainly played a part in the creation of the Offshore Supplies Office in 1973, but enthusiasm was no substitute for the sort of accurate appraisal, analysis of comparative performances in other countries, and economic model-making to locate the macro-economic role of oil enterprise in the British economy, which the situation demanded.

Governing the Province

The Rt Hon. Richard Marsh was not everyone's cup of tea. 'Alfie', as *Private Eye* christened him, was an ambitious young man to whom ideology was secondary. He did not run with any of Labour's internal packs, and careerism eventually led him out of the party and on to the Tory benches in the Lords. Nevertheless, even he got a shock when Harold Wilson made him Minister of Power in 1966:

One of the chastening experiences of that period was to discover just how ill-equipped a Ministry is to intervene in detailed administration. This was nowhere more evident than when we came to negotiate North Sea gas prices with the oil companies. We had no experience as a nation in dealing with this. The oil companies had spent two generations negotiating with governments.[44]

Marsh got a young scientist to bone up on the business for him, and warily approached Angus Beckett, the head of the petroleum department of the Ministry of Power:

He was very able, but his qualifications for becoming the most senior civil servant in Britain, concerned with the whole future of the development of North Sea Oil, was that he had a very ordinary degree in geology, but a near-obsessive interest in the oil industry.[45]

Beckett recommended the oil economist Walter Levy in New York; the Treasury shelled out £7,000, and Levy undertook to train up the supervisory staff, concluding after he had done so, 'It is quite remarkable how these bright young men that you've got have just read up on this subject. There is no doubt about their competence to provide good advice on how to exploit your country's oil interests.'[46] Whether this bouquet was deserved was perhaps doubtful, given the revelations which later emerged about oil taxation.

Yet the government should not have been in ignorance. The prospect of offshore oil exploration had been edging towards the North Sea for a couple of decades, ever since 1945, when the Americans, on Harry Truman's insistence, had parcelled up the Caribbean and started getting the appropriate legislation passed to facilitate this. In 1958 there occurred the Geneva Convention on the Law of the Sea, ratified by Britain in 1964 (no one noticed) followed sharply by the Continental Shelf Treaty, which parcelled out the North Sea among the littoral powers, and British orders in council which delineated the spheres of Scottish and English civil law, respectively north and south of latitude 55 degrees 50 minutes.

The Douglas-Home and Wilson governments reacted to the oil with an awkward combination of intellectual lethargy and administrative hurry, taking their cue from the Atlantic Alliance, the residual dominance which British Petroleum enjoyed in international oil politics, and Britain's awful balance of payments situation. The first round of licensing followed immediately, in 1964. Fifty-three licences were given to 51 companies in 358 blocks. This 'sought to secure two aims: first to favour British companies like BP; secondly to accelerate exploitation'.[47]

The Norwegians in the following year offered only 78, although their blocks were twice the size of the British.[48] The principle of 'discretionary licensing' was loosely construed as the confidence of the ministry that the licensees had the resources to carry out the work, and would benefit onshore industry. Later on, the accusation was made that the majors had been given unwarranted advantages, because of their own colonization of the ministry. The then Minister of Power, Frederick Errol, more or less admitted this to the *Financial Times* eight years later:

I rushed these through before the general election . . . I was afraid that a socialist government would get in and refuse licences to private enterprise.[49]

The licence allocations by the Douglas-Home and Heath governments disposed of almost 80 per cent of the blocks allocated by 1980. The nationalized industries of Britain got only 12 per cent of the concessions; if British private concerns were added, this came to 30 per cent. Beckett, 'a powerful civil servant', was praised by the Earl of Lauderdale, the former Tory MP for Caithness and prominent in Westminster's 'oil interest', for having accelerated exploitation. But on the Labour benches Marsh's junior minister Dr Jeremy Bray recollected wilful obstruction from Beckett over issues of industry statistics. Lord Balogh growled that he would 'with great diligence follow the career of that individual'.[50] Beckett retired shortly after and became chairman of William Press, the module construction firm, which seemed to make Balogh's point for him; this was not the last time that the incestuous relationship between modestly paid civil servants and the vast and wealthy industry they were supposed to control was to attract controversy. Richard Funkhouser, who had known Beckett well when the latter was oil attaché in Washington in the 1940s, was more charitable in his recollection of meeting Beckett at an Institute of Petroleum dinner in 1980:

He was bemoaning his fate as target of the Liberals and leftists for selling out Britain to the multinationals during the first rounds of licensing and more recently for allowing oil to seep secretly into Rhodesia. I tried to reassure him that a monument should and would be erected to him for saving Britain from the disaster that would have hit, without the oil lifeline which he personally produced when at the Department of Energy. All the producing fields in the North Sea were licensed by Angus (I think I said). The greater the criticism from fools, the greater the compliment. He brightened up.[51]

In 1964 Britain had come to a quick deal with Norway; it might have done better by taking its case to the European Court. But uncertainty about area rights was the sort of thing that throttled exploration. The Germans, Danes and Dutch occupied years in determining their zone boundaries. This worked to the ultimate advantage of the Germans, who by 1970 had extended their zone to the Ekofisk–Argyll area – an area where there was more chance of a strike than elsewhere.[52] But this also meant that rigs kept away from the debatable zone. By the time Bonn had secured its full slice of North Sea, the party had moved on.

The Norwegians were very canny in their licensing; they offered few blocks, and disposed of fewer, only 42 – admittedly much larger than the British allocations – by 1977. On the other hand, the existence of the Norwegian trench – and, ultimately more important, the remoteness of Norway from oil markets – meant that much of Norwegian production would have to be landed in Britain. The government appointed a committee in August 1970, and it came to the conclusion that while a pipeline could be laid across the trench, this would require unprecedented technological adaptation and would probably lead to delays.[53]

No major alteration to the British procedure was made until the fourth round in 1971–2, when, after agitation from the free-market Institute of Economic Affairs, some of the blocks were put up for auction. The free-marketeers intervened but little in the oil business (maybe its no-holds-barred cartelization seemed too remote from the limpid simplicities of Adam Smith), but this was successful within limits, raising £37 million and signalling the real degree of interest of the majors. Shell-Esso bid £21 million for block 211/21. In fact their rigs discovered nothing there, but the neighbouring block contained the qualified jackpot of the 15 million-ton Cormorant field.[54] Yet the fourth round also indicated that, in such an auction, national interests, and smaller independents, would simply be elbowed aside by the multinationals. The practice of discretionary licensing was confirmed, though on a reduced scale (only 86 blocks were licensed in the rest of the 1970s). The auction of 1971–2 remained unique.

For a country with over a century's involvement in the oil business, and hosting two of the Seven Sisters, the British state reacted to the oil with remarkable naivety, as the House of Commons Public Accounts Committee found in 1972:

The first huge areas of the sea, of a hundred square miles each, were leased to the companies as generously as though Britain were a gullible Sheikdom, with concessions running for forty-six years.[55]

The Wilson government, despite its success in adapting the gas regime, let the oil business almost go by default. Wilson gave the Ministry of Power to Ray Gunter, an ailing right-winger, who had earlier been a flop at Transport and Labour. Wilson noted in his memoirs that he hoped that Gunter would be able to free the Ministry from a relationship with the oil companies too close to that of the Ministry of Agriculture and the farmers. Gunter did nothing. After his sacking in 1969, his successor – in the new 'super-ministry' of the DTI, was Eric Varley.[56]

Edward Heath, on coming to office in 1970, did not revive the Ministry of Power; although, with some successful strikes being made, a corner of the DTI under John Davies was an unobtrusive place for the controllers of a potential bonanza. Later, faced with the hostility of the miners, he would fling this policy into reverse. According to Peter Hennessy,

Heath was advised by his Cabinet Secretary, John Hunt, among others, that in these circumstances, the benefits of clearing the Cabinet's agenda by keeping as much policy as possible within the mega-DTI was, in fact, a serious disadvantage. Energy policy was so critical to the Government's political and economic strategy that the place for it to be determined was collectively within the cabinet room, which could best be achieved by reconstituting a separate energy department. Heath concurred and placed the new/old ministry in the hands of one of his heaviest heavyweights, Lord Carrington.[57]

This explanation would look a bit more positive and convincing if Carrington agreed with it, or even mentioned the episode in his memoirs – apart from claiming that this stint provided him with the worst weeks of his political career. For the six months in which he was in charge of the new department, he was being given the run-around by the miners. The government, preoccupied with overcoming chronic deficits in the balance of payments, and with an ex-Ministry of Power establishment sympathetic to the producers' lobby, continued to handle the allocation of licences for exploration ineptly. The Public Accounts Committee found in 1972 that

Between 1965 and 1973 the oil majors' corporation tax liability in the UK was £500,000. It is hard to believe that the profits made did not warrant a higher tax payment.[58]

No Oil but Plenty Profit

In a manner almost completely unanticipated in 1969, the North Sea was to become the second largest offshore producer after Saudi Arabia, with twenty fields on stream by 1982.[59] Signs of this scale of production were, however, appearing by 1971. Up to the discovery of the Forties field the companies had pursued a 'there probably isn't much there, and we're doing you a favour in looking for it' line, but the size of the investment involved – even before giants like Ekofisk, Forties and Brent had been detected – betrayed this. On the other hand it meant that the business of equipping the fields would put pressure on the industry and, all things being equal, push the price of material and wages up. There was therefore something of a hiatus; in 1972 there were only two discoveries – the medium-sized Beryl A and the second section of the Frigg gas field. Then a further wave of exploration coincided with two things: a British realization that the oil was serious business, and a major shift in American policy.

By January 1973 it was beginning to dawn on policy-makers that the Americans had been let in by default. The IMEG report argued that there would be a demand for oil-related goods and services running at an average annual rate of £1.3 billion until at least 1985. At that time about £190 to £400 million of this money was coming to UK contractors, a maximum of about 30 per cent of orders, when 40 per cent should be possible by 1979, and as much as 70 per cent by 1985. The IMEG shopping list demanded a wholly-owned UK offshore drilling company, at a cost of £25 million; an alteration in the British Steel Corporation's forward planning to create capacity for such products as pipes; assistance to UK shipyards to enable them to tender for rig construction; and partnerships with American firms to facilitate technology transfer. The last would be based on an obligation to foreign firms, operating in the UK province, to make technological information available. Overall, IMEG concluded, 'British industry generally remains extremely unsure of the facts about offshore requirements.'[60]

The reaction of politicians still seemed opaque. Peter Walker, who had succeeded the luckless Davies at Trade and Industry, shelled out £1.2 billion to propitiate the miners, but still showed a lack of urgency about oil. (Indeed, in his quite extensive bibliography the absence of any mention of oil is quite remarkable for a politician who was twice in his career, in 1972–3 and 1983–7, in charge of it.) Only in March did the issue make centre stage, with the devastating report of the Public Accounts Committee under Harold Lever. This disclosed that the majors were using their North Sea operations to get their overall profits almost tax-free:

The root cause of tax losses is the use in Middle East countries of a posted price as a base for tax calculations on oil production . . . this posted price has become considerably in excess of true market price but is nevertheless the price at which the production company in an oil group transfers its oil to the trading company. The effect is to increase the production company's profits while the accounts of the trading companies are correspondingly reduced. The UK does not receive any tax on the profits earned by the production companies because the credit for the foreign tax paid on those profits extinguishes any liability to UK tax; while at the same time the trading company builds up tax losses in the UK.[61]

Thus profits from North Sea operations – estimated at £1.5 billion – were already being made, although not a drop of oil had so far been extracted. The licensing procedures had been for the companies an added bonus. The *Economist* wrote:

For the companies, the affair has been a public relations disaster, strengthening the popular impression of a secretive and Machiavellian industry. That may not have been too damaging in the past, but increasingly the issues that dominate the industry are broad-based political ones.[62]

The report was not just music to the ears of the Labour Party. Edward Heath, whose hostility to the oil companies was well known, and who was reckoned by Edmund Dell to be one of the few men with any grasp of oil industry politics, had already passed legislation on the gas industry which gave the government drastic powers amounting, according to Tony Benn, to 'total control'; his own contributions, so much maligned by the companies, were well within this framework.[63] But Heath's other preoccupation, entry into the EEC, blocked out most of the 1973 parliamentary session. By the winter, the crisis unleashed by the Yom Kippur war had overtaken him.

Consul Funkhouser

As early as 1971 the government of the United States started quietly to panic about its fuel resources. In part, this was merely an aspect of a pervasive *angst*: Richard Nixon had got in past a divided Democrat party, but inspired even less trust than before. Tensions over Vietnam had riven the entire society; black enfranchisement was a complete imponderable; *détente* in Europe seemed more threatening than the certainties of the Cold War.

By early 1973 the fuel shortage was imminent. The native oilfields seemed rapidly to be approaching exhaustion, and the Nixon government, looking with apprehension at the renascent Arab nationalism demonstrated in the Ghadafi coup in Libya, suspended the import quotas which had traditionally protected the US oil industry. The oil majors shook their heads (and sidestepped swiftly into other energy sources). The *Observer* reported a mounting panic: 'The United States is on the brink of a fuel crisis unique in its history.' In June 1973, Mobil, no less, was telling US citizens to do the unthinkable and take the train. In itself, this was an index of hysteria: so nominal was the American passenger railway network that finding a train could involve a journey of hundreds of miles. By car.[64]

Henry Kissinger had already got the State Department started on a hunt for conservation options and oil provinces which would be profitable and, above all, politically safe. The State

Department reported confidentially to the White House about the overall situation on 9 March 1972. But the North Sea was only one among several possible areas – and technologies – for development. There was an element of departmental politicking here, as in Britain. The State Department had no wish to lose its functions to the proposed Department of Energy which various reformers were mooting. So in May 1973 a State Department official, Richard Funkhouser, one of the team which had produced the report, turned up in London for consultations. Funkhouser had been ambassador to Gabon, and before that to several Gulf states; he was a Princeton graduate, a geologist by training, and a Nixonian Republican by conviction. He had flown alongside the RAF in the Burma campaign and had won the DFC; and in the 1940s, as we have seen, he had been one of Angus Beckett's opposite numbers in Washington.

In London, on 9 and 10 May, Funkhouser conferred with civil servants from Trade and Industry, the Treasury, and the Downing Street 'think-tank'. He went on to Paris. His conclusions were sobering. Although there was a general will to present a common front against OPEC, this was vitiated by divisions among the European powers:

The third problem, relations with producers, seemed promethean to all. There was an expectation that despite unanimity for consumers' co-operation, major consumers would continue to seek national solutions for vital oil supplies. The cliché is that Americans have cash and position; the Germans have cash but no interest in buying oil concessions; the Italians will 'cheat' on any rules, and the Japanese will buy anything available regardless of price.[65]

Funkhouser had few doubts about his role: to help to get the oil out as fast as possible, from a 'safe' province. He had strong views on the Middle East, where he believed the USA would always be compromised by its support for Israel; he had also read Odell's arguments on the North Sea wealth, and believed them rather than the low estimates peddled by the majors. While Funkhouser was in London, Sir Dennis Greenhill, Under-

Secretary at the Foreign Office, had raised the one disruptive factor: the 'very serious threat' of the Scottish nationalists.[66]

In the summer, Funkhouser was posted to the Consulate-General in Edinburgh: technically a demotion – he had been offered embassies in Bucharest or the Gulf – but the world's best whiskies, golf courses and salmon rivers were more of a draw than Ceausescu's megalomaniac capital, or the absence of practically any form of human enjoyment in the lands of conservative Islam. Funkhouser took Edinburgh, believing 'North Sea oil is a vital factor in western economic survival if, as and when it leaves the sub-surface of the sea.'[67]

In June Funkhouser, with his wife and daughter, turned up at the tall, narrow building on Regent Terrace which housed the Consulate. In Guayaquil in Ecuador, he noted, the US had a staff of thirteen; Edinburgh had three, who had hitherto raised their eyes little above visa-issuing and passport renewal. Yet Funkhouser believed it was the best place to keep an eye on the billions of dollars which the United States companies had committed to the North Sea. Moreover, as an American conservative, he construed the Scottish national movement as a form of 'states' rights' and found himself comfortable with it. He stayed as Consul for two years, and then, after retirement, served Texas Eastern as adviser for a further four. An easy-going man with James Stewart looks, clubbable and with deft journalistic skills, Funkhouser was suspected by Tony Benn of financing the SNP, and by Billy Wolfe of running the CIA's operation, while retaining their respect as a performer in the Great Game of intelligence. He would turn out to be one of the shrewdest observers of the Game, in which oil was only one of the dancers in a ferocious highland fling.

Sheikh, Rattle and Roll

Funkhouser's appearance in Edinburgh was just one indication that a sophisticated exploitation regime had turned up, determined to get results quickly. The phase which commenced in 1973 tended to be rather more American-dominated than was to the taste of the Europeans. 'We did all the work in the North Sea . . . Exxon got rich on our backs,' commented a Shell director to Anthony Sampson. On the other hand, Shell and BP had already got by far the biggest fields.[68]

The key to the profitability of the United Kingdom's North Sea province lay thousands of miles away, not in Houston but in Beirut. A hundred and thirty years earlier, in an obscure novel, a young and ambitious English politician had seen the destiny of the Empire linked inextricably to the clan feuds of the Levant. Benjamin Disraeli's 1847 vision in *Tancred* of a British Middle East had ended in the tragicomedy of Suez. But one of his odder notions – that the Arabs were 'Jews on horseback', fully endowed with 'Semitic' qualities of intelligence and adaptability, suddenly became actuality, as a new generation, trained in American universities but still loyal in a *politique* way to their feudal leaders, used the oil weapon as a means of buying off radical assaults on their power.[69] Throughout the 1960s the rise of OPEC had been loosely connected with the rise of the political idea of non-alignment and the liquidation of the last vestiges of imperialism. After Suez, at conferences at Bandung and Belgrade, Britain was symbolically and ideologically evicted from her imperial role, much as the Americans had insisted on in 1945; but the next target turned out, with some encouragement from the Soviet Union, to be America itself. The conservative rulers of Saudi Arabia and the Gulf States distrusted this tendency, but had to play along. The oil majors sussed out ways of making a killing, whatever happened.

Nixon as President proved as unreliable as his Democrat opponents had prophesied. As the strange truth about the 1972 re-election campaign leaked out – the dirty tricks department, Watergate – his capacity to control events diminished; just at the time when foreign policy was acquiring a menacing degree of pragmatism in the hands of Secretary of State Kissinger, who allowed a mistrustful Israel again to drift out of American control, while Egypt, with frontier negotiations in mind and opportunistic Russian support, attacked across the Suez Canal on 6 October 1973. On its northern front Israel encountered Palestinian and Syrian troops reinforced by Russian weaponry. The Six-Day success of 1967 was not repeated. For several awkward days Dayan's army looked like being bogged down in an impasse; but for massive American support, there was even the prospect of defeat.

For the conservative Arab states the issue was plain. To abstain would favour Israel; to intervene would encourage the radicals and the Palestinian refugees. The moderate solution was to use the oil weapon against the West: an embargo against America and Holland, the major entry-point for European oil supplies, and an increase in price. Britain remained immune from the blockade. For the last four years it had been getting discounted oil from Saudi Arabia and Iran in exchange for technology, chiefly armaments; and the Saudi court feared a Labour government, which they assumed would be on better terms with Israel. These factors, however, didn't shelter Britain from price rises. Zaki Yamani, then forty years old, a graduate of Cairo University and Harvard, became overnight as visually prominent as anyone except Nixon, Kissinger or Moshe Dayan. The Arabs started to tighten the oil screw.

The Yom Kippur war ended in a strategic impasse, complicated rather than solved by the Camp David Agreement in 1978, between Israel and Egypt. Lebanon, 'the Switzerland of the Middle East', took the frustrations of all parties, and became the first but not, alas, the last dystopia. The tragedy was that this horror overshadowed the sort of thing the calculating Levantines had always been good at – the handling of Arab trade balances. Population statistics were vague, but there were perhaps half a million 'citizens' (leaving out immigrant workers and international oil people) in the United Emirates, 300,000 in Bahrein, 125,000 in Qatar, 650,000 in Kuwait, 900,000 in Oman, 9.3 million in Saudi Arabia: collectively far fewer than the population of the London commuter area. Even if the 13 million in Iraq and 37.5 million in Iran were added, the total only matched the population of England. This tiny proportion of the world's population had overnight become incredibly rich, without having the capacity to consume the additional revenues in ways which would continue to stimulate the world economy. The immediate effect of the oil price rise was to impose an indirect tax of 3 per cent on the industrialized world without, *pro tem*, providing it with new markets. It took time for the West to adjust – largely by selling arms to the Middle East's nervous conservatives – but meanwhile stagnation and inflation coincided jarringly with the need to equip the oilfields, and left a lasting *mortmain* in the shape of a deeply unstable financial system.

This almost fortuitous piece of bad timing proved traumatic for Britain.

4

On Stream

Insofar as the battlefield presented itself to the bare eyesight of men, it had no entirety, no breadth, no depth, no size, no shape, and was made up of nothing except small numberless circlets commensurate with such ranges of vision as the mist might allow at each spot . . . In such conditions, each separate gathering of English soldiery went on fighting its own little battle in happy and advantageous ignorance of the general state of the action; nay, even very often in ignorance of the fact that any great conflict was raging.

A.W. Kinglake, *History of the Crimean War* (1863–87)

The Battlefield

The winter of 1973–4 confirmed the future of the North Sea province, and thrust its principal owner, the United Kingdom, towards economic chaos. With oil prices up sixfold on 1970 levels, exploitation stopped being a marginal option and became highly profitable. That was the good news. The bad news was that the fuel crisis had managed to collide with an internal industrial struggle, entry to the Common Market, and the collapse of the Bretton Woods system of managed exchange rates. The first retarded North Sea exploration and construction; the second demanded a huge net contribution to EC costs in return, it seemed, for a flood of imports. The third made financial forecasting as hazardous as anything going on a hundred miles east of the Shetlands.

Oil policy had been something for grand South Bank board-rooms, ministry corridors, Westminster committees. It suddenly became highly charged with party politics. Not just because the general energy crisis, sharpened by the miners' work-to-rule, had brought down the British government: what A.J.P. Taylor called 'the revenge for 1926'. The OPEC action shifted the initiative, world-wide, from the Seven Sisters to national governments and the specific increase in demand for North Sea oil revealed that other regimes of exploitation were possible.[1] British and Scottish politicians, Consul Funkhouser reported apprehensively from Edinburgh to Washington, were increasingly inclined 'to look to Norway more as a model than as a dog in the Western manger'.[2]

The Norwegians argued for sitting tight on an appreciating asset: a slow-depletion policy seemed to them sensible, maximizing both reserves and revenue. Or was it? Might it not result in a situation in which a price collapse would leave the North Sea states with vast capital investments – platforms, pipelines, refineries – exploiting a low-earning raw material? The *Economist*, to some extent *parti pris* (it was owned by the Pearson conglomerate, which had substantial oil interests), was cool about gradual depletion, and indeed about the idea of oil as any sort of panacea:

Even this resource saving, though spectacular, would not bring about any miracles. It would merely take Britain back to the resource cost of oil in the late 1960s, and that at a cost of two years' growth . . . If the price of oil falls, to something like the marginal cost of producing it – which is what usually happens to most prices eventually – Britain could be left having invested considerable sums and built up heavy overseas debts in order to saddle itself with energy up to ten times more expensive than can be bought on world markets.[3]

This turned out to be true of every other commodity price. Why not oil? It depended whom you read. Many commentators – not least in the United States – regarded with vast suspicion the prospect of prices peaking and then collapsing. Oil companies had been as active as Arabs in pushing up the price of oil; their fat 1973–4 profits seemed to confirm this. To the maverick independent T. Boone Pickens, later to surface off Nigg with his Mesa Petroleum in the Beatrice field, the majors were 'swimming in money'.[4] Barry Rubin, in the *National Review*, reprinted in the *Spectator*, claimed that the crisis had been rigged. There had been 'phenomenal increases' in company profits. Exxon's were up by 80 per cent, Mobil's by 64 per cent, Getty's by 71 per cent. The majors now controlled through recent purchases 30 per cent of coal, 40 per cent of uranium and 72 per cent of gas reserves in the USA. They were playing down native American oil reserves, in reality ten times greater than those reported to the Federal Power Commission. The crisis was for them a bogey: a means of scaring consumers into switching to the other power sources which they owned, *and* being subsidized by government to do this. It also enabled them to get round the environmentalists; not least over the Alaska pipeline.[5] Once this manoeuvre had been carried out, ran this interpretation, realistic – if not good – relations with OPEC would keep the producers' cartel going, and prices up.

But the risk of things getting out of hand was still there, and this made the whole province a fairly ambitious gamble. The Norwegians' faith in slow depletion was reinforced by their history. Over 40 per cent of the country's energy came, anyway, from the unceasing and long ago depreciated resource of hydro-electric power-stations, erected after the First World War. And the Norwegian population, at only 4 million, devoted to patriotism, ecological uprightness, liberated but worried sex, and downright gloomy alcoholism, already enjoyed a higher per capita income. The country intended to keep its few licensed blocks under firm control, both directly and through Statoil.

In Britain the troubles of 1974 were mitigated by the fact that the early discoveries were being connected up with pipelines and coming on stream. Early in 1975 Hamilton Oil's Argyll field, using an old semi-submersible rig as a floating production platform, became the first to produce. A pipeline barge was dragging itself slowly from the Forties field to Cruden Bay in Aberdeenshire to link up with a land pipe being completed to the BP refinery at Grangemouth; pumping would start in the autumn.

In other, more northerly fields tankers started loading from buoys, pending the construction of pipelines. Within four years, it was estimated, the Ninian, Brent and Piper fields would be linked up by pipeline to their terminals; the first two to Sullom Voe in the Shetlands in 1978, the latter to Flotta in Orkney in 1976.

Yet nearly all these projects were running on average a year behind schedule. 'Excitement has given way to disappointment and disillusion,' Alastair Dunnett of Thompson Oil told Funkhouser in late 1974, 'not because of lack of oil reserves but because of political, industrial and mechanical problems which have risen even faster.' In a long cable to the State Department Funkhouser detailed seven retarding factors: extreme cost escalation, liquidity problems, fears about government taxation policy, the sheer mass of projects, failure of suppliers to deliver on time, technical problems with structures, and interference by environmentalists. As a representative from Conoco put it, 'these negative facts existed one year ago, but we had never expected them all to snowball concurrently'.[6]

Paradoxically, the weak pound favoured Britain, just as the weak Krone had favoured Norway, in the task of building up its command over the oil and associated investment. A high pound made the country more vulnerable to the export of capital and the inflow of imports. A slow-depletion policy – at the same time building up investment and expertise in alternative energy and supply industries – was a gamble; it would have fallen foul of the majors and of the EC, and would have required a considerable amount of state control, co-operation by the unions, and tolerance by consumers. Would it pay off in the first half of the eighties? That, and much else, remained obscure in 1974, the year of two general elections.

Money

In April 1974 the Department of Energy calculated reserves of between 8.5 billion and 14 billion barrels (1.13 to 1.9 billion tons), which might yield 3 million barrels per day. The companies had stopped arguing that the stuff was so restricted and expensive that they were doing the country a favour by trying to get it out on their own terms. Instead there was optimistic talk of at least four and possibly six 500,000-barrel-a-day fields. US incomers hazarded between 10 and 20 billion barrels; in 1975 Stanley Gray of Shell talked in terms of 35 billion in reserves.[7]

The heretic in this scene was Dr Odell, who had now gone from the London School of Economics to a chair at the Erasmus University, Rotterdam. Odell had moved from studying the offshore gas industry to write *Oil and World Power* (1970), a critical study of the cartelized policies of the Seven Sisters. In the North Sea, he argued, the companies were extrapolating reserves from their estimates of profit, not from what was actually under the sea. Odell claimed that there might be as much as 78 billion barrels in reserve, perhaps as much as 100 billion (10.5 to 13 billion tons). This did not meet with oil company approval. At all. Odell would become a close runner-up to Tony Benn as licensed offshore bogeyman, a position he continued to maintain until 1993.[8] Oil companies liked the idea of increases in reserves. But not huge increases; that might mean governments being a lot more choosy about policy.

Besides, the companies were having to revise upwards their estimates of costs, and not just because of the physical conditions they found. Inflation between 1974 and 1976 soared by over 50 per cent. They also claimed that government – especially Labour government – opacity about policy was frustrating exploration and planning. These protests were objectively justified, but also seemed self-serving as news of massive increases in profits came flooding in. The companies stigmatized the government as rapacious, but this was their line; it had little to do with their reasons for being in the North Sea, conveyed in a typically unvarnished way by T. Boone Pickens:

The North Sea finds dwarfed anything being found in the Gulf of Mexico where Mesa was working. I couldn't help thinking about the great possibilities across the Atlantic, especially when I learned that 50,000-acre tracts were being given free to companies willing to explore them. To oilmen used to paying millions just for the privilege of drilling, that was a real incentive.[9]

Exploration might, thanks to pre-1973 policy, be nearly free, but the price of getting the oil and gas out was at least ten times the cost of Middle East production: $1.50 instead of 10–15 cents a barrel. For an ultimate price of $8.75 a barrel, the going rate in 1974, there would have to be a capital outlay of £1,500 for every barrel produced. An output of one million barrels per day would cost £1.5 billion in investment, which came to 2.5 per cent of the UK's total gross domestic product.[10] So to meet the UK's needs alone from North Sea oil by 1980 would demand investment equal to two years' growth – at a time when the oil price increase itself was adding a symmetrical £1.5 billion to the country's balance-of-payments deficit.

If rapid depletion was the policy, then foreign participation was essential. But this inevitably moved costs in an embarrassing direction: every rig or supply boat which arrived in Aberdeen in response to an order from a UK-registered company set up by American oilmen was chalked up as an import. These rose to a peak of £1.2 billion in 1976 and 1977 – half the UK's total trade deficit, the *Economist* calculated.[11] The visible trade deficit in these years was £3.9 and £2.2 billion respectively, but this substantial component scarcely registered on commentators on the sterling crisis of the mid-1970s, then or since.[12] The *Economist* believed in 1974 that the oil-related balance of payments deficit ought to be separately identified: two years later, preparing to punish Britain for an economic crisis largely prompted by the volatility of Arab financial balances, the International Monetary Fund was curiously insouciant about the oil and its costs.[13] In *Goodbye Great Britain*, their account of 1976 – the fall, and equally dramatic rise, of the pound and the equally violent lurches in Treasury forecasting – Sir Alec Cairncross and Kathleen Burk content themselves with one mention:

North Sea oil is sometimes credited with changing the outlook. But the National Institute in November 1976 was already forecasting an expansion in output of North Sea oil from a negligible total in 1975 to £2.8 billion in 1977 as *part* of its forecast of the current account. The oil was there all along and had no rational association with the change in sentiment.[14]

Chancellor Denis Healey, the left's villain of the piece, subsequently wrote that he and the Treasury had underestimated the resilience of the economy.[15] Perhaps a closer knowledge of the oil industry and its economics, of the sort possible by 1978, would have given badly needed ammunition against the IMF.

It wasn't just government that had problems with an enterprise where $1 million tended to become the basic unit of currency.

In the normal course of financial enterprise, money was borrowed, either from banks or by issuing shares to sleeping partners. Oil wasn't like that. Only about 16 per cent of the capital requirement of American oil companies in 1972 – a total of $5.5 billion – was borrowed.[16] The multinational nature of the business, and the fact that much of companies' profits had traditionally been made – bluntly – by looting the Arabs and by taxation fiddles, meant that they had sufficient cash to invest themselves, out of current operations, with additional funds provided by American banks which were virtually in-house institutions, such as Morgan Guaranty of New York.

This of course applied to the established operators, the Seven Sisters, which also derived strength from the fact that in the United States the oil firms could also acquire permanent title to mineral rights, whereas in most European countries these had been nationalized – although doubt existed over the precise legal status of a block which had been licensed. According to the international lawyer Tony Carty,

In none of the depletion and participation renegotiations did the UK dispute that the companies had as complete a title as possible in the oil. Indeed, the object of renegotiation was to recapture the property.[17]

A position which seemed to be borne out by the company's version of the outcome of renegotiation:

... but the company will retain full beneficial ownership of all petroleum and related assets. The entire Shell share of foreseeable North Sea offshore oil production, all of which will be required to support Shell's UK refining and marketing activities, will be secured for the company's own use. Furthermore, there will be no change in the Shell position as operator responsible for the total management of all activities with the ability to exercise decision-making control.[18]

In 1974 American firms had secured 36.8 per cent of discovered reserves in the North Sea; British concerns had 41.2 per cent and the French had 11 per cent.[19] Expenditure was roughly proportionate. UK companies raised 37 per cent of the £1.7 billion which had been spent up to 1977 on exploration, plus £5.6 billion on development, and three-quarters of that came from British Gas, the British National Oil Corporation, BP and Shell.[20]

For the Americans, the North Sea was politically secure. Sure, it was also technically demanding, but such innovation as was required would be applicable elsewhere. Here it was necessary to go outside the normal oil financing structures and tap more speculative sources of capital. Even BP, strapped for cash because of its Alaska investments, had to raise for the Forties some £360 million (and eventually much more), which depended on elaborate new banking facilities: a consortium of sixty-six banks headed by Lazard's, Morgan Guaranty, and National Westminster.[21] Shell's usual bankers refused to have anything to do with the Brent field; Shell and Esso were, however, able to raise over £3 billion between 1975 and 1980, using their hitherto impressive profits as a form of collateral.[22] Another basic disadvantage was that since the province was in the United Kingdom, British firms could not claim the export subsidies that the Americans or French could obtain to supply equipment for use on foreign territory. In 1973 the government got round this by granting interest relief on money borrowed for oil purposes – something which would later on be a source of conflict with the Common Market.[23]

Overall, however, 35 per cent of the finance needed was generated by British banks. Barclays and National Westminster took on leading commitments, while the Scottish banks, particu-

larly the Bank of Scotland, played a pathfinder role, building up
extensive research and intelligence departments geared to oil
business. The Bank of Scotland (in which Barclays had a 35 per
cent stake) set up an oil division, assisted the formation of North
Sea Assets, and in 1973 combined with Barclays and other
European banks to set up the International Energy Bank (1973),
of whose potential assets of £52 billion the Bank held 15 per
cent. The Clydesdale Bank, actually controlled by the Midland
Bank, became strongly involved through north-east interests, and
put up the finance for Brown and Root's Nigg Yard (though this
got, surprisingly, no mention whatever in its official history).[24]
All in all, the Scottish clearing banks raised 10 per cent of the
capital required for North Sea operations.

How much capital was actually required? The pace had been
set by the two huge fields, Forties and Brent, whose annual
production was estimated at around 24 million tons. These involved multiple platforms, major pipelines and terminals. They
were also run by companies which were part of the metropolitan
oil establishment: BP, Shell, Exxon. American incomers suspected
that they had a tendency to 'gold-plate' their facilities, to invest
in equipment which went beyond the actual requirements. Forties
oil would cost 95 cents a barrel to produce; Hamilton's, on the
Argyll field, by contrast, would pay out only 16 cents a barrel.[25]
The companies, particularly the Americans, suspected that they
were being forced to instal expensive platforms to 'tether' them
to a field, when their own preference would be more flexible
forms of production which could subsequently be transferred
elsewhere. Pickens reckoned that Beatrice's pipeline cost $300
million more than was necessary.[26] In fact this didn't choke off
development. The heaviest investment was made in 1974–5,
when money was cheap and investment in the USA stifled
by the recession, while in Britain the state rescue of the aircraft,
car and shipbuilding industries inhibited other industrial investment goals.

The problem came when smaller independents and European
companies tried to get in on the act. They started off with some

advantages because of the expansion of banking enterprise in the early 1970s, but this carried, it turned out, more disadvantages in its train. The attempt to create more competitive industrial units in the late 1960s – such as the takeover of Associated Electrical Industries by Arnold Weinstock's General Electric Co. – had forced innovation on the City, and the period since 1970 had seen the merchant banking area boom with fringe banks, which obviated the staidness of the old institutions by offering finance for 'enterprise', usually company restructuring. This often amounted to buying concerns with undervalued property assets and selling these off. Hence the expansion of fringe banking concerns, often with a close connection to political personalities. The operation of outfits like Slater Walker Securities, in some ways a prototype, amounted – bluntly – to paying dividends out of the sums lodged with the firm by new subscribers, and the profits made by selling stripped assets, chiefly property, to new entrants to the game.[27] Bailing out the companies which became overcommitted to property speculation was to cost the Bank of England and the clearing banks £1.2 billion in 1974.[28]

But the cards were stacked *in principle* against any North Sea involvement leading in the direction of industrial reconstruction. This required a type of long-term commitment which was rarely considered. Typical enough was the *Economist*, announcing that oil company shares had risen 50 per cent since November 1973:

The shareholders should now get out. The way to play North Sea oil shares is to buy early, wait for discoveries to be announced and then sell at a fancy price ... So pick several prospective, if small, companies, and wait.[29]

The next four years, which involved getting the stuff ashore, would show low profits. The smaller investor should make his excuses and leave. Dr Colin Phipps, a petroleum geologist who was also a Labour MP, protested during the debate on the Petroleum bill about the lack of direction of oil finance policy. Government frowned on dealing in oil shares, because

Small firms and sometimes even individuals took a licence, bartered it and pocketed the money on their way back to Houston or Calgary.

Profit-taking discouraged the small investor, already doomed to play a minor role anyway. Most growth in this period was registered by insurance companies and pensions funds, and the City was scarcely helpful to raising capital:

I was astonished when the Hon. Member for Honiton (Peter Emery MP) said that finding money for a development was easy. I do not know whether he has spoken to many British banks recently, but I have. Many of them, including the merchant banks, say that they are not used to non-recourse borrowing in the way that banks, for instance, in Texas are. They are unwilling to take these risks and to raise these sums of money.[30]

Not for the first time would the British banking industry demonstrate that intriguing combination of Scrooge-like caution in assessing smaller enterprises on the cutting edge of new developments, along with an Errol Flynn abandon in financing huge and speculative projects. Luckily for it – and a big hand for Ayatollah Khomeini! – some of the latter paid off handsomely. Which was good for big oil, but not so good for the smaller firms which lived by equipment supply.

Charlotte Square

The City was not expert in oil finance, but it knew men who were. A new phrase crept into financial shop-talk: Charlotte Square. In this palatial segment of Edinburgh's New Town, built by Robert Adam in 1791, were found, behind silver-grey Craigleith stone and brass plates polished to anonymity, the masters of the Edinburgh financial universe. In fact the rise of the Scottish financial sector had been a by-product of regional de-industrialization. Its real boost had come in the 1880s, when it discovered the limits of industrial possibilities in Scotland, and set out after new commercial opportunities.

Charlotte Square awoke echoes of an earlier Scottish offshore oil boom. In this case the oil was animal-borne, got by the slaughter of whales. Dundee's prosperity rose on the North Atlantic whaling trade; the city's merchants realized that the oil could be used to process jute and hessian, and in the second quarter of the nineteenth century adapted linen machinery to the spinning and weaving of jute. Their business boomed remarkably in the 1860s, as the demand for sacking increased with world trade and linoleum was invented, which required a jute base. Yet it became evident to families like the Bonars and the Grimonds that Dundee's possibilities were finite. Jute could be processed more cheaply in Bengal, the country in which it originated. And bigger profits could also be made by prudent and professionally organized speculation in real estate and transport utilities.

Out of Dundee came the investment trust movement, in which funds were beneficially managed – in part by skilled financial employees of the jute firms, such as the Fleming family, originally clerks to the Bonars, who became English landed gentry in two generations (and produced Ian Fleming), and in part by the lawyers of Edinburgh. Firms like Shepherd and Wedderburn and Ivory and Sime built up a network of inter-connected holdings across the American Mid-West, in cattle, railroads and real estate.[31] Much of this was lost in both world wars, but enough survived – one-third of Scottish capital was invested in the USA in the early 1970s – to make some Charlotte Square firms sensitive to the rumours coming out of Texas.[32]

The one Scottish financier who really got on the wavelength of oil was James Gammell of Ivory and Sime. Besides being a lawyer in Edinburgh, Gammell was also a landowner near Blair-gowrie; and his interests in American asset management gave him thirty years' worth of Texas contacts, including the future president George Bush.[33] Gammell realized that the majors would dominate, but that, with independents already banging on the doors of the oil market, Scottish investments in key blocks might pay off. At a time when the stock market and the banks were slipping into what would become the chaos of the property market, Ivory and Sime and the sharp-eyed Edinburgh stock-brokers Wood Mackenzie were moving against the trend. But they were observed in the City of London, in particular by the blue-blooded firm of Cazenove, who were alert to the business as early as 1970.

Cazenove's report, *Investment Opportunities in North Sea Oil*, published in 1972, spurred London businesses, the investment trusts and individual entrepreneurs, into a London–Scottish link-up of small firms oriented to exploration and production. These interests took 37 per cent of London and Scottish Marine Oil (LASMO), 59 per cent of Scot Petroleum, 65 per cent of Caledonian Offshore (29 per cent of this coming from Ivory and Sime), 33 per cent of Caber (16 per cent of it Ivory and Sime), and 69 per cent of Pict Petroleum. Pict and Caber were created by Iain Noble and Angus Grossart, two young and, by City standards, rather radical businessmen; Caledonian Offshore and Viking Offshore – who commissioned the giant *Viking Piper* pipelaying barge – stemmed from the Ivory and Sime-inspired merchant bank Edward Bates, whose assets went up from £2.5 million in 1969 to £24.5 million in 1972.[34] Among those involved were Lord Balfour of Burleigh, of an old Tory dynasty; his kinsman Peter Balfour; Lord Clydesmuir, of the Lanarkshire steelmaking family of Colvilles; George Younger, of the brewers; and the ubiquitous Gammell.[35] Much the same team founded North Sea Assets in 1972, Ivory and Sime drawing finance from Edward Bates and Noble Grossart: its board also included repre-sentatives from Scottish investment firms such as Stenhouse Hold-ings, Christian Salvesen, and Oil Exploration. In turn it made funds available for such suppliers as Bett Brothers, Hewden Stewart and Seaforth Marine.

Such operations seemed important at the time. But the 120 foreign banks that opened up in Scotland turned out to be much more significant. The Scots financiers were only running a marginal show, although several finance firms turned to oil investment, and more investment companies were active than industrial concerns.

John Scott and Michael Hughes concluded, in their study of the evolution of Scottish capitalism, that

The lasting effects of the oil boom may prove to have been the restructuring of the financial sector which was already more consistently successful than the Scottish industrial companies.[36]

The track record of Scottish finance had always shown shrewdness in assessing investment running far ahead of sensitivity to the needs of domestic industry; and although Charlotte Square played a positive role in spreading information about the oil industry, of a sort lacking in English industrial regions which had long since lost their financial sectors, there were mistakes. The geography of ownership was one thing; actual success another. In 1973 and 1974 Edward Bates, like many another fringe bank, looked to enterprises other than oil, and over-committed itself in property purchases. As the market collapsed, its assets shrank. Bates lacked the £6 million it had promised to fund a London property takeover. It lost £9.5 million on an insurance company purchase. Attempting to attract *nouveau riche* Arab capital, it got rid of the prominent Jewish businessman Sir Max Rayne from its board. It was finally sold to National Westminster Bank and the London and Manchester Assurance Co. for £2 million. Bates and other speculative ventures foundered in a tangle of interlinked metropolitan property deals, few of which could be sold at a profit.[37] The upshot of these speculative traumas was to inhibit resources for investment, and for the sort of detailed research into technology and its transfer, business organization and joint ventures that the oil business required — even at a period when industrial assets could be cheaply purchased, with the stock market on the floor. *Faute de mieux*, the initiative passed to the state.

Guests and Hosts

Making money, the Scots had discovered in gold-rush after gold-rush in the nineteenth century, from California to the Rand, did not actually involve striking gold, but providing the prospectors with their essential supplies; which meant being in the right place at the right time, and noting how the market was shaping. The gas boom of the late 1960s had acted as a limited precedent. It brought sudden prosperity to the declining resort of Great Yarmouth and the fishing port of Lowestoft. Of eleven rigs in the North Sea in 1967, nine were serviced from Yarmouth. After 1965, in the month of March, ship movements had increased from 165 to 600, while ten-seater Westland Whirlwinds crowded the tarmac at the local airport.[38] The gas platforms were small and within sight of land; Yarmouth was only a couple of hours by road or train from London. Little independent enterprise was generated; even the inevitable night-clubs and prostitutes moved up from Soho.[39]

Was Aberdeen any different for the men from the multinationals who arrived five years later – professionals with years of experience in the Caribbean and the Gulf? For them, place tended to be immaterial: Aberdeen registered as awful weather, qualified by golf and whisky. And what was the reaction going to be among the locals? But perhaps 'locals' was a misnomer: particularly for the people of the Scottish north-east, that triangle of land between Aberdeen, Elgin and Peterhead. Remote and bleak it appeared, the 'muckle ferms' in their great parks, their black cattle sheltering under the windbreaks and dykes, and on the sea-coast the bright cottages of the fisher-folk, their painted gables facing the sea, dropping down steep braes to trawler-cluttered harbours. Men whose gear, in diesel engines and radar, ran to millions of pounds worshipped in grim Brethren chapels. They spoke a dialect which still seemed unfathomable to non-Buchan folk. But they were anything but isolated from the great movements of world history. Renaissance Aberdeen had two universities – the independent foundations of King's College and Marischal College – the same number as England . . .

There was, for instance, a very old man in Peterhead, Max Schultze, a German fish-merchant from Stettin, whose grand-aunt was a friend of Wagner, and whose sister married Yeats's friend, the mystic F.P. Sturm. Schultze had been the Labour provost of the burgh. And there was the convenor of Aberdeen County Council, Maitland Mackie, who organized a delegation of seventy-two north-eastern entrepreneurs to the United States almost as soon as rumours of the oilfield began.[40] On the surface a typical north-eastern 'muckle fermer', Mackie's wife turned out to be Texan. Not only this; one brother, John, had been a Labour MP for many years, was a close friend of Aneurin Bevan, and was the party's agriculture expert, and the other, George, had briefly been a Liberal MP and now led the party in the House of Lords. This sort of network was not untypical. The county, producing some of the best meat in the world, had long-standing connections with Argentina and the American West.

The Buchan fisheries had been transformed in the nineteenth century from foreign merchants to a co-operatively owned multinational monopolizing the salt-herring supply to Eastern Europe. Until 1914 the steam drifters supplied freight steamers which butted their way to the Baltic ports; after 1917 Fraserburgh fish-merchants swotted up on Marx, in an effort to get on speaking terms with the new Soviets. And in schools throughout Scotland a disproportionate number of teachers were, thanks to plentiful bursaries, Buchan loons and queans.

Would such people take the initiative? Would they be passive? Aberdeen and its hinterland produced their entrepreneurs: Ian Wood, of the John D. Wood company, and even more remark-ably R.B. Farquhar of Huntly, a man whose couthy delivery baffled even most of his Scottish business colleagues, but who established a near-monopoly in the supply of 'onshore modules' for office and accommodation use. But a lot depended on the precise civil society of the area. Aberdeen's was democratic and competitive; the city had been for years a Labour stronghold; the country areas harboured a strong radicalism: its whole political outlook was like something out of the American 'progressive' era.[41]

Two other cases brought distinct areas of Scotland into oil's firing line. In 1972 and 1973 the hunt was on for sites for building concrete platforms, and a committee of the Energy Department and the Scottish Office was set up to study this. Ten deep-water platforms were needed, of which the Cormorant platform, commissioned from McAlpine at Ardyne on the Clyde, which cost £35 million, was a mere tiddler. In particular there was a need for yards where the surrounding waters were deep enough for the Condeep type of platform to be floated off. Condeeps were made of concrete pillars and could draw anything up to 450 feet. The civil engineering firm R.H.W. Bullock reported to the Department of Energy in February 1974 that at least forty fathoms were needed to tow a Condeep out; the Clyde had only twenty-five. Loch Carron, Loch Hourn (earlier, the haunt of Gavin Maxwell and his otters) and Loch Broom were possible, but the last two were ruled out: Ullapool was too busy, and Loch Hourn accessible only over twenty miles of very bad road.[42] There were only a couple of sites round the Scottish coast where this sort of operation would be possible, and in 1972 the Scottish Office and its client Taylor Woodrow settled for the hamlet of Drumbuie on Loch Carron.

When you get off the diesel at Duirinish halt, the sea lies round a twist in the single-track, fenceless road, running above patches of bog and dwarf oak. Then you are in Port na hEora, five houses round its tiny bay — and in the distance, west of the great bluff of Applecross, the Crowlin Islands, then Raasay with its strange conning-tower, then the sawtooth ridge of the Cuillins. This was not just 'an area of outstanding natural beauty', but the heartland of the greatest modern Gaelic poet, Sorley MacLean; somewhere so symbolic of the Scottish highlands that the National Trust for Scotland took it over in the 1930s as one of its first properties, to be held 'in perpetuity for the nation'. The government proposed to sequester it.

It had its reasons, which were not wholly materialistic.

The future of the Inverness and Kyle of Lochalsh railway hung by a thread. The yard would bring enough traffic – cement and steel, and of course the workforce, to enable it to survive. A furious argument about jobs versus scenery, complicated by the railway factor, broke out.[43] The months ticked by. Taylor Woodrow moved off, but then another construction partnership, an alliance of the English Sir John Howard group and the French Doris, moved in, and this time the Scottish Office had another proposal: the lonely sea-loch of Kishorn, four miles by sea to the north and hidden by the peninsula of Meall na hAirde from the railway and the tourists. A concrete platform yard could be constructed there, served from a railhead at Strome Ferry, whence heavy supplies would be shipped in by barge. Howard-Doris agreed, and the delving of 'the big hole' started in January 1975.

At the other end of the Kyle railway, seventy miles and as many houses from Strome Ferry, was Dingwall and the Cromarty Firth, the great *fata Morgana* of an industrialized Highlands. A dozen miles north of Inverness the water was deep, without the disadvantage of precipitous sides. Dreadnoughts had anchored here in the First World War. After the setting-up by Labour of the Highlands and Islands Development Board in 1965 there were great schemes for a linear city between Inverness and Invergordon. An aluminium smelter came in 1970; it seemed that a number of chemical works were possible. But this was also aristocrats' country, and an old landed élite still ran the Ross and Cromarty County Council. In 1968 there had been an election for the Nigg seat which presaged a major confrontation. On one side was John Robertson, a local Liberal of arcane talents, including the ability to swim the Cromarty Firth and to understand Scottish local government finance. Robertson, a Cambridge graduate, had helped save the railway to Wick from Dr Beeching. He now campaigned on the slogan 'The time for industry is now!' against Mrs Pat Hunter-Gordon, on the Conservative ticket. Mrs Gordon was Robertson's sister: merely the first peculiarity in a fight which ranged over a couple of continents, and would involve the operations of one of the world's richest and most reclusive men.[44]

Although there was a strong vote in favour of development candidates, an arcane politics soon took over. Robertson sold off 220 acres in 1968 for £160,000; a year later the Hunter-Gordons sold their land for a cool million, and moved to Angus. In fact, by 1970 almost every riparian site along the Firth had gone, for a huge mark-up, to mushroom property companies. There was some reality behind this speculative frenzy. It was provided by Highland Fabricators, alias Brown and Root, who got contracts in 1972 for two of the four platforms for the Forties field, each 550 feet high, weighing 20,000 tons plus a 3,000-ton deck. These would be built in a dock 1,000 feet long, 600 feet across and 50 feet deep, which had been completed by mid-1972.[45]

The parent company, Halliburton, had done well out of the Vietnam War, and become the biggest supply company in the world. Nigg had 1,300 workers in mid-1973, 1,500 in early 1974, 2,000 by mid-1974. Wages were between £40 and £60 per week after tax. The locals were satisfied, but the incomers were not, neither the Glasgow engineers nor the 'white settlers'. Working conditions were poor, pay low, facilities in the local towns primitive.[46] Yet, as a local put it to George Rosie of the *Sunday Times*,

What are we supposed to do? Stand about being picturesque, being gawped at by tourists? Because that's what tourism does. I know a man who, in the summer, gets all dressed up in a kilt, feathered bonnet, takes his bagpipes and goes and stands in Glengarry: and charges the tourists for taking pictures of him. Is that what they want for us, these folk who talk about the bad effect the oil will have on the tourists?[47]

But bigger interests were eyeing the Firth, and, anticipating this, a colourful selection of Scots speculators homed in. *Private Eye* detected an old-fashioned con-man claiming to have a couple of benevolent sheikhs in tow, who would put up cash for offshore operations provided 10 per cent commission was paid *in advance*. The fact that this scam was run from a bungalow in

Troon did not increase its credibility.[48] A persistent fringe finance character called Eoin Mekie, who had once been a Tory candidate (in a solid Labour seat), conjured up Grampian Chemicals, which cavorted on the front pages for a bit and then evaporated. More seriously, the Cromarty Firth Development Co., alias Foulerton and Ivory and Sime, surfaced and spent £4 million on farmland. An imminent selling-on operation was rumbled by MPs and Cromarty Firth pulled out on the prompting of the fringe banking collapse. In the middle of all this Ed Loughney, former executive vice-president of Gulf, moved in, acting for Daniel K. Ludwig.[49]

Ludwig's firm announced a £180 million project for an oil refinery on 12 December 1973. All the local political parties were in favour, versus the old – and conservationist – order:

'The split was classic,' says one participant. 'The white settlers and the middle class were out in force agitating about the countryside being despoiled and the air polluted and so on. The locals were cautious, but inclined to approve.'[50]

There were two other refinery schemes on the go by now, one at Hunterston on the Clyde and another at Nigg. The planning committee of the local council threw Ludwig's out; a meeting of the full council reinstated it. The right was divided between rather high-handed environmentalism and making a quick killing; the left between the need for jobs and the suspicion that devious speculative motions were going on behind the scenes. Doubts remained because, world-wide, refinery capacity already existed in overabundance. Britain itself had only 60 per cent of its plant in operation.

The Aberdeen University oil economist Alex Kemp, close to the SNP, queried the Ludwig plan on precisely those grounds: there would, if anything, be a general cutback in oil refinery building. The government could end coughing up £30 million in subsidy, perhaps to fund a tax dodge, providing high-cost cargoes for Ludwig's ships with the refinery operating at zero profit, to set against liability for tax.[51] In December 1975 the

Reporter found against the plan, but the Scottish Secretary, Willie Ross, overruled his decision in March 1976, under strict conditions, and with permission not confined to Ludwig.

There then appeared the 'white settler' *par excellence*. A Kentish Tory, Michael Nightingale, who had made himself laird of Cromarty, 'an obstructive, nit-picking menace of a man', held a vital forty-seven acres opposite Nigg Point, and launched a series of objections to the project. It was to take Ludwig three years to get this piece of land. Meanwhile the Tory MP Roger Moate blocked the refinery bill on Nightingale's behalf, and Labour opponents of the project worked closely with such odd allies as the Conservative right-wingers Nicholas Ridley and Jock Bruce-Gardyne. The London press were hostile, arguing that only 450 jobs would be created for a state outlay of £36 million. Bruce-Gardyne gibed in the *Telegraph*:

This is a project of such commercial improbability that it may very well, like its previous manifestations, turn out to be stillborn. Nevertheless it tells us much about management of the nation's affairs over the past ten years. . .[52]

He need not have worried. It was to take until the summer of 1977 for work to start, continue desultorily for a few months, and end on 7 June 1978.[53] Promises of a gas-gathering pipeline kept alive the notion of downstream development until 1981. When this was given up, so too was the hope of a cheap electricity supply to the Invergordon aluminium smelter, which duly fell victim to Thatcher's first slump. Of the linear industrial city Sir Robert Grieve and the first members of the Highlands and Islands Development Board had foreseen, not much could be traced.

The Cromarty Firth was a developmental mess. The Nigg yard kept surfacing in the headlines as a battlefield between the Red Clyde's away team and whoever actually wanted to get the platforms into the water. A very large Welshman called Ivor the Bounce and a crony were hired to keep order on the old Italian cruise liner which accommodated 250 men in 6 foot by 4 foot cabins. Ashore there was one pub and that was that. Landowners and 'white settlers', exhibiting a snobbery which now seems almost beyond belief, barred the building of decent accommodation for the workers.

This was one shadow side. The other concerned the offshore rigs. The fortnight-on, fortnight-off life worked against the creation of a working community and of effective trade unions, always fundamental to Scottish industrial politics. Indeed the interpretations made of its impact divided more than they united: the 'gold rush' version – of desperate drinking in pubs and shebeens, of crowded alcohol-soaked trains – was set against the more enduring reality of families and communities under strain, scattered fairly thinly all over the country. The impact on specific areas was considerable, but these were isolated basins in a country whose politics were increasingly out of kilter with the two-party orthodoxy of the rest of Britain. The upheaval was to lead to differing political strategies, region by region, not straight-forwardly to any 'Scottish' view.

Despite, or perhaps because of, its dominance of Scottish politics, the organized working class lagged in its responses. It was not until 1972 that North Sea oil became of real concern to the Scottish Labour movement. Even then, the action taken by the Labour movement – the formation of the North Sea Oil Action Committee in October 1972 – was local and Aberdeen-based rather than Scottish. Only in January 1973 did the NSOAC meet with the Scottish Trades Union Congress, and it took until May for the latter to liaise with Labour MPs. Both were more concerned at this stage with remedying the immediate problem of working conditions on the rigs, and income differentials between American and British workers, than with strategic questions. Although these were ultimately ventilated at a conference on 22 June 1973, the Labour Party and the STUC now faced a formidable rival.[54]

Enter the Nats

Wagnerians will remember the scene in *Siegfried* when our hero is filling the wood with horn-calls, each one more brazen than the last, until a low, menacing roar indicates that he has upset something big and evil-tempered. Something like this happened in mid-1973. The Scots in general, and the Scottish National Party in particular, woke up to the oil. A year later the *Economist*, which had its own reasons for taking an interest in what was going on north of the border (Pearson's oil stake, and a Scottish editor, Alastair Burnett), was proclaiming:

The only clear-headed people, apart from the Ulstermen, were the Scottish nationalists: when the British economy is in trouble the best practical policy is to get Scottish hands on local resources. Nationalism has tended to advance and recede with the British economic pulse; oil may now be a more permanent factor.[55]

In 1970, following a revival which was more exciting than fundamental, and a poor performance in the general election, most political commentators had written off the SNP as a protest party, a Caledonian variant on the defensive populism which had London dockers demonstrating in favour of a classicist with a turn for portentous rhetoric. The flower of Scotland seemed to have wilted in the same wind that had borne away the dockers' chants of 'Ee-nock! Ee-nock!' – and for that matter most of their jobs. The SNP was lucky to keep a foothold in the fundamentalist outpost of the Western Isles.

But if the traditional social structure of Scotland had taken a battering, and with it the organized working class, there was perhaps space for a new movement. And the SNP lay second to the ruling Conservatives in five constituencies in north-east Scotland, precisely the area in which oil-related activity would become most densely concentrated. Conventional wisdom saw the 'age of affluence' of the 1950s and 1960s as undermining Labour's class politics, but in Scotland it ended the rural deference which had frozen the Scottish counties in the mould of 1931. The wiping-out of much of the railway system and the older sorts of rural employment – weaving, the labour-intensive farm, numerous military supply depots – knocked the basis from the Labour support which had traditionally divided the anti-Tory vote.

By-elections soon began to show this. Labour might have taken centre stage with the Upper Clyde agitation that summer, but in a by-election in its Stirling and Falkirk seat, on 16 September 1971, where the SNP candidate was the veteran Robert McIntyre (who had captured its first seat at Motherwell in April 1945), the oil issue already played a part in a qualified recovery.[56] Reacting to this, the established parties were not helped by two linked events. The transition to a new local government system – of regional and district authorities – was to take place in 1974–5. This was supposed in principle to diminish the dominance of the Scottish Office, and devolve its powers to a regional level. But a second factor supervened: the country was racked by a series of financial scandals, many connected with the Yorkshire architect John Poulson. Poulson's vast practice had been gained partly as a result of the 'motorway mania' which followed the Buchanan Report. His energetic bribery of local leaders hit the Labour Party. His activities around St Andrew's House brought down 'Gorgeous George' Pottinger, one of the high-flyers of the Scottish Office, who would certainly have carved himself a leading role in oil politics.

As a result, Edinburgh was losing power to the regions, and to London. The resuscitation of the Energy ministry could only be expected to rile the Scots, as the *Economist* reported in early 1974:

It is not the possible despoliation of part of the west coast that is galling to most Scots. For them the issue is the transfer of power over such matters from Edinburgh to London.[57]

There had been internal pressure at St Andrew's House for a Scottish Oil office since 1971, without effect; Heath's Scottish Secretary, Gordon Campbell, was an anachronism, a pleasant ex-diplomat, totally without flair. Might things change with his successor, the Glasgow populist Teddy Taylor, to the *Economist* 'a convinced devolutionist', whose agent had even (briefly) joined the SNP? The Scottish bourgeoisie he represented sought a return of respect through oil, yet the decline of its industrial power was starkly evident in Tory Party finances. It effectively had its autonomy removed in 1975, just when Margaret Thatcher, the 'English patriot', took over in London.

The Barber of Govan

There was a time when by-elections didn't count. The Labour government of 1945–51, with a huge legislative programme and unending economic and industrial problems, didn't lose a single seat. But by the 1970s things had changed. The SNP's rise had been due to mid-term volatility; this revived after 1970. Labour ought to have benefited from Heath's problems, but the Labour Party in Scotland contemned home rule, which remained obstinately popular. So the SNP had its opportunity – particularly when George Thomson, the former Labour Colonial Secretary, fall guy for BP's Rhodesian duplicity and MP for Dundee East, went to Brussels as commissioner in 1972. There was a six-month by-election campaign, which started with Labour selecting, after much internal conflict, a Sheffield trade unionist who had no connection with the place. The SNP ran Gordon Wilson, its vice-president, who was also a local solicitor. Charged with supervising the 'Scotland's Oil' campaign, he launched it on 5 September 1972.

Wilson appeared a rather dour figure, but though he was not utterly persuaded that it was ethical to concentrate on such a materialistic argument for independence, he underscored a strategy which cannily homed in, through 'action packs', on the local consequences of the oil: Dundee, he argued, could be £28 million better off through its quota of Scotland's oil income. By sticking doggedly to the issue, he ran Labour very close on

1 March 1973, and was chosen by the party to transform oil into a second, full-blown campaign, launched on 16 March.[58]

When the $5 barrel shot to between $12 and $16, the SNP's 1980 projections were already being more than met. The party had hit a jackpot it had never expected, and Scotland had stopped being a debtor nation. The 'Scottish balance of payments' theme had effectively been the parent of the oil campaign, in a long-lasting dispute about economic viability. This had its origins in pre-war attempts by the Scottish Economic Committee to assess Scotland's component of UK public income and expenditure. The economist James A. A. Porteous, who had been assistant-secretary to the Committee, had argued in a paper written for John MacCormick's briefly influential Covenant Movement of 1948, *Scotland and the South*, that taxation took from Scots more than government policy conferred on them.[59] This remained the SNP position in the 1960s, and provoked the Labour government to commission a 'Scottish budget' in 1968, which calculated that the opposite was the case. This line was also put over by Dr Gavin McCrone, while an Oxford economist, in *The Economics of Nationalism* (1969), which saw Scotland in deficit to the tune of between £56 and £93 million annually.[60]

This sum was very important. The SNP had long ceased to be – if indeed it ever had been – a party of Lallans poets and simple-lifers. Its research department had been since 1969 under an able young economist, Donald Bain, an Aberdeen graduate who had done research in Canada and observed how recent oil discoveries in Alberta had been exploited by its Conservative state government. Under premier Peter Lougheed its 2 million people were in 1974 reaping $2,000 million in oil revenues, against $300 million in 1972, after a rise in oil's domestic price from $4 to $6.50 a barrel.[61]

To Bain, oil and gas resources could alter the equation in favour of the economics of independence, *and* establish Scotland's international presence. With the Cambridge and Chatham House graduate Stephen Maxwell, the SNP's head of publicity, and Wilson's experience as organizer of the SNP's pirate Radio Free

Scotland, the SNP so collared the oil issue that, between 1972 and 1975, businessmen and journalists wanting information on oil policy came to the SNP rather than to government departments, as the SNP was factually better briefed. Oil wasn't just a potential benefit to Scotland; it also exposed the failings of the centralized British state. Hence those edgy dinners at embassies as Foreign Office personnel tried to find out exactly how Gordon Wilson and Bain were using their technical knowledge and international contacts to develop relations with OPEC in Vienna and the Norwegian government.[62]

The impression grew during 1973 and 1974 that a sort of Tartan Katanga policy was germinating, whereby the majors would get further with an independent Scottish government than they would with UK governments of left or right. But the result of the SNP's international consultations and party discussions was an oil policy whose main points were derived from Norway: (1) The oil would be the property of the future Scottish state; (2) annual output would be limited to 70 to 100 million tons; (3) there would be more local participation in oil-related industry; (4) and there would be a Scottish state oil company, resembling Norway's Statoil, with 50 per cent participation in fields to be developed in the Scottish sector.[63] This was distinctly less reassuring.

Yet events didn't rule out the prospect that the companies might have to deal with an SNP regime. The report of the Kilbrandon Commission on the Constitution was due in autumn 1973. So too was a fresh by-election, in the exceptionally run-down seat of Glasgow Govan, only days after the publication of Kilbrandon. The Yom Kippur war intervened, and also Labour's enduring facility to choose the wrong candidate. Harry Selby, an elderly barber who passed for a stalwart of the tiny party, greeted Kilbrandon's proposals for devolution with unqualified hostility. The SNP countered, as in Hamilton in 1967, with a young, articulate and progressive woman. Margo MacDonald ran a well-planned campaign with party resources – already in high gear – effectively concentrated. On 4 November Selby lost, the new MP attained instant celebrity, and the winter of crisis began.[64]

The SNP's oil campaign was more than an exercise in acquiring and spreading information. It also presented one option in the strategies of British and Scottish oil-oriented groups, at a time when government strategy towards the North Sea was inchoate and unpredictable, mingling the 'extract as fast as possible' of the Conservatives, the state-participation inclinations of Labour, and the unpredictable possibility of a depletion policy. When no one among the bigger oil firms knew quite what was going on behind the classical façades of sandstone Edinburgh and granite Aberdeen, the comings and goings of the SNP activists and the exploration, extraction and finance interests were a guide. Some figures in stockbroking and merchant banking, notably Robin Angus of Wood Mackenzie, and the Pict Petroleum partnership of Iain Noble and Angus Grossart, were known to be sympathetic to home rule. Sir Hugh Fraser, son of the chain-store tycoon, joined the SNP in April 1974.[65] In June he hosted a presentation of the party and its policies to a further 170 businessmen.[66] The banks there were several closet Nats. The chief economist at the Royal, the largest of the Scottish banks, Grant Baird, who produced a quarterly commentary on oil issues from 1970, was close to the SNP. Peter Chiene, the proprietor of Q magazine, a lively intellectual nationalist magazine which enjoyed a brief flourishing between 1974 and 1977, was from a great fund-managing dynasty. The nearness of SNP headquarters to Charlotte Square was not utterly coincidental.[67]

In time most observers would find out, to their satisfaction or otherwise, that articulateness about oil finance didn't actually amount to financial clout. But perhaps the most important of the observers were to be found in that huge lump of Edinburgh rococo which stares down on Waverley station and the provocatively named North British Hotel: the offices of the *Scotsman*.

'No one alive will see the end of this'

Roy, first Lord Thomson of Fleet, proprietor of the *Scotsman*, a screed of Canadian provincial newspapers, Scottish Television and (in an act of hubris) *The Times*, was legendarily mean. Asked by Armand Hammer and Paul Getty to join them in an oil venture, decided on when BP had struck the Forties field, he demanded to be grubstaked, and offered the job of running Thomson Scottish Petroleum to his friend Alastair Dunnett, editor of the *Scotsman*, without extra pay. Dunnett, being a patriotic soul, agreed. 'Keep on saying that, Alastair!' was Thomson's response. The three multi-millionaires celebrated their alliance in an untypically chic London restaurant, with neither cash nor a credit card between them. A passing millionaire had to bail them out.

Thomson's choice was a brilliant one, as Dunnett was a true insider, a practical journalist with a minute knowledge of the interstices of Scottish society, who had assisted Thomson to transform the *Scotsman* from a dry, conservative provincial daily to a radical and campaigning broadsheet, and to launch Thomson's capture of Scottish Television, the celebrated 'licence to print money'.[68]

Dunnett did not care at all for Hammer – 'a man who vulgarized everything he touched' – and indeed there was much about Occidental's operations which caused raised eyebrows in circles which were wider than merely financial. The company had nearly been felled by the fall in tanker rates in 1971, and its stock was down by 75 per cent; the *Economist* claimed that the company didn't disclose the facts about its losses on tankers, something which kept the lawyers busy for a few months until it had to retract in April.[69] Following on links made back in the days of the New Economic Policy with Lenin, Hammer was helping the Russians to build fertilizer plants and a trade centre as part of a $580-million programme, a connection strong enough to bring the CIA's James Jesus Angleton across to London, denouncing him to sceptical British intelligence chiefs.[70] The Thomson organization itself, capitalized on £30 million, had profits down from £5 to £1 million on tourism losses. Still, the drilling-rig *Ocean Victory* was hired, and operating out of Peterhead in December 1972 it detected, on its third well, a large 94-million-ton field (though this was only half the size of Brent or Forties) in block 15/17, 130 miles east of the Orkneys. Occidental christened it the Piper.

How to finance the building of the production platform, 475 feet from sea-bed to water level, and the associated pipeline? The majors had their own internal sources; the Piper partners would have to raise their cash in a financial market which was poised on the verge of a major collapse. They managed it, just in time. In October 1974 the advertisements were posted for the Piper field's finance – $150 million for Occidental, $100 million for Thomson. Finance would be underwritten by the Republican Bank of Dallas and the International Energy Bank. Production drilling, at a depth of 470 feet, would be carried out by 1976, giving an output of 220,000 barrels per day from mid-1977. At $10 a barrel, its annual share of the gross revenue would be £67 million.[71]

A month later, after the Yom Kippur war had made its mark, this could have been difficult. But Dunnett and his banking allies pulled it off just in time. Practical problems now took over: notably finding a landfall for Piper. Dunnett and his staff spent weeks flying about the north of Scotland in light aircraft. The Caithness coast was no more friendly than in Thomas Stevenson's day – there had been 5,000 wrecks off the north of Scotland. Orkney was more promising. Had not the Grand Fleet anchored in Scapa Flow – and the German High Seas Fleet destroyed itself there? The trouble was that, of two possible sites, one was the main nesting place for the world's population of long-tailed duck. The other was the grave of the battleship *Royal Oak* and several hundred sailors, torpedoed there in 1940. A decision would have to be made at the big Offshore Engineering Exhibition in Houston in 1972. On the plane going out, Dunnett encountered Admiral David Dunbar-Nasmyth, spending his retirement helping the Scottish Council in its efforts to attract oil business. They started talking, and Dunnett raised his problem. Easy, said Dunbar-Nasmyth, where I could take a Dreadnought, you could take a tanker. Flotta's the place.

Flotta was free of birds and drowned sailors. The following day Dunbar-Nasmyth explained this to Occidental, and the decision was taken. Dunnett went into action, becoming 'an Orcadian for several years', persuading the crofters to sell up; prowling around the Edinburgh banks, whom he persuaded to put up most of the $200 million that Thomson wanted; trying to galvanize the unions (not all that difficult, given the unemployment situation) and put some backbone into a Scottish business class which seemed to have given up.

By 1977 the Piper–Flotta project had been set up, but Thomson was dead. Dunnett had not been transformed into a millionaire; he still lived in his Victorian house in Colinton Road, in Britain overshadowed by the enormous popularity of his wife Dorothy and her historical novels, but in Scotland and Edinburgh a lively propellant of progressive and nationalist politics into his eighties. 'Can any good come out of Nazareth?' he mused. He concluded that, all in all, it had.

MCMLXXIV

Those long uneven lines
Standing as patiently
As if they were stretched outside
The Oval or Villa Park,
The crowns of hats, the sun
On moustached archaic faces
Grinning as if it were all
An August Bank Holiday lark . . .

– Philip Larkin, 'MCMXIV' (1960)[72]

For Philip Larkin, whose poems were secreted somewhere remote from the grouch projected in his letters, 1914 had been a sacrifice by ordinary Englishmen: 'Never such innocence again'. This was one view of a whole past – Orwell's people with their 'kindly, knobbly faces' and devotion to warm beer and foul language, Thackeray's Major Dobbin, Bunyan's Pilgrim: the land-living, insular, decent English. There were other, more 'British', metaphors associated with the sea, which involved the transfer of such qualities into grimmer, less calculable circumstances: 'The Ballad of Sir Patrick Spens', the last fight of the *Revenge*, Conrad's *Typhoon*, Richard Hughes's *In Hazard*: desperate situations in which dour fortitude was the only thing that could win out, or at least make an honest end.

Such a metaphor would have fitted 1974: the country as a drilling rig trying to keep station in a hurricane. The crew were variously dedicated and mutinous, new officers boarding from helicopters in breaks in the weather. Different samples came from the borings, some exciting, some depressing; conflicting instructions crackled over the wireless from a headquarters which itself seemed in turmoil. In retrospect 1974 was the crucial year, in both the politics and economics of oil. The decisions taken then saved Britain, at least for two decades. Their associated consequences were to haunt the polity for as long.

127.5 million tons. Keep that figure in mind, because it was a horizon of sorts. This was the output of the UK shelf at its maximum, eleven years later. The instruments in the rig's control-room would show various conjectural figures on either side of this, and these would determine policy, in so far as it could be determined in Britain alone. Signals from elsewhere were anything but straightforward. Even at the beginning of the year, as the City of London stood on the brink of 'a terrifying collapse of confidence in the banking system', share prices were dropping to half their 1972 level and fringe financiers were going bust. The country struggled under the miners' work-to-rule and the three-day week.[73] While futurologists were insisting that the energy age was coming to an end, there was a run on candles.

The prescient could, however, sense that the next transportation revolution would be to do with information transmission by electronic means, thanks to the microchip, invented in 1971.

Who, actually, was in charge of the rig? Carrington's Department of Energy might have 'an amount of power staggering under a Tory government in peacetime', but the *Economist* found the City obsessed with its own troubles: 'Britain is still not excited about the North Sea. British companies tend to approach the oil cautiously, hesitating to invest large funds.'[74]

Meanwhile, American firms were ignoring the UK government's modesty and making their own estimates. The Japanese – with only four factories in the UK at that time – were taking an interest. But what *Spielraum* did the UK government really have? What changes in energy policy were implied by entry in 1973 to the EEC?

On 11 February the command changed. Heath had moved from the free-market position of his early days and now represented a sort of right-wing social democracy, qualified by the consequences of having unleashed a speculative boom which had gone horribly wrong. As well as his enthusiasm for Europe, he still held by a scheme of constitutional reconstruction, and thought that this would benefit his party, not least through gains in Scotland, with Labour's vote divided by the SNP's inroads. The *Economist* agreed. It found Labour weak: 'particularly in the West, its election machine is as rusty as ever, many of its candidates are poor, and far too many are trade-union sponsored'.[75] In fact the SNP broke through, doubling its vote to 21 per cent and capturing seven seats. The Western Isles was retained, and although Margo MacDonald lost Govan, Stirling East and Dundee East were captured from Labour; Argyll, Aberdeenshire East, Moray and Nairn, and Banff from the Tories.

A devolution opponent from Wales, Neil Kinnock MP, attributed the SNP's success exclusively to oil, and indeed in oil-less Wales the Plaid Cymru vote declined although its MPs rose from one to three.[76] Yet a *Scotsman* ORC poll on 28 February found that North Sea oil scarcely registered as an election issue, and a later poll by System 3 in 1977 found that only 13 per cent of those surveyed had heard of the SNP's oil campaign. Instead, two things happened. The positive trade balance that the oil gave Scotland made the overall stance of the SNP credible, and the competence of its oil campaign reinforced its already effective publicity efforts. The issue was not oil in itself, but Scottish home rule.

The SNP was now calculating oil revenues at a possible £800 million a year by 1980: and promising to remove income tax on incomes of under £2,000. This had only a limited impact. Although Labour candidates taunted the SNP with exploiting emotionalism and racism, the Labour vote remained, for the moment, well ahead of that of the SNP. The Tories had been the miscalculators. They assumed that the winners in the oil-affected areas would settle for vague promises of devolution and a possible oil fund; they wanted more of both, and voted for the SNP.[77]

Did the Downing Street incomer, Harold Wilson, know or care anything about oil? The question is worth asking, because his biographers, fastidious about the strange ménage that was restored, are utterly silent on it. What faced him was a battlefield, but one out of Kinglake's description of the Crimea, and all too similar to that last British North Sea battle: Jutland. Something was wrong with the ships – *literally*, as launchings from British shipyards continued to fall, while the Swedes took theirs from 750,000 tons in 1960 to 2.5 million tons in 1973; and the French, with little previous experience, and no oil, cornered much of the rig and platform market.[78] More seemed wrong with the command. In February, Edmund Dell had pressed oil on Wilson as a vote-winner; Wilson had done nothing. Harold Lever had thought in terms of a consortium of industries which could secure their own oil reserves at beneficial prices; the *Economist* suggested an oil bond – a first shot at popular capitalism.[79] The time cried out for someone with the magisterial sweep of Keynes, who in 1940 had restrained the sort of inflation which now threatened by forcing such a policy of compulsory saving. But there was no Keynes around. The government's economic counsels were divided; as was its appraisal of Britain's future.

The issue of the Common Market remained under debate, to be settled by referendum in 1975. In May, one hopeful venture had come to grief, when a Protestant workers' strike destroyed the power-sharing executive Heath had set up in Northern Ireland. Wilson feared similar reactions in Scotland, should the Nationalists scoop the home-rule pool and get the upper hand. Wilson was no silent, masterful Captain MacWhirr; dissent on the rig's control-room would be combated, after noisy conspiracy, by buying-off the dissenters, if need be at the expense of the Scottish Labour hierarchy. This was one track of a famously empirical policy. The other was that, once in office, Wilson's government quickly started to draft its Petroleum and Pipelines bill, to provide a framework for controlling the industry – a stage passed two years before in Norway, but one which inevitably consolidated the rights of the central state, and diminished the alternatives to it.

A new phase in the saga was about to begin, complicated by this second political issue, oil-related, not Britain-friendly, but manageable. The near-mutineers might hold the bit of the rig near the oil. But what mattered was keeping control of the oil itself. This done, the rig would come through.

5

'The Biggest Movable Thing on Earth'

> ... when you see the Queen in action, everything is just
> absorbed into this frozen feudal hierarchy. All the old big-wigs
> are brought out into the open as if they were somehow
> responsible for a great industrial achievement, while the workers
> are presented as natives and barbarians who can be greeted but
> have to be kept at a distance ... this great Scottish occasion was
> just an opportunity for the London Establishment to come up
> and lord it over the Scots.
>
> Tony Benn, *Diaries*, 3 November 1975[1]

Royalty or Revolution?

On 3 November 1975 the Queen came to Aberdeenshire to preside over the landing of the first oil from the Forties field at Cruden Bay. The grand hotel had vanished from where her great-grandfather Edward, King Emperor, had taken to the golf links, his entourage brought from the station by a private tram, but something of that style persisted. The new Secretary of State for Energy was unimpressed.

Tony Benn's views were echoed by the natives. Kenneth Roy, of BBC-TV Scotland, recollected being shunted to one side – 'if you don't mind, dear boy' – to make way for Raymond Baxter, master of the technological ceremonies at Television Centre.[2] Perhaps in reaction to a couple of small bomb-blasts along the course of the pipeline, the work of militant Scottish nationalist splinter-groups, the fact that the province was 'British', not Scottish, territory was none too subtly emphasized.

There was symbolism in all this. The oil business *qua* money had been ingested by the British establishment; it had stopped being rough and disruptive and potentially revolutionary. For all Baxter's superlatives, the public – not to speak of the press – were beginning to find it boring: a safe bet for royal patronage. After 'a phase of collective euphoria' it started to lose interest.[3] The oil was there, but like the Queen, it was kept at a distance; neither in 1975 nor in 1976 did it seem to be able to remedy the country's oil-induced depression. Apathy wasn't confined to the tabloids. In 1974 the Social Science Research Council had set up a panel under W.G. Runciman to survey the oil-related scene and, where necessary, commission research. In 1975 it found that

Current research coverage of the social effects of North Sea oil is, at best, patchy; much of it is of a general nature, and throws little light on the questions raised by the social impact of oil ... Virtually no multi-disciplinary research is in progress.[4]

'Multi-disciplinary' was for once more than a slogan. Technologies and organizations of every description were being thrown at the province, each of which had its own economic and social implications. Could they act 'synergically', as Patrick Geddes would have put it? The North Sea shelf was expensive; once the decision for rapid exploitation had been made, the relevant technology was totally altered to suit. This might have implied an 'industrial revolution' in much the same way that the machine production of textiles, the steam railway, or the automobile assembly-line had done. But where was the imaginative 'capture' of the industry, the phrase or symbol which summed the whole thing up?

An industrial revolution does three things: it creates a new technology, with hitherto unforeseen capabilities; it consumes vast quantities of capital; and it completely alters the market for its product. In the eighteenth century textiles had demanded, firstly, the sequence of water-powered machines which transformed bales of cotton into thread; secondly, entrepreneurs needed the money to purchase the machinery, and even more important, the huge quantities of raw material needed for optimum production; thirdly, a market for cheap cottons had to be created. In the North Sea the situation was in no respect so symmetrical, but there were some resemblances.

The application of technology radically expanded the dimensions of the province. By 1977 known discoveries ran to 22 billion barrels (3 billion tons) in reserves. The UK had between 16 and 17 billion barrels, Norway had 5–6 billion. The Danes had found only one small field, the Dan, in their sector; the Germans, after a decade of drilling and several million Deutschmarks, were still looking.[5] Most of the oil and gas was concentrated in a few very large fields: Statfjord, discovered in 1974, accounted for 50 per cent of the Norwegian reserves; Brent, Forties, Ninian and Brae for two-fifths of the UK reserves. In 1977, fourteen fields with reserves of 9 billion barrels were under development; a further 5 billion barrels might possibly be extracted. Exploitation of the remaining 5 billion was deemed unlikely. But this would change as means were devised of exploiting smaller, and even very small, fields. So a revolution in the commodity itself was possible.

The North Sea was an expensive oil province. Even in 1983, when prices were at $30 a barrel, production costs in the North Sea came to $1.50 a barrel; in Saudi Arabia production costs were a mere 5 cents.[6] The financial crisis of the mid-1970s, moreover, meant that costs escalated. The original estimate for developing the Forties field had been £300–350 million; by 1975 inflation had driven this up to £650, and by 1976 to £800 million. Between 1976 and 1979 capital for the North Sea was amounting to around 25 per cent of annual British industrial investment.[7] What, in general terms, *happened* to economies faced with such a challenge, and such a concentration of investment? And what would happen in the particular case of Britain?

But to turn to the third factor, the market, was to face a problem. The foregoing factors – technological innovation and capital input – when mixed together in such volumes would usually send production and consumption whizzing off the graph at the upper right-hand corner. But energy, the production of which was the name of the game, had peaked in the early 1970s.

Could you have an industrial revolution in a context of the 'managed' decline of a productive sector? Or where the selling of oil was determined by an international cartel?

The Iron Roughneck

Charlotte Square's smarter brother, Peter Chiene's Q magazine, had a quirky science correspondent who roved across the terrain of energy, environment and what we now know as 'information technology'. He called himself 'Wheech!', a Scots expression equivalent to 'Eureka!', 'My God!', or 'Eppur si muove!'. Offshore, there was a lot to exclaim about. Under pressure of a hellish environment, drastic steps in innovation were required, and accomplished with much cash and marvellous rapidity. Speed, as the Edinburgh legal scholar Kit Carson argued, created its own political economy.[8] But it would not have got as far as it did without two external factors: the growing capacity of microprocessors, which enabled more and more sophisticated computing, and satellite communications. The main application of the first was three-dimensional seismography; this meant that – at a cost of $30 million a ship – comprehensive modelling of the oil-bearing strata below the sea–bed was possible. Something which would have taken months – or required the use of drilling rigs – could be done, by the mid-1980s, in hours, and far more accurately, on a computer.[9] The increasing use of satellites not only improved links between rigs and shore stations, but could be combined with computer-controlled thruster propellors to enable rigs to keep station to within a few square metres of sea. Mediated through defence-contracting firms like Ferranti and Racal, the American space programme (which put men on the moon within a few months of the first commercial oil discoveries) had one of its biggest pay-offs in the North Sea.[10]

In fact, the parallels between offshore engineering and space exploration were continuous, with the former, if anything, more predictable. In both there was the same debate between exploiting hi-tech robotics and using manpower, as could be seen in NASA's unmanned satellite and Discovery programmes. Paradoxically, in the North Sea, the glamour of 'one small step for man' was discounted altogether, although many more men met their deaths at the frontier of technology at sea than in space; not least beneath the waters.

Even in an age of stone blocks and sailing ships, the diver had been essential to North Sea engineering. As a teenager, Robert Louis Stevenson was clad in a weighted suit, crowned with a heavy brass helmet, and lowered into the waters around Wick pier.[11] He did not proceed with his family's ambition that he follow his father as an engineer, but he was fascinated by this plunge into a quivering green world. Little of this technology had changed, 150 years later, when the deeper waters of the North Sea were tackled. Diving remained essential, and an area of maximum risk. Divers were needed to install pipeline junctions, to maintain the complex control networks, and to safeguard the rigs against the ever-present threat of corrosion. In the 1960s the maximum depth reachable in a wet-suit had been fifty feet. One hour below could still mean a day of decompression. By the 1980s this had changed radically:

Divers now spend roughly four weeks in saturation, living in a specially pressurized habitat on Stadive's lower deck, and moving directly from it to the similarly pressurised diving bell that takes them down to the sea-bed. They work for twenty-one days in eight- to twelve-hour shifts, without ever breathing ordinary air, then decompress for three or four days. At the end of that time, they spend four well-earned weeks back on the beach.[12]

Because the helium–oxygen mixture which they breathed removed heat from the body, divers at 450 feet or more now wore 'hot-suits' with water circulating at 50–60 degrees Celsius. Increasingly, the divers were followed and assisted by Robot Operational Vehicles, known as ROVs or 'Snoopies'. These little humanoid, unmanned submarines, powered by electric screws and with computerized control equipment and mechanical arms and hands, took over more and more of their tasks. But specialist diving support ships were also built which accommodated the decompression suites required for long-term submerged activity; they often doubled as support and fire-fighting vessels. As Alvarez found in 1986, the *Stadive*, purpose-built in Finland, had, within its unprepossessing 'floating coffee-table' bulk,

the largest commercial diving spread in the world: two bells, a small submarine, a divers' escape lifeboat, and room for twenty-eight men in saturation – two six-man chambers, two eight-man chambers.[13]

Divers believed that the companies always lagged behind in technology, because it interfered with profits. Innovation was always something that had to be forced on them. The level of diving deaths was always serious, and was not improved by innovations elsewhere. The propellor-thrusts of dynamically positioned craft could entangle divers' control and power lines; the coupling of the pressurized bell to the surface compression chamber was subject to human error. This happened on the *Byford Dolphin* support ship in 1984. Five divers were killed.[14]

The mastery of the depths impelled further innovations in extraction systems, visible in the exploitation of the Highlander field, first discovered in 1976. Here Texaco devised an unmanned underwater 'template' or production centre which pumped oil to the Tartan production platform thirteen kilometres away. This platform in turn communicated with the Claymore production centre, and ultimately with Occidental's Flotta terminal. As the 1980s progressed and the price of oil fell, it seemed that the future of the oilfield would increasingly lie in the exploitation of small fields by underwater satellite units, up to 50 kilometres away from their 'mother' platforms, which could be 50 per cent less expensive than manned production platforms.[15] Robot-controlled multiphase pumps, which separated oil, gas and water, moved from fantasy towards reality. Even where platforms remained *in situ* and without satellites, 'deviated drilling' could now enable fields to be tapped up to 13 kilometres away; in 1977 the maximum deviation had been about 6 kilometres.[16]

Alternatively, there were modifications of the dynamically positioned drill ship. Experimentation by Weir Pumps of Glasgow, subsidized by BP and the Energy Department, produced the 'downhole' pump, operating from the sea-bed. This could operate with the single well oil production system, or SWOPS, installed on Shell-Esso's Cormorant Centre in May 1983, whereby at the modest cost of £120–150 million, a vessel could drop a pipe to an underwater manifold to extract oil.[17] Or the Norwegian *Petrojarl*, which started to exploit the small Angus field in 1986, a tanker-like vessel which relied on dynamic positioning and transferred its load periodically to its 'dedicated' shuttle tanker, the *Petroskald*. The Angus field becoming exhausted in 1992, it moved to a new site on Amerada's Hudson field.[18]

Government was apprehensive about mobile extraction systems. A fixed platform was a commitment to exploit a particular field; a floating system might skim off the oil which was easiest to reach – as little as 12–14 per cent – and then move off elsewhere.[19] Moreover, almost ten times the number of oil spillages arose during oil loading than during pumping to platforms. But by the mid-eighties there was a further, compromise technology: the tension-leg platform. This was a massive concrete pontoon barge which floated, held captive like a concrete balloon by wires under tension from the sea-bed. It had the stability of the metal-jacket and Condeep types, but when the oil was exhausted, it could be towed to another field, and its wires would flop harmlessly to the sea-bed – *over two thousand feet below*.

Beryl B, commissioned in 1983, had a new invention. This replaced the tough guys on the drilling floor who swung drill pipe into the hole with a computer-controlled hoisting and clamping mechanism called an Iron Roughneck. As if to emphasize the change to a hi-tech regime, with the VDU taking over from brawn and skill, the platform was the first in the British sector to have a substantial female crew.[20] At the International Offshore Exhibition in Aberdeen in 1993, a red-faced man with a loud shirt and a louder Texan voice was demonstrating a set of pincers and wrenches which looked as if designed for a monster dentist. 'Ah ripresent low technology!' he bellowed. But he might have been representing drystane dyking or the Clydesdale horse at an agricultural show. The future lay with the iron roughnecks, and behind them the omnipresent computer screens.

Notes from the Province

In 1982, imagine flying north, from Southend to the Shetlands: quite possible, given the expansion in the civilian light-aircraft business – albeit with strong warnings to keep your height, above Europe's densest helicopter routes. If you start off flying at about two degrees to the east of the Greenwich meridian, you will, with only a few deviations, pass all the oil and gas fields in review. Skirting the Norfolk coast just east of Yarmouth, the platforms of the gas fields appear. The Hewett, Leman and Indefatigable fields dispatch their gas to processing plants at Bacton, near Sheringham, and thence to the British Gas grid. The step from successful drilling to production has taken, in most of these cases, only as long as it takes a pipe to be laid: about a year. What is visible at sea, in about 150 feet of water, is relatively simple platforms, manned by only five or six men. Further to the north, the Viking sends its gas by pipe to Theddlethorpe in Lincolnshire, and the Rough and West Sole fields to Easington, near Hull. In 1976 these six fields were already producing 98 per cent of Britain's gas needs. The town gasworks was by then a museum piece: in the case of those of Lauder and Biggar in Scotland, quite literally so.[21]

At 55 degrees 50, the plane crosses the line of demarcation between the English and Scottish courts. Around 56 degrees north, on the latitude of Fife, irrupt the platforms of the smallish Auk, Fulmar and Argyll fields, in production since 1975. These stand in about 250 feet of water and load oil directly on to tankers which take it to the Teesport refinery. To the east is the giant Norwegian Ekofisk field, with eighteen major platforms, various satellites, a 36-inch pipe to Teesside and a gas line to Emden, and a great concrete storage tank. Not without its troubles: scene of the first major blowout in 1977, and later of subsidy problems which threatened its very existence.

More grey-blue sea, flecked with sharp wind-waves. A few rigs about, their tenders trailing towards them like tiny red slugs. There are possible small fields here; to the west, Amoco's Montrose, with its single platform, producing since August 1976, awaits a 'dedicated' 50,000-ton shuttle tanker. Twenty miles to the north are the four huge steel platforms of BP's Forties, since 1975 pumping their oil towards Cruden Bay and ultimately Grangemouth. Beside their reserves of 261 billion barrels, Montrose is a tiddler at 12 billion.

A few more small, tanker-served platforms – Maureen, Buchan – and then the Tartan platform, standing in 465 feet of water, looms up. An outrider, with the Claymore platform, of Occidental's, and Getty's and Thomson's, Piper complex. The big Piper Alpha platform is its Clapham junction, bringing in crude from the two satellites and pumping it through ninety miles of 30-inch pipe to Flotta in Scapa Flow. Its history has been less than happy; design flaws have meant that its jacket has had to be rebuilt; a mishandled positioning – thumping it down on the sea-bed – has set up severe internal stresses; it requires considerable strengthening to stop it falling apart. Its reputation among offshore workers is not high.

Now we are 58 degrees north, and altering our course slightly to the north-east. Mobil's *Beryl A* stands by itself, a concrete Condeep platform installed by a Stavanger firm, served by a shuttle tanker. *Beryl* is just into the British sector, though it looks Norwegian, like the Frigg gas field, only six miles away to the north-east. Frigg has no fewer than seven platforms of all sorts, built all over the place – Scotland, Sweden, Normandy, Norway – oddly recalling exactly where all these trading and slaughtering Northmen got to a millennium earlier.

Night is coming on from the Norwegian coast, and the biggest complex is yet to come: almost 60 per cent of the North Sea output, beginning to show up as a cluster of light. This is very deep water: 480 feet at the Alwyn platform, 465 at the three-platform Ninian field, 470 feet at the Heather platform. All these

are linked together and deliver via the southern 36-inch pipe to
Sullom Voe. From Heather the South Cormorant can be seen
blazing away, the junction for the four Brent platforms, depleting
the biggest field after the Forties, at 230 million tons of reserves.
To the north, further subsidiary fields – Dunlin, Thistle, Murchison – pump into the Brent system. Close by, the Statfjord
field, with its tanker-loading buoys and three massive concrete-
jacketed platforms, their accommodation modules showing up
like a block of Bergen flats. Finally, surrounded by tenders and
safety trawlers and the massive 'hook-up' barge towed north
from Rotterdam, which is lowering its modules on to the deck,
the Magnus platform, newly-built at Nigg. In August, Mrs
Thatcher will pull a switch in London which will turn its pipeline
(to Ninian) on. Two years later she will sell it off. Ten years later,
she will forget about it, and all these other lights glittering against
the wind and the dusk, completely.

As, indeed, would all but a few hundred thousand of the
British public. Here we come to a problem in social psychology.
Despite the similarity of the sums concerned to those which built
the British railway system, the analogy with it breaks down. For
there is no problem in being interesting when writing about
railways; the informed and expert, and the plain besotted, will
follow every word and detect every mistake. Moreover, railway
history leads easily to the history of the industries the lines served.
In the 1950s and early 1960s a man called Eric Tonks traced every
siding and line which had ever served the oolitic ironstone field.
His book, *The Ironstone Railways and Tramways of the East
Midlands* (1964), which logs every line and locomotive, when
opened, when closed, when built or bought or scrapped, also
describes the central technology of exploiting and transporting a
natural resource, and evokes the regional impact the iron industry
made, the communities it created, the industrial archaeology it
left behind. The same could be said of books about the lead mines
of the Lake District, the tin mines on their Cornish cliffs, the slate
quarries of North Wales, and the building of the reservoirs of the
Pennine chain. They start off with machines, but form a way into

a fascinating human history: the mining villages, the navvies' camps, the chapels and shebeens, the overseers and speculators. Even when the last deep pit in the South Wales coalfield has closed, the mining-based community is something more than a part of the 'heritage' industry.

Railway enthusiasts number at least a quarter of a million; there are equivalent but smaller groups fascinated by buses or coastal ships. In the 1980s there grew up the cult of the computer-freak; publications catering for their particular interest dominated newsagents (Ian Jack found in 1982 that Wigan people bought twenty copies of the *New Statesman* each month, and 2,500 copies of computer journals). But despite its huge social and technological impact, oil culture never became more than 'shop'.[22] There were never group excursions to travel on a vintage supply boat of a particular type, or visit a unique Condeep platform; there hasn't even been an industrial archaeology interest in the huge sites left at Kishorn or Portavadie. A project by Aberdeen District Council to create 'Offshore World', a 'living museum' of the oil industry, first advanced when the slump of 1985–6 hit the place, has remained on ice. Although the number of museums in Scotland rose in the 1980s from 170 to 430, a museum of oil is, at least so far, not among them.

Why? Oil companies were notoriously secretive about their operations, and this didn't improve over time. Even in 1994 the majors were still wary of allowing film crews aboard platforms. Secondly, the technology itself was temporary and recyclable, built largely of standard components and the ubiquitous concrete. The local intimacy of the railway age, the blending into the landscape, was not repeated. Finally, one can't avoid the conclusion that because the oil business did not occur in, and did not create, a community, and was largely American in ownership, it seemed almost a colonial imposition: something inherently alien.

Oilfields, to paraphrase Tolstoy, were boring when they were successful; interesting when disastrous. And the North Sea fields were, to a remarkable degree, successful, although not perhaps as successful as some companies had suggested in the mid-1970s.

There were 2 in production in 1975, 15 in 1980, 29 in 1985, and 43 in 1990. A total output of 3.5 million barrels a day had been forecast for 1980. In fact only 2.2 million a day were being recovered in that year. Tony Benn had been thinking in terms of 4 to 5 million barrels in 1985, but in fact the highest production reached, in that year, was 2.7 million.[23] Argyll, Beryl, Dunlin, Montrose, Claymore and Piper peaked between 1980 and 1985; so too did the mighty Forties. By 1990 Brent and Forties were well down, and Piper and Claymore right out, because of the July 1988 disaster.

Although a host of new fields had come on stream, they were all rather small. So too, however, after 1985 were the platforms. In 1992 Shell estimated that the jacket for its Gannet platform would have weighed, using the technology of 1987, 15,000 tons; instead it weighed 5,000, and drilled its wells by using a remote-controlled semi-submersible instead of a conventional derrick, which considerably reduced the need to strengthen the structure. In comparison, Forties Alpha seemed, at 30,000 tons, a giant, and Ninian Central at 600,000 a dinosaur.[24] But even these were being challenged, not just by SWOPS and *Petrojarls*, but by rig-like 'floating production facilities' such as the German-American owned AH-100, which worked the Hamish, Ivanhoe and Rob Roy fields.[25] These were the ultimate and logical development of a mobile, rational and exploitation-oriented industry. For various reasons, such an industry is not likely to leave much in the local memory.

In the Orkney Islands, north of Stromness and twenty miles or so from Occidental's Flotta terminal, archaeologists found in the 1890s the settlement of Skara Brae. It had been deserted by its inhabitants 2,000 years before, but their life could still be reconstructed through their middens and latrines. Then as now the Orkneys were devoid of trees, so stone panels had done the work of wood, and thus the assembly had been preserved through the centuries. Wood rots, metal rusts or can be sold for scrap. Even concrete gradually erodes. And much depends on the memory of the industry: the extent to which it has awakened loyalties, to which people have felt it was theirs, and not a remotely controlled form of exploitation. No one is very sentimental about car or washing-machine factories, but there are countless 'Miner's Arms' or 'Quarryman's Arms'. Despite the bears' taste for alcohol, you will look in vain for the 'Roughneck's Arms'.

On the western coast of Harris stand the remains of an earlier oil industry, a whaling station. Everything has gone save the slip-ways up which the victims were dragged, and the smokestack for the furnace which was used to boil down their blubber. Ling and heather and bog-myrtle have covered the bones and the ash, the bricks and iron bolts. One literal monument remains, a gravestone:

Meine troste Hund

Sam

gest. 20. II. 01

Georg Herloesen

For all its billions, will the oil industry leave much more behind?

Sourcing from Britain

'Basically it's all American technology, just a bit bigger.' The man who said this was the British executive of one oil production company, who had done well out of the industry, but whose tolerance of the field itself was limited. The platforms were grim; Aberdeen an absolute hell-hole: 'the armpit of the universe'. Oil bankrolled Britain, but it always provoked feelings of guilt rather than pride. Britain was getting too few of the orders which were coming from the North Sea: the usual proportion was reckoned in 1974 at only about 35 per cent, or £525 million out of £1,600 million of purchases to date.[26] The drilling rigs were overwhelmingly American, Norwegian or Dutch; the same went for the supply vessels. Most of the production platforms *had* to be built close to their intended sites, at least in the first years, and here the British had a better chance – but only two of the main platform yards were British-owned: Methil in Fife and Graythorpe on Teesside, and both were marginal operations. The pipelines came from Japan, which had the only capability of rolling the high-quality non-corrosive 36-inch pipe required. The picture wasn't all black: Andrew Neil wrote in the *Economist* that

British companies have actually been rather good at . . . much of the more traditional heavy engineering products such as cables, pumps, generators, steel structures, cranes and valves. Industry has adapted easily to these demands because it has required little modification to existing production patterns.[27]

But the quota of orders, particularly for the new types of offshore-specific technology, might have been better. Under two circumstances: had the rate of extraction been slower, and had there been an adequate response by British maritime manufacturers and contractors. Still, there is something of a mystery regarding gas. Here the British government, that of Harold Wilson, was successful in imposing tough 'national interest' conditions on the companies, but seems to have failed totally to make any contingency plans for the likelihood that success in gas would be followed by success in oil. Perhaps this was due to the separation of energy from trade issues, in its own Ministry of Power. Anyhow, it was left to the Conservatives, under Edward Heath and the ex-Shell man John Davies, to make belated plans.

In 1972 Davies' Industry minister, Christopher Chataway, ex-athlete and one of the first generation of television figures who had gone into politics, commissioned the IMEG report. Its rather hurried inquiry into the amount of oil business – out of an anticipated total of £300 million annually between 1973 and 1985 – that could be brought to Britain, produced distinctly sobering results; in 1973 it appeared that the American dominance of areas like pipeline and refinery installation was such that the British would be lucky to take more than 25 per cent of the orders for such installations.[28] As a result of the IMEG recommendation to establish a Petroleum Industry Supplies Board, the Conservative government set up the Offshore Supplies Office in early 1973, mandated to direct as much business in this field as possible to Britain. In 1974 Labour moved this administratively from Trade and Industry to the Department of Energy, and physically from London to Glasgow.[29]

Consul Funkhouser was sceptical about this ploy:

Oil industry equipment has always been as American as Scotch is Scottish, and protectionism would appear to set a poor precedent for nations that live by trading.[30]

Other observers were equally despairing about the consequences of inertia, especially in Scotland. 'The only things that we are supplying oilmen with are whisky and whores,' lamented a Church of Scotland minister from an Aberdeen parish in 1975.[31] There was an element of Manichaean gloom about this, but the actual situation was less than impressive. In 1975 the Scottish Council: Development and Industry predicted that in the six years to 1981 equipment worth £3 billion would be required, 61 per cent of it for operations in the British sector; but even the Council reckoned that in 1974 only 40 per cent of British-sector work had actually gone to UK firms. Although purchases went up by 12 per cent after the Code of Practice introduced by the Department of Energy and the Offshore Supplies Office, there were doubts about how 'British' some of the successful firms were.[32]

For example, in 1984 Tony Mackay calculated the actual input of production factors into firms which were supposed to be British, and compared them with the returns of the Offshore Supplies Office. The result was sobering:

	OSO	Mackay
1973	35	30.5
1975	51.7	44.4
1977	65	52.3
1980	70.8	52.6
1982	72.2	49.4

In other words, 'British' input was being overestimated by anything up to 25 per cent.

To look at one promising sector: supply vessels. Four hundred supply vessels would be needed by 1980; by 1977 only four had been built in Britain. And that was largely because at Seaforth Marine Iain Noble, who had formerly been an official with the Scottish Council and was dynastically connected with Vickers-Armstrong, had a deliberate policy of ordering British. He was not encouraged by the fact that his main supplier, the Drypool Yard at Hull, went bust while completing its first contract for him. British supply-boat construction improved in the later 1970s, partly due to government subsidy, but while this was going on, record tonnages in Sweden, West Germany and Norway marked those countries' diversification into the North Sea market. UK output declined by 216,000 tons between 1970 and 1977, and its yards were beaten by Norway in tonnage.[33]

Britain, and in particular the older industrial areas such as Tyneside, Yorkshire, and Northern Ireland, were more successful with the hardware that went into the production modules of the platforms – gas turbines, generators, compressors, electrical switchgear. After a slow start, pumps and sub-sea control equipment started to prosper, as did 'services' in general – notably the helicopters which provided virtually the only means of getting to the rigs. Again, history helped; the helicopter had been the workhorse of the Vietnam War, and many veterans thereof found a second life working for Alan Bristow or British Airways out of Dyce and Sumburgh.

Helicopters were by no means popular, and there were several disasters. Alexander MacKay, a veteran rig-worker, hated the sensations they induced:

You see the platform appear, grey and massive, flare burning normally, gas compression's OK. Ding-dong, brace for landing, down we go. Swallow hard, we're safely down again. Doing this now for more than fifteen years, but it still bothers me.[34]

Norwegian workers were also unenthusiastic about them.[35] There were attempts to rationalize communications with the rigs and platforms. In 1976 Shell and Esso served the Brent field with a former car ferry from which staff were helicoptered to individual rigs, but this lasted only one summer. Seaforth Marine's project for a floating airport, the STOLport (short take-off and landing), a giant converted tanker on which jets could land and take off, recurred from year to year but finally vanished in 1979.

One problem was gently pointed out by Tony Benn when the American ambassador, Elliot Richardson, visited him in August 1975 to complain about aggression by British government bodies against the interests of the American majors. Benn repeated the complaint made frequently by British entrepreneurs that their attempts to break into the oil-equipment supply business ran up against protectionism, practised notably by the United States.[36] Sir Iain Noble confirmed the penal quality of this inhibition, in his attempt to expand the overseas business of Seaforth Marine.[37] Other entrepreneurs didn't even attempt to enter the business.

In Norway things were different. If anything, the shipbuilders over-reacted: conventional shipbuilding, already in grave difficulties because of the slump in demand for tankers after 1973, almost died as companies set out to exploit the opportunities generated by oil. The Aker Group in fact provided an overcapacity in production for North Sea purposes, but only captured 15 per cent of the Norwegians' own offshore market; seventeen of the twenty-two platforms installed by 1977 had to be imported, although this situation changed in the 1980s as companies such as Kvaerner Offshore captured the initiative with a new generation of 'tension-leg' concrete platforms. Dutch and West German success was wholly disproportionate to these countries' oil possessions, and the French, who had no oil at all, established a commanding position in rig- and platform-building.

Training for work on rigs and in diving and pipelaying was more successful, through the Offshore Petroleum Industry Training Board. But this took time to appear. Research and Development was, to Tony Mackay, 'much more depressing and is undoubtedly one of the weak points of industrial policy as far as the North Sea is concerned'. He contrasted the underfunded British institutions with the situation in Norway:

The visitor to Norway cannot fail to be impressed by the research centres there. Trondheim, for example, has just completed a new deep-water test tank and a two-phase pipeline test station. Bergen has a new underwater training and research centre. No such facilities exist in Scotland and those in England are generally inferior to their European counterparts.[38]

One of the few Scottish successes based on oil was that of the old Aberdeen firm of John D. Wood. In 1970 fishing and ship repairing brought it an annual turnover of £4 million. There were 600 employees. The company's young managing director, Ian Wood, cottoned on to the possibilities of oil-rig supply; by 1975 turnover was up to £16 million and he was employing 1,350. In 1982 turnover stood at £80 million, generated by 2,600 employees. While its stake in traditional industry (still a good earner) had fallen to only 25 per cent of its business, it had moved into onshore and offshore logistics, and petrochemical engineering. Ian Wood put its success down to three factors, none of them simple to achieve. The first was to buy expertise from the industry, which was by definition expensive, given the interest of the majors in retaining their expertise and monopoly position. The second possibility was joint ventures: but these had only a 50–50 chance of success because of the imbalance of size between multinational and smaller Scottish concerns. The final and most successful was the acquisition of small specialist companies: the problem here, however, was that this might simply create a medium-sized Scottish concern, ripe for international acquisition itself.

Sir Iain Noble had to appoint a chief executive in 1972 for Seaforth Marine. Out of eighty applicants, he whittled the contenders down to five, and then three. Two of them were professional marine managers, but the other, one of the least likely, had stayed the course. Least likely because he had no maritime experience, and was running a milk delivery company. Yet he had researched the business of Seaforth Marine, had realized the originality of its concerns, and had turned his own logistic abilities to bear on its problems and requirements. His name was James Hann; he got the job, and performed with great success. Noble cited this as an instance of the new type of management that the offshore business required; an ability to discard preconceived stereotypes. But he also saw the role of the state as something which inhibited logical organization. Resources were being concentrated in the Energy Department in London; the local information and contacts which the Scottish Office and Scottish regional authorities could contribute were being neglected.[39]

Outer Space, with Bad Weather

In the middle of winter when conditions are exceptionally rough, it must be absolute hell to work there. It is a complete science fiction world and it is a sobering thought that our future as a nation depends upon the Forties Field and others like it in the North Sea, and how vulnerable they are to foreign attack.[40]

Thus minister Benn, on first encountering the Graythorpe platform on the Forties field, in July 1975. A production platform – and there were twenty-four of them in the British sector by 1980 – was a huge space-station of a place. It was distinguished by standing on many thin legs, if its 'jacket' was metal, or on between one and four very thick legs, if concrete. These platforms supported a derrick for drilling the production wells, up to thirty 'risers' which brought the oil from the sea-bed, the pumps which dispatched it to the mainland (or to storage tanks in and around the legs, in the case of most of the concrete platforms), the complex control apparatus to separate water and gas from oil, and to ensure uniform pressure in the pipelines. All this depended on a power-station, one or more cranes to hoist supplies from the supply vessels, a helideck for the delivery of the labour force, and accommodation for the workers who had constantly to man the equipment and maintain the platform and its pipes against the assault of wind and sea.

Giant gas turbines, literally jet engines attached to electric generators, produced the power required for a middle-sized town. Not only were they incredibly noisy, 'like having Concorde where your garage is', but their design usually assumed a prevailing wind, to carry the heat and fumes away. Should the wind veer, all this would be thrown back at the platform. Of energy-saving technologies – windmills or wave-powered generators – there was no sign, for the obvious reason that the gas which drove the turbines would otherwise be flared. Modules, unlovely assemblies of tubes and girders – 'at best, functional' was what Mobil called Beryl Bravo in 1983 – had cabins on the standard pattern of shipping containers slotted into them, innocent of the hand of the design engineer, or of the ideas of the Modern Movement. Gangways and stairwells, as the Cullen Report found, had awkward corners and steps, ill-adapted to rapid or convenient movement.

Locomotives and their train-sheds, cars and factories had expressed some sort of Bauhaus-like flair in their construction; or had even inspired other branches of architecture. Something like this did, to some extent, happen in the North Sea: could Richard Rogers's exhilarating Centre Pompidou have happened, had it not been for these precedents? But most of the North Sea platforms were monstrous and, as it turned out, also dangerous.

Rogers's latest success, Lloyd's of London, would have to pick up the tab of $1.4 billion for Piper Alpha.

Production platforms usually had two crews, averaging 200

workers each. In Norway this was a legal maximum; additional workers had to live on 'flotels'. This labour force accounted for about half the total of 25,000 workers 'offshore', drilling, pipe-laying, and maintaining the ever-threatened fabric. The standard terms were a fortnight on, a fortnight off, on the rigs and production platforms; six weeks on, six weeks off, on the supply vessels. The workers lived spartanly in the cabins of the rigs; rather more luxuriously in the 'hotel' modules of the production platforms. The notion of the oilman as a sort of Davy Crockett of industry, a primitive taken on board in an early state of technological evolution, was partly correct. The crews of the drilling-rigs tended to be 'recruited from all over Britain, and beyond – from the reserve army of the unemployed', bossed by Americans as 'tool-pushers' who seemed always to have the top jobs 'by right of nationality'.[41] In drilling and exploration activity, brawn and resilience counted: for the roustabouts who acted as the rigs' general labourers, carrying supplies from the cranes which unloaded the supply boats; hoping to become the higher-paid 'roughnecks'.

Rigs were the most speculative undertakings loose on the waters. They were up for hire, and their price depended on demand. If a lot was going on, and there were only a few rigs around, then the going rate could rise to $70,000 a day; if there was a glut on the market, it could fall to $10,000. In these circumstances rig-owners combine to press down wages and conditions in a part of the industry almost wholly non-unionized. For those of the crew on firm contracts, rewards could be reasonable – over £7,000 a year – but most of the crew were non-contract on less than half of this:

The non-contract men were a mixed bunch in background and nationality. Many came from the Commonwealth travelling crowd – Kiwis, Aussies, South Africans, Rhodesians, Canadians. Some, like myself, were English. The Scots were in a minority. One trait the majority shared was rootless-ness. All of us were single, with few personal commitments.

I can't recall anyone who felt that we were adequately paid or reasonably treated. None the less, most were indifferent or hostile to the idea of joining a trade union. Simply, they were not joiners. The drilling industry is a home for what remains of the world's hobo migrant workers' society.[42]

Many rigs recruited cabin staff from low-wage countries, and with no attempt to level up rates, they seemed almost a microcosm of transnational exploitation:

Figures for a particular barge show that rates of pay for Lebanese and Indian cooks and stewards, Spanish welders, British engineers, and US contract men were in the ratios 3:10:30:45 ... Lebanese and Indians worked one year on, one month off; Spaniards worked six months on and fifteen days off; British and Americans three months on, one month off.[43]

There was little attempt, outside of the few rigs owned by the British majors, to promote British staff into skilled positions; but here at least there were contracts. In Norway, in which there had been agreements with the trade unions from the beginning, there was union representation. Elsewhere,

By controlling a closed and tightly policed environment management has largely succeeded in selecting, excluding, confusing, indoctrinating, insulting, infuriating and – significantly – rotating workers in such a way as to prevent their combination and maintain their fragmented, isolated condition.[44]

This was not fanciful, as many construction firms used the services of the far-right Economic League to vet their workforce, a practice defended by Shell's Personnel Director, Peter Linklater, in 1978:

They give us pretty good value. We are interested in identifying overt opponents of the system to which we are committed. The last thing we want to do is to have political subversives on our payroll or on sites in which we have an interest.[45]

On the production platforms, the requirements were more the sort of routine of patience combined with disciplined responsiveness that was closer to everyday life in the services than to manufacturing industry. Not surprisingly, many offshore oilmen were ex-service, accustomed to the kicks and ha'pence that life (in the navy in particular) customarily provided: endless strings of orders, good food, and cheap fags. Alcohol was banned completely – though some spectacular binges were recorded around Christmas, when the limited rations then allowed could be traded. There was little news or entertainment in the early days: Robert Orrell's crew made do with ancient Westerns on 16mm film in the 1960s, but video came in within a decade; then satellite transmission made reception feasible and unlimited phone calls 'to the beach' were possible.[46]

Much was made of the 'frontier' quality of rig or platform life, but Carson showed that offshore accidents resembled the sort of thing that happened in shore factories. There were just more of them. The same thing went for the ailments and worries of platform crews. The study undertaken by Bergen University with the co-operation of Statoil and Mobil about life and health on Statfjord Alpha, under Odd Hellesoy, showed disturbed sleep, boredom, limited communications with shore, physical work environment problems (chemical hazards, noise, weather, heavy lifting), worries about social problems, career opportunities, organizational disputes (particularly with onshore control), and industrial relations. Forty-three per cent of the crew logged their health as excellent, 45 per cent as good, 11 per cent as fair, and only 2 per cent as poor – although, inevitably, there was a propensity for epidemics to sweep through the platforms.[47] The chief mental problems were worry about home: 22.4 per cent; irritation, 10.7 per cent; and depression, 10.9 per cent. Only 1.9 per cent reported claustrophobia; but then no claustrophobic would have gone out of his or her way to work on an oil platform.[48]

The left-wing journalist Mervyn Jones found that in 1976 – after two years of Labour government – unionization had made little progress. This was not just because of an anti-union prejudice, emanating from the southern states of the USA, which was pervasive, but because it was difficult to organize a labour force which at the end of its tour of duty dispersed all over the country:

Only one company, on a single occasion, has allowed a trade union representative to visit a rig. Generally, the companies say they will be delighted to agree to recognition when the unions have recruited 50 per cent of the workers.[49]

That put the matter quite succinctly.

Given the omnipresent risks, particularly on the drilling rigs, there was an alarming absence of safety provisions and arrangements for emergency hospitalization. Although many rigs carried a larger crew than a merchant ship, which by law had to have a medical officer, the only possibility of treatment after a serious injury offshore was a flight to a hospital 'on the beach', which could often involve four to six hours, even in good weather.[50] There couldn't be many nurses, as women didn't arrive offshore on the British continental shelf until Beryl Bravo was staffed in 1984. Mobil, which had hitherto operated in the Norwegian Statfjord, where women were encouraged and where there were hundreds in the labour force, carried on with its standard practice and broke with a ban which the British had, in typical fashion, grounded on the threat of sexual disruption. Two geologists challenged BNOC in 1978 and got a selection of curious responses from the state oil company: men might go around in the nude, crane-drivers might lose their concentration, wives of crew might get upset, contractors might object. The women persisted, claiming that their professional development was being inhibited by the ban; and Elaine Field, an analyst with BNOC, managed to get a ruling from the deputy Energy minister, Dr Dickson Mabon:

The Sex Discrimination Act of 1975 does not apply at present to offshore employment, and will not apply until an Order in Council is made under Section 10 (5).[51]

Given the universal nude pin-ups – Alvarez found that the Offshore Installation Manager's office was usually the only one lacking its quota of centrefolds – this seemed special pleading on behalf of a threatened machismo. By 1979 the Norwegians had literally hundreds of women on their platforms, and were philosophical about it:

The addition of women to the offshore work-force led to a 'polish' of language, dress and behaviour, and to an even more orderly social interaction.[52]

Women were mainly in catering and on the 'flotel' staff, but by 1994 the OIM on one of the main Statfjord platforms was a woman. Norway had, of course, a female premier, but Britain had had one since 1979 . . .

Such enforced celibacy was, perhaps, a partial explanation of the huge circulation in Britain of 'adult' magazines no one ever admitted to reading. It certainly did oil-workers' marriages little good. A 1991 report found that while wages were only 20–30 per cent higher than onshore, there was a 25–40 per cent increase in the threat of a marital break-up. Wives complained that the 'fortnight off' was like their husbands continually coming off night-shift;[53] what psychiatrists, after surveying 268 wives, called 'intermittent husband syndrome': 'in loss through death the process of adjustment is not continually interrupted by the loved one's return'.[54] Wives complained of sexual demands ('He seemed to want it all the time; you know, every night. Two weeks non-stop. I don't like refusing him, because then he gets moody and bad-tempered') and of the results of 'endless hours watching pornography'. Around 20,000 marriages were under strain, and rather more than a third collapsed.

Alvarez regarded the society of the platforms as gentle, sensual, and visceral, with its enforced socialization (no one was allowed a cabin to themselves, in case they suddenly broke down and ran amok). The result was that

In an environment as hostile as that of the North Sea the virtues that matter most are friendliness, good humour, and the kind of resignation that is learned in the armed services: a willingness to obey orders, however pointless they seem, and to accept the hierarchy. Imagination for anything except the job in hand is as great a handicap as excessive aggressiveness or a thin skin. During the time you are offshore, you are defined solely in terms of your work, and if the work does not satisfy you there are no other compensations.[55]

Most men had little time to socialize while on the rigs − a 'clique' of mates or chinas which held together round its own mess-table or functions − while once off them they dispersed rapidly over the face of the country. This was a major difference with Norway, where not only was recruitment to the rigs organized *through* the trade unions of the 'Labour Organisation', but most of the offshore work-force − 16,000 out of 25,000 − was concentrated at Stavanger. The Statfjord Alpha platform study put great stress on the resulting social solidarity:

Social support is clearly an area with both positive and negative possibilities. Poor social support makes the individual and organizations vulnerable to a number of disagreeable and harmful effects of environmental demands and limitations. Good social support protects against health and safety risk factors, improves learning and coping and clearly contributes to improving the quality of work life in the offshore environment.[56]

Not only does this sense of solidarity seem less evident in Britain; no study along Hellesoy's lines was ever allowed or, it seems, contemplated.

Onshore

The platforms had to be built, and from 1971 on there was a scramble for sites for platform construction along the northern Scottish coastline. Helicopters and hired cars disgorged surveyors and engineers; planning applications thudded on to the desks of county officials used to vetting schemes for loft conversions and garages; the phone lines buzzed with messages from landowners to lawyers and vice-versa. The sites had to be close to the area of operation because of the size of the structures and the difficulty of assembling them in bad weather. In the next couple of years twenty-four bays and sea-lochs were earmarked for development, and seven proceeded to yard construction: Kishorn on the West Highland coast, Nigg and Ardersier in the Moray Firth, Hunterston, Ardyne and Portavadie on the Clyde estuary, and Methil in Fife. Of these, Howard Doris at Kishorn and MacAlpine at Ardyne built in concrete; Highland Fabricators (Brown and Root) at Nigg, and McDermott at Ardersier, fabricated metal jackets.[57]

Ardersier built the jackets for the Brae, Heather, North-West Hutton, Murchison, Piper, Clyde, and part of the Hutton platform; Methil built the Auk, Beatrice, Brent A, Fulmar, Tartan and Beryl A; Nigg built Forties C and D, Magnus, Ninian North and South, and Hutton; Kishorn's contribution was limited to the central Ninian platform and part of the Maureen platform; Ardyne built the South Cormorant platform, which was also the main pumping platform for the Brent field, and the Frigg gas field platform. Hunterston was limited to a part of the Maureen platform; Portavadie, which cost £15 million, built nothing at all. The dock was completed late in 1975, along with a workers' village of a couple of hundred houses, on the shore of Loch Fyne opposite Ardrishaig. It lay empty for six years, and then rumours started that it had been bought as a holiday camp. This was a red herring. Eventually the government sold the by now ruinous development for £7,500.

Daniel K. Ludwig and his operations apart, the Cromarty Firth was more active. By 1974 Highland Fabricators were employing over 2,000 workers on the Forties platforms at Nigg. George Rosie of the *Sunday Times* did a breakdown of their origins: 10 per cent came from farming and fishing, 7 per cent from electrics, 15 per cent from engineering, 2 per cent from woodworking, 4.5 per cent from transport, 11 per cent from local construction. Wages were £40 to £60 per week after tax, compared with a national average of £35. For the locals, this was a notable improvement on the going rates. Incomers were less satisfied; the works were remote, unionization was limited and discouraged, accommodation was primitive, and working conditions were poor. The unions claimed that coercion and violence were shown to their organizers; the management claimed that deadlines were frustrated by poor workmanship and frequent strikes.[58] Industrial relations could certainly have been better, but the early 1970s were boom years in which industrial disputes could be expected; the alternative, to recruit and train up local men, ran into the problem of lack of expertise. Much of the welding on the Forties platforms carried out at Nigg had to be re-done.

By contrast, the construction of pipelines was swiftly and effectively carried out. There were three main routes: from Cruden Bay to Grangemouth for oil, from St Fergus to the gas grid, and from Crimond to Moss Morran for natural gas. The companies rapidly came to agreements with local farmers and the routes were built with a minimum of trouble, even though five parallel pipes were eventually laid from St Fergus. But the 'green field' refinery expansion that was hoped for never occurred, save at the natural gas processing plant at Moss Morran in Fife, which came on stream in 1984. Refinery overcapacity already existed, and in fact increased in the 1970s as fuel was more efficiently consumed. Sir William Lithgow's 'Oceanspan' scheme for the Clyde remained as forlorn a hope as the various schemes proposed for the Cromarty Firth.

The semi-farcical outcome of the scramble for platform-building sites wrong-footed the Scottish Office, and may have accounted for its subsequent relative sidelining. Certainly, it ended up a spear-carrier to the Energy Department under Tony Benn, with its flagship project, the Scottish Development Agency of 1975, specifically barred from oil-related activity. There were strange mistakes in overall infrastructure planning. Scotland remained isolated from the British motorway system — access being only via the restricted and dangerous A74 — but a dual-carriageway road was built to connect Perth and Inverness, although it would have been quicker to have developed the existing railway. (In fact, British Rail was paid a government subsidy to remove the double track on the line in the 1960s, and another subsidy in the 1970s to reinstate it.) Aberdeen's airport, at Dyce, was the only one in Scotland to have a rail connection, despite the building of new airports at Edinburgh and Glasgow close to, but not communicating with, main railway lines. There was no attempt to install roll-on-roll-off ferry routes to Europe and Scandinavia to avoid the congestion on the English motorways.

Aberdeen remained ill-served by road, and its railway to the south was not electrified; many local lines had been closed down under the Beeching regime, but there were hopes that the branches to the large towns of Fraserburgh and Peterhead, with about 40,000 people between them, could be reinstated. Peterhead's line was never reopened, and Fraserburgh's, after a brief period carrying pipelines, was ripped up. Although the railways showed themselves flexible in meeting new demands (a pipeline siding at Invergordon took only three weeks to install in 1972), the oil business, with its demands anticipating 'just-in-time' industrial organization, turned out a victory for road transport. By 1994 there was only a handful of freight trains running north of the Scottish central belt. The suspicion remained that the government was more concerned to keep Scottish local authorities and planners away from the oil than it was to create an effective infrastructure.

The Loch Kishorn Monster

The press were for once in demand. They were summoned north to Toscaig pier on 1 May 1978. Here they would see something to their advantage: 'the biggest movable object on earth', all 601,200 tons of it. The central platform for the Ninian field was about to start its slow journey north, hauled by seven tugs and 80,000 horsepower, to its resting-place in Block 3/8.

Oil had been located in this block, by drilling rigs on contract to Chevron Petroleum, four and a half years earlier, in January 1974. Eleven fields had already been detected and about £1.25 billion spent, but Ninian was a biggish one, estimated at 155 million tons. Following the manoeuvres which had produced rather more platform-building yards than there were projects, and which had delayed development by a year, government was anxious to get the concrete construction side under way. The Ninian platform was a sophisticated project; it was supposed to drill for oil, to extract it, to re-inject sea-water when the pressure began to fall, to gather gas, and to pump the oil into the pipeline to Sullom Voe. And it had to be ready for the weather window in May 1977.

At Drumbuie on Loch Carron there had been protestors. At Loch Kishorn there was nothing, save a shooting lodge and a few crofts and cottages, where the great granitic massif of Applecross toppled into an inlet of the Minch. Above the site, one road climbed over a desolate pass to Shieldaig on Loch Torridon, while another zig-zagged over the 2,400 feet of the Bealach na Ba, the Pass of the Cattle, to Applecross village and Loch Toscaig.

The Howard men arrived at the end of 1974; the Doris men remained in Paris and designed the thing. The Howard men started literally by stumbling through the heather and the fore-shore rocks, staking out the ground for a dry dock which would itself cost £20 million. This was finished in seven months. At the same time another work-force turned the sleepy village of Strome Ferry, which had lost its *raison d'être* when a new road made the ferry redundant in 1975, into the railhead. Over half a million tons of cement were going to arrive there by train, and be shipped on by barge the six miles to Kishorn.[59] There were supposed to be 400 workers, and a camp was built for them, but within six months re-specified designs, and the need to enlarge the dock, had boosted this number to 850: the extra men were put up on an old Greek ferry, the *Odysseus*. There was union recognition and organization, and wages were better than on the rigs, at £150 for a seventy-five-hour week, against £120 for eight-four hours. Apart from saving up, there was little to spend the wages on; most of the men saved. But labour relations became steadily more problematic – largely because of the distance many workers had to travel, and because of the continually changing work patterns. An attempt by the management in the summer of 1976 to alter the bonus system led to a strike, and the effective breaking of the union. The 1977 weather window was missed.[60]

At the beginning of that year Ninian Central was beginning to resemble a gargantuan drawing-pin, 140 metres broad at its base, and with a shaft of 236 metres. The first seventy metres from the bottom saw the shaft encircled by further tanks – not, as in some other designs, for storing oil, but as containers for water-ballast. However, only the first 18 metres of this – which still managed to weigh 150,000 tons (twice the weight of the QE 2) – were actually completed in the dry dock. It was then towed out into open water at the southern end of the Sound of Raasay and, as each additional metre of concrete shaft was poured into the wooden shuttering, the assembly sank lower in the water. In September 1977 the concrete work was finished, and the huge structure obediently sank almost completely beneath the waves to allow the Heerema crane barge from Rotterdam to add the 6,300 tons of upper works and modules. The deck on which these were positioned was larger than a football field, eighty by fifty metres, and was supported by a grid of great steel tubes, two-and-a-half metres in diameter. The tower would be held in place by five miles of anchors and chains, as well as its own weight.

The American Offshore Installation Manager, Jimmy Carter from Louisiana, arrived. He was used to pumping 560 tons a day in the Gulf of Mexico; now he would be handling 57,000 a day on Ninian, with a crew of 120 and three gas turbines generating enough power to supply Aberdeen. This would be used to pump oil from forty-two drillings. The tug commander, John Gray, had to get the tower, now drawing 252 feet, northwards through the Minch, at one point only just clearing sandbanks at 270 feet,

and take it a total of 875 miles, north of the Shetlands and then
north-east, to avoid the Brent pipeline, before looping southwards
again, to its final position.[61]

Perhaps because of the Drumbuie controversy, perhaps because
of its size and the remote place of its construction, the Ninian
platform caught the general imagination. Unlike most of the
other platforms, it was also rather handsome, with some evidence
of conscious industrial design. In five years its production rose to
a 300,000 barrels a day maximum; in 1993 that had fallen to
65,000. But worse happened to Kishorn. It was not the government's fault that an outbreak of disasters involving concrete
structures, and a large fall in the price of steel, meant that the
Ninian platform was the only one that Kishorn ever produced.
After a couple of small contracts, the yard was mothballed in
1978; concrete platforms came back into vogue, but the Norwegians had now cornered this market in their Stavanger yards. By
1988 it was derelict, as eccentric an industrial monument as the
crumbling concrete walls of the ironworks on Raasay, six miles
off Drumbuie, built in the First World War.

Oil Capitals

> If you find that anything is missing in your room, please ring for the
> proprietor, who will show you how to do without it.
>
> (Notice in a hotel in Aberdeen)

Aberdonians hated the Aberdonian joke, yet it was often repeated
by the journalists drawn north by the oil. At the least it reflected
the acumen of a regional capital with a trading tradition going
back to the Vikings; the hard bargaining which, from commerce
with the fjords and the Baltic, had built the granite terraces
which marched out into the rich farmland of Gordon. This civic
virtu stood the place in good stead when the oilmen moved in.

Aberdeen was not necessarily the best site for an oil base: the harbour was narrow and controlled by locks; there was little space for warehouses and lorry parks on the quays. Dundee's broad sweep of quay, built for the jute ships, was better fitted to the needs of the supply boats. But Dundee, with its huge textile factories, absentee owners and ill-paid workers, was a town class-divided: 'a city of helots', Gavin McCrone called it, with a Labour Party rather too often in the courts.[62] Legends persisted of Texans greeted by Labour councillors who promised or threatened to 'see them right' for enough folding money; enough to prod them further northward.[63]

Radical politics in Aberdeen were erudite and cosmopolitan. Thomas Reid, the great philosopher of the Scottish enlightenment, had taught at one of the town's two universities, Marischal College; in the nineteenth century James Bryce of *The American Commonwealth* had been MP for the city, and his friend the scholar Robertson Smith had written there the first great Western study of Arab custom and society. Britain and the Empire might have been ruled, for a week or so every summer, from Balmoral, but Aberdeen had also been an early centre of the socialist movement. Henry Champion had helped set up the local Labour Party; more surprisingly, that strange poseur who was Father Rolfe and, fictionally, the super-diplomat Pope Hadrian VII, had passed through, leaving behind a trade-union banner and a mass of debts. Aberdeen socialism thereafter offered few surprises, but was honest. The Labour Lord Provost, bearing the confusing name of John Smith, joined the Callaghan government as oil minister in Scotland, going to the Lords as Baron Kirkhill.[64]

Grey Granite was the title of Lewis Grassic Gibbon's novel about the city and its folk in the 1930s, when the life of the land and the fisheries gave way to 'the greater herd and the great machines', and Gibbon's young hero ended up leading the hunger-marchers. By 1976 it was prosperous. Unemployment was low, and a local capitalism survived – more than in the rest of Scotland – with, so Iain Noble observed, a notable suspicion of lawyers and merchant bankers.[65] Then, by 1976, its 185,000 people became hosts to 5,000 Americans. The impression that the latter made was discreet; they had their own stores, their ranch-style villas in the farther suburbs, their Petroleum Club. They were not unwelcome, but in themselves they changed the place little. The same could not be said for the impact of the oil industry.

Symbolically almost, Aberdeen Council sent bulldozers into the fishing village of Torry, which had thought itself safe under a preservation order. Wages were pushed up. A powerful and unusually compact local oligarchy retreated in good order, doing rather well in the process but surrendering its leading position. New firms came in, not just from the United States but from elsewhere in Scotland, notably Strathclyde. Local firms could not match what the incomers offered, and either went to the wall or were taken over: 'Control had passed to three main areas, Glasgow, London and the States, particularly California.'[66] By 1980 Aberdeen-owned capitalism consisted of a few paper mills, the Wood Group, and not much else.

Things were even more drastic in Peterhead, whose name was an internal Scottish joke, on account of the great, bleak jail – the Scottish Dartmoor – which stretched along its cliffs. Convict-quarried stone had built the breakwater which, after 1884, had made it a harbour of refuge for the herring fleet on its southward course to Yarmouth and Lowestoft. By 1974 the supply vessels were packing its harbour, while the rigs sheltered behind the breakwater from the nor'easters. In the pink granite houses, a lot of money was being made; not least by Mr Ferrari.

Ron Ferrari, one of Scotland's small but gifted Italian community (Tom Conti, Eduardo Paolozzi, Ricky Demarco, etc.), took account of what he heard in his fish-and-chip shop: what the oilmen wanted, and what they were prepared to pay, then shrewdly moved to corner the hotel market in Buchan.[67] Yet the town experienced no re-industrialization; beyond property, ware-housing and the less sophisticated levels of the service industries, there was no autonomous economic growth. An inquiry under Professor Robert Moore of Aberdeen University found that the locals considered themselves 'more a commodity than a community'. This was in no sense as brutal as the multinationals' assaults on third-world societies:

... we found no job destruction, little absolute immiseration, hardly any unemployment and the conditions we described as potential features of underdevelopment were nowhere near as devastating as those found in a third-world country.

But it was a variant of what the Dutch sociologist Johann Galtung had called the 'international division of labour', which was ominously indicative of future inequalities. In these, outside the technological metropolises, only low-level economic activities would prosper: encouraged not by the sophistication of the host society, but by the opposite. It was the weakness, not the strength, of UK environmental legislation which encouraged such rapidity of development.[68]

The oil impact was in no way confined to north-east Scotland. Indeed, the salience of that area may have been due as much to the aggressiveness of its politics as to actual economic developments. The demands of the oil business were almost as significant elsewhere, particularly in the north-east of England. Indeed, oil seemed uncannily well adapted to the development strategies of these local authorities, such as the new county of Cleveland, which were already well served by steel and chemical works. Already in 1969 the government's regional ports survey had suggested a major expansion. This led to the Maritime Industrial Development Scheme to drain and build on the Seal Sands off Middlesbrough. This was promptly followed by a working group of the county authority. Seal Sands attracted the building sites for the Graythorpe platforms of BP's Forties field, and for the onshore terminal of Phillips Petroleum's pipeline from the Norwegians' Ekofisk field. And that was that. Refinery rationalization removed more jobs than the oil created. Victorian Middlesbrough was bulldozed and concreted over to accommodate service industries, but these failed to turn up:

By the end of 1983 almost 200,000 square feet of office space was standing empty in central Middlesbrough, while only about 15,000 square feet of additional office space [was] taken up *annually* in the *whole* of Cleveland County.[69]

Local politics were much slower to adjust to the oil challenge. In 1974 the local government system was in upheaval, with an almost complete change of guard. In Scotland this was drastic, with the old county, burgh, and landward councils being replaced by regional councils with responsibility for strategic planning, and district councils for housing, libraries and local services. In general, this provided a much more adaptive framework for managing big infrastructural investments, training schemes and housing projects – and for liaison with European bodies – but it took roughly a decade for the new regimes to work themselves in, and the new regional establishment proved deeply hostile to devolution. Few local MPs knew much about oil. Aberdeen's two members were Robert Hughes, a left-wing Labour man, an exiled South African, who supported union campaigns but did not have a detailed knowledge of oil matters, and was opposed to devolution, and Iain Sproat, a noisy and inept right-winger. The co-option of Lord Kirkhill into the government was an elegant method of 'incorporating' an Aberdeen point of view into an industry-dominated scene. The SNP's Douglas Henderson, in the Buchan seat, was emotional and inexpert. Just what the combination of an able MP and an expert council could do was vividly demonstrated in Shetland.

'It's Shetland's oil!'

'Miles and miles of bugger all': the Shetland archipelago was less than seductive; a chain of bleak, treeless islands 200 miles north of the Scottish mainland. In contrast to the whale-backed Orkneys, circled round the anchorage of Scapa Flow, the Shetland mainland formed a narrow spine, about fifty miles long, from the island airport at Sumburgh in the south to Isbister at the northern tip. Together, the two groups of islands resembled Norway more than anything in Scotland: the Orkneys the rich farmlands around the Oslofjord, the Shetlands the bleak and infertile Norden. Unlike Orkney, the Shetland involvement in the two World Wars had been limited: no great anchorages, but the headquarters of 'the Shetland bus', the Norwegian guerrilla attacks on the German occupiers. The Orkney population was stable; in Shetland it had been steadily falling, from 30,000 in 1901 to 17,000 in 1971. Economic activities, such as they were, involved cattle-rearing on the rough grazing which was more than nine-tenths of the surface area, fishing, fish-processing, and knitwear – and remittances from the numerous Shetlanders in the merchant navy. Which may account for the fact that family and local relationships, customs and traditions endured to an extent that every one of its islands seemed to have its own social anthropologist.[70] Even so, in 1968 12 per cent of the work-force was on the dole.[71]

By 1973 unemployment had fallen to 5 per cent. With the northward progression of exploration, visits by supply vessels were rising; from seventy-nine visits in 1971 they reached 1,879 in 1978. Four or five service vessels were handled at nineteen quays, most of them to the north of the grey county town of Lerwick, along the western side of Bressay Sound. The onshore labour force rose from twenty-one to 316. The handsome old passenger ship which connected the islands to Leith and Aberdeen was sold, to be replaced by a bigger roll-on-roll-off ferry run by P & O, the company which had been founded by the local MP, Alexander Anderson, in the 1830s. Aircraft movements to the awkwardly sited airport, nearly thirty twisting miles south, started to climb; from 3,895 in 1971 they reached 50,666 in 1978, half of which were helicopters, shuttling to and from the rigs.[72]

By then the sight of the rigs and supply boats ploughing up Bressay Sound, past Shetlanders sailing their traditional clinker-built yachts – almost unchanged since Viking days – in their regattas, must have seemed like the confrontation of dhow and supertanker in the Gulf, transposed into the severities of the North Atlantic: only a few hours of daylight during the winter months, yet no night at all during the 'simmer dim' in June and July. But there was hardly any port project in the Gulf equal to the Shetland pipeline terminal at Sullom Voe, designed to handle 1.2 million barrels of crude every day, an oil port on the scale of Rotterdam.

Shetland's importance became patent after March 1972, particularly when Shell-Esso offered £21 million for block 211/21 in the auction element of the fourth licensing round on the British shelf in 1971. The Brent oilfield was announced in August 1972, and in 1973 the Dunlin and Thistle fields followed. Charlotte Square showed an interest; Iain Noble came north to talk about folk-fiddling with Tom Anderson, the genius of the islands: a cover for getting his hands on a strategic farm in the interests of a private company, Nordport.[73]

In the next few years the Brent system took shape, consisting of the Brent, the three Cormorant fields, the Dunlin, Hutton, North-West Hutton and Thistle fields. All but Brent were medium-range; Brent itself was very large. These would pump oil to the South Cormorant platform, whence it would proceed to Sullom Voe. Here, after 1981, the gas separation would begin. Brent was soon joined by a southern complex, the Heather, Magnus and Ninian fields, discovered in 1973 and 1974 and also linked to Sullom Voe by 36-inch pipeline. The cost of that alone came to £200 million. The gas of the Brent field was, however, pumped south to St Fergus, near Peterhead. St Fergus opened on 6 October 1982, piping gas to a processing plant at Moss Morran, near Cowdenbeath in Fife.[74]

In no part of the North Sea was activity so intense. But where, by then, was Nordport?

Nowhere. For by this time the initiative in oil matters had, uniquely in Britain, passed out of the hands of the majors and almost out of those of government. It lay with the Shetland Islands Council, whose predecessor, the Zetland County Council, had in April 1971 presciently decided to acquire land and go into the port business. Why did Shetland seize for itself an initiative of almost Norwegian proportions?

As the sagas would begin, there was a man in Shetland, and his name was Ian Clark, and he was clerk to the Zetland County Council. Clark was no Shetlander but came (like the present writer) from the far-away and unlovely town of Motherwell, where he managed to combine an incredible gift for political negotiation with an interest in theology of a robust but fundamentalist sort. Even today his opponents, as respectful as his many enthusiasts, see a shadowy Almighty perched at his shoulder. As clerk, and aware of the fact that the Council had, under the Scottish local government act, but a short time to live, Clark anticipated the demand for sites and appointed the consultants Transport Research Ltd to prepare a report on it, tabled in July 1972. This argued for the concentration of oil activity, and settled on a former naval depot on Sullom Voe as the centre of operations. Sullom Voe was a long, meandering sea-loch which almost bisected the mainland, about twenty-five miles north of Lerwick. Its advantage was the proximity of a low coast to very deep water; its disadvantage the tides and skerries of the Sound of Yell.

Nordport was seen off. In November 1972 the islands' MP, Jo Grimond, promoted an Order in Parliament, but so extensive were the powers envisaged that a private bill was substituted. Despite being 'municipal socialism' of an ambitious sort, the County Council gained the approval of Heath's Oil minister, Lord Polwarth, and the bill survived the February 1974 general election to become law in April, just before the Zetland County Council gave way to the Shetland Islands Council.

Construction of the Sullom Voe terminal began in 1974. Two work camps were built, and supplemented, at the height of construction in 1978–80, by two old ferries, the *Rangatira* and the *Stena Baltica*. Ten million cubic metres of rock and peat had to be shifted and a harbour built before actual construction could begin in 1977. At the same time its equipment was being prefabricated on the mainland, which halved the construction time to seven years. The total cost in 1975 had been guessed at £600 million, with 1,800 employed; by the time the Queen opened it on 9 May 1981 this had risen to £1.2 billion, with 7,200 workers on site. Sullom Voe was not totally operational – with three tanker movements in and out daily – until the end of the year. At Sullom, ethane and methane were separated from the crude. The methane powered the electricity generating station; butane was liquefied and dispatched by ship, and the remaining 'dead' crude stored pending dispatch by supertanker. If after completion only 650 workers ran it, this was good going for Shetland.

Initially the use of the terminal was lower than expected, owing to 2 million tonnes a month – half Sullom Voe's throughput – being loaded offshore at the Brent Spar loading buoy.[75] Not having to pay their harbour dues at Sullom made sense to the companies, but raised the problem that there was no place for the contaminated ballast water of the tankers to be treated. At Sullom this was possible and by 1982 most of the Shetland Islands Council's income came from the rates on Sullom; almost 85 per cent of the Council's rates bill was met by the companies, with only 3.4 per cent coming from private ratepayers. But there were also harbour dues and a 'disturbance fund' – an initial £2 million plus a levy of 2p per ton passing through the Voe. The dividend came to the pensioners as a supplement to their income; it came to the youth in the form of subsidies to schools and a sports complex. Powers were successfully kept from central government, but at the price of considerable confusion. But oil also meant a falling-off of local industry, and the suspicion grew that any advance in Scottish nationalism meant a threat to Shetland's rights in the oil business.

Shetlanders didn't discourage this. They *had* little to do with the remote Scottish mainland, and even less with Orkney. It was thought to be more expensive to reach Sumburgh Airport from London than to reach New York. As the most extreme example of a rural community beset by instant industrialization, the islands attracted sociologists in droves, eager to chart the impact of the new order. They were intrigued and even heartened to come across a toughly independent localism. As one of the islands semi-resident colony commented:

Members become conscious of their culture when they reach its boundaries – such as when intrusion occurs or is threatened – and in that consciousness they become aware of its values. Having done such accounting, neither they as individuals, nor their culture, can ever be the same again.[76]

The point was, all this had happened before. Shetland was only remote from London or Glasgow, not from Hugh MacDiarmid's 'winds wi' warlds to swing'. In the nineteenth century its men had crewed ships in all the seven seas. Alexander Anderson, MP, a proto-Clark figure, had manned the Brazilian navy with them in the 1860s. The elaborate festival of 'Up Helly Aa!' which took place at the end of every January, with a torchlit Viking procession followed by the immolation of a longship, and with parties and dances, was an invention of the 1870s, aimed at bringing the seamen home for the seed-time on their crofts. The Shetlanders were very clever with their bounty.

By the mid-1980s BP was paying £53.4 million a year to the Shetland Islands Council, and 80 per cent of the Council's domestic rate. Yet Shetland considered that, as a consequence of earlier agreements, it had spent over £150 million on accommodating the oil companies and was owed £320 million by them. It brought an action against them in the Court of Session in Edinburgh to secure this, which dragged on inconclusively until 1988.[77]

The majors, and to some extent the British and US governments, were intrigued by Shetland developments. Richard Funkhouser's 1975 telex to the State Department served almost as Shetland's equivalent of the Declaration of Arbroath:

The irony of the North Sea allegedly was that the tyrant which bestrode it was the Shetland County Council, a tiny group of home-spun farmers led by 'Fuehrer' Ian Clark who had reputedly hornswoggled some of the biggest multinationals and most sophisticated leaders in Britain out of terms which would make Scottish Nationalists pale with envy.

Not only had these 'amateurs' pushed a private bill through Parliament, giving them reportedly unprecedented autonomy to make their own critical industrial decisions, but had forced the majors into giving them a highly profitable partnership for which they had put up no funds and over which they had won significant control.[78]

Could the islanders be expected to acquiesce in the proposition of 'Scotland's oil' when 60 per cent of the stuff was in 'their' territorial waters? The local MP, Grimond, was an unpredictable quantity. Looking like a Viking, but an Etonian and kinsman of Asquith, he was one of those Dundee jute dynasts who had sidestepped cannily from industry into finance. Grimond was a local oligarch while in the north, a radical democrat in those London suburbs which his Liberals always seemed on the point of taking over, and in economic terms a proto-Thatcherite of the Institute of Economic Affairs variety. Although pledged to Scottish home rule, he was not above mischievously playing the Shetland card against it.

Shetlanders didn't let him or the anti-devolutionists down. By the end of the 1970s they had generated an independence pressure group of their own, the Shetland Movement. Jonathan Wills characterized it as a variation on the subsequent Social Democrat secession from the Labour Party, by *soi-disant* socialists fed up with an uphill battle against the control of the Liberals and the local oligarchy.[79] Still, it was strong enough to prompt the Council into commissioning – at £45,000 – an inquiry under Lord Kilbrandon into the islands' political future.[80]

A more agonizing and longer-lasting problem was that the owner of an oil terminal resembled the proprietor of a bar. He had responsibility for keeping the premises tidy, but only a limited control over the clientele. And the international oil trade was, almost by definition, a very rough sort of trade indeed. This was rapidly demonstrated by the terminal's first weeks in service. The first vessel to berth was the 70,000-ton tanker *Donovania*, on 29 November 1978; but its arrival was premature as ballast-water cleansing equipment had not yet been completed, and this was to cause a lot of trouble. Only a few weeks into operation the ageing 193,000-ton *Esso Berenicia* crashed into a loading jetty and lost 1,174 tons of fuel oil.[81] Two-thirds of this was recovered, but the costs of subsequent processes were formidable. The clean-up cost BP £1.75 million and the Shetland Council £200,000; £300,000 had to be paid to locals; repairs to the jetty cost a further £200,000. And 3,702 birds of forty-nine species were killed by the oil. A formal oil-spill plan was not produced until February 1979, and the construction of a system of oil-retaining booms followed, with the number of tugs rising from three to five. Spillage incidents thereafter averaged about one a month, but many indicated the menace of ill-equipped and poorly maintained tankers under flags of convenience.[82] A report of 1981 was reassuring about the pollution threat – a spill on the west Shetland coast once every forty-eight years; off the east coast once every 167 years.

Eleven years later the supertanker *Braer*, with over 60,000 tons of oil from Norway, crashed into the cliffs off Sumburgh.

6

Benn and the Defence of Britain

Some oil companies are comparable in strength and wealth to national governments. In 1977 Shell earned $55 billion from 4.2 million barrels per day, while Exxon earned $58 billion producing 4.9 million. By contrast the revenues of Saudi Arabia were only $38 billion and 9.2 million barrels per day, and the revenues of Iran were $23 billion and 5.7 million barrels. As Secretary of State, I learned that relations between governments and oil companies were rather like treaty negotiations.

Tony Benn, *Diaries*, 11 January 1977[1]

Quap

A group composed of several hundred men, offshore, living in a huge metal-framed structure, only fitfully conscious of events in the outside world: some qualities were common to the oil industry and to the Palace of Westminster. Indeed the Victoria Tower, the first skyscraper when it was built in the 1850s, was the generic ancestor of the jackets of the production platforms. Women were, as on the rigs, all but absent save in ritualized form; the iconography of the place was, however, supplied not by centre-folds but by late-nineteenth-century *Punch* cartoons. Where these did not feature either Queen Victoria or various breastplated national deities, they depicted Sir William Harcourt. Harcourt, intelligent, arrogant, lazy, had once – incredibly – held the chair of International Law at Cambridge. He led the Liberal Party in the Commons in the 1890s; slipping on and off his front bench like a great complacent sealion, he persisted in the 1970s as a role-model of sorts.

Harcourt appeared as Sir Ethelred in Conrad's *The Secret Agent*, where his confident complacency saw off the frantic reactionary Mr Vladimir, the conspiratorial Russian diplomat in London who had tried to provoke the expulsion of anarchists from the city. Conrad, the victim of Russian repression, marvelled at this 'you be damned' English effectiveness, this refusal to become either enthusiastic or obsessed. During the 1960s there was a revival of interest in the Edwardian period. The last of its survivors, Winston Churchill, had just departed, but Harold Macmillan conspicuously modelled his style on such as Arthur Balfour. Roy Jenkins wrote biographies of Sir Charles Dilke and Asquith; Julian Amery was still working on Joseph Chamberlain (later on he would advise the Bank of Credit and Commerce International); Enoch Powell, a scholarly throwback to the imperial 1900s, remained a populist force in the land.

This veneration was not altogether shared by the Edwardians themselves. H.G. Wells, a man whose spiritual home might have been an oil rig, denounced the Edwardian House of Commons as 'Bladesover', its ostensible English country-house values a carapace of *rentier* decadence:

In that great pile of Victorian architecture the landlords and the lawyers, the bishops, the railway men and the magnates of commerce go to and fro – in their incurable tradition of commercialized Bladesovery, of meretricious gentry and nobility sold for riches.[2]

In *Tono-Bungay* the last chance of retrieving the Ponderevo family fortunes – and the Ponderevos are all too obviously symbolic of Britain – is a deposit of a wonder mineral called (even more symbolically) Quap, like Roy Jenkins trying to be rude. Was Mr Jenkins, and the Commons, any better fitted to cope with the quap which had turned up off the British coasts? Alastair Dunnett commented that if the oil had been at the mouth of the Thames, Parliament would have taken notice of it.[3] In fact it – or at least gas – was in 1965 not all that far away from the edge of the London commuter belt. And Parliament had reacted with near-total indifference.

Yet oil was moving in on the politicians, whether they wanted it to or not. Edith Penrose, the doyenne of oil politics studies, sees the period from 1973 to 1985 as the last act of an epic drama: world management by OPEC, and a move from multinational to national companies:

In 1970 the seven international majors owned about 60 per cent of the crude produced in the non-communist areas of the world, and another 30 per cent was produced by other private international companies. By 1982 the majors' share had fallen to about 16 per cent and other private companies' to around 21 per cent.[4]

Britain was affected as much as any other power. With this caveat: Britain also had two majors in the house, so to speak, and the other five grazing, so far contentedly, on the back lawn.

Oil and the Politicians

Turn to the sections dealing with energy in any university library and you are confronted with shelves full of volumes on oil and foreign policy, oil and diplomacy, oil and defence: almost exclusively of American provenance. Although the rise of 'sunbelt America' as a political factor was only just beginning in the 1960s – an early, unpropitious marker being the assassination of John Kennedy in Dallas in November 1963 – the oil business was as central to American diplomatic pedagogy as, say, the Ottoman Empire had been to British diplomacy in the age of Lord Salisbury. Who else would pay the salaries of so many of Washington's most skilful lobbyists?

In 1970 there was no longer any British parallel. The 'transition' in British politics which veterans like James Margach and Francis Boyd had observed while political correspondents of the *Sunday Times* and the *Guardian* in the 1950s meant the replacement of the 'high politics' of foreign policy and defence affairs by issues of domestic policy, which now accounted for two-thirds of the annual expenditure of government.[5] As a result, an internationally traded commodity such as oil fell almost out of sight. BP was notionally a semi-state company, but its two government directors were traditionally men of straw – as the messy history of Rhodesian sanctions had proved. Shell, so Anthony Sampson found when he visited its South Bank citadel in 1965, was conscious of being patricianly Anglo-Dutch, and kept the government at a distance.[6] Given Britain's political problems in the Middle East after Suez, this was tactful.

But as a result there were few people in British politics during the 1960s who knew anything about the oil business; or, for that matter, about the sort of political framework into which it fitted. Washington was a city of lobbies, London was – at that stage – not. It was favoured by the majors for this very reason. The sort of internal groupings within parties which might favour lobby activity were ideological on the left and rather more social on the right. The diaries and recollections of the 1960s and 1970s show the self-obsession of the leading performers, and their almost total obliviousness to factors which did not come under their immediate purview. There was a coal lobby, no longer personified by Tory coal-owners but grouped around the MPs sponsored by the National Union of Mineworkers: ponderous and conservative, as they had always been. There was a nuclear lobby, split awkwardly but powerfully between the service chiefs and the scientists; but there was no 'oil lobby' distinct from those pressure groups which urged the interests of its various applications, notably the well-heeled British Road Federation and its satellites.

Was the Conservative Party the place to look? The Trade minister in the Heath government had been John Davies, Director-General of the Confederation of British Industries *and* a former Shell executive. But Davies, and the hard-line market policies he represented, was always an outsider and in office a flop. There were Conservative directors of oil companies, of course, but the party itself regarded the oil companies as less than loyal — Edward Heath's relations with Shell and BP during the 1973 fuel crisis had been even icier than the winter — and was reluctant to make an issue of protecting them. Conversely, there were no examples in Britain of the huge political donations — the Lockheed or Exxon bribes — widespread on the continent. The majors were traditionally skilled in public relations, but they were conscious that opinion polls showed the political feelings of the people were unfriendly, favouring 'national' action to secure oil revenues for Britain. As motorists the people had little appreciation for the companies' interest in keeping prices high.

The political situation in the mid-1970s also seemed set in a particular direction. The Conservatives had shot their bolt. 'Selsdon Park' Heath had tried confrontation with the unions and the welfare state and failed; his Keynesian excursion had been catastrophic. This left Labour, capable of polling about 36 per cent; the Liberals, sure of between 15 and 20 per cent; and assorted nationalists and Ulster unionists, totalling about 7 per cent. Labour had come into office with a left-wing manifesto but a reassuringly right-wing cabinet.[7] After October 1974 it was clear that it would be dependent on the Liberals, and even more moderate. With the Thorpe scandal hanging over them, the Liberals had little room for manoeuvre. Devolution of some sort to Scotland seemed likely; and after this was accomplished, the betting must have been that a continuing system of 'co-operative federalism', based on proportional representation akin to that of West Germany, would give continuity to centre-left politics.

This apparent centre-left solidity, and the oil industry's general unpopularity, affected its pressure-group activity. The majors had set up the United Kingdom North Sea Operators' Committee in 1964. In 1973 it became the UK Offshore Operators' Association (UKOOA), with a full-time staff. By 1977 it represented thirty-seven companies operating on the continental shelf. By that time the smaller British-based independents had come together as Brindex, the Association of British Independent Oil Exploration Companies. The latter, however, represented only 4.4 per cent of proven reserves.[8] UKOOA was palpably successful in imposing its will on the Department of Energy, although it tended to be marginalized after the Petroleum and Pipelines Act, and the accession of Tony Benn. It was not admitted to the government's Energy Commission until 1978.

The oil company lobby was discreet, but not wholly effective. Funkhouser reckoned its activities did little to alter the Pipelines bill, or change attitudes in the Tory Party.[9] This was in part because it was construed, by government and public, as offshore in word and deed; remote from British social and economic affairs. Its attempts to purchase support in Parliament were, as we shall see, absurd. Where onshore consequences were expected, things were different. In the early 1970s the most persistent oil lobby groups were to be found in Scotland.

They were not just or even primarily to be found in the SNP. The Labour Party Scottish Council had also taken an early interest, proposing an oil-funded Scottish Development Agency at its 1972 conference. The Liberals wanted 50 per cent of any revenues from the North Sea to go to a Scottish Oil Development Council. Both groups were flanked by those Scottish businesses, organized in the Scottish Council: Development and Industry, which hoped to do well out of oil, and produced activist business-men such as Iain Noble and Angus Grossart. The SC:DI ran an International Forum on offshore oil in the autumn of 1972, and contact-making delegations were already on their way to Texas and Norway.[10] At the General Assembly of 1972 the Church of Scotland took the trouble to commission a report on the social and economic consequences of the oil discoveries from John Francis and Norman Swan, the latter being, usefully, a former Burmah manager who had gone into the ministry.[11] From her mansion at Carradale Naomi Mitchison, who seemed fated to grasp in a sensible and humane manner all sorts of points which 'rational' politicians regularly contrived to ignore, responded to the excitement as well as the danger of the whole thing:

For the twentieth century the oil rigs represent what the Forth Bridge did for the nineteenth – the achievement of what had seemed impossible; the work of man. We have not adjusted to this kind of beauty, which undoubtedly exists ... They remain, not only superb constructions, but also providers of danger and excitement and skill, which might otherwise turn to violence and war.[12]

Mitchison came from a family of scientists and politicians: her brother J.B.S. Haldane had pioneered escape methods from stricken submarines, and had headed the Communist Party's capture of much of the leadership of British science in the 1930s; her uncle Viscount Haldane, Liberal War Minister and Lord Chancellor, a state-socialist of Bismarckian stamp, had even dared in 1919 to attempt to rationalize the British 'machinery of government' along lines that Lord Balogh would have approved.

The Westminster parties were uninterested in rationalization, and deeply ignorant of technology of any description. This suited the oil majors and their entourage, which had an interest in keeping things calm and were, like Shell, intractably and agreeably WASP-ish. Yet this produced an intriguing side-effect. Their Arab dealings meant that the Jewish element which had characterized – and frequently energized – British economic activity was absent: a lack of something which massaged a particularly metropolitan style of conservatism. On the other hand North Sea oil gave a chance to perform to one group on the margin of the Labour Party: Harold Lever, Robert Sheldon, Joel Barnett and Edmund Dell formed a competent northern financial group – largely Manchester Jewish. Its members had once been on the far left, but now used oil to shift, literally as well as metaphorically, to the political centre. MPs didn't usually, in those days, know much about money, or were too busy making it. Lever, Sheldon, Barnett and Dell did, and this command served them well in 1972.

Lever, a millionaire Manchester businessman on the right of the party, had been alerted by the £40 million bid for fifteen blocks at auction for the fourth round. Following recent reforms, the Public Accounts Committee was allowed to pick one 'big' topic every year and in 1972 Lever insisted on oil. The Committee's first meeting helpfully coincided with *that* article by Lord Balogh in the *Sunday Times* (not an utterly disinterested source, as it was owned by Lord Thomson) in February 1972. Balogh accused the oil companies of deliberately playing down the prospects of North Sea oil. Why was it that when the Arabs got 75 per cent and the Dutch 76.5 per cent, the UK tax and royalty take made up only 50 per cent?[13]

After the Committee's first meeting Lever suffered a stroke, but was succeeded by his deputy Edmund Dell. Dell's was an unusual background. He qualified as an historian at Oxford and joined the Communist Party, writing with Christopher Hill a study of English radicalism called *The Good Old Cause*. This career was far behind him when, by then firmly on the right of the party, he served as a junior minister under Wilson. The Committee – or, more precisely, Dell himself – interrogated civil servants in the Board of Trade and the Inland Revenue in 1992 and 1993.[14] The exchanges recorded showed a regime of alleged 'control' breaking down.[15] The deputy chairman of the Inland Revenue admitted to the Committee that with the rise in Middle East posted prices, the losses of UK-based companies had risen from £90 million in 1966 to £470 million in 1972. As a result, 'The total accumulated losses which are available for relief against profits of these companies is now £1,500 million.' UK tax income from oil in 1975 simply would not exist:

Mr Dell: You were talking about the existing tax losses, which are very large in amount, and indicating that Parliament might be unwilling to take retrospective measures to deal with this? – *Mr Lord*: Yes, I was.

But these tax losses are so large that they might, in fact, eliminate liability to tax for a significant number of years to come? – That is true.

As it is clear that little will come into the UK exchequer in the way of tax revenue from North Sea oil in the early 1980s, and perhaps later as things stand at the moment, maybe there will be benefits because the oil firms are British? – Well, no – most of them are not.[16]

In America this tax kickback was a means of subsidizing the majors for carrying out a sizeable chunk of the country's foreign policy. Such a justification was scarcely possible in Britain.

Dell made the running. The only other Committee member who had much to contribute was Dick Douglas, the Labour MP for Clackmannan, who had been a marine engineer, had lectured on economics, and was close to Scottish trade unions in the oil business.[17] The Tories on the Committee were silent. The report was a triumph for its Labour members, but one with a barb. Dell urged on Harold Wilson that oil be made the major part of Labour's 1974 platform, and was disappointed when this didn't happen. However, Wilson then gave him, as Paymaster-General, the responsibility for creating the new Petroleum Revenue Tax.[18] Douglas, the only Scottish Labour MP who knew anything about oil, lost his seat to the SNP in the election.

The Scottish Snake

By mid-1974 the politics of the oil issue had divided itself into two main areas, and should have produced a third. The first was the technical business of taxing the stuff adequately, which involved giving government a degree of oversight into the way the industry was run. The second – what to do about Scotland? – became active politics after the Govan by-election of November 1973. The third, appraising the technology of oil, remained a dead letter.

The Commons Select Committee on Science and Technology inquired into offshore engineering in early 1974, in the wake of the IMEG report. It had no one on it as dominant as Dell, it made no direct connections with the Public Accounts Committee's financial case, and its warnings remained unheard:

As witnesses reminded us, compared with France our record of endeavour and achievement, especially in the area of 'the man in the sea' has been abysmally poor. Added to this is a more understandable backwardness in developing specialist support for offshore oil recovery.[19]

Prima facie, the Select Committee's report ought to have been even more damning than that of the Public Accounts Committee. Gas exploration had been going on for over a decade; its extraction had been a financial success, if also a technological failure. Both BP and Burmah had attempted to get in on the rig and supply-vessel market. The problems that they ran into should have been instructive. But the report sank without trace.

It is the habit of élites – especially failing ones – to define as the business of politics the areas that they can cope with, and forget about the others. Technology could be forgotten about; but not the Scottish National Party. With a thin majority making another election inevitable, it had used the oil weapon effectively, and seemed bound to go on doing so. Asked at a Washington press conference in 1976 why Britain didn't give Scotland its independence, Anthony Crosland, Foreign Secretary, would murmur, 'Because they have a lot of oil.'[20] Elsewhere, embassies warily entertained SNP functionaries on trips to OPEC, Statoil or the State Department. After February 1974, if the SNP could, for whatever reason, build on its poll performance, it could gain a majority of Scottish seats. This would provoke a constitutional crisis, and all bets – technological or otherwise – would be off.

The Commons – and up to February 1974 the leadership of Edward Heath – could not be expected to know or care much about the internal dynamics of Scottish politics. For decades Scottish MPs were there to be ignored: on the Labour side, town council mediocrities from the Glasgow area, and a Tory clutch of equally dim public-school and Oxbridge lairds and farmers. Heath did have some insight; he had set up an advisory committee on Scottish government in 1968, which had recommended a Scottish Assembly. This had been shelved, partly through the flagging performance of the SNP in 1970, partly through Heath's other preoccupations – local government, the energy crisis, entry to the EEC. Suddenly, and just about the time when, after the PAC report had concentrated people's minds wonderfully on the need to control oil production, this reassuring landscape was transformed into one of menace. Suppose the Scots voters saw what the SNP saw – and what Westminster saw – and acted thereon?[21]

Hence the salience of the home rule rather than the oil issue in 1973 and 1974, which posed the question: how much could the independence threat be neutralized by the offer of qualified home rule in the Kilbrandon mode? It was evident that oil in Scotland unloosed a great deal of emotion, but even a Westminster front-bencher could see that the fundamental attitudes of the Scots, both *qua* oil and *qua* the United Kingdom, were conciliatory. They wanted a re-negotiation of the Union, and they wanted some allocation of oil revenues for Scottish purposes. How was the Labour Party and, after February 1974, the Labour government to react?

The answer was, with as much tribulation as 'this great movement of ours' was capable of bringing on itself. Wilson took over a semi-formed devolution unit in the civil service from Heath, and delegated the business to his former Chief Whip, Edward Short. Short and the unit's head, Sir James Garlick, drafted a White Paper promising a severely limited sort of legislative devolution, and published it on 3 June.[22] But Labour had recaptured Govan in February, and the local elections in early May turned out to be nothing special for the SNP. The pressure seemed to be off, at least as far as the Labour Party faithful were concerned. Labour's Scottish oligarchy was a mixture of 'sweetie wifies' – long-serving local worthies – trade unionists, and articulate and interesting zealots of what could be called a proto-Bennite tendency. They wanted the full strength of the Conference-sanctioned economic strategy, modified by a development agency to dispose of some of the oil revenues in Scotland's interests (which they got – albeit *indirectly* financed – in the Scottish Development Agency of 1975). Otherwise they preferred to let the new regional system of local government run itself in.[23] They saw the Assembly as a distraction from the Bevanite goal of co-ordinated economic planning; and they loathed the SNP. At a thinly attended meeting in Glasgow on 2 June – about half the comrades were away watching a World Cup qualifier – the Scottish executive rejected the White Paper.

Home rulers in the Labour Party in Scotland were a minority, but a growing and increasingly fractious one. After the Scottish Executive's provocation, rumours seeped out of secession or even – in the case of John Mackintosh – affiliation to the SNP. A private MORI poll carried out for the party showed that the SNP would take thirteen seats from Labour.[24] This was bad enough, but should there also be a *Labour* secession before the next election, the result could be the much-feared SNP jackpot: thirty-six SNP MPs, or enough to enable the party to secede from Westminster and form its own administration in Edinburgh. Wilson and the Cabinet were forced to act.

The crucial Cabinet meeting was held on 24 July 1974, on the eve of a Labour National Executive meeting. The Scottish Secretary of State, Willie Ross, was both panicked and unconstructive, muttering that his past warnings had been ignored, but making no suggestions. Roy Jenkins, the future constitutional radical, was deeply hostile to any change; Tony Crosland was mutinous but silent. Edmund Dell was concerned at the way things were going:

The issue in Scotland was restricted primarily to the prospects from North Sea oil and I argued that a minimal scheme of devolution which my colleagues seemed to think would suffice would in no way satisfy the demand arising from North Sea oil. The best thing was to stand up and fight.

Despite the despair of the right, no one else spoke thus. Dell regarded the whole project as a diversion:

The frivolity with which the question of devolution in the UK was treated . . . reduced hardened civil servants to despair.[25]

At the same time contacts with Scottish colleagues – Mackintosh, Dickson Mabon – who gave the UK ten years were scarcely reassuring. Wilson was empowered to go to the National Executive, along with the Trades Union Congress, and force the Scottish Council of the Labour Party to hold an extraordinary general meeting on 16 August. The union block votes duly reversed the Scottish Council's policy on devolution. Labour's unionism was deployed to promote home rule. On 17 September a White Paper, *Democracy and Devolution*, was issued, and in October Labour fought for the first time on its own Scottish manifesto.[26] It held the line, dropping only 0.3 per cent, although four more Conservative seats fell to the SNP. The latter, however, now held 30 per cent of the Scottish vote.[27]

Wilson and his weighty biographers are as silent on devolution as they are on oil, although the two were together to dominate the 1974–9 Labour government, and the critical decisions were taken during Wilson's tenure. The style of the prime minister was non-interventionist, in contrast to his earlier ministry, and yet this period achieved one notable strategic victory for Whitehall. The oil issue was split from devolution, proposals for a dedicated oil fund were ditched, and a minimal home rule offer was made. The government calculated that the Scots would concentrate on the latter and ignore the former. The Scots, or most of them, swallowed the bait. Wilson's constitutional adviser, Norman Hunt, had been a dissident member of the Kilbrandon Commission, who rejected the majority report's neo-nationalism in favour of a system of largely executive regional councils. The lack of printed sources, the absence of access to internal papers, and the early death of Lord Crowther-Hunt make it difficult to confirm the following, but my hunch is that Crowther-Hunt sold Wilson a formula whereby a type of devolution was promulgated which might be appropriate all round, to English regions as well as to Scotland and Wales. In this way, through the general constitutional debate thus provoked, the oil issue would be defused.

In the House

Quite a lot of people had expertise and opinion on the constitutional issue, although few were consulted. (Irony of ironies, Professor John Mackintosh, who had been advocating devolution since 1968, is mistaken in Barbara Castle's memoirs for George

Cunningham, the author of the amendment demanding a 40 per cent 'yes' vote, which torpedoed the bill in 1979.) But according to Bernard Donoughue, policy adviser to Callaghan, only two people had any semblance of understanding of the energy crisis: Heath and Lever.[28] There seemed little evidence of the former during the government of 1970–74, and its economic acrobatics. Labour could argue that John Davies was an oil insider, but Davies was sidelined before Heath revived the Ministry of Power as the Department of Energy and put Lord Carrington in charge of it. Much of the subsequent oil taxation legislation was sketched out under Carrington.

Which was probably more than happened under Labour. Between 1970 and 1974 the Shadow Cabinet élite left the radicals on the National Executive to their own devices, and (beyond the usual intention to nationalize wherever possible) these did not include oil. Donoghue comments that, even when in office, 'the Cabinet never really discussed economic policy before the October election', bearing out Adrian Hamilton's comment of February 1974 in the *Financial Times*:

Save for a few notable exceptions like Lord Balogh and the Public Accounts Committee of the Commons, North Sea decisions over the last nine years have been taken in an atmosphere of little criticism and a general lack of public discussion.[29]

This abstention could not survive the miners' work-to-rule and the three-day week. Heath was patently pulled up short when Sir Eric Drake told him that Britain had no priority in oil supplies, despite BP being an almost state-owned company, and despite the government's self-presentation to the Arabs as a 'friendly' power.[30] Lord Rothschild, who headed the Central Policy Review Group, told Dell that as a result of this act of 'treason', Heath had become perfectly open to the proposition of state participation.[31]

But as with devolution, Heath didn't appear to be doing anything about it. Wilson did not make oil an issue in the election, but included a Lloyd George-like flourish in a speech at Oxford:

God gave the land to the people, he gave the seas to the people and the treasures beneath the seas. There is no record that when God made the firmament and the seas he ordained that the profit from the wealth beneath the seas should accrue in full to private investors or rich multinational oil companies.[32]

With Wilson in power after early March, Balogh became Minister of State in the Energy department. Despite his earlier radicalism he, as well as Colin Phipps and Dick Douglas, opposed outright nationalization; they turned out to be representative of the party, for what that was worth. As usual, the left's ambitions had not been filtered through any detailed planning. It was preoccupied with industrial policy; and in so far as it thought of energy, it thought about expanding coal production and left it at that. For those in the Labour Party who had studied the oil business, the threat of a pull-out by the majors persisted, constraining more radical ideas.

With the minister, the 'reliable' Eric Varley, concentrating on coal, a committee composed of sonorous archaisms – Balogh was Minister of State, Dell Paymaster-General, and Lever Chancellor of the Duchy of Lancaster – set about drafting legislation. Although they drew on preliminary work carried out by the Conservatives, they stressed participation, on the Norwegian precedent, as well as taxation. They had a relatively easy passage. Heath, a spent force after October, had moved into one of his huffs, and had lost interest in opposition. When Margaret Thatcher defeated him on 11 February 1975, she was only gingerly moving to lead an opposition which saw her purely as a stop-gap. This may account for the Conservatives' qualified and unconvincing attack on the legislation.

Labour's very brief White Paper came out on 11 July 1974. It proposed an additional revenue tax on petroleum production; majority participation in future fields; and majority participation in existing fields – using the precedents of the British Gas Corporation and the National Coal Board; a British National Oil Corporation was to be set up, with its headquarters in Scotland. The government would thus have control of production and pipelines.[33] The drafting of the Offshore Petroleum and Pipelines bill was put into the hands of the joint ministerial-official committee. Debate now centred on the cost of state participation. How prohibitive was it? Adrian Hamilton, writing on 29 November, put the costs of the state share as high as £3 billion, a figure much repeated by Conservative spokesmen.[34] The inevitable government response was that the people now complaining about such costs were those who had already allowed the majors to get away with billions more.

Government action from here on took three parallel courses: the Petroleum Revenue Tax bill was tabled on 19 November 1974, and enacted on 25 February 1975. The Offshore Petroleum and Pipelines bill followed on 30 April; and parallel to these were detailed negotiations on state participation. For the first, Dell had invented a 'no better and no worse off' formula. If PRT were at 51 per cent the companies got rid of that proportion of their obligation by turning that fraction of the risk as well as the income over to the government. Much of the detail of this was missed by a public transfixed by the awfulness of the economic situation, with inflation totalling 50 per cent over two years. But this gave ministers a chance.

Dell felt it necessary to gain the confidence of the industry. He was aware that the conditions encountered in the North Sea were much worse than the industry had expected. This had to be set against its skill in avoiding taxation. That said, the personalities of the various oil companies varied enormously. Dell recorded that Exxon sent him a letter 'so rude that I could only assume it was drafted by someone accustomed to addressing banana republics'.[35] Amoco harangued the public in newspaper adverts. This the United States Embassy saw as counter-productive and tried to cool down.

In discussion the American companies, now used to this sort of thing world–wide, became co-operative, if mistrustful; the British majors fumed, but realized that Heath loathed them more than they loathed Labour.[36]

Dell found in fact that Balogh, the former *bête noire* of the companies, was conciliatory, believing that 45 per cent – rather than his own 55 per cent – was the most that could be taken in tax; with his fellow Hungarian Nicholas Kaldor, Balogh put forward a formula – the Varley memorandum – which safeguarded marginal fields by allowing the companies to recoup their outlay before becoming liable. Recollecting that the British regime was no worse than the Norwegian, the companies complied. Dell rode out the rest of the bill's stages in the Commons:

> The left in the Parliamentary Labour Party and in the media attempted to give me a hard time, as did the Scottish Nationalists. But their intellectual energy was unequal to the task of challenging me in the House of Commons on something as complex as a tax bill. They made their protest. Then they disappeared from this scene without trace.[37]

Two months after the enactment of the tax bill, the Pipelines bill came up for debate in the Commons on 30 April 1975, with a government majority of only four. Dell continued to fend off the companies on taxation, while the UK Offshore Operators' Association, in the person of Bob Dyk of Hamilton Petroleum, fed amendments to the press as much as to the government. This campaign of making the public 'well and timely informed' had some effect. The Under-Secretary for Energy, John Smith, who handled most of the legislation in the Commons with great flair, became doubtful about making government rights retrospective, leaving Lever to appear more radical.[38]

Heath (surprisingly, given his attitude to the majors), and initially Thatcher, faltered in their choice of parliamentary spokesmen. In the debates on the oil bill, the direct hand of company influence appeared too obvious. Patrick Jenkin, the main Tory speaker, was regarded, even by the Americans, as weak as Smith was strong.[39] A former director of the Distillers Company,

Jenkin's arguments were dubiously researched and his rhetoric tended to be overblown:

He [Varley] is sometimes accused of assuming the mantle of a modern oil sheikh, but here he looks like a sort of eighteenth-century Middle Eastern despot, with BNOC as his pampered, privileged eunuch.[40]

Jenkin in debate admitted that the Heath government had thought of participation, but dismissed it on grounds of cost.[41] He quoted the cost of participation at double the government's estimates, and insisted that the accountants of BNOC were being outrageously masked from parliamentary scrutiny. After some ineptness on the government side, it transpired that the latter terms were the same as those in the Heath government's gas bill of 1972.[42]

Jenkin's supporting speakers were disappointing. Davies had the mark of failure on him; Ian Sproat, the MP for the oil-enriched seat of South Aberdeen, Peter Viggers, a director of Edward Bates, and Peter Emery, a director of Phillips Petroleum, were too deeply involved in oil-related business to sound judicious.[43] Subsequently, as Gerry Corti and Frank Frazer reported in their study of the participation negotiations, Jenkin was defensive:

[John Smith] says that Patrick Jenkin as the chief opposition spokesman was absolutely flooded by material from the oil companies. Patrick Jenkin says that during the period he picked up the opposition portfolio in the summer of 1974 he got a lot of teach-ins from the oil companies, notably BP and Shell, and to a lesser extent some of the large American independents. He went out of his way to stress that he did not, and still does not, feel that he was in the companies' pockets.[44]

Jenkin made matters worse by the relations he then cultivated with the majors. He went in the spring of 1975 to the USA, with four Tory colleagues. Their expenses were paid by the majors after an approach from the politicians. The sum of £750 was forthcoming from each, delivered in a somewhat offhand, not to say condescending, manner, one company paying in used pound notes. Jenkin also visited the Middle East with another group, and Brazil on his own.[45] The inevitable result of such trips was the accusation that the Tories were being run by American oilmen; this was voiced by Smith on 26 June 1975:

I sometimes wonder just how confidential these negotiations are, since the Rt Hon. Gentleman seems to have information given to oil companies immediately at his hand when he speaks in the Committee.[46]

The debate echoed the earlier Select Committee activity in concentrating almost exclusively on financial issues. Certain themes were, when raised, remarkable for being otherwise ignored. The merchant banker Viggers alluded to safety, which was more than any Labour MP ever did:

No one can say that the safety record in the North Sea is exemplary. The work done there is very dangerous. It is carried on in hazardous conditions, and the commercial pressures on those working in the industry are extreme. Britain leads in some areas, particularly diving, an area of particular danger. It is right that there should be extreme safety measures. The government should take them, and we should back them.[47]

And the young Glasgow Labour MP James Craigen stressed, equally uniquely, the environment:

After the scars left by the mining industry in the course of its exploitation in the last century in the west-central part of Scotland, it is most important that we should not now be creating oil slag heaps on the bed of the North Sea.[48]

But the distinctive aspect of the debates was absence of interest on both sides of the House, and the dearth of intimate knowledge of the industry, even on the part of those who were tediously prepared to be its spokesmen. Alone in the House was one maverick Labour geologist, Dr Colin Phipps, who had actual experience of running a small oil company, and who had put forward the idea of a National Hydrocarbons Corporation in a Fabian Society pamphlet eight years earlier. He complained about the lack of a financial base for oil enterprise and the lack of enthusiasm from British banks.[49]:

Such contributions were noted for the record, and that was that. The same went for the intervention of the SNP's oil spokesman, Gordon Wilson:

As soon as there is a directly-elected Scottish Assembly and as soon as Scotland has its own chief executive, whether he be called Prime Minister or something else, his very first action will be to telephone the Prime Minister of the United Kingdom and say, 'Prime Minister, I should like to see you soon to discuss the question of Scotland's share of oil resources.'[50]

At a later stage in the debate Gordon Wilson proposed an amendment which would have regionalized BNOC. This did not even get the length of a division, and was venomously opposed by all the Scottish Labour MPs who spoke; evidence of the division between devolution, to which such MPs paid lip-service, and the delegation of any real degree of economic authority over the oil.[51] After the Commons had considered Lords' amendments, the Offshore Petroleum and Pipelines bill became law in November 1975, under a different minister, Anthony Neil Wedgwood Benn. Consul Funkhouser found him 'a charming, extreme left-wing intellectual' – with (even more alarmingly) a 'liberal' American wife. Up to no good, by defini-tion. But he was anything but reassured by Margaret Thatcher's choice of John Biffen as Benn's opponent. As the companies and the Department got down to discuss participation, a nationalist of the left would be faced by a nationalist of the right. The two obviously got along famously, and it was almost impossible to see where their policies differed.[52]

In the Corridors of Power

The parliamentary debates were not even for show. The sort of issue which could bring mobs out on the streets in South America or in the Middle East was not one to fill the House of Commons. MPs alluded to the emptiness of the place and the Scottish Nationalists in particular were harried for their absences. The real discussions were taking place elsewhere, carried on by ministerial–official negotiating teams at the Department of Energy.

The crucial problem confronting the British government was that foreign holdings had fallen only from 70 per cent to 60 per cent over the first four rounds: the Americans were needed to accelerate the development of the province, but their dominance was reflected in the tax giveaway and the import of equipment. The British reaction was to go into partnership with the smaller against the larger companies.[53] Moreover, they began to massage operators who were exploring more marginal fields – which, with the prevailing inflation, would cost double to start up – and, at the same time, to stand guard against attempts by the companies to create two or three fields out of one, in order to claim tax breaks on them. Poker was, according to Funkhouser, a favourite game among oilmen. One could see why. When John Smith's door was opened to negotiators, Funkhouser's future boss entered: Governor Connally, who had survived the Kennedy assassination in Dallas a decade or so earlier, and now represented Texas Eastern, the first of the transatlantic clients, and probably also a stalking-horse for the interests of the US government.[54]

Some majors were already partners with the National Coal Board, and in their haste to forge links some majors were prepared to be more tolerant of government than their British counterparts. The breakthrough involved Jack Reynolds of Conoco, James Longcroft of Tricentrol, Frank Kearton (not yet chairman of BNOC but only chairman of its Organizing Committee) and three Department of Energy officials, John Liverman,

Gerry Corti and Robert Priddle. The outcome of their negotiations was for long uncertain:

As Dick Mabon, later the Minister of State in the Department, commented
quite spontaneously, nobody who started off with a concept of participation
or a commitment on the lines of the White Paper of the summer of 1974
could have conceived that we would finish up with the form of participation
we did by late 1975.[55]

'These were swashbuckling times', according to John Smith.[56]
From the recollections of the participants, recorded in Corti and
Frazer's fascinating account, the whole business had the atmosphere of particularly robust horse-trading in some Texan town,
with the limeys giving as good as they got, and being respected
for it. A well-honed tactic was for some Labour moderate, Lever
or Smith, to enter breathing radical fire, putting the wind up
the companies, and then for the Secretary of State to appear,
giant mug of tea in hand, pipe in mouth (a combination which
appalled and fascinated his interlocutors), as the spirit of compromise.[57] The government team started to reach agreements with a
handful of companies, some small, some feeling vulnerable: Black-
friars, Berry Wiggins, Consolidated, Tricentrol, Burmah. Dem-
inex, with its Thistle field interests, was a special case, being
effectively owned by the German state. Was Helmut Schmidt
conceding here in order, in the longer term, to insist on a
European right to North Sea output?

The government side in the negotiations was helped by the
fact that oil companies were much more unpopular in the UK
than in the USA, yet its own case was badly projected beyond
the negotiating table and it had to endure repeated attacks from
the British majors. Why was this? Was Bernard Ingham too far
adrift from Tony Benn as Energy's publicity chief?[58] Why did
Shell, otherwise circumspect, become so extreme an opponent?
Its Chairman, Sir Frank McFadzean, was notably uninhibited.
Despite coming from British Airways, he was a free-enterprise
economist of the Institute of Economic Affairs school, who saw
the economic situation as a *Schicksalkampf* between the state and

the market. In this sense relations were almost bound to be worse between the UK government and UK companies than between the government and the Americans.

After the Petroleum and Submarine Pipelines Act reached the Statute Book in November 1975, it was followed by a softening-up of some of the bigger independents, with participation agreements in mind. Lever entertained the Piper partners, Hammer and Thomson. A Hammer tirade was followed by a clever Lever counter-attack, which crushed him; Roy Thomson then believed he would have to do business. Another observer remarked of this phase:

. . . it was only about this time that it became absolutely clear that it was the obtaining of control over oil without total expropriation of private property rights that was the name of the game.[59]

In the winter of 1975–6 the meetings began again, with a small and overworked negotiating team – Edmund Dell, Lever, Balogh, Kearton (who had only one assistant at BNOC). BNOC paid £83 million to take over 2 per cent of Ninian field, and would later take over 16 per cent of Thistle field.

BNOC was officially born on 1 January 1976; Kearton moved into the empty Stornoway House in St James's, once the head-quarters of Lord Beaverbrook and his press empire. BNOC's birth, however, had already been facilitated by the near-decease of another monument of Scots capitalism. On 3 December 1975 the government bought the North Sea assets of the Burmah Oil Co.

Burmah

James Lumsden, a director of William Baird, Weir Pumps and the Bank of Scotland, was a Glasgow businessman of a type as imperilled as the Atlantic passenger liner. He was also the chairman of the Burmah Oil Co., another of those Scottish ventures into imperial capitalism which had marked the economy of Asia, along with the Irrawaddy Flotilla and Jardine Matheson. Burmah was a very old, brass-plate company which proved the key to the government's intervention.[60] Small shareholders, not utterly remote from little old ladies in Firth of Clyde villages, controlled 80 per cent of its shares.

Formed to exploit the oil deposits of Burma, the company had in the early 1900s bought into the state-dominated Anglo-Iranian concern, which became BP: 'a small concern with big assets', according to Iain Noble.[61] But in the 1960s and early 1970s, under the aggressive management of Nicholas Williams, it became an early example of something which was subsequently to burgeon: the 'mini-conglomerate'. It had sunk £100 million on capital projects since 1966, out of a market capitalization of £600 million. It dragged behind it a clutch of enterprises whose resources had never been properly valued, and critics estimated its individual shares at £3 over their current value of £4.30, if Burmah were to rationalize its acquisitions. Instead of this, it kept on pouring money into eccentric and unproven projects:

It was Williams' rapacious taste for acquisition and diversification that led to the company's downfall and not – as some have suggested – simply a bad year in the tanker business ... The management had been spending money like drunken sailors and had precious little to show for it.[62]

Burmah built a refinery, to use an as yet unproven process, in the late 1960s at Ellesmere Port in Cheshire. It took four years longer than estimated to construct, and cost £43 million instead of a planned £10 million. According to Williams, the blocks the Department of Trade granted it in the North Sea in the first round were a reward for this investment. Burmah speculated in Australian natural gas. It poured money into liquid pressurized gas tankers, which cost well over estimates. But it failed to digest or rationalize the firms it took over. One of its acquisitions, Quinton Hazell, had won Queen's Awards, but at the Burmah board its managing director felt himself insulted: 'He went to three meetings of Burmah top brass and was totally ignored.'[63]

Such trading activities would, according to Williams, catch up with the operation that paid the dividends, Burmah's 20.5 per cent share in BP, by 1975. But the share in BP, regarded as a hostile sign by the US administration, had already accounted for Burmah's failure to merge with Conoco in 1971. It was not deterred, and £208 million was offered for the American concern Signal Oil and Gas on Christmas Eve, 1973:

Some Burmah men put a different complexion on it all. 'The acquisitions are really a means to an end. We had to do them to generate the cash flow to allow us to go into the oil game on a bigger scale.'

They did not. Burmah borrowed from the Chase Manhattan and Orion banks on the collateral of its holding in BP, then valued at £440 million. But during 1974 the BP share price fell, because of BP's commitments in the North Sea and in Alaska, and the general slump in the British stock market. By December the value of the Burmah stake in BP was down to £180 million, and its profits, which in 1973 had been £57 million, almost vanished. The creditors closed in. The slump in tankers was not to blame: it cost only £15 million; the culprit was incompetent and arrogant management.

The twenty-fifth largest company in Britain, hitherto eleventh in the European profitability league, came so unstuck that Harold Wilson was flown back from his Christmas holidays in the Scilly Islands to cope with the emergency. The Bank of England had to guarantee £300 million of Burmah's outstanding loans, largely in the interests of the North Sea project:

... its intervention ... prevented the massive loss of confidence that would have resulted from the collapse of a company with such a large stake.[64]

The alternative, as Dell recollected much later, was quite blunt: either bail Burmah out, or face a run on sterling.[65] By early January the Bank was in possession of Burmah's shares in BP, and Eric Varley was examining a short list of three to succeed James Lumsden as its chairman. Williams resigned, and a new slimmed-down company was administered by a drastically purged board. The casualties included one director, of whom his wife was subsequently to say:

His industrial experience was invaluable to me. Not only was he familiar with the scientific side (something which we had in common); he was also a crack cost and management accountant. Nothing escaped his professional eye – he could see and sense trouble long before anyone else. His knowledge of the oil industry also gave me immediate access to expert advice when in 1979 the world experienced the second sudden oil price increase.[66]

Denis Thatcher – he of the golf-club bar and the tinctures, the ferocious right-wing views – has been projected as a sort of Surrey Pooter. That he was a great deal more was shown by the substantial fortune that awaited his wife when she quit politics. Denis Thatcher, indeed, was an oilman. His family firm was bought out in 1965 by Burmah; he was a director of Burmah, and an active one, driving daily to company headquarters at Swindon in his Rolls-Royce until 1975.[67] The fact that Mr Thatcher had shared collective responsibility for this industrial catastrophe, and the resulting capitulation to a 'socialist' government, was unobserved by the political commentators who covered his wife's unexpected victory in the Conservative Party's leadership contest on 11 February 1975.[68]

Bringing up BNOC

For several of Corti and Frazer's interviewees it was the Burmah crisis which turned BNOC from a shadow into a real concern. Shortly afterwards London and Scottish Marine Oil (LASMO) and Scottish and Canadian Oil Trading (SCOT) were in negotiations with government, and got short-term guarantees. Chevron and Tricentrol followed them in conceding.

The system of oil options was now in place. Whether the government's anticipation of the future was accurate was another matter, as the *Sunday Times* reported on 25 January 1976:

What really worries the government, as opposed to what it complains about, is the likelihood of a world oil shortage in the 1980s with the

Iranians and even the Russians running short and the US still importing heavily. Nobody wants then to find that Esso has contracted all its North Sea oil to an overseas refinery. The options should give the underlying security.[69]

Opponents of the sort of participation proposed were more worried that the price of oil might instead fall, leaving the government and taxpayer with expensive investment in a depreciating asset. But the underlying motive of participation was broadly accepted:

Oilmen have said that once they were satisfied that the intention was to have a true market price then the monetary effects of participation did indeed look like being truly neutral as far as the investors were concerned.[70]

One example of a participation agreement involved Tricentrol's stake in the Thistle field:

The participation agreement provides the Government with nominal title to 51 per cent of Tricentrol's stake in Thistle and an option to purchase 51 per cent of Tricentrol's share of the Thistle oil at market price as soon as production starts. It also gives the Government 51 per cent of Tricentrol's vote on the Thistle Operating Committee.

BNOC set out with a stake in the Thistle, Dunlin, Hutton and Brae fields, as well as Burmah's North Sea interests. It had four main functions: to manage its shareholding in the oil business; to use its supplies of petroleum; to give the government experience in controlling the oil resource, so that its calculations and judgements would be informed (its experience, for example, could be used to assess companies' claims of offshore expenditure to set against tax); and finally, to give expert advice to government. As well as this, it was to move business in the direction of British onshore suppliers, and, by establishing its head office in Glasgow, it was to demonstrate sensitivity to the Scottish issue. It was only in February 1978, when the Thistle field came on stream, that it started selling its oil to the companies.[71]

Eric Varley's successor, Tony Benn, would have preferred

outright nationalization along the (very successful) lines of British Gas. At BNOC, Kearton's board personified the consensus politics of the 1970s. His managing director, Alastair Morton, would later go on to manage the Channel Tunnel. Benn had insisted on the trade unionist Lord Briginshaw; Scottish opinion was to be mollified by the appointment of Ian Clark, after his Shetland success, and the Engineers' union leader Gavin Laird, who had come a long way from his early days as a Young Communist in Clydebank.

On 6 January 1977 BNOC finally reached a participation agreement with Shell and Esso. This was a particularly strenuous negotiation. Jim Garvin of Esso and Peter Baxendell of Shell were very tough, Garvin particularly. Esso's reason was hostility to Benn, which seemed to have persisted from a meeting in the autumn of 1975 at the Department of Energy between Jim Dean of Esso, Baxendell of Shell and Tony Benn. The majors had then deployed the gambit of using US anti-trust legislation against the partnership with BNOC. This didn't work with the politician who was, of all his colleagues, best informed on American administration:

The Secretary of State very quietly came back on the lines that it was news to him that US legislation concerns of Congress ran as writ in Britain and that Britain had lost its sovereignty.[72]

Ultimately Esso was offered a compromise position: it could keep the oil as long as it was refined in the UK. According to the *Financial Times*, this would leave BNOC effectively with only 30 per cent of the oil. But the agreement would also give the Secretary of State a *force majeure* clause enabling him to override the detailed participation provisions. Clause-by-clause negotiations covered eighty to a hundred pages of text, occupied sessions which lasted beyond midnight, and were particularly complicated concerning fields with multiple partnerships. Kearton, sixty-five in 1977, was satisfied with participation terms, and deeply unpopular with companies who regarded him as a gamekeeper turned poacher. Yet his had been an essential appointment, and came almost to be romanticized in retrospect by such tough opponents as Swede Nelson of Chevron and Jack Reynolds of Conoco.[73]

A dissident was the Texas freebooter T. Boone Pickens, who had announced his acquisition of the Mesa field, the Beatrice (named after his wife), by buzzing Balmoral Castle. Confronted with BNOC and the unappetizing prospect of 'participation', Pickens sold the field to them in 1978. For a man to whom life was the driving of hard bargains, BNOC and its elderly chairman appear to have been too much:

He was crusty and sometimes amusing, but I had the feeling he would screw you to the wall if he got the chance. Kearton was, to use a phrase from 'L'il Abner', 'an inside guy at the skunk works'.

Pickens sold out for $1 a barrel, a profit of $31.2 million: 'We had just sold our interest in the biggest oilfield we had ever found at a wholesale price.'[74]

BNOC was not the nationalized hydrocarbons corporation that the left had wanted, but in its participation and information role it became increasingly formidable. Through discretionary powers, it became effectively an extension of the ministry – what would later be known as an agency – which remedied the earlier deficiencies of the Petroleum Department.[75] To Funkhouser, in mid-1978,

Perhaps even more important than its crude control, BNOC's brainpower was compounding at a faster rate than even its manpower. Soon, no oil company in the west would be able to match its intellectual background, compiled from the accumulated knowledge of all its partners in the North Sea.[76]

With over 1,000 employees – 450 in Glasgow, 350 in London, 250 abroad or offshore – BNOC was formidable. Nor did there seem, to most observers, much sign of the Tories abandoning it, should they be elected; particularly after the escalation in prices in late 1978 transformed its initial losses into formidable profits: £309 million in 1980 alone.[77]

Citizen Benn

18 June, 1975: To Tower Pier on the Thames for the first landing of North Sea Oil . . . we boarded the hydrofoil for the Isle of Grain. On board we found a complete cross-section of the international capitalist and Tory establishment and their wives – Fred Hamilton of Hamilton Oil, Sir Mark Turner, Deputy-Chairman of RTZ, Elliot Richardson, Ronnie Spiers, the American Minister and Vere Harmsworth from the filthy *Daily Mail.* I was so glad Caroline was there to talk to.[78]

At the beginning of 1976 his American wife Caroline gave Tony Benn, the British Energy minister, a copy of Karl Marx's *The Communist Manifesto.* There were two remarkable things about this. First, that Benn took the young Marx's rather jejune declarations seriously, in an age in which Marxism meant Althusser or Habermas or at least Gramsci; second, that he had never read it before.

In the following decade Benn would become the bogeyman of British politics; despite his wit, lucidity and unfailing courtesy, the press – centre as much as right-wing – made him into a monster only slightly less repellent than Ghadafi and Khomeini. But the point about Benn was that he was not a Marxist, but a radical patriot in the style of Stafford Cripps – whose grandson was in fact his political adviser.

The Energy portfolio did not imply promotion for Tony Benn, appointed to it by Harold Wilson a week before the Isle of Grain ceremony. Since February 1974 Benn had been in charge of the Department of Trade and Industry, to which, not long before, Energy had belonged. As Minister of Technology in the 1966–70 Labour government he had been identified with an essentially capitalistic reconstruction of British manufacturing, seeking to create large units which would be competitive in Europe. Subsequently, no one had swung further against this. Benn had become the advocate both of workers' control and of economic nationalism. Within the Wilson government he had taken the lead in opposing the Common Market, and had won most of the Labour Party rank-and-file to his position.

In deference to this grass-roots militancy, Harold Wilson made two constitutional innovations which, in any context other than the convulsions and inflation of the mid-1970s, would have seemed revolutionary. The country's entry into the EEC would be sealed by a referendum, the first ever sanctioned by Parliament, and in debating Europe Cabinet members would not be tied by the convention of unanimity. Benn led the 'anti' camp, and was defeated on 5 June 1975. His demotion to Energy, and replacement by Varley, followed.

Almost immediately Benn found himself involved in the Committee Stage of the Petroleum bill, and in the North Sea Re-negotiation Committee. In these Varley had played only a marginal role, leaving matters to Lever and Dell, Balogh and John Smith, along with the senior civil servants Jack Rampton, Leo Pliatzky, Kenneth Berrill and John Liverman. Dell had now shifted against participation by a state oil corporation, but the others were uncommitted:

Leo Pliatzky said, 'There is no financial gain in this either way. We want control, especially in an emergency, a public sector capability and a seat on the operating consortium. How much oil do we need for that?'[79]

The slate of problems was to remain constant during Benn's tenure. Balogh and Berrill were preoccupied with relations with the EC and the extent to which a European fuel policy could intervene in the North Sea. The other issue was the extent of government control of its own oil interests. Sir Eric Drake of BP was deeply hostile to the government exercising ownership rights through the Burmah shares which had been purchased by the Bank of England. Benn decided against giving him the chairmanship of BNOC; he was also suspicious that Dell and Lever were both fundamentally taking the oil companies' line.

Noises from the United States were also ominous. On 1 August Benn received a visit from the American Ambassador, Elliott Richardson, which made him uncomfortably aware just how closely Washington was paying attention. Richardson voiced concerns expressed by US companies over changes in licences, the control of development, provisions for compensation, and any slowing of extraction. He stressed the need to keep up the pace of development, and to maintain the traditional international law demarcations, which had always favoured the United States. Were its majors, for example, to be forced into buying British equipment? When Benn pointed out that British offshore boats could not be used around US coasts, this was news to Richardson.[80]

Benn's initial objective was to strengthen the chief of BNOC. Kearton, candidate number forty-six (he said) for the post, had been former managing director of the textile and artificial fibre manufacturers Courtaulds. Courtaulds had never been in the state sector, and Kearton called himself a Tory, yet the company represented that 'Butskellite' centrist approach to British industrial policy which had featured prominently in the 1950s. Butler himself had married into the family.

When, on 27 October 1975, Benn saw Kearton, the experience was sobering:

He apparently went to see Harold Lever and Edmund Dell when he was first appointed because the PM had led him to believe it was a real job. They said, 'Oh the petroleum revenue tax is getting us all we need, you don't really need to bother.' Harold Lever more or less indicated that he shouldn't take the job too seriously.

The same line was taken by the US government and the oil companies. With oil concessions tied up under the Varley memorandum for seven to ten years they assumed that 'we would only get the residual oil'. Benn, on the other hand, wanted 25 per cent participation by Shell, Exxon and BP, 'with no pledge on petroleum revenue tax or future policy'. He set up a BNOC organization committee with Balogh, Richard Briginshaw and some bright young men – including Martin Lovegrove, the acknowledged expert on the technology and economics of oil extraction, and a Labour Party member, and the battle started, company by company, to determine the level of UK state participation.[81]

Benn made a disconcertingly positive impression on the oil companies: 'open, courteous, funny, sure-footed, and one of God's gifts to easy communication', according to Ingham, he had his doubts about the overall direction of government policy. What had been achieved in participation was 'a fraudulent scheme, all done by mirrors', which by itself was nugatory.[82] This judgement was borne out by Funkhouser:

Above all, the government position on participation was substantially eroded by early 1976. The option to buy 51 per cent of a company's production at market prices was a long way from a demand for 51 per cent of equity. Finally, the Labour government was moving right in financial and economic policy without the extreme left being able to stop it.[83]

This seemed to be reflected in the overall approach of the government. A strategy conference at Chequers on 5 November showed that behind Wilson's attempts at policy co-ordination was the threat to emasculate the left. Benn concluded: 'The so-called consensus is a front for a monetarist, lame-duck policy.'[84] In moments of despondency it seemed to him that his defeat of 5 June had been bigger than he first thought: 'The Department of Energy is really a side department.' The power of the Prime Minister was still being exerted to keep him off key Cabinet committees. Yet he had to remain diplomatic and centrist, even when dealing with issues which saw his trade-union allies in the oil industry disadvantaged.[85]

Between Europe and the Sisters

On 25 January 1976 Harold Wilson summoned the directors of BP to Chequers. Benn found the Prime Minister coarse and inept:

Harold got into a long rambling metaphor about the virginity of BP, how the original marriage had not been consummated because the bride was frigid and how rape was involved – how would they cope with a more randy customer, in the person of Frank Kearton? It was vulgar and thoroughly embarrassing.[86]

The point at issue was whether BNOC and BP could be effectively integrated. Kearton argued that without BP co-operation it would take BNOC between twelve and fifteen years to develop. Wilson was willing to press on BP the formation of a North Sea subsidiary which could deal with BNOC.

I said there are several options. We can do nothing; or have a BNOC takeover, which I think we should rule out; we can go for minimum consultation; a middle way in which we can set up a subsidiary; or we could set up a partnership between BP UK and BNOC which I think is the best option.[87]

Neither this, nor government attempts to stop gas being flared off from the Forties field, got anywhere. Benn found Kearton subdued, 'because BNOC is so weak and there was no indication of support from the PM'. Esso, deeply aggressive, had to be handled with extreme tact.[88] After the BP negotiations in June 1976, Shell and Exxon turned up in October. Benn put a brave face on this at the American Embassy in September:

I described our oil policy, how it was preferred by the oil companies to confiscation in OPEC or divestition, and I joked about Henry VIII taking a 51 per cent participation in the Vatican and setting up the British Episcopal Corporation which became the Church of England. They laughed at this.[89]

They laughed even more when the government was forced in December by the IMF's terms to sell 17 per cent of its BP shares. This was done in May 1977. In January 1977 Benn was more sanguine. He flew to the Orkneys with Armand Hammer. In the aircraft the old man handed round biographies to everyone, and endeared himself to the minister ('He's a historical figure, very charming, extremely modest. Angry about rearmament') with reminiscences of his father, a De Leonite socialist in New York, and Lenin, with whom he began trading during the Russian civil war. Lenin had told him communism was no good, hence the 'capitalist' input of such as Hammer into the New Economic Policy: Hammer built a pencil factory then, and still kept up links with Brezhnev, whom he said he admired. Benn was impressed; he was also satisfied with the outcome:

The whole thing, if you include the Piper and Claymore fields, has cost $1.3 billion, which in current prices would be about £600 million, and they will get their money back in two years, and we'll get 70 or 75 per cent of it through the PRT.[90]

Hammer being legendarily adept at telling politicians what they wanted to hear, his Lenin reminiscences went down well. In his memoirs he was respectful about Benn and – unsurprisingly – ecstatic about 'that majestic lady', Mrs Thatcher.[91]

Benn's next fight in Cabinet was in a sense foredoomed by the sterling crisis of late 1976, and the deflationary policy then adopted at the behest of the IMF. The creation of a dedicated North Sea Oil Fund at Cabinet had figured in the manifestos of all the parties in the 1974 election. In early 1978 the Cabinet Office, with its own views well signposted, produced a for/against paper, tabled on 16 February. Benn favoured what he regarded as a minimal project: a fund of £5 billion rising to absorb 50 per cent of oil revenues, which would issue an annual report on their specific allocation. Even this would only account for 2 per cent of public expenditure. A committee consisting of Peter Shore, Bruce Millan, Harold Lever and Joel Barnett were instructed to report. On 16 February, in full Cabinet, Barnett, Varley, Rodgers and Lever were hostile, the latter favouring tax cuts only. David Owen, the Foreign Secretary, earlier favourable, changed his mind:

Michael Foot suggested we discuss it with the party first. Someone said you couldn't discuss it with the party until you had a clear view. In the end it was agreed that there would be a party meeting to explain why there couldn't be a fund.

So that is the end of the saga of the oil revenues. They are now a part of the general public expenditure. Now that we have got money, we are doing a sort of IMF in reverse. We are not putting it into capital expenditure or public investment of one kind or another; we are going to give it away in tax cuts. That is the measure of the Labour government.[92]

The White Paper, 'The Challenge of North Sea Oil', which came out on 23 March 1978, recommended tax cuts, increases in public expenditure, and specific funding for education and training. There would be an annual report on the use of North Sea revenues, but no separate fund:

55. After much consideration the Government have concluded that it is not practicable to do things in this way. The difference is between attempting a prior allocation (which is what a fund implies) and rendering an account of how the North Sea resources have helped the nation to achieve its economic objectives.[93]

To add insult to injury, in July the Cabinet sanctioned expenditure cuts in breach of even the generalized assurances of 'The Challenge of North Sea Oil'.[94]

But most wearing and troublesome of all was the attitude of Benn's old enemy in Brussels. Benn had opposed entry to the EC from a self-avowedly socialist position, not far from that of the Norwegians. Entry meant a surrender of control over industrial and energy planning. He shared this position with Kearton, who in conversation in 1976 argued that

There is a minority in the CBI and a growing minority in favour of protection. We have got to protect the country . . . There is one problem. Upper management have suffered a 30 per cent fall in their standard of living and they are worried. If you could get management with you, then you could ignore the shareholders. As for the City of London, they are rolling in money and doing absolutely nothing about it.[95]

The European Community presented itself to the Secretary of

State in two guises, neither of them construed as friendly. First, it was the defender of free-market policies, which took particular exception to Britain's attempts to subsidize its oil-related industry. In 1975 Benn flew to Luxembourg over this issue, and was unimpressed. Over time, his concern at interference grew:

We [Benn and Raymond Vouel, the Commissioner for Competition] again discussed the interest relief grant scheme, which the Commission is trying to stop. The scheme allows firms in Scotland to borrow money slightly below the going rate for equipment for the North Sea oil industry . . . I went over the arguments, particularly in relation to the severe unemployment in Scotland, but he just went on about the Treaty being against discrimination, and so on. I felt we were a prisoner of this Treaty theology.[96]

In the summer of 1977 news came in that the European Community was offering subsidies for drilling in the seas around Rockall, without ministerial consultation. With conciliatory intent, but a similar lack of finesse, it had offered to invest in BNOC. The Secretary of State was scandalized:

The thing is outrageous, and this is how the Commission is eating and eating away at independent control of our oil resources.[97]

The dispute over subsidies to oil equipment manufacture dragged on, and the appointment of Roy Jenkins as President of the Commission in 1976 did nothing to help matters. In fact, in Benn's eyes, it made them worse:

Vouel wanted to reduce our capacity to produce platforms and North Sea equipment, and he was not prepared to make any concession on EEC components. It all came out. Commissioner Etienne d'Avignon had complained that we were violating the free movement of goods, and Roy Jenkins had demanded an inquiry into our oil policy. This is clearly a major attack on our energy policy . . .[98]

In March 1979, shortly before the general election, the Commission finally banned the UK's interest reliefs, giving the Energy Department two months to amend the scheme on pain of referral to the European Court of Justice for prosecution. Benn offered to extend the scheme to companies from other EC countries at 50 per cent of the UK subsidy rate, but without effect. Not content with this, the Commission went further, investigating the UK's insistence that all oil be landed in its territory.[99]

The impression that Benn gained, early on in his tenure, was accurate. Dealing with the oil companies was a form of diplomacy. The Department of Energy had in fact waxed into the sort of importance that it had held, for all the wrong reasons, in the 1960s, because of the Rhodesian issue. Its concerns overlapped more than ever with those of the Foreign Office and the Department of Trade and Industry. But the problem was that both of these were firmly in the hands of the pro-European right wing, David Owen in the Foreign Office and John Smith in Trade. And (although conservative Americans feared his suspected links through his wife with the Carter administration) foreign affairs was not an area in which Benn had either expertise or inclination.[100]

Benn's one plausible break-out could have been through negotiations with Norway, to enable the two North Sea oil powers to act as negotiators between the OPEC and OECD countries. Such a strategy was outlined by Oystein Noreng, Professor at the Oslo Institute of Business Administration, who had been a senior planner in the Norwegian Ministry of Finance and Resources and planning manager of Statoil:

These kinds of concessions mean that the OECD countries would have to accept a greater OPEC presence in their own economies, and in economic, finance and trade policy take OPEC interests more explicitly into account. This might seem to be a tough bargain, but something along these lines is probably necessary to induce the oil exporters to accept an agreement that in essence implies relinquishing the oil weapon.[101]

Towards the end of 1978, there were indications that such a positive policy might be possible. 'Oilgate' – the revelations about the intrigues of the Foreign Office and the then Ministry of Power about Rhodesian sanctions – discredited both ministries and left the initiative with Benn. In February 1979 Benn got his way on oil flaring, after furious protests from BP. It was to be cut to 45 per cent. In this way he was moving policy closer to the Norwegian norm on control and depletion. On 28 February he met Zaki Yamani at Yamani's country house at Windlesham, and the two got on well; Yamani wanted a reformist Mossadeq-type government in Iran.[102] But there was no chance of further collaboration. The next day the devolution referendum flopped and the Callaghan government fell apart. The Offshore Operators rapidly offered their co-operation to the new government, and measures previously judged abhorrent became negotiable. A representative explained their change of tone to the *Financial Times North Sea Newsletter* with disarming candour: 'Yes, we blew our trumpet rather loudly, to help bring down the house of Benn.'[103]

Conviction Politics

Went for a long walk with Melissa and visited Westminster Abbey, the first time M has been inside. Of course the whole of Westminster is my village. That's where I was born, went to school, where Father and Mother were married, where Father died and his memorial service was held, and where I work. It is a strange place, Westminster, very dull in the sense that there are no natural centres or shopping areas but I've been around there for fifty years.[104]

Above Tony Benn's collection of miners' lamps and Labour posters is hung an RAF crest. His father, Viscount Stansgate, was Air minister; his brother was shot down and killed in the war. It is important to remember this: the man was closer to being a revolutionary patriot of the Cromwellian sort than any sort of scientific socialist. In this militant nonconformity, his politics of conviction seemed close to those of Mrs Thatcher. Both talked about 'securing a change of ownership in favour of working people'; both distrusted the liberal intelligentsia, Europe and the Common Market; both talked much, and without embarrassment, about 'Britain'. But there the resemblance ended. Benn's utopia was collective: working people should be given control of their industries; all Thatcher wanted to do was to 'liberate the individual' (if necessary with public subsidy), and dismantle those aspects of the state which might enforce collectivism.

Both were figures beloved their parties' rank and file. Where Benn failed was in overestimating the capability of his own brethren; the commitment of trade unionists to self-discipline, real democracy, and an open, experimental style of decision-making. The trade union élite tended both to be authoritarian and to have goals which were as individualistic as anything the Tories applauded at their conferences. Thatcher could count on the fact that divisions *within* the working class were greater than its solidarity; and that, since families *in work* were now usually taxpayers, they would be disinclined to make sacrifices for their poorer brethren.

Benn regarded the shift to Energy as a demotion, but he performed remarkably effectively. According to Dell, inevitably hostile, 'the unobjectionable Varley' was the loser by the exchange.[105] However, he was still inhibited by three factors. The first was the continuing imbroglio over atomic energy, where he could not rid himself of earlier commitments, which in turn isolated him from the environmental lobby. The second was the small size of the petroleum branch of the department, and its nearness to the oil industry, which meant that its belief in a limited life for the province and the likelihood of price decline – and thus in the imperative of rapid extraction – could not be budged. Finally, the Energy Department was prospectively an earner, not a supplicant for government funds – *but not yet*. And expenditure departments, then as ever, found it difficult to make common cause against the supply departments, which were in the hands of the Labour right.

The oil story up to 1979 showed that, for high wages, or simply to be in work, workers were prepared to sacrifice certain of the things they had earlier struggled for: trade unionism, strict safety regulation, socially tolerable working hours. Benn's blend of Fabianism and 'Marxism' (a disturbingly potent mixture) ostensibly seemed to suggest that once a certain level of intervention had been achieved, the economic structure would be ratcheted on to 'full' socialism. Funkhouser, representative enough of American conservative opinion, agreed with the persuasiveness of this, and advised Texas Eastern to get on good terms with BNOC. Thatcher, in 1978, was at best an each-way bet.[106]

Thatcher's economic ideology – culled from a few apophthegms of Milton Friedman – was as simple-minded as Benn's and in practice probably more disastrous.[107] But she saw the potent psychological combination of high-wage 'enterprise' and low welfare – the 'authoritarian individualism' projected by the militarized command structures on every oil platform – even if she only stumbled on this prototype by chance. In a forgettable movie of 1979, *North Sea Hijack*, Thatcher orders a commando group led by Roger Moore to re-take a production platform captured by international terrorists. This they do, with the usual bloodbath. There was a factual parallel to this in June 1982, when the British re-took a collection of desolate islands in the South Atlantic (owned, ironically, by Coalite, the company of which Eric Varley would shortly become chief). The Falkland Islands had 1,200 civilians (later guarded by troops), 700,000 sheep and no oil (although offshore fields were recurrently hypothesized). But the battle for them won Mrs Thatcher the 1983 election.

7

The Mature Province

My people think money
And talk weather. Oil rigs lull their future
On single acquisitive stems. Silence
Has shoaled into the trawlers' echo-sounders.

The ground we kept our ear to for so long
Is flayed or calloused, and its entrails
Tented by an impious augury.
Our isle is full of comfortless noises.

Seamus Heaney, 'Sybil'[1]

Downstream All the Way

In 1970 the tiny port of St Davids, on the Fife coast about three miles east of the Forth Bridge, seemed still trapped in an enchantment of decay. As late as the Second World War, horses had shunted antique railway wagons here which had come down by the Fordell Railway, an eighteenth-century fossil which had survived until 1946, from the days when Scots colliers were serfs. The Earls of Buckinghamshire, and the Lord Hobart who gave his name to both the capital of Tasmania and the headquarters of the National Coal Board, had once ridden to their mansion, four miles inland, in a private carriage attached to the coal trains. The era of such domestic energy sheikhs was long drawn out, but now over. The Earl of Buckinghamshire was famous for being 'the working-class peer', a corporation gardener in somewhere like Eastbourne, Fordell House was a ruin, at the coast the stables

Before the storm: the Belfast-built BP *Sea Quest* fitting out at Queen's Island in 1967, one of the very few rigs to be built and owned in Britain.

The rig *Ocean Prince*, built for the Burmah Oil Company, being launched on 29 July 1965 at Teesside.

The same vessel breaking up in hurricane conditions less than three years later on the Dogger Bank.

A roughneck positioning a drill on the rig *Mr Cap* in 1965: the classic image of the pre-high-technology oil industry.

A pipe-laying catamaran barge, *Chocktaw*, which laid the Ekofisk pipes to Teesside for oil and to Emden for gas.

The jacket for Forties One being towed north from the Greythorpe yard at Teesside in 1972. This weighed over 20,000 tons and was 460 feet high.

The Heather Platform, opened in 1984, standing in 470 feet. This was a middle-sized field with 107 million barrels, an outlier to the Ninian field, pumping oil via a pipeline to Sullom Voe, and gas to St Fergus. In 1992 only 9 million barrels remained.

'As I told Lenin': Energy minister Tony Benn, Joe Grimond and Armand
Hammer at the opening of the Flotta terminal in 1977.

Prime Minister James Callaghan thanking God for the bounty of North Sea
oil, on the Forties field in 1977.

Red Adair arrives to cap the Ekofisk blowout, 29 April 1977.

Tender dousing the Ekofisk blowout.

The Norwegian 'flotel' *Henryk Ibsen*. A 'Pentagon' rig with hotel accommodation erected on the deck. Norwegian platforms were not allowed to accommodate more than 200; so such vessels were anchored next to them, and linked up by gantries. The *Alexander Kielland* lost one of its legs in a storm on 27 March 1980 on the Statfjord field, and capsized. 123 men drowned.

The oil terminal at Sullom Voe under construction in 1977.

One module with the platform's flare-boom: all that was left of Occidental's Piper Alpha platform on the morning of 9 July 1988.

'It's no' fish ye're buying, it's men's lives': survivors are landed at Aberdeen from Piper Alpha.

and offices were overgrown, the harbour silted up. You could still find old wagons sprouting in the woods, and the stone blocks which had carried the track underlay the farm road it had now become, to send the cyclist flying.

This backwater, which despite its nearness to Edinburgh was almost more withdrawn from the modern world than Sullom Voe, was to undergo an almost total upheaval and become one of the relatively few continuing industrial landmarks created by North Sea oil. The Fordell area would be transformed by 1985 into the ethylene plant at Moss Morran in Fife and its marine terminal. And over the next decade much of rural Britain would bear the mark of its products, in the fragments of plastic bags and sacks and insulation and packaging which lodged themselves in every hedge, cluttered every foreshore.

Moss Morran was 'downstream', meaning a project which utilized the North Sea oil and gas for industrial purposes, and 'downstream' became increasingly salient as the oil came ashore in greater and greater quantities, at the same time as Britain's industrial situation worsened and unemployment increased. The year 1977 was the first in which really large amounts of oil – 38.3 million tons of it – were produced; this was just under half the country's demand, of 92.8 million tons. Gas output almost matched national needs, at 35.8 million tons oil equivalent. In 1978 it was 54, in 1979 nearly 78, and in 1980 80.5 million tons, almost exactly equal to demand. Gas production was virtually static, while demand for it rose from almost 37 to almost 42 million tons. The value of North Sea output, however, increased spectacularly, thanks to the Iranian-inspired price hike; £2,226 million in 1977, it had hit £8,851 million in 1980, a fourfold increase in sales income.[2] The horrors of 1976, which had led to the intervention of the International Monetary Fund and a major government crisis, evaporated with remarkable rapidity, causing several ministers to think that they had been diddled all along by the Treasury.

There was still uncertainty about strategy, as in the period after 1976 the government began to take energy conservation seriously and, for the first time, subject industrial projections to open analysis.[3] The Royal Commission on Environmental Pollution was set up in September 1976. Wriggling free of his now-regretted nuclear commitments, after ordering two advanced gas-cooled reactors, Tony Benn set up an Energy Commission, with twenty-two members, in June 1977, to do some brainstorming about future energy policy. All the major fuel contractors and the relevant unions were represented, but oil had representatives from BNOC and the Petroleum Industry Advisory Committee, not the Offshore Operators' Association who – with some justification – felt outraged.[4]

Openness to an energy policy meant, however, a more restrained attitude to the rate of oil extraction. In October 1977 Tony Benn took on the oil companies' *bête noire* Professor Peter Odell, now attached to the Erasmus University in Rotterdam, as an energy consultant to the ministry. In late 1978 he was to come up with a plan for oil which involved an increased rate of extraction coupled with investment in downstream capacity, refineries, petro-chemical plants, and competitors for BNOC in the shape of new private companies. Benn was not enthusiastic. Odell 'didn't do well' in sustaining his thesis that the reserves were much larger than the companies had claimed; and his advocacy of accelerated exploitation was at odds with Benn's desire to award only a few blocks in the fifth, 1976–7, round as a means of enforcing a measure of depletion control and of protecting BNOC until it was up and running.[5] But the Callaghan government permitted itself a brief triumphal moment with its White Paper, *The Challenge of North Sea Oil*, in March 1978.

The musical chair might look increasingly attractive, but 1977 also showed the other face of the oil business. On 22 April drillers on the Ekofisk Bravo platform put on a blowout preventer upside down, and the riser pipe blew out, spilling 3,000 tons a day – Norwegian, admittedly, but no less pollutant for that – into the sea. Mercifully, the torrent of oil and mud did not catch fire, and all the crew got away in their dinghies. The imperturbable and (by Texan standards) courtly Red Adair – well known

beforehand as he had been played by John Wayne in *Hellfighters* –
along with Boots Hansen became folk heroes for their skill in
capping the well after a week, but not before 22,500 tons of oil
had spread out over 900 square miles of the sea.[6]

Onshore, however, the good times were only beginning to roll
for some. The shift from exploration to production altered the
pattern of economic activity within the industry. The province
belonged to Britain, but the Scottish Office was allowed to
calculate its associated activities. It worked out that in 1977 oil-
related firms generated £518 million, or 4.8 per cent of Scottish
GDP. It estimated total economic effect as the result of a 'multi-
plier' of about 1.5, which gave £738.5 million. Of this total, 24
per cent went to manufacturing, 45 per cent to oil-related services,
18 per cent to platform and module construction, and 11 per cent
to wages for offshore work.

Numbers employed in the oil industry totalled 27,000 in 1976;
the figure would rise to 61,000 in 1982, 63,292 in 1983. The oil-
related economy registered 20 per cent annual growth for three
years after 1976, but thereafter it tended to tail off. Almost three-
quarters – 73 per cent – of the jobs it created were in Grampian
Region, centred in Aberdeen; here were the shore bases, the
transport and administration offices, the warehouses. Twelve per
cent were in Highland, mainly the big platform yards around the
Cromarty Firth, with outliers in Kishorn, Orkney, Shetland and
the Western Isles. Only 4 per cent of the new jobs had been
created in Strathclyde, mainly at the platform yard at Ardyne,
near Dunoon. On the platforms and rigs, 60 per cent of the
workers came from Scotland, 33 per cent from England; 26 per
cent came from Grampian, but only 14 per cent from
Strathclyde.[7]

The quantitative growth appeared formidable, until seen in
certain other contexts. Oil had been consuming about 25 per cent
of new capital investment, and yet the yields from it in job
terms, after the construction phase, were minimal; already,
platform-building yards, their orders fulfilled, were being put on
a care-and-maintenance basis. Moreover, there appeared to be no

connection between advanced technology and job creation. That the former could actually militate *against* employment was seen in the 1979 battle between BP and the other majors, who wanted sea-bed 'templates' – remote-controlled pumping stations – and the Department of Energy which, for employment reasons, favoured platforms. The South-East Forties field was developed by BP, under pressure from BNOC, with platforms, but BP was plainly none too happy about it. Nor was there much comfort from the export market. The same 1977 Scottish Office survey showed that 14 per cent of oil-related activity was geared to overseas markets (Norway took 14 per cent of such exports, Europe 24 per cent, and the rest of the world 21 per cent). But the total value added by these exports was only £50 million.

The hope had been that the bounty of the North Sea could be converted into profitable downstream developments, refineries and chemical plants. But this depended either on factors beyond the control of any British government, or on government policies which could be in themselves antithetical to the oil industry. Conservation measures taken since the crisis of 1973 meant that there had been a fall in the demand for oil: down from nearly 95 to 80 million tons. The amount of oil required per unit of GDP had decreased by 26 per cent. The unexpected increase in the oil price after 1978 seemed a windfall, but after 1978 the petro-pound started to increase in value (by 1983 the exchange rate was 36 per cent up on 1976), and this lessened the prospects for exports in general. Added to this was the fact that the OPEC countries had steadily been investing in refineries during the 1970s, with the object of exporting refined products rather than crude. The result was that there was now an overcapacity, especially in Europe.

Far from the North Sea boosting the British refining industry, the opposite was the case. In 1938 refining capacity was only 1.9 million tons, but this grew to 11.5 million in 1950. In 1970 it stood at 112 million tons, with twenty-three refineries. In 1980 £400 million was invested, which took British refining capacity to its peak of nearly 132 million tons.[8] Utilization, however, remained well below this level. From the start, this level. From the start, the oil companies had known that the low-sulphur 'light crude' of the North Sea was not as satisfactory a refinery feedstock as the heavy crude of the Middle East. There was pressure for more gasoline refining to be based in Britain, but such was the international overcapacity that BP's Grangemouth plant was the only one to be expanded in this direction.

As raw material for petrochemicals, the gas of the field was much more attractive. But even this had its difficulties, as was shown by the story of the one major new project undertaken, the ethylene and polypropylene plant constructed by Shell and Esso. In 1977, after building their gas pipeline to its landfall at St Fergus, the companies proposed a chemical plant for Peterhead, but two years later sited it instead at Moss Morran. Gas would be piped to the plant from St Fergus, and the refined ethylene and polypropylene (used in the manufacture of polythene and poly-urethane) would be pumped to a sea terminal at Dalgety Bay, next to St Davids.

Moss Morran may have been desolate, but Dalgety Bay had been developed as a commuter suburb for Dunfermline and Edinburgh and its well-heeled inhabitants were unenthusiastic about being close to the sort of substances which in 1972 had blown a Spanish town apart, killing 200 people. The planning process was fiercely contested.[9] Nevertheless it got through — as ever, in Scotland, the promise of jobs proved the clincher. Construction work started in 1979 and was completed on 16 November 1984, six months ahead of target and 5 per cent under budget.[10] By 1987 it was producing over three million tons a year; but the total staff was only 700. A study commissioned by the firms reported in 1990 that a further 1,500 jobs had been created, 620 of them in Fife, but only 140 of these were in manufacture.[11] So much for the 6,000 jobs promised when the site was first designated in 1977.[12]

At least Moss Morran meant expansion. Elsewhere the opposite was the case. Britain's twenty-three refineries in 1970 were down to twenty-one in 1980, and there were only thirteen in 1990; capacity peaked at 132 million tons in 1980 and had fallen to 92 million by

1990. Particularly drastic was the reduction in British-owned capacity: Shell's was down from 30 million tons in 1970 to 17.5 million in 1990; BP's even more drastic, from 26.5 million down to 8.8 million.[13] American companies now owned 43 per cent of British capacity. Downstream development in fact became a mirage, consuming 'enormous amounts of regional aid' at Grangemouth and Moss Morran, but providing few jobs and, worse, diverting resources from projects which might provide them:

In the first quarter of 1982, Shell and Esso at Moss Morran were paid £19 million in Regional Development Grant, and BP at Grangemouth over £2 million. Along with the BP development at Lerwick, which attracted an astonishing £92 million, these oil and petrochemical projects accounted for 61 per cent of total UK Regional Development Grant Payments in that quarter.[14]

Nor were matters much better on the oil industry supplies front. In 1980, on quitting the Offshore Supplies Office to return to merchant banking, its former director-general Norman Smith was bitterly critical of British industry:

The UK's worst record is probably in marine activities requiring very large capital investment – drilling rigs, dual-purpose diving support vessels, heavy lift and pipelaying vessels, for example.[15]

As reasons, Smith cited the lack of risk capital for large projects in markets which were seen as volatile; and too many 'conglomerate entrants' moving from the City into the market who lacked the understanding to adjust with the speed required. There were not enough well-financed medium-sized contractors, and far too many undercapitalized market entrants. This made it difficult to compete with established American firms, while persistent industrial relations problems resulted in time slippages and cost overruns.

Thus far, Smith's indictment would have got broad support in Scotland, but he went on to claim that the OSO itself had suffered from a politically inspired division of its base. The result was too much time being spent commuting between London and

Glasgow, servicing a devolved operation which was too small to be self-sustaining and too large to be ignored. Much the same sort of thing was being said about BNOC. In the efforts of Whitehall to buy off the Scots, always stopping short of giving them real control over oil resources, the advantages of devolution were being lost, while the Scots failed to see any perspicacity resulting from the centralization of power in London. With reason, if the example of Norway were to be invoked.

Statoil

It stood in the middle of the Oslofjord, unavoidable, as if something from the world of H.G. Wells had stalked into the city of his tormented contemporary, Henrik Ibsen. It was visible from practically every angle, at the end of those frenchified streets which dropped down to the harbour from the Royal Palace, from Vigeland's writhing nudes on his fountain in the park. It was a drilling-rig for the Statfjord field, possession of the Royal Norwegian Government's newly created Statoil Corporation.[16]

Statoil was based at Stavanger, five hours from Oslo by train. The railway line had only been completed in 1957, the year in which King Haakon died, the first monarch of the country, independent – at last! – from Sweden in 1905. Fifteen years after 1957 Mr Arve Johnsen, a graduate of the University of Kansas who had experienced the American industry at first hand, and an assistant arrived in the town of 81,000 souls – about the size and significance of Perth – to set up the business; a decade later, 16,000 out of a population now grown to 191,000 would live by oil.

Norway had always lived by the sea, anyway. The cultivable area was 3 per cent and as late as the 1960s the journey from south to north could only be made by steamer, so frequently was the road system breached by fjords and apparently impassable mountains.

In the nineteenth century, chiefly by dint of buying sailing-ships from the British as the latter turned over to steam, and from Americans menaced by Confederate commerce-raiding, the Norwegians had held on to their maritime business, and gradually traded up until they possessed the world's fourth-largest merchant marine. They also took a close interest in the sea *qua* oil province. Jens Evensen, Minister for Commerce and Shipping in 1974, had led the Norwegian delegation to the Law of the Sea conference at Geneva, and was an authority on international oil politics.[17] He co-operated closely with Per Keppe, the Minister of Finance, who was the former policy chief of the Labour Party and the Trade Union Federation. In their sober, poker-faced way, they came out of the division of the North Sea rather better than their British counterparts, who were too anxious to get the legal business out of the way and the exploration started. The Geneva conference's decisions theoretically applied only to depths of up to 200 metres, or 600 feet, which might have terminated Norway's sphere at the edge of the trench, up to 800 metres deep, but largely because of Britain's haste to conclude an agreement, Norway was in 1965 allowed to ignore it and extend her boundaries westwards to the point of equidistance.[18]

The result must have seemed to British ministers and civil servants, for a few nail-biting months, a diplomatic Battle of Jutland. In 1969 a rig drilling slightly east of the demarcation line with Britain struck the Ekofisk field. This was very big, a field of 2.8 billion barrels of reserves. It would be two years before the British had similar good fortune with Forties (2.5 billion) and Brent (2 billion).

The discovery, which was succeeded by several other major finds, was timely for Norway, as a large merchant fleet was not necessarily the best sort of investment to have when the oil crisis bit into the tanker market. In 1974 various fjords played host to a quarter of the tanker fleet, laid up for want of orders. This depression persuaded the Norwegian government to exploit its giant Frigg gas field, in 1972 producing half the UK's total output, and its Statfjord oilfield, discovered in February 1974, the

North Sea's biggest at 3.5 billion barrels, sooner than it had wanted to. But the bargain that Statoil made with Phillips at Ekofisk, securing 50 per cent participation, established a strong position – explicitly social-democratic in its linking of the oil to industrial acquisition and welfare extension – from which the country only retreated (temporarily, as it turned out) in the mid-1980s.[19] 'Norwegian policies,' wrote Thomas Lind and Tony Mackay admiringly in 1980, 'are less concerned with maximizing oil revenue and production, and more concerned with maximizing the benefit to Norway.'[20]

Devotees of more exciting, 1968-style socialist ideology always used to take the mickey out of the 'Royal Norwegian Labour Party', but the Norwegians thought very seriously about energy policy. They were in the fortunate position that most of their fuel bills were already covered; 40 per cent of national energy requirements were met by hydro-electric plants. The Labour government of Trygve Brattelli settled in 1970 on gradual depletion of the reserves, at 1.8 million barrels per day, six times the country's own requirements. Two years later, by a unanimous vote of the Storting, Statoil was set up.

From the beginning, the Norwegians appeared to know how much oil they wanted, and on what they intended to spend their revenues (estimated as exceeding 25 per cent of the national budget by 1980). As with Britain, they were in deficit in the mid-1970s because of the additional cost of Middle East oil and the need to import materials for their own oil programme, but they could finance this on the collateral of their subsequent oil exports. Norwegian licensing policy was, in contrast to that of Britain, ultra-cautious. By 1970 only 42 blocks had been licensed for exploration, compared with 583 in the British sector. Norway's target was 90 million tons a year by 1980, of which 75 million would be exported. Sixty rigs had been ordered by 1974, of which twenty-seven were constructed in Norwegian yards, together with five Condeep platforms and a fleet of 150 supply vessels.[21]

Statoil started out with small shares in the Frigg and Heimdal gas fields, but also half of the pipeline which connected Ekofisk to Teesside.[22] In the third licensing round in March 1975 Statoil was granted a share of between 50 and 70 per cent of all new developments. And then came the news of the possibilities offered by Statfjord. Statoil was patronized – gingerly – by the left, and opposed, half-heartedly, by the right. Even Statoil's chief competitor was state-owned: Norsk Hydro, in which the country had a 51 per cent interest. There were mistakes: a project for a 90 per cent oil tax in late 1975 which was badly drafted and bit the dust in the Storting. This was modified to come in at 75 per cent with various tax offsets which would put the actual tax take at about 60 per cent. Because the Norwegian government took things slowly, and because its reserves were, in proportion to annual output, vast, it dominated negotiations. The analysts Lind and Mackay commended this in their 1980 study:

It may be argued that the process of consultation and debate has led to lengthy delays, but it has permitted extensive discussion of the issues and alternatives, and has ensured that many of the mistakes made in the UK were not replicated. The latter arose mainly from ignorance and inadequate discussion.[23]

This statism might seem to threaten the private sector, and indeed was interpreted in this way by the Americans.[24] But it was friendly to native Norwegian capitalism. By 1975 the Aker company, which was building the rig in Oslo harbour, had captured orders for 20 per cent of drilling-rigs; sixty-eight were active in that year. The programme of slow depletion didn't depress this; instead the Norwegian firms went abroad for orders, actually aided by the fact that the country's foreign debt – to purchase equipment to exploit the fields – kept the krone at a level low enough to facilitate exports. The same applied to supply ships, which the Norwegians effectively invented, and to platform production: Norway developed its own type of concrete oil-storing platform, the Condeep, and successfully sold them, even when the course of economics favoured the steel platform.

From the start the government, with its 1970 'white paper',

'The Petroleum Industry in Norwegian Society', concentrated on restraining and directing the course of oil industry development although its child, Statoil, pressed for a faster rate of development in order to build up its financial basis as a means of competing internationally. But tension built up, particularly as the oil started to induce population movements from the north to areas where the oil gave the promise of jobs. Gradually, policy shifted to favour a higher rate of depletion, coupled with greater investment in the infrastructure. The Norwegian political élite had, before September 1992, invested its hopes in adhesion to the EEC. Rejection of this in that month's referendum seemed a setback. In fact, as Tony Benn ruefully admitted, it allowed the state far greater freedom to develop and control its resources than Britain had as a member of the Community.[25]

Dirty Story

In the private language of the oilmen, the North Sea province was, in the late 1970s, 'gold-plated'; in other words, no expense was spared on platforms, pipelines and terminals. In particular, Sullom Voe, which had consumed around £2.5 billion, dripped with the stuff. Almost immediately after its commissioning, however, a lot of goldplate fell off. A ten-year-old turbine-powered tanker, the *Esso Berenicia*, 190,600 tons deadweight, collided with mooring 'dolphins'. The weather on 30 December 1978 was foul: snow-laden, blowing a 30 mph gale. One of the tanker's three escorting tugs, the *Stanechakker*, caught fire in its engine-room. The result was that 1,174 tons of fuel oil poured out. Attempts to control the spillage with a boom failed and it drifted into the Sound of Yell, with results best conveyed by Jonathan Wills's injunction: 'Try cleaning a piece of carpet with a toothbrush and a teaspoon after you have spilt molasses on it.' The oil killed over 3,000 seabirds, and caused damage estimated (conservatively) at £2.25 million. The tanker was a write-off.[26]

The *Esso Berenicia* was towed off to the shipbreakers and, within a few months, recycled into cars, videorecorders and what have you.

Shetland Islands Council and the owners were still fighting over compensation in the courts a decade later. But it may be generations before the loons and great squaw ducks return in large numbers to their breeding-grounds in the Sound of Yell. This episode gives some idea of the complexities which the oil business imposed. Within a couple of years the Council had five tugs, anti-pollution vessels, a helicopter patrol which contacted ships 200 miles away from the islands; and a database with the pollution history of every vessel likely to use the terminal. None of this came cheap.

Fourteen years later, the ten-year-old tanker *Braer*, with 95,000 tons of light crude from Statoil's Mongstad plant, went out of control south of Shetland and was wrecked near Sumburgh. But a collision such as this was only one of the more obvious aspects of a deeply suspect confrontation between commercialism and the environment. The early 1970s had been boom years for tankers; they were not repeated. As a result, corners were cut, ships were out-flagged. BP rejected 30 per cent of tankers inspected in 1992, but as it cost only $30,000 to charter a 250,000 tonner for a day, and one could speculate on the oil while the cargo was in transit, the low-cost business increased. The owners of the *Braer*, Bergvall and Hudner, seemed to have come straight out of Ibsen's *Pillars of Society*, with a policy of running their forty-seven old boats to death. The *Braer*'s engine breakdown was repeated with its sister ship *Celtic* a week later.[27]

Because of a profile about as obtrusive as that of a plaice, to coin an ecological simile, the British Minister of Transport at the time of the wreck of the *Braer*, John MacGregor, had the reputation of being 'a safe pair of hands'. How safe was open to question. Coastguards and lighthousemen had been made redundant in scores and replaced, at best, by automatic equipment. Government ministers had repeatedly stalled on safety and double hulls. Most spectacular of all was the collapse of tanker inspection.

The ministry's official target was to inspect 25 per cent of tankers. In 1990 the ministry itself claimed to have inspected only fifteen tankers at Sullom Voe, which it estimated to be 10 per cent. But Shetland Islands Council had records of 459 tankers docking at the Voe, Britain's busiest port, in that year. Nine were inspected out of a rather higher total in 1991, and only four in 1992. In other words the numbers inspected had declined from 3 per cent in 1990 to 0.77 per cent in 1992.[28] Jonathan Wills's observations on this were all the more damning for being qualified:

The statistics of the world tanker fleet are a scandal. It is estimated that one-fifth of the world's 3,200 tankers are unfit to be afloat, let alone put to sea. More than half the ships are over sixteen years old. Although many older tankers are well maintained and well managed, three-quarters of all those lost in 1991 were built before 1976.[29]

Tankers were the chief menace in the oil business, because much more oil was lost in transport than in actual production. Authorities were unsure of the precise amounts, but perhaps as much as 35,000 tons was spilled every year, according to a Dutch aerial survey in 1987, while 1,000 tons leaked from terminals.[30]

Yet the platforms themselves were not absolved as polluters. At Ekofisk Bravo, in April 1977, between 15,000 and 22,000 tons of oil were spilled before Red Adair managed to cap the well; 3,000 tons escaped when an anchor damaged a pipeline on the Claymore field in 1986, and 1,500 tons escaped at Piper Alpha in July, although this was overshadowed by the appalling loss of human life. One ton of oil could kill 1,000 birds.[31]

Pollution could take unexpected forms. The explosions of seismic survey vessels apparently caused bafflement among whales, whose sophisticated method of communication was fouled up. But the most recurrent problem stemming from the platforms was mud: 1,000 tons of mud were needed to drill a single well, and one platform might dump 4,000 tons per year. This consti-tuted 76 per cent of pollution from platforms, totalling 22,555 tons in 1988. Diesel-based muds were killers, and were only replaced by low-toxicity muds in 1985, largely through pressure from the Norwegian government. As well as mud, the drills also brought up naturally radioactive scale, which was dumped back into the sea.[32] Less spectacular than this, but even more worrying in the longer term, was the oil in 'produced' water, used for cooling or domestic purposes. The oil in this was increasing to between 0.5 and 3 millionths of a gram per litre – minute quantities, but adding up, and having an incalculable but certainly negative effect on the plankton-breeding necessary to sustain the fish stocks.[33]

In truth, oil was only one among the menaces converging on the defiled sea, and, in comparison with others, relatively minor. With a catch of 3 million tons of fish annually, down to 2.5 million in 1992 (50 per cent of catch being Danish, 15 per cent British, 20 per cent Norwegian), and in particular the assault on the sand-eel population, much used in fish farms, the numbers of pout and sprat collapsed, and with them those of their natural predators, the Arctic tern and puffin. The whole ecosystem of the sea was completely disrupted, as evidenced by the spread in the late 1980s of poisonous algae, encouraged by ever-mounting discharges of nitrates from the littoral countries. And where did nitrate fertilizers – or the foul tide of plastic foam and packaging – come from, but out of the feedstocks provided by the oil and gas fields?[34]

The Road to Piper Alpha

Only three weeks before he found himself struggling to cap the Ekofisk Alpha blowout, Red Adair was scathing about the emergency services in the North Sea:

Whatever precautions are taken, there'll be a disaster in the North Sea, sooner or later. There are no proper facilities for coping with it. The thing is time, to get trained personnel there. By then, a well might have caught fire — then it gets larger and larger . . . The more wells you have, on any platform, the more difficult it gets, because the heat will go on to the next tree . . . The hardware to deal with a disaster? At the moment, for a real blowout, you don't have anything . . .[35]

Ekofisk Alpha was scarcely a textbook response. BP's fire-fighting ship, a converted tanker on station in the Forties, sailed south but wasn't much use. The four Vicoma surface skimmers which it brought were supposed to scoop up 300 tons, but managed between them only 60 tons. Never one to shy away from publicity, Dr Armand Hammer of Occidental announced the ordering of a composite firefighting and diving support vessel for the Piper field, called the *Tharos*.

Yet when seven years later, in March 1984, gas exploded on Occidental Petroleum's Piper Alpha platform, and four men were slightly injured, Occidental kept quiet. As the official report on the blast didn't recommend prosecution, it was never made public. A proposal to 'wrap' the gas condenser with a steel blast sheet was considered by the company, but turned down as it would close the Piper field, along with its tributaries Tartan, Highlander and Claymore, for six weeks. It was even less likely that such work would be taken on two years later, following the price slump of the winter of 1985–6.

The North Sea province was from the start a dangerous region:

By the mid-1970s, the likelihood of being killed in the course of employ-ment on offshore installations operating in the British sector of the North Sea had risen to around eleven times that of accidental death in the construction industry, to nearly nine times that of becoming a fatal casualty in mining, and to nearly six times that of being killed as a quarryman.[36]

With the capsizing of *Sea Gem* on 27 December 1965 — thirteen lives were lost out of a crew of thirty-two — exploration did not get off to the most auspicious start. Twenty-three years later the peak of operations would be marked by the explosion which destroyed the Piper Alpha production platform, with 167 deaths.

In between there were two major disasters – Ekofisk and the overturning of the *Axel Kielland* on the Ekofisk field during a gale on 23 March 1980, when 100 men were drowned. In the British sector alone over 100 men had been killed by 1984, and over 400 seriously injured. By mid-1988, over 300 men had been killed in twenty-three years.

In November 1965, three men died in an explosion on a half-built barge at a Teesside shipyard; in December of that year *Sea Gem* capsized, killing thirteen. Throughout the 1970s there were regular casualties among divers – some calculated that this numbered almost one a week. In April 1975 the survey ship *Compass Rose* and eighteen men went down in a force ten gale while on contract to Menard Marine, surveying the Total pipeline to Fraserburgh. An old corvette, built in 1944, the *Compass Rose* was badly undermanned, according to the unions. In March 1980, two died in an explosion on Cormorant Alpha; in November 1983, five died when a diving-bell on the Frigg field was totally decompressed. In June 1984, three workers were burned to death on Shell's Brent Bravo; in January 1985, two more were killed on the rig Glomar Arctic II. The accidents seemed to increase as the province aged: in May 1985, six workers were killed in a blowout on Auk Alpha; in November 1986, forty-five were killed when a Chinook helicopter crashed *en route* to the Brent field; in February 1988, two were killed by a falling crane on the rig Whisky Charlie.[37]

Safety was always sensitive in an industry dealing with inflammable-to-explosive material, in a province in which weather conditions could change violently in the space of an hour, and where communications were dependent on helicopter transport. But in a detailed study of accidents and safety in the province, the Edinburgh University criminologist Kit Carson argued that the 'frontier' quality of the fields was exaggerated. The safety issue largely concerned problems which were standard to any industry, but which were aggravated on the North Sea by the imperative of rapidly extracting the oil and gas. Safety measures were lax, and were further hampered by a

battle between various under-financed and ill-equipped government agencies and each other, as well as with the majors. The
trade unions were, from the beginning, firmly marginalized, and
authority over the large number of foreign vessels on station in the
province was limited, sometimes to the extent of black comedy.
Carson recorded the evidence of one of the Department of Energy's
inspection staff, reporting on accidents on pipelaying vessels, who
sounded as if he had strayed in from a play by Joe Orton:

These are reported to us on a sort of courtesy basis . . . I say to whoever, 'It
would be nice to know what accidents you are having. You know, there's
an enforceable procedure under the Factories Act, you know, do you think
we could go along with it?' So it's a question of whether they do so. I
don't know how soon he's going to do it; I really have no idea. I've only
had one from X and there's not been a dickie bird from anywhere else.
This maybe indicates that they are being terribly safe or it maybe indicates
that they are not reporting the accidents. I don't know, and really I have no
way of finding out other than asking them.[38]

The main factor here was the conflict between the Health and
Safety Executive established by Michael Foot's Health and Safety
at Work Act of 1975 and the Petroleum Engineering Division of
the Department of Energy. It was Foot's intention to get the
remit of the HSE extended offshore, but this was opposed by the
operators. Responsibility was further divided between the Marine
Division of the Department of Trade and Industry (rigs and
supply vessels) and the Civil Aviation Authority (helicopters),
and complicated by the divisions between Scots and English
law.[39] Even when the HSE was finally given offshore authority
in July 1977, this was diluted by being made subject to an agency
agreement with the Petroleum Engineering Division.

This meant that two aspects of onshore safety regulations, for
example in the mines, were instantly lacking. There was no
obligation to consult the unions, and there was no regular inspection on the fortnightly basis of the Mines Inspectorate. As the
Petroleum Engineering Division staff numbered only sixty-three
in 1977, it's difficult to see how this could have been entertained.[40]

Yet in a report by Professor J.N. Burgoyne, undertaken after an inquiry lasting from September 1978 to January 1980, this arrangement was criticized but, overall, upheld.[41] There would be safety committees, to be elected by those 'employed for the time being on the installation', and these would have the ability to liaise with other committees on the companies' installations; Department of Energy supervision would continue. To Professor John Foster of Paisley University, this had

... every appearance of a stitch-up involving oil companies, consultants and their professional bodies, together with Department of Energy civil servants.[42]

The unions opposed the Burgoyne recommendation:

A government department substantially responsible for the direction and control of an industry should not in any way be responsible for standards and enforcement of occupational health and safety in that industry ... It is our view that any unification of responsibilities under the auspices of the Department of Energy, as the sponsoring department, entails a continuing risk, to the possible detriment of safety standards.[43]

How thorough the stitch-up was would be shown in the experience of the Piper Alpha disaster.

Some sort of objective comparison was needed, and it was provided from the Norwegian sector. The Hellesoy inquiry found a generally high level of satisfaction, but doubts about promotion prospects and evacuation safety.[44] The *Axel Kielland* crisis led to greater criticism. There was, overall, an absence of stereotyping, even among the roughnecks:

Despite their bravado and ostensible disregard for personal safety, the drillers' basic attitude is in fact quite sober and oriented toward accident prevention and safety instruction ... They may well like to play the part of dare-devils, but they watch their step.[45]

In 1979 a further Norwegian report detailed eighty-two fatal accidents between 1966 and 1978; thirty-four of these had been in helicopter crashes. Accidents worked out at twenty times the fatalities on land, but industrial comparisons were favourable. On platforms there was only 0.5 fatalities per 1,000 man-years worked, compared with 0.8 in mines.[46] The need was for better training on an unemployed rig and regular non-punitive report-ing. Although the *Axel Kielland* disaster subsequently took place right at the beginning of the Hellesoy inquiry and the Statfjord Alpha platform had earlier been regarded as 'a hotel on a volcano', the Norwegian workers believed that the precautions under the Work Environment Act of 1977 made for a satisfactory situation in relation to security.[47]

Norwegian solidarity plainly benefited from an elaborate secu-rity regime, based on a safety supervisor plus three technicians and three nurses, under a safety committee. Moreover, the plat-form staff were mostly on a two weeks on/ three weeks off regime, and came from the nearby shore regions of Hordaland (Haugesund) and Rogaland (Bergen), a helicopter flight away.[48] Part of the British problem was the sheer distance of the oilfields both from the homes of many of their workers and from London. Out of sight tended to mean out of mind, a situation not altogether remedied even after the major disaster that Adair had forecast.

Tony Benn's other concern, when visiting Forties Alpha, was the defence of the platforms. The need for security was made patent by the frequent attention of Russian reconnaissance trawl-ers, drawing various reactions — from the ribald to the obscene — of platform crews. A German study of the province's technology paid great attention to this, and then cited as a counter-weapon the newly commissioned vessel *Jura*. This was a Fisheries Patrol cruiser belonging to the Department of Agriculture and Fisheries of Scotland, built like a trawler and mounting, against the might of the Soviets, a single Bofors gun.[49]

In the event of a world war, and the use of nuclear weapons, the fate of the platforms would be irrelevant; they would, anyway, be sitting targets for torpedoes. More alarming was the prospect of terrorist attack. A bomb had gone off during the royal opening of Sullom Voe in 1978, and the IRA was known to have agents on onshore plants. Against this was a plethora of small and elegantly old-fashioned patrol and research vessels, a museum of those responsibilities taken unto itself by what had once been the greatest naval power. 'At present the apparatus of government is riddled with "private" navies,' complained Donald Cameron Watt, the London School of Economics' Professor of International Relations.[50] The Royal Air Force, Royal Navy, Departments of Trade, Environment, Energy, Agriculture and Fisheries of Scotland, Customs and Excise, Commissioners of Northern Lights, Coastguard, and Port Authorities had all got police powers, some of them up to and including authorization for the use of firearms. In 1980 two oil patrol vessels were ordered from Hall Russell at Aberdeen to join a score of warships and fifty-six research or survey vessels already operating in the North Sea, but no attempt had been made to co-ordinate all these craft, least of all with research, supply and life-saving functions.[51]

Disorganized Labour

There was also the 'enemy within', which was in the 1980s to become the shorthand for the Labour movement:

Consensus: although union activity is currently subdued, industry expects matters to get worse under Minister Benn and the 'Code of Conduct'.[52]

Consul Funkhouser's telegram to the State Department in 1975 raised a perennial American preoccupation, not mollified by the reputation of the new minister, and by the spectacle of Arthur Scargill directing his shock troops against the Saltley coal depot in Birmingham during the coal strike. Yet fourteen years later, after Piper Alpha, the unions were lamenting their impotence. Roger Lyons, deputy general secretary of the Manufacturing, Science and Finance Union, condemned Mobil, Phillips, CONOCO, Britoil and BP for conceding the worst negotiating rights in the world, save Libya and Saudi Arabia. The Offshore Operators, as usual, were defensive:

We believe that our companies do have satisfactory safety committees offshore. There is no reason why the people on them should not be union members even though they are not there as union representatives.

In 1988 the MSF union was still failing to get any response to its demand that legal limits be set on working hours, following cases in which 48-hour shifts had been discovered. Tommy Lafferty, the Engineers' Union organizer, was despairing:

The oil companies have eliminated anyone hostile to them and there is now complete disillusionment with the trade union movement offshore. The men are now becoming masochistic. The more punishment they get, the more they are prepared to take.

Lyons's Norwegian opposite number, Lars Myhre, of the Norwegian Offshore Workers' Union, attributed his country's higher standards to the fact that unions were represented on statutory union–management safety committees.[53] Norwegian corporatism didn't damp down labour disputes, which could be severe, partly because of inter-union conflicts, complicated by the fact that the platforms were regarded as dry land while the rigs and 'flotels' were 'ships'. The Statfjord Workers' Union was affiliated to the OFS (Oil Workers' Joint Committee) and the drillers were in the Norwegian Oil and Petrochemical Workers' Union and the Norwegian Oil and Energy Workers' Federation, while the 'flotel' crew were in the Norwegian Seamen's Federation.[54] This caused repeated strikes around 1980, but eventually a reasonably smooth bipartisan regime evolved. When the proto-Thatcherite policies of Willoch's Conservative government ran into trouble in 1985, it was to be the unions – voicing a 'national' opposition – that brought it down.

The comparative disadvantaging of the British unions was inevitable, given the tenor of policy throughout the decade, and their overall decline in membership from 13.2 million in 1979 to 10 million in 1988.[55] Yet the interesting thing was that their isolation from effective power started under the Labour government. Although the oil companies feared that Benn would force unionization, by 1979 he had gone no further than putting two trade unionists – Gavin Laird of the Engineers and Richard Briginshaw of NATSOPA – on the board of BNOC, and had opened to discussion the issue of unions on safety committees. Unions in such hazardous areas as diving had to wage an unending struggle for recognition.[56]

Trade unionists in the Aberdeen area got early experience of the authoritarian style of the rigs and supply business, and the patent existence of an offshore cartel in labour issues, the Association of Chartered Rig Operators (British Chapter), setting up their own organization, the North Sea Oil Action Committee on 19 October 1972.[57] This local Trades Council-based organization had a lot of early success, but in 1974 it gave way to a committee of organizers from eight unions, the Inter-Union Off-shore Committee. Unfortunately this had the effect of replacing grass-roots enthusiasm with the inertia of the metropolitan union élite. Although the IUOC came to various agreements with the UKOOA after 1976, *after* the two most important years in the province's history, such agreements were not taken seriously by the employers. The union side complained to the Burgoyne Committee:

A battery of devices are used to minimize the trade union presence amongst permanent platform employees involved in production. To this date [1979] there is only one collective bargaining agreement offshore, covering gas platform staff in the southern sector, and that was only secured after several years of resistance. Elsewhere, pressure, intimidation, temporary bribes and other means are used to hold back the development of bona fide trade-union organization and recognition.[58]

Much of this weakness came from within the union movement itself. Although its leaders – Jack Jones of the Transport Workers, Hugh Scanlon of the Engineers, Clive Jenkins of ASTMS – had a higher profile than many Cabinet ministers, the union side of the corporate industrial order, inevitably members of committees of the great and the good, was marked not by aggression but by inertia. Vic Feather, general secretary in the mid-1970s, was typical in serving on no fewer than eight quangos. But to what effect? According to one observer, Robert Taylor, 'Until recently most of those public posts were treated as sources of extra income rather than as opportunities for hard work in the trade union interest.[59]

'Seniority, union muscle, competence' counted, not prescience or imagination, and perhaps least of all socialist conviction. Not surprisingly, the national unions were slow off the mark. In 1975 Benn had words with Jack Jones on the failure to organize on the rigs.[60] In 1977 Benn met Sir John Boyd of the Engineers' Union and was appalled at his conservatism and anti-semitism. In fact Boyd represented one of two streams in the Scottish trade-union movement: Catholic populism. The other, the communist tradition of the Red Clyde and of much of the executive of the Scottish Trades Union Congress, and of the local trades councils, was in no circumstances likely to be acceptable to the Americans. In the oil industry, the right was generally in control. The unions were content to negotiate centrally with the operators, and inhibited the organization of the platforms and rigs on a shop-steward basis. As Carson found in 1983, these were content to acquiesce in an authoritarian management style and 'the political economy of speed'. Only in 1990, with growing restiveness after the Piper Alpha disaster, would there be a major rising against the control of the companies, and one which ran into as much hostility from the union hierarchies as from the companies themselves.

The safety framework in which unions and companies worked – or attempted to work – had been created by decisions made during the tenure of a radical socialist minister. But it also reflected the fact that the Department of Energy, and even the minister, were prepared to keep the oil province 'special', and in particular remote from the intervention of EEC authorities. Benn, in fact, was caught rather guiltily between two stools; his support for the trade unions on the one hand, and his hostility to the Common Market on the other.[61]

In the early 1960s the oil industry had been seen as the precursor of collective bargaining by a new and confidently affluent working class. The 'Fawley Agreements' of 1962 between Esso and the Transport and General Workers' Union were the type of compact which legitimized both a popular capitalism and trade unionism, along the sort of New Deal lines applauded by Anthony Crosland in his 'revisionist' *Future of Socialism* (1956) and *The Future of Socialism* (1974). Yet even at this time trade unionism in American refineries was declining, and offshore operations, with the possibility of creating a labour force which was both disciplined and dispersed, offered the prospect of a new and much more subservient labour force. The irony was that if Denis Healey had introduced monetarism by conceding to the International Monetary Fund in June 1976, Tony Benn was (involuntarily) to preside over the first seaborne steps towards the blunting of trade-union power.

8

It's Not Scotland's Oil After All

What is more, in Britain's case, our luck has not deserted us. Like the beautiful young lady, we have discovered that we are sitting on a fortune. From my inquiries in the North of Scotland, I am convinced that Britain is the centre of one of the largest deposits – perhaps the largest – of natural energy in the world.

I often tell my continental friends, who spend their time listening to sterile bureaucratic arguments in Brussels and Strasbourg, that they could learn much more about the future in such places as Aberdeen, Inverness and Oslo.

Paul Johnson, in the *New Statesman*, 28 June 1974[1]

The Crest of the Wave

Bliss was it in that dawn to be alive, and to be young, with a reasonable degree and a Social Science Research Council grant, was very heaven. The lack of interest in oil affairs which the *Economist* mourned was not replicated in Scotland where, although academics, publicists, economists and journalists might know little about the weird technology on hand, and could scarcely have endured a fortnight on a rig, they had realized the size of the business afoot. Scottish nationalism, denounced only a decade earlier, on one of his northern progresses, by the selfsame Paul Johnson, as 'a totally new kind of boredom', remained a bit arcane; those in search of state-of-the-art enlightenment from Bain, Maxwell and company, could still knock on the wrong door and be regaled with a recital of the grievances of the folk from Galcagus on.

Academics and nationalists were alike in being tuppeny-ha'penny performers; the cost of a mile of pipeline, or a small submarine, would keep them scribbling away for months, yet at this juncture they were important. If politics moved in a particular direction, companies and governments would have a lot of rethinking to do.

It wasn't just the SSRC shelling out its thousands to measure the impact of the oil business; there were international and business initiatives, sometimes paying more; and various more-or-less exciting freelance characters, male and female, thought to be working for MI5 or the CIA. The social research community was in its infancy, still collectivized in university departments; not yet the province of sharp private research partnerships whose slim papers would flap down on City desks at £500 a throw. There were groups of interested and interesting academics at the Scottish universities, especially Edinburgh, Strathclyde and Aberdeen, not only economists but international lawyers and political scientists, whose expertise could be tapped for the price of a good lunch and nebulous promises of an article, a TV documentary appearance, a trip abroad, or help with an application for a research grant. Donald Mackay soon gained a chair at Aberdeen, and went on to help devise a television series for the BBC – with an associated book – on *Scotland 1980*, based pretty directly on the premise that an independent state was not just possible but inevitable.[2] Professors Tom MacRae and David Simpson at Strathclyde, based in the Fraser of Allander Institute for applied economics, were equally quotable, and supportive of a nationalist line. Lawyers such as Neil MacCormick, Tony Carty and Sandy MacCall Smith, in the Edinburgh faculty who tended to have a strong defensive attitude to the Scottish legal tradition, were also intrigued by the implications of the issue for international and commercial law, and Scotland's legal relations with Europe.[3] As for political scientists and historians, who among them was likely to reject an issue which gave their work international interest, the bounty of the SSRC and the British Council?[4]

There were also the journalists. In the mid-1970s Scotland

even ran to a Scottish Society of Political Correspondents, graced by one of Europe's most elegant and perceptive performers, Neal Ascherson, who had come north from the *Observer* to the *Scotsman*. But the oil issue developed a cousinhood of its own, particularly those working for the Scottish broadsheets, such as Alf Young who went from the Labour Party to the *Glasgow Herald*, and Frank Frazer, who became the doyen of oil correspondents. The financial papers and the 'Insight' team of Thomson's own *Sunday Times*, notably George Rosie, grasped early on how much of an upper hand the oil multinationals had over the government, and how deeply that hand was dipping into the public purse.[5] Adrian Hamilton, Chris Baur and Ray Perman of the *Financial Times'* Scottish staff were both attuned to oil issues and sympathetic to the SNP. Less sympathetic, but still insistent that the SNP and its ideas on oil ought to be taken seriously, was the Scottish correspondent of the *Economist*, Andrew Neil, a former Tory Club debater at Glasgow University, who had become a protégé of Alastair Burnett and close to Peter Walker.[6]

Confronted with Labour and Conservative public relations teams in Scotland which were disunited – particularly over devolution – when not second-rate, journalists found a rapid affinity with the very professional SNP outfit. It was from such quarters that the scenario of Scotland as a 'tartan Katanga' began to emanate, particularly after Labour took power in February 1974. The Scottish Council: Development and Industry responded to the Green Paper which followed Kilbrandon, suggesting substantial Scottish deviations from UK legislation in the interests of business, and the adhesion to the SNP of Sir Hugh Fraser also seemed to indicate that a switch of allegiance by powerful Scottish business leaders was a real possibility. These signals were actually no more than a reluctant business community, dragooned by Edward Heath into accepting devolution, making the best of it. But they seemed convincing at the time. In 1975 Richard Funkhouser estimated the odds against an SNP takeover and a Benn premiership at five to one, construing the second as the greater menace to North Sea exploitation.[7] He put this later to Neal Ascherson: '"What political force would *you* back if you had a few hundred millions to invest in the North Sea?" The SNP were the work-ethic party.'[8]

This line, also taken by the Hudson Institute in its report on the future of the British economy in mid-1974, was double-edged. It might appeal to some refugees from 'socialist' controls, but native capitalist growths were, apart from the financial sector, weak. Promises of increases in pensions or cuts in petrol prices were more generally attractive to the Scotsman or woman in the street, but raised the problem of equity with the rest of Britain and of an overvalued Scots pound. Nevertheless, in 1974 and 1975 the volatility of Scottish politics was such that a fresh election could mean either of two things: the SNP could push its vote above 36 per cent, leave Westminster and convene a Scottish parliament in Edinburgh; or the Labour Party could split over home rule. Both would have incalculable consequences for the future of oil exploitation.

Papering the Country Red

But matters were not quite so straightforward. Once in Parliament the SNP ran into increasing opposition from the Scottish Labour establishment, bloodied but not unbowed by the events of 1974, which had seen it shanghaied on to a devolution bandwagon on orders from London. The nationalists, realizing that they had done as well as they could hope to against the Tories, now tended to play down their old 'not left, not right, but Scottish' approach and shift to a generally social-democratic position, hoping in this way to make inroads into Labour's not utterly reliable Clydeside fortresses. In turn this forced an accelerated course of self-criticism among the Scottish lefties. John McGrath's *The Cheviot, the Stag, and the Black, Black Oil* had become the Bible of resistance to the oilmen, but as many interpretations could be made of it as of the Book itself. McGrath at this stage saw nationalism careering off on its own trail of false consciousness. His *Little Red Hen* (1977), a strip-cartoon history of the Scottish labour movement since the brave days of John Maclean, continued the American dance metaphor of the *Cheviot*, satirizing the SNP and its oil politics as the fabulously talentless Scottish rock group, the Bay City Rollers, capering cluelessly in their tartans while being ripped off by their managers.

Les McKeown and his gang, enjoying their fifteen minutes of world fame, wouldn't – couldn't – have known that the name they selected with a pin stuck in an atlas was the Gomorrah of Raymond Chandler, the city of misrule whose values were wearily spelt out by Philip Marlowe's friend, the 'good cop' Bernie Ohls in *The Long Goodbye*:

'There ain't no clean way to make a hundred million bucks,' Ohls said . . . 'Big money is big power and big power gets used wrong. It's the system. Maybe it's the best we can get, but it still ain't my Ivory Soap deal.'

'You sound like a Red,' I said, just to needle him.

'I wouldn't know,' he said contemptuously. 'I ain't been investigated yet.'[19]

The symbolism was appropriate. The Upper Clyde crisis, which produced a political analogue to McGrath in the Communist Jimmy Reid, had been in a way 'solved' – by the conversion of John Brown's into the Marathon rig-building yard – by the arrival in Scotland of international capitalist imperialism at its most robust and unreconstructed. This concentrated the Scottish left's attention on the national question. Indeed it impacted directly on the careers of two young men who occupied a uniquely Scottish *point d'appui*.

In 1972, for the first time, Edinburgh University elected a student as Rector – chairman of the University Court Jonathan Wills was editor of *The Student* newspaper, where he represented a belated Scottish version of the 'spirit of 1968', a landscape of manic if ineffectual Guevara-like activity. There was a counter-attack by the lawyers and councillors who feared for their dominance on the University Court, and Wills had to hold them at bay. Then in 1973, with a commune in tow, he set off for the Shetland Islands, to set up a co-operative crofting venture on the bay of Haroldswick, on Unst, as far north as you could possibly get. Within two years he had Sullom Voe on his hands, had stopped crofting, and become editor of Radio Shetland.[10]

His successor as student Rector of Edinburgh University was even younger: the son of the minister of Hamilton, who had arrived at the university at the improbable age of sixteen, and graduated with first-class honours at nineteen. Poorly sighted, communicating by a near-hieroglyphic hand, or by flailing at typewriters whose corpses littered his flat – yet flanked by a formidable media-minded entourage and a girlfriend from the Romanian royal family – Gordon Brown edited the Student Publication Board's *Red Paper on Scotland* (1975).[11] The thirty authors of this fundamental and distinctly challenging testament of a Scottish 'intellectual left' stretched from McGrath, on the fringes of the Socialist Workers' Party, to the increasingly mutinous figure of Jim Sillars in the Labour Party. Tom Nairn, coming north from Munich and Italy, recanted his earlier hostility to the home rule cause – 'Scotland will be reborn the day the last minister is strangled with the last copy of the *Sunday Post*' – and signed up with this army of this new Covenant.[12]

The *Red Paper* appeared in May 1975. It looked, and often read, like a telephone directory. Moreover, the more one read, the more disconcerted one became about what 'Red' or 'the Scottish left' meant. Brown's introduction and a piece by Robin Cook were standard productions of what would later be known as the Bennite tendency. As they later elaborated in a further work, the 'real divide' they recognized in Scotland was one of class, not of nation. This they opposed, rather politely, to the mild social-democracy of Billy Wolfe, rubbing their hands when they could launch themselves on some unreconstructed SNP wild man like Douglas Henderson MP. Him they disliked as much as the Crosland–Jenkins grandees of Balliol social democracy, who cared little for Scottish identity, and knew about it even less.

The rest of the contributors broke down rather obviously into two distinct schools: nationalist and communist. Bob Tait, late of *Scottish International*, and – always in the grand manner – Owen Dudley Edwards, were nats of the literary sort; Jim Sillars seemed to be moving in their direction. Otherwise the most coherent group – John Foster, Peter Smith, Donald Cameron – followed the line taken by the Scottish Committee of the Communist Party of Great Britain. This insisted that the government, and in particular the Labour right, was in cahoots with multinational capitalism to use oil as the collateral for an entry into the European Economic Community. In such a calculation British social issues, let alone the reconciliation of oil development with Scottish needs, came way down the list of priorities. The Communists were on the fringes of electoral politics, with tiny votes outside a few 'little Moscows' on the coalfields, but they were well informed about their subject, and their influence had always been substantial within the Scottish Trades Union Congress. Given the confrontational nature of offshore and onshore labour relations, this was important.[13]

The Communists had backed Scottish home rule for some thirty years. They regarded the slippery slope towards independence as a threat to British working-class solidarity, but this was balanced against the possibility of a would-be independent Scotland making things hot for the Americans, both on the oilfields and on their Polaris submarines on the Holy Loch. In a thriller called *Scotch on the Rocks*, written in 1968, Douglas Hurd, then Edward Heath's political secretary, had seen the Reds behind a Scottish nationalist uprising.[14] This was a fantasy, but it was a fact that the Communists knew something about oil, and something about where they were going, and Labour, on the evidence of the *Red Paper*, did not.

From Oil to Devolution

The burden of the *Red Paper* was not the 1960s conviction that the SNP was lightweight and romantic, but that its 'straightforward message to the people of Scotland' in February 1974 'Do you want to be "Rich Scots" or "Poor British"?' was an all-too-rational capitalist strategy.[15] The oil campaign had established the SNP as a highly professional force, whose presence in Scottish politics would be of permanent significance.[16] Gordon Brown, then writing with Henry Drucker of the Edinburgh University politics department, conceded in 1976 that the SNP 'was guided, if not dominated, by men of business and commercial experience. Anyone could see that they could run an establishment.'[17]

But the SNP then began to play down the oil issue, to back away from its own brainchild.[18] Why was this? In part it could be put down to the close result of the October 1974 election. Labour was determined to hang on to power – if necessary with Liberal aid. The Liberals, going through the horrors of the trial of Jeremy Thorpe, were in no position to do otherwise than enter a semi-coalition with Callaghan. It would be some time before the SNP could again gear itself up to a full assault. Moreover, the only way that the SNP could develop was to attack Labour seats in the central belt, and this meant that it had to appeal to Labour supporters who suspected any entente between it and the leaders of Scottish commerce.[19]

One problem – from the SNP's point of view – was that there were not enough of these. The Nobles, Grossarts and Frasers were in a small minority, and not a very reliable one at that. The government's creation of BNOC and the Offshore Supplies Office – and three of the BNOC's eight-man board were Scots, Iain Clark, Gavin Laird and Alastair Morton – offered the serious oil businessmen a partnership which was at least sensitive to regional development issues. Sir Hugh Fraser had seemed a catch at the time, but proved a financial incompetent whose business empire was falling to bits. The trouble was that, apart from a few staples, there was little autonomous business in Scotland. There were the very large players of international finance, in Charlotte Square, who had never thought in national terms, and the very small, the shopkeepers who did weekly battle with Labour councillors.

Elsewhere, oil-powered autonomy movements, like that of Alberta or for that matter Texas, had mobilized local conservative businessmen. Similar figures had also backed regionalist movements in continental Europe, notably in Italy, Spain and the German *Länder*. Norway built on the basis of a social-democratic bureaucracy as well as a nationalist tradition, but this sort of evolution was not yet perceptible in the Scottish Office. The SNP's insistence on a low rate of extraction was already deterring some previous supporters, notably the *Economist*, which commented critically about its 1974 conference:

Arguments about the potential of the North Sea are important because they influence government policy and the attitude of British industry. Over-conservative government predictions have probably held back industry's urge to invest in North Sea oil. Scottish businessmen seeking funds do now parade regularly in Houston and other oil banking centres, but even the record of Scotland is lamentable. Everything should be done to encourage investment in the equipment and supplies side of the business. Discouraging remarks such as Mr Wolfe's should be opposed.[20]

Nationalism subsequently became even thinner on the ground among Scottish businessmen. They had anyway usually been embattled supporters of the Conservative party, whose capacity for independent action had collapsed since the Declaration of Perth. After 1975 it proved very easy for the new leadership of Mrs Thatcher to bring them into an anti-devolutionist line.[21]

Moreover, any possible rapprochement between business and the SNP was inevitably complicated by the issue of entry to the EEC and the campaign which preceded the European Communities referendum on 8 June 1975. The SNP took an even stronger line than the Labour Party against the EEC. In 1975 at its Perth conference William Wolfe declared that the Common Market would be looked back on as 'a tragic blunder, comparable in its effects with the unification of the German States a century ago', and received considerable applause.[22] Other nationalists formulated a line 'No – on anyone else's terms!' which was subsequently to resurface in the 1980s as 'An Independent Scotland in a United Europe'. But despite the fact that the SNP and Labour had shared over 70 per cent of the popular vote in 1974, both went down to a heavy defeat, by 64 per cent to 46 per cent. This failure to mobilize their vote was surely borne in mind by Conservatives when appraising a referendum on Scottish devolution.

Yet the internal logic of oil economics imposed its own constraints on what any future Scottish government could do, and this was apparent by the SNP's conference in May 1975. Douglas Crawford, the new MP for Perth and East Perthshire and a former official of the Scottish Council, who was usually taken as representing the free-enterprise right wing of the party, hinted in a *Scotsman* story that a high pound Scots would penalize traditional Scots exporting industry, and that Scotland ought therefore to move to a 'Swiss' economy based on financial services, tourism and high-quality, high-price manufacture.[23] This had a lot of sense to it, but it met a scandalized reaction from the parliamentary party leader, Donald Stewart MP, since it suggested that the oil income could be a poisoned chalice; the future of the country, according to him and most party members, lay with the decadent arcana of the service industries, rather than the honourable toil of bashing metal and weaving tweed.[24]

The pound Scots issue was soon taken up by Christopher Smallwood, a Cambridge economist seconded via Edinburgh University to the government's devolution unit. Smallwood favoured devolution as providing an effective instrument for regional economic policy, but denied that independence would be any sort of panacea. He saw a gain of between 5 and 15 per cent in the Scottish standard of living largely cancelled by an overvaluation of the pound Scots.[25] Donald Mackay countered with the argument that a Scottish government could control the rate of exploitation of the oil resources, and invest abroad such excess income as was received, in order to hold the pound Scots down. Nationalists might – ironically but quite correctly – observe that such 'British' critiques never allowed the Scots to win: they were unviable either because their national income was too low, or because it was too high. This rather technical debate did not in itself marginalize the notion of oil as a panacea, but it accompanied the rather dispiriting experience of seeing the obvious activity surrounding oil coexist with severe inflation and then with mounting unemployment, after the deflationary measures required by the IMF in mid-1976. As far as ordinary voters were concerned, oil wasn't what it had been cracked up to be.

Hard Labour

The SNP was also encountering strategic problems. In the early 1970s it had had great room for manoeuvre. After February 1974 this was constrained by the adaptation of the Labour Party, which still framed Scotland's political culture. Only two of the SNP's seven seats had been Labour. Further gains from the Tories would be limited, yet it was now second to Labour in a further thirty-six seats, mainly in West Central Scotland. When West Central Scotland moved, as Hamilton and Govan showed, it could move far and fast; and Labour was also acutely conscious that the seats which it traditionally dominated it also traditionally neglected. Since it was evident from polls taken at the time of the February election that a substantial majority of Scots voters wanted self-government but were only marginally interested in independence and were prepared to be generous with the oil, Labour tailored its response appropriately.

Labour had been tripped up by such limited autonomy as it allowed its Scottish organization but, ironically, coped well through its centralized initiatives. The British National Oil

Corporation and the Offshore Supplies Office were both substantially located in Scotland, even though this posed problems for the co-ordination of the state oil operation; and in early 1977 BP also announced a huge investment scheme – of over £1.8 billion – for its Scottish operations, both offshore and at the Grangemouth refinery.[26] With further measures in April 1976 by the new Callaghan government to bail out the ailing Chrysler car plant at Linwood, there was some evidence that Scotland still stood to gain by the Union.

The right in the Cabinet, and the largely left-wing unionist element in Scottish Labour, still strong, both wanted to deny the proposed Scottish Assembly economic powers. By moving to meet them, the government managed to offend the 'high profile' devolutionists, several hundred of whom formed the Scottish Labour Party under Jim Sillars and John Robertson in mid-1975. The interesting thing about the 'Magic Party's' short but disastrous career was that – besides showing the ineptness of the Scottish intelligentsia in nitty-gritty politics – it recruited almost exclusively from the existing left, and picked up hardly anyone from the SNP. And, as far as is revealed in its instant history written by Henry Drucker in December 1977, the oil issue played no part whatsoever in its gestation.[27] The route of its most prominent members would lead to the SNP, but at a critical stage it gravely weakened the forces within Labour who might have accommodated the SNP's growing inclination to compromise with devolution. John Mackintosh, a man of greater abilities than most members of the Cabinet – only in Britain could the leading authority on Cabinet government be excluded from one – might have been the man to broker this, but he now felt himself in the wilderness, and semi-retired from Westminster politics by taking a chair at Edinburgh University.

The Liberals were more ambiguously affected, in part because they were the SNP's natural rivals in rural Scotland; in part also because their areas of strongest support were the Borders and the Northern Isles, where conventional Scottish nationalism was at a discount. The Borders had links to England which might be

broken if independence became a reality; the Shetlanders, salivat-
ing over the bounty of Sullom Voe, and encouraged in this by
their MP, Jo Grimond, had developed a 'bourgeois regionalism'
of their own. Moreover, if the Liberal leader David Steel in the
Borders was essentially a middle-of-the-road social democrat, Jo
Grimond in the northern isles was more a *laisser-faire*-minded
anarchist. Oil registered little enough on Steel, preoccupied with
keeping on some sort of reasonable terms with the government.
Grimond's Orkney and Shetland and Donald Stewart's Western
Isles had been the only constituencies which had voted against
entry into the EEC; but the Shetlands evidently also intended to
vote against any measure of Scottish home rule, which they saw
as affecting the deal they had made with the oil companies.
Grimond was not the man to discourage them. Indeed, in 1977
and 1978 Shetland in particular became a breeding-ground of
various activist Tories – Robert Underwood, Ewan Marwick,
Alan Massie – who realized that they might have a useful weapon
here to furnish against Scottish devolution.[28]

After 1974 discussions of devolution outweighed those of oil
policy in the Scottish press (in 1976 by almost six to one), and
subsequent interest in oil diminished almost proportionately to
the rise in the amount of the stuff coming ashore.[29] Even the
SNP itself was stepping back from the 'rich Scots and poor
British' scenario, and in the 'edgy' Annual Conference of May
1976, held in the steelworks town of Motherwell, oil figured not
at all in the president's, chairman's or parliamentary leader's
addresses.[30] Margo MacDonald, the most prominent figure on the
left of the party, was the only major speaker to address the oil
issue, and this she did while commending a two-stage political
process which involved a compromise with Labour's devolution
plans, and an attempt to come to terms with the concerns of the
depressed English regions like the north-east.[31] The discussion of
oil in Gavin Kennedy's symposium *The Radical Approach*,
published in April 1976, by Prof. David Simpson, the SNP's
leading economist, had already concentrated on the benefits to
England of Scottish exploitation of oil resources. The pound Scots

would be 'tethered' through Scots 'overseas investment' in the English economy, facilitated by preferential English access to Scottish oil surpluses.[32] It was evident by that time that, even within the SNP, the pull of solidarity with the rest of Britain (every Scottish family had around a quarter of its members south of the Border) counted for more than fantasies about independent Scottish defence forces.

Polls showed that oil was, even in 1975, being perceived by Scottish voters as a British resource, albeit one from which the Scots ought to draw specific advantages.[33] In October 1974 all parties had met this position by offering funds which would channel oil revenues back into the Scottish economy, as well as various forms of devolved legislature. The impact of the SNP was, initially, to move this general political consensus further in a devolutionist direction. But this had its limits. The Scotland and Wales bill which Michael Foot introduced in the Commons in autumn 1976 was cumbersome, and conceded very few powers to the assemblies it envisaged. It was cold-shouldered by the Nationalists, vehemently opposed by a minority of Labour MPs, who drafted amendment after amendment, and more or less ignored by the rest. Foot was the wrong man in the wrong place – not for the last time. The gentle Hampstead pacifist and *littérateur*, wrapped in his cloak of parliamentary rhetoric, wasn't up to bullying the House which he revered. When he tried to timetable the bill, Parliament rejected the guillotine on 22 February 1977. The SNP's popularity rose in the polls to an all-time high of 36 per cent. The question was: could it convert this to decisive electoral support'?

The Last Mazzinian

One of the very few Labour MPs to take any sort of interest in the Scotland bill had been the otherwise obscure William Small, of Glasgow Garscadden. He died suddenly in early 1978. At the by-election in April 1978, the SNP had the chance to convert its poll results – and its dominance of the district's local government seats – into electoral success. Its candidate Keith Bovey was a gentle Christian pacifist, the last person I ever remember describing himself as a follower of Giuseppi Mazzini and his moralsitic republicanism. Against him Labour put up a strong candidate: Donald Dewar, a former MP who had always been committed to legislative devolution and was not tainted with earlier manoeuvrings. This was enough to bring such of the party's home rulers who had not joined Sillars' SLP – myself included – into line. Moreover, Labour's austerity economics, somewhat tempered to the Scottish winds by the creation of the Scottish Development Agency, launched in 1975 under Professor Kenneth Alexander, another home ruler and one-time Communist, seemed to be working. The SNP lost badly.

The SNP challenge had been a combination of the macro-politics of oil, skill in handling by-elections and ineptitude on the part of Labour. This combination unravelled in 1978. The SLP collapsed in acrimony, and the voice of John Mackintosh was stilled, first by serious illness, then by death, while still under fifty. John Smith, former junior Energy minister, and hitherto a sceptic about devolution, successfully piloted a redrafted bill through the House. The SNP parliamentary party, fronted by the anachronistic figure of Donald Stewart, a pro-hanging, Calvinist fundamentalist from Lewis, became increasingly split within itself on left–right lines and over its attitude to devolution, and quarrelled with the party hierarchy in Scotland. Further by-elections in 1978 at Hamilton and East Lothian – and regional contests in which the SNP fell back to 20.9 per cent – strengthened Labour's position, while the decline of the SNP also allowed the strong anti-devolution wings of *both* parties to regroup and organize opposition to compromise which satisfied few and mobilized fewer. Persuaded that the Scotland Act was, for the moment, the best that could be got, Labour's home rulers put such resources as they had (not a lot, in view of an impending election) into fighting for its approval in the referendum specified by the Act, crossing their fingers that the winter would be short, the unions would keep their members in order, and Scotland would win the World Cup. Nothing was said about the oil, because the Scotland Act's drafting made sure there was no possible way in which the Assembly could affect it.

The weather was hellish – it was still snowing on General Election day in May – the unions laid on the 'winter of discontent', and Scotland were pulverized in Argentina. The home rulers swung from euphoria to near-despair; the anti-devolutionists on the Scottish Council, led by the fanatical Janey Buchan, pinned down Gordon Brown, who was in charge of the campaign. Tony Benn came up to Scotland campaigning for a 'Yes' vote, although he had earlier expressed misgivings about devolution. It seemed part of a process which was weakening Westminster authority – which he saw as the instrument for achieving socialism – to the benefit of the Scottish Assembly on one side and Brussels on the other.[34] He was virtually alone in the Labour leadership in actually taking seriously the issue which had occupied a bored and mischievous Parliament for nearly two years. The engagement of front-bench politicians was nominal, while *frondeurs* such as Robin Cook, Neil Kinnock and the indefatigable Tam Dalyell flung themselves on the hapless piece of legislation. Neither they, nor the Labour devolutionists, nor the SNP – all of us being tyros at a Scottish political game which had only started in the 1960s – had realized that what matters in politics is not taking part, but winning. Mrs Thatcher, Sir Alec Douglas Home, and the senior civil servant who said a couple of years later that devolution had been worth it, as it kept the Scots quiet for the vital period of securing the oil, didn't have to be taught that lesson.

Of the regions most affected by the oil industry, only Highland voted in favour of devolution in the referendum of 1 March 1979. This despite the fact that the oil was now being landed, that 100,000 jobs had been created, and that the balance of payments was steadily improving. Shetland's rejection of the Scotland Act was particularly emphatic.

'Turkeys Voting for an Early Christmas'

Under Mrs Thatcher the Tories had retreated from devolution and, at least in the short term, they acted with lack of scruple and great skill. She and her Scottish spokesman, the *ci-devant* devolutionist Teddy Taylor, pursued their own strategy – of tax cuts rather than an active industrial policy – and swung into opposition to any degree of Scottish autonomy. This was tough enough to lose the support of two junior Scottish affairs spokesmen, Malcolm Rifkind and Alick Buchanan-Smith, who campaigned mildly for a 'Yes' vote. The Tories let Labour, now devolutionist but not enthusiastic about it, outmanoeuvre the SNP, and then exploited Labour's internal divisions. The Scotland Act was finally passed in 1978, and as the referendum on it approached, Lord Home, who had chaired Heath's constitutional committee, was produced to announce that the Tories had 'something better' on offer. He may have been sincere in demanding proportional representation and taxation powers for the Assembly; he was certainly influential. The Callaghan government went tactically to pieces: it had convinced international finance by acceding to the IMF's terms in 1976, but it failed in the 'boom' situation of 1978–9 to convince the unions of the menace of the alternative, and no senior trade unionist had the prescience to see it either. When this was added to nationalist misgivings, government unpopularity and organizational ineptitude on the 'Yes' side, the wonder is that a majority of any sort was found for the bill on 1 March 1979.[35]

The referendum was purely advisory, but Callaghan was obliged by the terms of the Scotland Act to move for the repeal of the legislation if it got less than 40 per cent of the votes of the total Scots electorate. It got just under 33 per cent, barely 2 per cent ahead of the 'Noes'. The eleven SNP MPs decided to move a vote of no confidence in the government, and persisted in their hostility, even when by various devious means Callaghan got the support of the three Plaid Cymru MPs and Jim Sillars and John

Robertson of the Scottish Labour Party. By this vote, carried ultimately by a majority of one on 28 March, the SNP virtually wrote itself out of Parliament. 'Turkeys voting for an early Christmas' was the premier's exasperated response, and traditional Labour voters in the north-east and elsewhere swung back to their old allegiance. The SNP vote fell nationally from 30 per cent to 18 per cent; of the eleven MPs only Donald Stewart and Gordon Wilson in Dundee survived, and the Scottish Labour Party was wiped out. Later that year the Conservatives enjoyed a boomlet of support, and even took five out of the eight Scottish seats in the first elections to the European Parliament.

It was Mrs Thatcher's oil, to do with as she thought fit.

9

Oil Culture

If a city hasn't been used by an artist not even the inhabitants live there imaginatively.

–Alasdair Gray, *Lanark*[1]

Let us lie once more, say 'What we think, we can'
– The old idealist lie –

Louis MacNeice, 'An Eclogue for Christmas'[2]

The Offshore Islanders

The oil derrick was the most obvious symbol of industry since the factory chimney or the colliery headstock. And yet in the 1980s that seemed to be all most people knew about an industry which was gobbling a quarter of British industrial investment. Offshore oil was discreet, geographically withdrawn from the main population centres. Although its owners were literally household names, presenting themselves at every filling-station, it was shy about projecting itself as a producer. Rigs and support ships and production platforms were Meccano structures innocent of the hand of the industrial designer, let alone the corporate logo people.

Offshore oil communicated in a technobabble which was, even by the standards of shop-talk, inscrutable. Academics returned from the University of Stavanger talking of courses called *Boring* and *Advanced Boring*. Technical journals were throttled by phrases like 'maintenance of downhole umbilicals by intelligent pigs':

grievous bodily harm was done to the grammar and syntax of the English language. All the more so when what was being communicated could be put in decent English and, when explained, was often fascinating. Offshore oil's technology outdid in ingenuity the looms and mules and jennies of the industrial revolution which kids learned about in school. Ironically, thanks to progressive teaching methods – projects and 'hands-on' instruction – and the heritage business, kids knew more about Richard Arkwright and James Watt than they did about what was going on to the east of Hull or Aberdeen.

They were not alone. The impact of the oil on the British metropolitan intelligentsia and its imagination was practically zero. Mervyn Jones of the *New Statesman* wrote a sharp piece of reportage, *The Oil Rush*, in 1976, with grim photos by Fay Godwin; then there was silence. In 1979 a novel called *Offshore* won the Booker Prize. It was a gentle satire by Penelope Fitzgerald about a collection of middle-class eccentrics living on houseboats off Chelsea, rather like Joyce Cary's *The Horse's Mouth* forty years earlier, minus Cary's demonic Gully Jimson. Nothing in the way of metaphor was implied – least of all along the lines that the 'real' offshore business meant a collection of highly commercial operators living (and working) off an island inhabited by middle-class eccentrics.

In 1986 Al Alvarez wrote a book, also called *Offshore*, describing a trip to the platforms. Or rather, he republished a long *New Yorker* essay, itself a significant point. Alvarez seemed concerned to emphasize the downbeat quality of the whole experience: the contrast between 'outer space with bad weather', and the banality of what was actually going on. On one hand the battered, dishevelled affluence of Aberdeen, the necklaces of lights out to sea, viewed from the helicopter, the incredible statistics. On the other hand the tedium of day-to-day rig life – 'The atmosphere in the mess hall and coffee shop and recreation rooms is subdued, friendly, undemanding' – the noise, the lack of 'culture', of society *and* of individual space. Together these suggested not adventure, but something numbing in its normality:

In a way, the Diving Control Room is a model for the whole offshore enterprise. The first time you see the banks of gauges with their flickering needles, the digital read-outs, the levers, the switches, the coloured lights, and, above all, the images on the video screens . . . it seems like the greatest show on earth, a technological miracle, a justification of every boast about man's ingenuity and his ability to organize. But within an hour, you treat it as the people concerned treat it – as just another job, more complicated than most, more difficult than many.[3]

Did this reflect Kit Carson's picture of avoidable injuries caused by 'the political economy of speed': the loss of life in helicopter mishaps and diving accidents, the disruption to older communities and local and regional ecologies? Piper Alpha was yet to come. Others, though not in London, would later demand a 'creative treatment of actuality' which dramatized the hopes of prosperity raised and shattered, the testing and rejecting of local and national political élites. But at a 'British' political level, whose instabilities were provoking repeated and lurid fictionalizations, this refused to arrive.[4] Even the airport fiction of the likes of Jeffrey Archer failed to come up with anything other than *North Sea Hijack*, 'an asinine *Boy's Own Paper* adventure story with the very minimum of thrills and a totally miscast hero'. It did, however, have a tough female prime minister, double scotch in hand, knocking baddies for six from Downing Street. Prescient, for 1979 . . . There was a Bennite political thriller – Chris Mullin's *A Very British Coup* (1983), much more successfully filmed – with energy politics as a central theme, but it homed in on nuclear power, and ignored oil.[5]

This non-critique induces first curiosity and then suspicion. How could something that big be so boring? Was the British intelligentsia so parochial and apprehensive that it couldn't comprehend what was happening, or was a canny campaign of obfuscation going on? The first was always more than a possibility. If poetry, as F.R. Leavis said, ought to be at the most conscious point of the race in time, then Philip Larkin, at Hull, pretty well coincided with North Sea oil at its most unavoidable.

And avoided it. Drink, porn and general churlishness apart, the man wasn't blind to his surroundings: eyeing from his compartment the boozy miners on Retford or Doncaster platform, thinking of sad Mr Bleaney from 'the bodies' – the Coventry car body plant. Asked to write a poem for National Environment Year, 1972, he obliged with a pasquinade which, although second-grade Larkin, would have been acceptable to social critics as alert to industrial change as Ruskin or Carlyle over a century before:

> Things are tougher than we are, just
> As earth will always respond
> However we mess it about;
> Chuck filth in the sea, if you must:
> The tides will be clean beyond.
> – But what do I feel now? Doubt?
>
> *
>
> On the Business Page, a score
> Of spectacled grins approve
> Some takeover bid that entails
> Five per cent profit (and ten
> Per cent more in the estuaries): move
> Your works to the unspoilt dales
> (Grey area grants)! And when
>
> You try to get near the sea
> In summer . . .
>   It seems, just now,
> To be happening so very fast;
> Despite all the land left free
> For the first time I feel somehow
> That it isn't going to be the last,
>
> That before I snuff it, the whole
> Boiling will be bricked in
> Except for the tourist parts –
> First slum of Europe: a role
> It won't be so hard to win
> With a cast of crooks and tarts.[6]

Lady Dartmouth, for the Tory government, blanched at the 'spectacled grins'. Out they went, though Larkin didn't make a fuss about it. But of the industry which permitted this assault on old England – and gave men and trawlers from Hull, turned off the Icelandic fishing grounds, the chance of work providing safety watch around the rigs? Nothing.

From 1953 to 1961 there had been a smaller oil boom, on and off the coast of Sicily. For a few years the port of Syracuse contributed to a rise in Italian production from 18,000 to 7 million tons. There were tenders, tankers and rigs. It ended. Sicily continued, dogged by crime, *omertà*, the unwillingness to change; as its great writer, Giuseppi Tomasi, Prince of Lampedusa, had forecast in the book he laboured for decades to complete, *The Leopard*, which appeared in the middle of this period. Visited by a delegate from the northern capital of Turin, mandated to secure his membership of the Italian senate, Lampedusa's hero, the Prince of Salina, declares that he and his island are too old to change: 'it doesn't matter about doing things well or badly; the sin which we Sicilians never forgive is simply that of "doing" at all.' They will react to the modern world like a senile old man trundled in his wheelchair round the glories of the Crystal Palace in London.[7]

History was too much for Sicily. It bore the island down, numbed its responses. As oil activity rose, similar things were being said about Britain. In 1981, two years into a Conservative government whose 'radical' measures seemed to be intensifying the economic crisis, some relief seemed to come Mrs Thatcher's way from an interpretation of British history, emanating from Texas, which suggested that the slobberer in the wheelchair was already immanent in the grandeur of the Crystal Palace itself. Martin Wiener's *English Culture and the Decline of the Industrial Spirit, 1850–1980* argued that the English, even at their zenith, had never really liked commerce and had retreated as soon as possible to country life, political deference, and paternalistic social legislation which had progressively clogged the hard-and-fast dictates of the market economy.[8] Wiener met with academic opposition, but ministerial applause; Mrs Thatcher was believed to have distributed copies to wavering Cabinet wets. Something of what she believed the country was up against can be seen from the remarks of Armand Hammer of Occidental Petroleum:

Great Britain, sliding politely into post-imperial and post-industrial decline, seemed the least likely candidate on earth for membership among the great oil-producing nations ... The British government treated the potential bonanza as carelessly and complacently as any untutored sheikh and, in those early days, practically threw it into the hands of the Seven Sisters.[9]

Uncommercial Travellers

In terms of responses to something as big as the railway mania of the 1840s, Wiener had a point. In fact, apart from Jones and Alvarez only three writers based 'south of the M62' – the road which ran from Hull to Liverpool – seem in any sense to have reacted to the oil: Jonathan Raban, Paul Theroux and, later on, Linda Christmas. Christmas's book was in the tradition of J.B. Priestley's *English Journey* (1936). Both the others seem to have been determined to do something conspicuously odd: in 1982 Raban sailed around Britain and Theroux, following on his success in *The Great Railway Bazaar*, made the trip by train. All three were writing in a marginal mode – the home travel journal – albeit one which had had a long history, going back not just to Orwell's *Road to Wigan Pier* but to Dickens's *Uncommercial Traveller*, and before him to Defoe. However risky the 'self as oracle' was, the results might be illuminating. Were they?

Christmas's *Chopping Down the Cherry Trees* (1990) was the last and slightest. Although projecting herself as an 'absolute floating voter', sorrowfully concerned at the axemen's assault on British society, she remained oddly unanalytical about her own reactions

– although she had been eight years the wife of a Conservative politician, once part of that family that Norman Fowler famously wanted to spend more time with. She found that oil was simply a Shetland experience, just as there was a nuclear menace at Dounreay and a singularly dull and unforthcoming Scottish nationalist, Gordon Wilson, in a shabby office in Dundee. She made no attempt to articulate these issues in terms of the common factor of energy policy, or even to recollect that in 1972–9 Wilson had been the business end of the SNP's oil campaign. Granted Christmas's central metaphor, it didn't seem to occur to her that in terms of the real resources of the country, Mrs Thatcher – here in her 'stern nanny' guise – had been less Chekhov's Lophakin than the spendthrift Madame Ranevsky.[10]

Both Raban and Theroux were more committed, and angrier. Theroux's journey, undertaken in the middle of the Falklands War, contrasted the shabbily low-key decency of railwaymen keeping their branch lines going, and the understated heroics of the 'bracing' British holiday, with the ululations of triumph emanating from Whitehall. Otherwise baffled about nationalism, the American found the crofters and gamekeepers of desolate Sutherland representative of qualities of intelligence and honesty otherwise in short supply, but was appalled by Aberdeen, its mixture of ferocious respectability and empty exploitation. Oil had not improved the place:

We reached the coast. Offshore, a four-legged oil-rig looked like a mechanical sea-monster defecating in shallow water. It was like a symbol of this part of Scotland. Aberdeen was the most prosperous city on the British coast. It had the healthiest finances, the brightest future, the cleanest buildings, the briskest traders. But that was not the whole of it. I came to hate Aberdeen more than any other place I saw. Yes, yes, the streets were clean; but it was an awful city.[11]

Theroux hated the sort of obsessive money-making that Wiener thought propelled economic growth. The cultural void which was Aberdeen, the absence of civilized eating and drinking, were repellent to him, in comparison with the 'British' virtues of quietness, reflectiveness, savouring the slow passage of time along the threatened railway tracks.

Aberdonians being reading people, they were incensed at Theroux's assault. Jack Webster hurled Aberdeen intellects, from Thomas Reid to Annie Lennox, back at Theroux in the *Scottish Daily Express*.[12] This may account for what happened to Jonathan Raban.

Raban's line was that of the furious English left-liberal clerisy, what the Murdoch press would later dismiss as 'the chattering classes'. Encountering at Lyme Regis a copy of the *Sun* blaring about the Falklands, Raban

... saw hatred mass-produced, bigotry put up for sale under the benign eye of the government whose cause the bigotry was designed to serve.[13]

His boyhood haunt of Lymington had been sacked by speculative building; there was £25 million-worth of glittering yachts on the river:

Behind each mean-eyed boat there lay the rich pickings of the property business, the money markets, North Sea oil, silicon chippery or the legerdemain of tax accountancy.[14]

The Tory-voting clergyman father who had once sculled with him had now swung far left; a Rural Dean of Southampton living in the red light district and organizing the unemployed and the nuclear disarmers. In Hull he met Larkin, his old mentor, and found that that monument to political incorrectness indeed never elevated his range above a 200-yard circuit of flat, university library and off-licence. Against this, as his motor-boat chugged north, past angular, semi-alphabetical shapes on the eastern horizon which were rigs and platforms, Raban encountered a persuasive and Webster-friendly mirage:

But to the north there was still a living city whose amazing renaissance was talked of in places as far away even as London. People spoke of its lordly wealth as if it was the imaginary Dallas of the television serial. Its jewelled inhabitants walked ten feet tall. In the decaying industrial fabric of Britain, the city was a marvel, a promise of the good life to come . . . an astounding counterworld to Hull and Blyth. There'd be . . . there'd be . . . there'd be all-day, all-night saloons, their granite walls drumming with the amplified sound of Dolly Parton and Johnny Cash. You'd be able to buy Manhattans and Tequila Sunrises in dollars and cents. The deep, ravine-like streets would be solid with low-slung Cougars and Chevies, their chrome faces cast in the contemptuous grin that goes with big bucks . . .

The success of Aberdeen was an essential part of my own plot. After touching on so many failures and disappointments, the story needed a crock of gold somewhere.[15]

But Aberdeen gave him the slip, remained an imagined post-industrial Xanadu. Fog, a mass of birds at the sewage outfall, and the threat of being rammed in the mêlée of oil-rig tenders and tugs scared him off.

This seems ominously symptomatic. Oil failed almost totally to surface in the imaginative literature of Anglo-Britain. Where was the novel or the poem of North Sea oil? Or the play – although hadn't Ibsen arguably already written it in *Pillars of Society*? Where was the solemn moral accountancy of Leavis's Great Tradition?

Or was this to expect too much? Industrial change usually took a long time to register on the literary imagination. Jane Austen had the moral conscience of the Evangelical revival, but was indifferent to mules and jennies, if she ever knew what they were. Sir Walter Scott lived through the industrial revolution at its most intense and alarming, when poverty-ridden weavers and former soldiers could have plunged Scotland into insurrection, but only in his last serious work, *The Chronicles of the Canongate* (1827), did he even mention a cotton mill. Dickens got railways into *Dombey and Son* (1844), but as a discouraging symbol of death.

Perhaps the Scottish experience of oil those basins of onshore activity, as isolated from one another as the rigs themselves – was in its way suggestive. Raban himself had written in an earlier book, *Soft City* (1977), that people's view of their environment was not so much civic as highly subjective and discontinuous. The trend of modern communications created a compartmentalized life in which, say, the Los Angeles kid's notion of Los Angeles was limited to what he saw from his parents' car when being run to school or the supermarket: a couple of blocks looming into focus out of the motorway city.[16] This supplemented an earlier observation by the American historian of early industrialization, J.U. Nef, in *War and Human Progress* (1940): the increasing specialization of knowledge had itself made it impossible to take the 'synthetical' view necessary for an imaginative capture of economic and social change; even the intellectual was in the position of Kinglake's soldiers in the Crimea. The bigger the change, in fact, the more inadequate the conceptual response.[17]

Earlier, the moral maps had been more comprehensive. In *Mansfield Park*, Jane Austen could slap down the arriviste and probably Scots-nabob Crawford duo as representing behaviour toxic to the high thinking and plain living of her own sort – the sort of thing which could bring the Jacquerie to the lodge gates. However archaic his convictions, Scott had provided a template for the recovery of national histories throughout Europe. Once Thomas Carlyle had stated the 'Condition of England Question' in *Chartism* (1839), no writer could remain indifferent to the power of Mechanism and the Cash Nexus. Now it seemed that this collective consciousness, alive as late as Orwell, was disintegrating.[18]

Not because of hostility or falsity, but because of the same unmanageability of history of which Lampedusa complained? In Doris Lessing's autobiographical novel *The Golden Notebook*, published as a 'condition of England' work in 1962, Anna Wulf, Lessing's neurotic heroine, plagued by unfulfilled sexuality and disillusioned by communism, has a fling with an American businessman who satisfies her, sensitively and enjoyably. This much truth gave mutual respect and affection. The American's straightforward affection and hedonism – the mark of a younger and more confident society – cut across Anna's own obsessive history, cramped and bruised. Two people, enjoying one another physically, remain far apart politically but, as Raymond Williams would have put it, the distance is measured. This, however, implied metaphorically that the need to analyse checked the ability to organize: that the future lay with the unreflective but energetic Americans. Even when *The Golden Notebook* enjoyed a revival in the 1970s, it was not because of its reflections on history but because of its feminist connotations – something not wholly acceptable to its author, who saw this appropriation as part of an increasingly divided, depoliticized, sensibility.[19]

In the 1970s, the worlds of learning and of politics seemed almost as remote from one another as Britain and America. In 1977 Tony Benn visited Cambridge, and wrote in his diary of meeting Raymond Williams, 'a quiet middle-aged academic' apparently unknown to him.[20] If this was left speaking to left, what chance was there of a unity of view on the complex issue of the oil? This situation was made even more extreme since some authors were vividly conscious of the implications of the oil, particularly for politics, and nearly all of them were Scots.

McGrath's Rising

The rigs and platforms irrupted off a highly literary coastline, from the sagasteads of Shetland and the place of Hugh Mac-Diarmid's exile, south to the Orkney of St Magnus and Edwin Muir, the Cromarty of Hugh Miller and the fabulous Sir Thomas Urquhart, translator of Rabelais and proponent of a universal language, and the Aberdeenshire of George MacDonald and Lewis Grassic Gibbon. Eric Linklater lived long enough to sell his house at Nigg to Brown and Root for more than he made on most of his novels. Neil Gunn died in 1973, just as the first strikes were being made, MacDiarmid in 1978. The writers of the inter-war 'Scottish Renaissance', theoretically progressive, had looked with suspicion on 'the greater herd and the great machines'. How would they have reacted – how would their successors react – to the dimensions of this new assault?[21]

A tradition of Scots political fiction existed, but it was always 'extra-parliamentary'; its theatre of politics was both intimate and cosmic, with a satire, irony and obliquity which were turned on the individual's ideological and psychological involvement with the political. In the early nineteenth century John Galt, Walter Scott and James Hogg didn't just comment on but were *part* of Scotland's 'willed' modernization: from near-medieval subsistence to technology in under two generations. This impulse transformed itself into the 'popular print capitalism' of Victorian newspaper novels, like those of William Alexander, alert to the agricultural capitalism of Buchan, the 'muckle fermers' and fish merchants who were the forebears of Maitland Mackie and Iain Wood.[22] If Scottish politics in the 1980s had a slogan, it would come from a novel, Alasdair Gray's injunction to observe civic virtu: 'Work as if you were living in the early days of a better nation', from the climax – in every sense of the term – of his *1982 Janine*.[23]

In Scotland the first wave of SNP success, in the 1960s, had already energized a discussion about the country and its future in symposia and broadcasts, and in 1966 the magazine *Scottish International* was set up by a Catholic undergraduate, Bob Tait, with the assistance of Father Anthony Ross, Catholic chaplain to Edinburgh University, the historian Christopher Smout, and the poet and translator Edwin Morgan. *Scottish International*'s elaborate 'What Kind of Scotland?' conference, held in Edinburgh at Easter 1973, had two intriguingly distinct impacts. Dr Donald Mackay disclosed the unpreparedness of government departments when confronted with the challenge, and the hasty and incompetent taxation policy which had resulted in huge revenue losses: a début which was to give him a high profile for the rest of the decade.[24] And, perhaps more significantly, John McGrath's 7:84 Company's *The Cheviot, the Stag and the Black, Black Oil* – history, political cabaret and *ceilidh* – set out on its remarkable consciousness-raising career in the Highlands.

Commissioned by Bob Tait for the occasion, *The Cheviot*'s première was in the George Square Theatre in Edinburgh on 31 March 1973. McGrath had only assembled his troupe on 16 March; he wrote the last act on the night of the 30th. In the next couple of years there were to be 100 shows, seen by 30,000 people, in a 17,000-mile tour.

McGrath, a Liverpool man, was where the 'theatre of anger' met the spirit of 1968. 7:84 was dedicated to the proposition that 7 per cent of the population owned 84 per cent of the country's wealth, and fitted into the 'theatre as agitprop' British-style, minibuses doing the part of armoured trains. But McGrath also knew the Scottish bourgeoisie intimately; his wife Elizabeth was the daughter of the magnate Sir Hector MacLennan and sister of the Labour MP Robert MacLennan. She was also a fine actress, and with Alex Norton, Bill Paterson, the Gaelic singer Dolina MacLennan and John Bett, 7:84 set out north by minibus, along with another talented pair: John Byrne, who built the 'pop-up book' which served as a set, and Dave MacLennan, who provided the light show. The story could draw on the talents of a collective authorship spawned by a Narodnik-like movement of student radicals northwards, with the input of Brian Wilson, David Craig, Ray Burnett and James Hunter, several of whom were involved in the launch of the *West Highland Free Press*, edited from Broadford in Skye, within sight of the Howard Doris yard at Loch Kishorn.

The Scottish Committee of the Arts Council didn't believe that Highlanders wanted theatre; they were to be sharply disproved. In part, *The Cheviot* became that long-awaited Scottish sequel to E.P. Thompson's *The Making of the English Working Class* (1965); a story whose narrative, as much cultural as economic, could all too easily have become a grim recital of the circumstances of agrarian oppression. The McGrath collective's achievement was to balance this tragic element against the lyricism of the Gaelic tradition and the absurdities of the inept conquerors, sheep-graziers, tourist entrepreneurs, 'sportsmen', and the tartan-festooned dolts – chiefs, politicians, mad ideologues – who accommodated them. The climax comes when a Texan, Elmer Y. MacAlpine the Fourth, is ushered on stage by politicians and bankers. He sings 'Grannie's Heilan' Hame', drenching the audience in kitsch, then begins calling the company to a square-dance:

> Take your oil-rigs by the score,
> Drill a little well just a little off-shore,
> Pipe that oil in from the sea,
> Pipe those profits – home to me.
>
> I'll bring you work that's hard and good
> A little oil costs a lot of blood.
>
> Your union men just cut no ice
> You work for me – I name the price.
>
> So leave your fishing, and leave your soil,
> Come work for me, I want your oil.

The pace increases, the lyrics change, the dancers drift from the sets and watch open-mouthed as the caller goes solo:

> One 2 3 4 5 6 7
> All good oil men go to heaven
>
> 8 9 10 11 12
> Billions of dollars all to myself
>
> ★
>
> 27 28 29 30
> You play dumb and I'll play dirty
> I'll go home when I see fit
> And all I'll leave is a heap of shit.[25]

The first paying performance was at Aberdeen, then Rosemarkie. After the satire, the songs and the history, the evening would end with a *ceilidh* and a dance. Some places were more full-hearted than others. At Inverness Sir Andrew Gilchrist and a suspicious Highlands and Islands Development Board hierarchy turned up, as did the Countess of Sutherland, putting a brave face on things. At Lochinver the white settlers were out in force, also on Skye. There was 'a strange one at Alness, now oil-struck'. Not for the first time, the Clearances were to become the metaphor for the destruction and dispossession wrought on Scotland:

An ancient, near-blind Gaelic poet, the Bard of Melbost, came up to us after a show in the Outer Hebrides, and said: 'I have heard the story of my people told with truth. If I die tonight, I die a happier man.'[26]

McGrath admitted that the process was for his troupe as much an educational experience *for them* as a didactic exercise. They were seeing the Highlands getting off their knees, breaking out of the 'lament syndrome'. The play ended with the words of Mary MacPherson, a Highland Land Leaguer of the 1880s, which helpfully combined Gaelic, socialism, and the land issue:

> *Cuimhnichibh ur cruadal*
> *Is cumaibh suas ur sroill,*
> *Gun teid an roth mun cuairt duibh*
> *Le neart is cruas nan dorn*
> *Gum bi ur crodh air bhuailtean*
> *'S gach tuathanach air doigh,*
> *'S na Sas'naich air fuadach*
> *A Eilean Uain a' Cheo.*

> Remember that you are a people and fight for your rights –
> There are riches under the hills where you grew up.
> There is iron and coal there, grey lead and gold there –
> There is richness in the land under your feet.

> Remember your hardships and keep up your struggle
> The wheel will turn for you
> By the strength of your hands and the hardness of your fists.
> Your cattle will be on the plains
> Everyone on the land will have a place
> And the exploiter will be driven out.

The Cheviot reached Oban in July, where the SNP was holding its conference. Jim Lynch in the *Scots Independent* remarked on its

impact, although christening the McGrath troupe 'the International Young Socialists'. 'How can they put on a play like that
and then say they are not nationalists?' he asked Billy Wolfe. 'If
we knew the answer to that,' Wolfe replied, 'we would sweep
Scotland tomorrow.'[27]

Nisi Dominus, Frustra Aedificabit

Was oil to power a new autonomy, or was it simply increasing
external control of the country by big money and the American
superpower? This quandary provided much meat for discussion
on the left, the burden of Gordon Brown's *Red Paper*, in 1975,
and tended to emphasize the gulf between 'revolutionaries' and
'home rulers'. The former, rebelling against nationalism's 'false
consciousness', found unusual allies among Conservatives, who
were shifting away from the decentralization of Sir Alec
Douglas-Home's committee, towards a 'Britishness' which was
all the stronger for feeling itself in a minority.

Alan Massie, a leading realist and deeply political novelist,
inherited a sceptical line from Scottish novelists of the 1950s such
as James Kennaway and J.D. Scott. He had a European awareness:
the kidnapping and murder of Aldo Moro in *The Death of Men*
(1981), and Vichy France in *A Question of Loyalties* (1988). He
also intervened frequently in politics, moving from fringe devolution in the 1970s – as an associate of Robert Underwood and
Euan Marwick and their Nevis Institute – to embattled unionism
in the 1980s. This transition was reflected in his one fictional
encounter with contemporary Scottish politics, *One Night in
Winter* (1984).

Despite the Grand Guignol of its theme, the tone of the novel
is elegiac and pessimistic. Massie's narrator, Dallas Graham, returns to his family mansion in Kincardineshire and joins the
louche entourage of a rising SNP politician called Fraser Donnelly.
Donnelly, a haulage contractor, represents the enterprise culture

(soap, rope and dope) parasitic on oil. A monster of the permissive age, sexually voracious, he is killed off by his wife while *in flagrante*. As a handy Marxist friend assures Graham, Donnelly is what small nationalism will turn out to be: nasty, brutish and Scots.

The most sympathetic figure in a deeply off-putting *galère* is an old merchant banker, whose view is that

> ... the world is for the big battalions. Small countries cannot withstand it, especially when they are not protected by the barrier of a different language. Their geographical fate determines their nature ... Scotland will grow ever less Scottish and ever less stimulating; we live in a withered culture. Sounds of energy are the energy of a death-rattle. The Union may not have been the end of an auld sang, but it led us into the last verse.[28]

This lecture – which represents Massie's own view – shows the limitations of his 'novel of ideas'. The ideas – rather elderly ones at that – simply crush out V.S. Pritchett's 'determined stupor' out of which great novelists work, something vividly evident in their contrast with the perjink defence of the Union by Bailie Nicoll Jarvie in Scott's *Rob Roy*. Jarvie and his cronies would have taken oil in their stride, with a real energy behind them which would never stay put in Charlotte Square. Ultimately *A Night in Winter* was derivative where it was not melodramatic: Lampedusa, Anthony Powell, John Fowles leave their prints on too many episodes. Only the final section, when Graham, now an antique-dealer in London, tries to make contact with Donnelly's widow/murderess, conveys a sense of individual experience. Massie's point was perhaps that real life could only be lived away from the Scottish phantasmagoria; but delineating the Scottish situation – even if only to reject it – required greater empathy.

Massie did not lose by being the one articulate voice of Scottish intellectual unionism, the inevitable balancing opinion called into play by the national media. But, *The Cheviot* apart, politics rather than literature was dominant in the 1970s. In 1977 Neal Ascherson observed that little cultural efflorescence seemed to accompany the political activity.[29] Indeed one of the last declarations of Hugh MacDiarmid was that, if spared to vote on 1 March 1979, he would vote against the Scotland Act as betraying 'real' nationalism. This sense of *ennui* was imprinted on James Campbell, whose *Invisible Country* (1984) was an attempt to combine the discursive observation of Theroux with something of Edwin Muir's social criticism in *Scottish Journey* (1935). Campbell chose to leave Edinburgh for *The Times Literary Supplement* in 1982, believing that there was no cultural life worth speaking of in the north.[30] This informs both the tone of his book, and his encounters with the oil — an insensitive executive in one pub, a trip to a rig, a couple of whores in another pub:

It was the Boom. But booms come and go in a country where pessimism is a native faculty. On 12 August 1982, the *Scotsman* published an article by a local journalist which foretold the withering of Aberdeen's oil industry. On 13 August, the same newspaper had a report based on a new Scottish Economic Bulletin, which glowed with 'the sustaining effect of the North Sea oil industry'. The reason for the contradiction, which in a similar form can be found, week in, week out, lies not in the ineptitude of journalists, but in the nature of the economy itself.[31]

The fact that the *Scottish Economic Bulletin* was a government publication, and that the journalist might have been trying to pre-empt what he thought was propaganda, didn't seem to occur to Campbell. His notion of the country's 'invisibility', its ingrained contradiction and pessimism, was predicated on the failure of 1979. Scottish politics, to Campbell, was a bore; but without politics, others felt, a rhetoric of confusion became self-fulfilling.

Campbell shared the conventional wisdom in the South that the Scottish question was exploded; and indeed the resumption both of agitation for home rule and any growth in the fortunes of the Scottish National Party took two parliaments to achieve. Yet as the cultural historian Cairns Craig wrote,

Instead of political defeat leading to quiescence, it led directly into an explosion of cultural creativity, a creativity coming to terms with the origins of the political defeat and redefining the nation's conception of itself. The eighties have been one of the most significant decades of Scottish cultural self-definition in the past two centuries.[32]

Parallels could be drawn with Ireland after the death of Parnell in 1891 – the foundation of the Gaelic League, the Irish Literary Theatre and, in 1908, Sinn Féin. W.B. Yeats's later image of Parnell visiting Jonathan Swift's dark grove, and there drinking 'bitter wisdom that enriched the blood', seems telling. Of all these cultural developments – in painting, the revival of representational art in a new Glasgow School; in plays, the work of John McGrath, Liz Lochhead and Iain Heggie; in television, John Byrne's *Tutti Frutti*; and the films of Bill Forsyth – perhaps the success of Alasdair Gray's *Lanark* in 1982 was the most vivid, not least because Gray stated that the traumas of 1979 had knocked away a writer's block that had afflicted him for years.

In Gray's frontispiece to *Lanark*, the oil rigs twinkle in an inky sea, out of which rises a version of Hobbes' Leviathan – 'Man, greatest among the beasts of the earth for pride'. *Lanark* was a heady mixture of *Bildungsroman*, science-fiction and political allegory, stylistically suspended between James Joyce and Lewis Carroll, and in time between the 1950s and 2000. It has been compared with *Ulysses*, but in fact is both more realistic and fantastic. An artist, Duncan Thaw, attempting and failing to paint a mural of the Creation in a Glasgow church, passes after his suicide into a strange subterranean world in which the wealthy literally live off the poor – who are recycled into food. Reincarnated as Lanark, and projected into a world of international negotiations, severed from the messy, creative reality of working-class Unthank, he ultimately plays a confused part in saving his own community, the doomed industrial town.

Lanark is about the struggle of love and what Adam Smith called the 'social affections' against impersonal forces which have changed the institutions of politics into those of destruction. It also reflects the experience of many Scots in the oil years – of being plucked from a country suddenly grown interesting, and set down in pleasant and privileged places where food, wine and women became magically available: the provincial suddenly subject to the seduction of power. *Lanark* is, and is not, about oil (or, God help us, the Oil Experience). At one level it harks back to Henryson's fable of 'The Toun Mous and the Uponlandis Mous', and a traditional discourse anent affluence and morality. It nearly ends pessimistic, and yet the glimmerings of a small-scale socialist future show through. When the author, rendered as Nastler, appears, he tells Lanark that he had originally intended the book to be a socialist epic:

... what the Aeneid had been to the Roman Empire my epic would be to the Scottish Cooperative Wholesale Republic, one of the many hundreds of small peaceful socialist republics which would emerge (I thought) when all the big empires and corporations crumbled.[33]

The socialist city, run by 'makers, movers and menders', what David Marquand would call the 'principled society', is saved: '*Nisi Dominus, Frustra Aedificabit*'. The theme resurfaces in Gray's shorter and more savage *1982 Janine*, which he claims to be 'a sadomasochistic fetishistic fantasy'. This is the black night of Jock MacLeish, one-time 'lad o' pairts' and electrical lighting wizard, now an alcoholic supervisor of security installations, tied to pornographic fantasies of power over women which are a combination of *Playboy* and *Dallas*. America, that expansive, Whitmanite continent of democracy and opportunity and jazz, the demotic civic justice of the Western and the hard-bitten private eye, had still been around in the early impact of the oil. But now it had, in the Thatcher-Reagan alliance, calcified into modes of exploitation and repression; of barbed-wire installations, corrupt cops, and flesh for sale: a confederacy of the rich and the brutal. MacLeish's calvary is even more agonizing than Lanark's.

Gray's achievement in a way endorsed Massie's criticisms. Scotland, and Scottish nationalism, was no longer an adequate container for the civic. The menaces to the virtuous life were themselves international, and required appropriately complex responses. But they also had to be grounded in a cultural community which was directly conscious, not one in which artistic response was mediated through a print-capitalism which had long passed beyond the possibility of individual control. One, authentically Scottish, response was to surrender, to sell oneself to the highest international bidder. The eponymous hero of Gray's *The Fall of Kelvin Walker* (1984) does precisely this, recruiting himself into the media which is, *inter alia*, conspiring to play down the economic benefits which could flow from the oil. Walker had his factual analogues, notably in the career of the charmless but energetic Andrew Neil, who moved from being an advocate of 'oil-powered independence' in the *Economist* in the early 1970s to becoming lieutenant of the ubiquitous Rupert Murdoch in the following decade.

The alternative to the 'cultural supermarket' which Neil peddled in the *Sunday Times* was the engaged culture of the post-industrial city of Glasgow in which Gray's eccentric career was sustained by the richness of painting, jazz and rock groups, drama and broadcasting; not unlike 1920s Berlin, a slightly ominous precedent. Again there was the concern with the response of individuals, the encapsulation of social change in their own histories. Liz Lochhead's monologues were a new type of social criticism, penetrating the cocoon of the *Sunday Times* reader who deadened the uncertainties of fitful affluence with conspicuous consumption. They shifted away from the easy target of the former schoolteacher Verena complaining that, 'When He comes back from the rigs after a fortnight he can think of only one thing. A sheet and duvet set in navy blue is not a good idea', to something much darker and metaphorical.

21 March
Course, I'm used to it now, after all these years, never give it a thought. Well, from the word go, ever since He first went up there on the rigs it's been much better. Definitely. Well, financially speaking anyway, I mean see before, with his other job, before, on shore . . . honest to God, the mortgage was a millstone.

We first flitted here, I thought we were going to be clomping about on the bare floorboards and sitting on orange boxes watching a wee black-and-white portable for ever.

Him away, the diet is a piece of cake. Well, you've no distractions. Although it's much easier now that I'm only on the maintenance anyway. But see when He's home and he gets the munchies and he's up at midnight frying eggs and spattering grease all over my new ceramic hob I could see him far enough – but och well, I just try and tell myself that he's not home for ever, and I bite my tongue.

But you don't tend to bother cooking for yourself, do you? And I am out a lot. Tend to just slurp down a wee cup of slimmasoup while I'm waiting for my carmens to heat up.

Och just round to my mother's basically, just to get out of the house. Although He is that jealous, vernear divorce proceedings he phones up and I'm no in!

Although as I try to tell My Mother and Our Joy, I'm convinced it's with us having the none of a family ourselves I've adjusted so well. Means I'm a free agent. Moira was just asking me when I was round there the other day, she says: Did you never think to *investigate* it, if that's no too cheeky a question . . .

I says, No, I don't mind telling you, I says, it was a *night*mare Moira, I says, you know nothing about indignity if you've never had your tubes blown.

Doctors! Och it was into the ins-and-outs of everything.

Could find nothing wrong. Nothing wrong with either of the two of us. Not that they could put their finger on. Suggested might simply be missing the moment, what with the two weeks on, two weeks off, mibbe he should think of changing his job, or something?

But och, it's security isn't it . . .

And is a kid compatible with an off-white fitted carpet, that's the question . . .? [34]

Liz Lochhead, like Gray, went to the School of Art in Glasgow: and went there from the doomed steelworks town of Motherwell. A miniaturist with a knife, she did not constrain herself with realism, as the sub-title implies. The narrator is a thirtysomething former schoolteacher, not in work but well off. Her husband is on the rigs, her society determined by the positional goods he enables her to own. There is a sexual relationship of sorts, nothing else. Her fecund sister Joy lives in a 'scheme', with five kids and an unemployed husband, but fights her corner in tenants' and anti-poll-tax groups. Verena tries to persuade Joy to act as a surrogate mother and give her her last, unexpected child. But at the birth Joy refuses, and her sister breaks with her and everyone else. The child will be called Felicity. Verena and Joy are not just two Scotlands, but two unequal halves of the world, two incompatible moral codes. Nothing in Scotland was simple; as with Carlyle a century and a half earlier, the didactic point was made with satire and grotesquerie.

Resurrection or Brigadoon?

Political disenfranchisement meant an absence in Scotland of the 'politics as theatre' novel, but it encouraged this migration of political and economic themes into the metaphor or the fable; as in George Mackay Brown's *Greenvoe* (1972). To Brown, as to his teacher Edwin Muir, the whale-backed Orkneys were an Eden, and one which, unlike Muir, he never left. But now mechanism was moving in on them, too. *Greenvoe* was written evidently with Occidental's Flotta terminal in mind. The Orkney island of Hellya, whose quiet, co-operative life is celebrated in the early chapters, is taken over to house a project called Black Star. Its people are dispersed, its houses, church and school bulldozed to make way for tanks and piers and 'installations'. Yet at the end, when Black Star is itself evacuated, the islanders come back to act out the ceremony of the death and resurrection of the harvest king:

The Lord of the Harvest took the black cloth from the niche where the horse-shoe had been secreted. The horse-shoe had vanished. In its place was a loaf and a bottle.

The Master Horsemen raised the Harvester to his feet. They put a white cloak over his shoulders. They brought him over to the niche where the whisky and the bread stood.

Slowly the sun heaved itself clear of the sea. The cliff below was alive with the stir and cry of birds. The sea moved and flung glories of light over Quoylay and Hrossey and Hellya, and all the skerries and rocks around. The smell of the earth came to them in the first wind of morning, from the imprisoned fields of the island; and the fence could not keep it back.

The Lord of the Harvest raised his hands. 'We have brought light and blessing to the kingdom of winter,' he said, 'however long it endures, that kingdom, a night or a season or a thousand ages. The word has been found. Now we will eat and drink together and be glad.'

The sun rose. The stones were warm. They broke the bread.

Despite the social changes, the Christian faith – which Mackay Brown shared with Muir – would persist, as indeed would the interpretive sophistication of an intellect which could juggle with economics, ecology, and Frazer's *Golden Bough*.[35]

English novels about the political and economic crisis of the late 1970s – by Melvyn Bragg, Margaret Drabble or Mervyn Jones – were portentous. A nation-shattering crisis appears to be both imminent and unresolvable, with the likes of Drabble's *The Ice Age* (1978) showing Fabian meliorism in full retreat. The Scots, on the other hand, treated the crisis imaginatively and even playfully. This may sound like a contradiction in terms, given the importance of what was happening. But they realized that the oil had triggered a very complex transformation, at once local and international. It was worth treating experimentally, using it as a means of focusing Scottish history. Thus while the thing itself was local, occurring in specific basins of activity, it was incorporated into the national repertoire of metaphors.[36]

Two young Americans are lost in the mist in the Scottish Highlands. The mist clears and they see a village. They also see a limping rabbit on the road, and wrap it up and carry it with them in the car. The village of Ferness has been slumbering for years, and they are about to waken it with a surprising announcement. The little rabbit appears at dinner, in a casserole. Bill Forsyth's film *Local Hero* (1982) became perhaps the most widely distributed cultural artefact about the oil business. By turns poignant and sharp, it was a playful meditation on Scotland's uneasy love affair with America. For Forsyth this was a particularly Scottish issue, not just in its subject-matter:

The way that I go about making films is a reaction against what you could call the traditional English dramatically structured film, and also, especially, the English form of film acting. I'm doing that because of the relationship that Scotland has had with England. I suppose it's that inferiority that we feel, the Scots people, vis-à-vis England.[37]

The roots of the plot were derived from almost documentary instances: the Drumbuie case in 1972, in which Taylor Woodrow wanted to move in on Loch Carron; the operations of Daniel K. Ludwig at Cromarty and Armand Hammer in Orkney. But Forsyth used these as a structure on which to weave a complex pattern of Scoto-American parallels, divergences and misunderstandings – and he derived the manner of their presentation from sources ranging from Vincent Minelli's tartan-kitsch *Brigadoon* (1950) and Sandy Mackendrick's black comedy *The Maggie* (1955) to Mackay Brown and McGrath.

Most of the Ealing comedies of the 1940s started from a firm conviction of Englishness. 'It's because we're British that we want to be Burgundian,' Margaret Rutherford insists in *Passport to Pimlico* (1949); Mackendrick, however, lacked this confidence. In *The Maggie* his vision of Scotland was altogether darker and more corrupted: the hero, the 'wee boy' who 'saves' the disgraceful Clyde puffer and its crooked captain, will be doomed to see American money poured into similar hopeless enterprises. Forsyth is somewhat more optimistic: the Ferness villagers are quite prepared to trade their easy-going life for oil, with its wealth, pollution and stress. They will even kill for this, if necessary. But they are saved by a literal *deus ex machina*: Happer's fascination with the aurora borealis, which makes him preserve Ferness as an observatory. (Not utterly implausible: think of the use to which Sir Iain Noble would put his wealth in Skye in the 1980s – the revival of the Gaelic language.) The film's last sequence, when the oil executive dials Ferness from the hectic of Houston, and the phone rings in the telephone box on the empty pier, suggests that the Arcadian fantasy of *Brigadoon* is as dead as the distance that once divided the two continents. To avoid a hideous outcome, for many more places than Ferness, responsibility and imagination would be needed on both sides.

In 1976 Alastair Dunnett observed three very old men walking slowly about the parterres of a great English country house. Sutton Place, near Woking, had accommodated a royal mistress and, in the nineteenth century, the republican and radical Frederic Harrison. Now, as the jets (which he hated) from Heathrow roared overhead, Paul Getty escorted Roy Thomson and Armand Hammer, his partners in the Piper field, round his estate. Within a year Getty would be dead, his profits endowing the Getty Museum in California with an annual income from interest alone that dwarfed that of the Arts Council of Great Britain. Gradually, like some huge vacuum cleaner, this fund would loosen old masters from the walls of English mansions and art galleries, and suck them across the Atlantic to Malibu.[38]

Oil had this sort of protean impact, and North Sea oil was important to the UK economy, but at the same time it marked only one part of the United Kingdom, a remote area in a period when most of the population had edited remote areas, especially troublesome ones, out of their concerns. It was a large-scale construction and extraction project, at a time when the British economy was tilting further towards the service sector. So its impact was, in a cultural sense, patchy. The Scots picked it up and wove it into their own complex national revival, partly because it was unavoidable for them; but their revival was itself intellectual and civic as much as political. They also had traditional links with America, which meant that the oil business was never impossibly alien. Even the great Satan of Texan megalomania shared the good Scots name of Ewing with the figurehead of the

SNP. If the Scots wanted convenient villains, they turned not to the oilmen but to the financiers and speculators of the City of London.

The oil business was American; so too was the sort of enterprise society which Mrs Thatcher wanted to enable. Yet somehow the two didn't coincide. British business society became more multinational, more controlled from America; but at the same time it stressed its southern English credentials; it projected the 'heritage' that could be marketed to a wealthy but insecure and increasingly unenterprising American plutocracy. The discovery made by T. Boone Pickens after his brush with the Beatrice field became common currency: more money could be made through speculating in oil than in getting it out of the ground.

Some years later the British prime minister, John Major, paid his first visit to the new president, Bill Clinton, in Washington. He took with him a first edition of Anthony Trollope's novel of 1876, *The Way We Live Now*. In this a fraudulent speculator, Augustus Melmotte, involves all levels of respectable London society in an overblown American railroad scheme, and the most prestigious scramble over one another in the race for easy money. We have never been told what the president thought of his gift.

10

Oil and Mrs Thatcher

At every turn the significance of North Sea oil and gas seemed to compound. Margaret Thatcher went to the EEC summit and took the limelight. She went to Tokyo and played a key role ... Why? Oil! Not British industry, not British political acumen, but because the UK was the only Western industrial country with oil to burn. No longer the weak sister, no longer the Seven Sisters, but Margaret Thatcher, apparently holding the trumps ...

Richard Funkhouser, interview, 21 March 1994

Without the oil, the Thatcher experiment would almost certainly have been cut short as early as 1981 or 1982 after the unmitigated disasters of the first year or so of the new dispensation.

Sidney Pollard[1]

Behind the Miracle

At the end of his election campaign in 1979, driving wearily back to Downing Street in his official car, James Callaghan remarked to Bernard Donoghue:

You know, there are times, perhaps once every thirty years, when there is a sea-change in politics. It then does not matter what you say or what you do. There is a shift in what the public wants and what it approves of. I suspect there is now such a sea-change – and it is for Mrs Thatcher.[2]

Such profundities were unusual, especially for Callaghan, a

thorough political professional. The Labour complaint had usually been that just when they had got the balance of payments sorted out, generally by hammering their own supporters (who then started to desert them) the Tories came in and blew the proceeds on loose financial living. When Labour fell from power in June 1970, it had done so partly because the April balance of payments showed an unexpected current account deficit of £36 million – largely due to British Overseas Airways' purchase of a couple of Boeing jumbo jets; the annual deficits of the Wilson government between 1964 and 1970 had been at their greatest in 1965, and had actually been overcome by 1970, with a surplus in that year of £821 million.[3]

The deficit in 1974, after the Arabs' oil price rise had joined itself to the hangover after the Barber boom, had been a horrendous £3,186 million; this had gradually come down, impeded partly by oil-industry-related imports, until a surplus was recorded in 1978, a year in which oil production, totalling 53 million tons, yielded £2,800 million. The revolutionary Iranians then helped by causing the oil price to double in 1979–80. That this bonanza was now presented to the Conservatives, through the indecision of the Scots and the bloody-mindedness of the unions, might have accounted for Callaghan's gloom. But even he could not foresee the fact that this surplus could be turned into a deficit of £4,482 million in 1987, of £6,321 million in 1991, *and* that the Conservatives could still win an election at the pit of a depression in 1992.[4]

Much remains obscure about the Conservative governments of the 1980s, even after their ceaseless drive for publicity. Which of their measures were calculated? Which were gambles, barely thought through, succeeding – or having their failures masked – through sheer chance? Which of these gambles worked because the political structures which might have facilitated a critique were too far gone in decay?

And not the least mysterious was Mrs Thatcher's relationship to the oil wealth which had come into her hands.

The Importance of Being Denis

The Winter of Discontent, one of those semi-suicidal frenzies which 'this great movement of ours' was so expert at inflicting on itself (and regrettably it was not the last), masked the fact that Britain was, for once and thanks to the oil, experiencing a boom and not going bust. Even the mayhem inflicted on the economy by Mrs Thatcher's first year only pushed the country into a modest trade deficit of £550 million in 1979. The oil kept on coming.

There were no discoveries in the later 1970s on the scale of Forties' 261 million tons of reserves, or Brent, with 230 million tons, but the development work of this period paid off, with many smaller or medium-size fields starting up in the early 1980s.

North-east of the Shetlands, in September 1980, the Murchison field began pumping oil to Sullom Voe, followed in November by Ninian North. Further south, in the complex developed by Hammer and Occidental, Texaco's Tartan started in January 1981, supplying Flotta via the Piper Alpha platform. BP's Buchan, a western outlier of the Forties field, started in May 1981, and Boone Pickens's once-upon-a-time and isolated Beatrice field in the cleft of the Moray Firth – now a BNOC prize – started in the autumn of that year. Shell's North Cormorant, a Brent outlier, and Fulmar, near Ekofisk, both started in February 1982.

Production, 77.9 million tons in 1979, had reached 103.2 millions in 1982. Then came 1983, which was, in terms of new fields, an *annus mirabilis*, with Amoco's North-West Hutton starting in April and Marathon's Brae South in July. Mrs Thatcher switched on BP's Magnus, with the tallest platform of the lot, in August. Phillips's Maureen started in September, Hamilton's Duncan in November. Of all the post-1979 oilfields, Brae South, Fulmar, North Cormorant and North-West Hutton had between 40 and 50 million tons in reserves; Magnus around 75 million; the rest were small.[5]

The effect of all this was very timely for the government.

Thanks to the Iranian crisis, the value of the oil soared from £5.69 billion in 1979 to £14.43 billion in 1982.[6] Oil was contributing 4.75 per cent of British Gross National Product, and almost 8 per cent of taxation income, which was boosted by Geoffrey Howe screwing the Petroleum Revenue Tax rate up from 45 per cent to 75 per cent.[7] This had the happy consequence that in 1981 the UK surplus on trade was £6,628 million and in 1983, £4,587 million. In the game of musical chairs, Thatcher had landed on one with a particularly deep velvet cushion.

A decade later Lady Thatcher in her memoirs would try to settle a few old scores. In *The Downing Street Years* the apostasy of the Scots figured as 'Thatcherism Rebuffed'. Another section saw Thatcher, culture-patriot, open up on the school history curriculum, blazing away for a couple of pages – 'I was appalled . . .', etc. – about how children were not (because of the wimpishness of Baker and MacGregor and 'progressive educational theorists') being taught names, dates, and the centrality of 'British' history.[8] Odd, therefore, that in 914 pages one huge theme was disremembered as thoroughly as some awkward bit of the Ingsoc past in Orwell's *1984*: North Sea oil and the bounty that it had brought her.

Denis Healey could not be expected to be generous about the early Thatcher years:

It would have been impossible for Britain to have survived these disasters without North Sea oil. When I was Chancellor, it had given me little benefit, either in revenue or in foreign exchange, until 1978. During Mrs Thatcher's first nine years it brought the Treasury £62 billion in revenue, while its contribution to the balance of payments was nearly £100 billion. Without it, she would never have won even her second term; Britain would have been bankrupt by 1983.[9]

Against this sort of assault, the silence of *The Downing Street Years* on the oil issue meant that no defence was offered. Alone of the horde of Conservative apologists and premature autobiographers, Nigel Lawson rose to the challenge in *The View from Number 11*, implying that the oil was becoming more of a nuisance than a resource, and the quicker it was flogged off, before the price fell, the better.[10] Lady Thatcher, in fact, seemed clumsy when confronted by oil. Among pre-1983 privatizations she cited 'Britoil (a nationalized North Sea oil exploration and production company set up by Labour in 1975)'. But *she* set up Britoil when she sold the British National Oil Corporation in 1982. Lawson's 'largest denationalization in British history' occupies one inaccurate line. The mighty 'British' achievement – by state and private concerns – in creating the rigs, platforms and pipelines: a project comparable with those of her revered Victorians, was totally ignored. Nor were even the tragedies commemorated, such as Piper Alpha: the result – partly – of 'management's right to manage' not being construed as involving safety. Falklands sacrifices were real; North Sea sacrifices apparently were not.

Why was this? Ignorance of and boredom with a highly technical agenda? Surely not, from someone who prided herself on being the first trained scientist in Downing Street. A 'Little Englander' distrust of foreigners? Perhaps: the Norwegians and the Dutch, who had the bad taste to get rich out of oil and gas, figure little in *The Downing Street Years* (particularly odd, since the 'Dutch disease' of too much welfare and not enough manufacture was the malady to which Thatcherism had announced itself as the cure).

Or was it Denis, whose involvement with Burmah must have posed one of the biggest risks to her career? Financial journalists are not dedicated historians; they rarely revisit the scenes where their advice boosted a business which subsequently went wrong. There are no breast-beatings over 'what I told you about Slater Walker, BCCI, Polly Peck, in 1974 or 1984' in the financial supplements. But Denis had been granted a peculiarly charmed life, considering that he had been one of that Burmah board which had sold out on a low valuation to the Bank of England at the end of 1974. Had this buy-out of its North Sea interests by the Labour government – a cave-in to the state by the Burmah directors, their shareholders unconsulted – left its mark? Had Burmah's shares then collapsed, his wife's career might never have got off the ground.

The recovery of BP shares after the purchase of Burmah's BP holdings and North Sea concessions, and a long-running lawsuit, in which neither of the Thatchers appears to have concerned themselves, caused much unrest among former Burmah shareholders – who saw the company's former BP shares rise by £117 million in a month.[11] But if oil industry *realpolitik* made Denis Thatcher seem closer to J.R. Ewing than to John Wells's Wodehousian creation, no way was 'the Boss' going to be Sue Ellen.

Richard Funkhouser was a paid-up Reaganite-Thatcherite, deviating only in a quixotic support for Scottish home rule, regarded as something closer to good ol' states' rights than to the Scots intellectual idea of a socialist commonwealth. At the same time he was alert to a family influence; being married to an ex-Burmah executive 'should not hurt'.[12] This fusion of personal and political concerns may also help to account for Mrs Thatcher's devious and manipulative attitude to political and industrial issues, which lasted throughout her career: Westland, Iraqi rearmament, aid to Malaysia. It was a predilection, however unfortunate, which was encouraged by the decay of any sort of overall grasp of the interlinking processes of government among commentators and historians of politics, not to mention the official opposition.

Balance Sheet Blues

Other commentators came to conclusions about the Thatcher years which were more articulate about the oil, and less indulgent. Professor Sidney Pollard had been scathing about the state of the economy in 1982, after a decade or more of largely Labour governments:

After having led the world for two hundred years, Britain is no longer counted among the economically most advanced nations of the world. A wide gap separates her from the rest of industrialized Europe. The difference as measured in national produce per head between Britain and, say, Germany, is now as wide as the difference between Britain and the continent of Africa. One short generation has squandered the inheritance of centuries.[13]

He was not disposed to be any more indulgent ten years later:

... for the eleven years of the Thatcher experiment there need be no ambiguity of verdict. All the signs point in the same direction: the experiment ended in almost unmitigated failure. By the end of the period, in 1990, Britain had the highest rate of inflation among advanced economies, though the curbing of the inflation had been the Government's declared priority number one. It had, correspondingly, the highest interest rates; and it had also high and rising unemployment; large-scale bankruptcies of firms in all sectors of the economy; falling output and declining national income; and the largest deficit on the current balance of payments in history. Over the period as a whole, despite the oil, Britain has, unbelievably, a slower rate of growth than in comparable periods before. In other subsidiary respects also, such as the number of hours worked in industry, environmental pollution, the morale of the Social Services, and many more, Britain was at the bottom of the developed world. The exception was the one aim which, curiously, the government did not stress in its statements of policy, though it clearly played a large part in its programme; the transfer of income from the poor, and especially the poorest, to the rich, and especially the richest.[14]

Pollard, like the present writer, had moved from British to German academia in 1979. German GDP grew sluggishly in the 1980s, at about 1.7 per cent per annum. But even with the oil, the UK rate was only 1.8 per cent, while between 1979 and 1992 the £ sterling almost halved in value, from nearly 4.5 Deutschmarks to around 2.5. Pollard's politics were broadly Fabian, and Sir Iain Gilmour, an erudite Macmillanite Tory who served Thatcher as Lord Privy Seal, did not share them. His response to the new order was, however, deeply critical:

North Sea Oil could have been used to finance a massive increase of investment in industry and in the infrastructure; the social repercussions of economic change could have been cushioned, and industry restructured and made more competitive; at the same time the tax and benefit systems and the system of pay-bargaining (all interconnected) could have been reformed. All that, in the view of the dissidents, might well have produced a decisive change in the British economy.[15]

North Sea oil had been only part of a very complex British scenario in the 1970s. Fundamentally, there was the balance of payments problem, and its relationship to the low productivity of British industry; but to this was added the world depression which stemmed from the OPEC price rises, and the entry into the European Community in 1973. This last resulted in a change in Britain's patterns of imports and exports.

Traditionally Britain had imported large quantities of food and raw materials: 78 per cent of imports in 1951. Such primary product imports, largely from less developed countries, fell by more than half over the next three decades, both because of North Sea oil and because of the effect of EC barriers. Of these imports, 30 per cent of foodstuffs had come from the former 'white dominions' in 1972 and 32.7 per cent from EC countries. The former dropped by half in 1982, the latter rose to 52 per cent. This brought prosperity to Britain's farmers, who benefited from the Common Agricultural Policy, and burdened British consumers, who paid for it. In 1984 the gains to UK farmers amounted to 6.7 billion ECUs, and the loss to consumers through higher prices amounted to 8.7 billion: thus the net loss to the UK was 2 billion ECUs.[16] In terms of exports, the UK maintained its overall position, but largely through primary product exports, mainly fuel. These rose over this period from 13.8 per cent to 31.3 per cent of exports, a gain which was almost completely accounted for by oil – up from 3.1 per cent of exports in 1973 to 21.7 per cent in 1983.[17]

Manufacturing exports, on the other hand, joined manufacturing output in a sharp decline between 1973 and 1983; from 83.1 per cent of total exports to 66.1 per cent. Imports of manufactured goods – mainly from other EC countries – increased, from 39 per cent in 1972 to 51.2 per cent in 1983. In the next year, for the first time since records began, their value overtook that of manufacturing exports.[18] Put bluntly, at a time when other industrialized countries were moving in the direction of increased manufacturing exports and high value-added services, Britain in the 1980s appeared to be regressing, a situation which had ominous precedents because the fate of primary producers worldwide was to be faced with ever lower incomes and ever slower growth. The exception was the OPEC countries (only a partial exception, as two of the biggest of them had been sucked into an appallingly destructive war). What had happened was that certain interests in Britain had done well out of EC entry: the farmers (always a powerful group in the local organization of the Conservative Party), the British representatives of multinationals, of which the oil companies were always prominent, and the City of London and its penumbra of financial services, property development and advertising and media outfits. The City hoped to prosper, and indeed largely did prosper, through entry to the EC and through handling much of the $80 billion of balances deposited by the oil producers; not least because the fringe banking collapse of 1973 left it in a situation where up was the only way it could go.

A catastrophe is something to be avoided, as is a government which promises a catastrophe. Yet if something devastating does happen, but most people live through it, any subsequent mitigation is seen as a positive good. Thus did soldiers react to surviving one of their generals' crazy offensives in 1914–18. Mrs Thatcher was similarly placed to Robertson or Haig. Between 1979 and 1981 she took a petro-pound which was already overvalued because of the Iran-induced price-doubling, and forced it further up by policies dogmatically directed at curbing the money supply. What happened to sterling was exactly what Christopher Smallwood said would happen to the petro-pound Scots. High interest rates propelled it further upwards, throttled industrial investment, and decimated exports. A decline of 2.5 per cent in the size of the economy, and of nearly 20 per cent in manufacturing capacity, was the result.[19] Yet the result was less politically devastating than it appeared at first. Voters' memories are short; the opposition was memorably divided; and a world of remarkable and rapid gain in financial services had opened up. Not least in the case of oil.

In the turmoil which had followed the end of the Bretton Woods system of managed currencies and the drive into speculating in currencies and commodity futures, oil joined the carousel, at first tentatively, and then, once the Thatcher programme of deregulation had been carried out – rather belatedly – after the end of 1982, with growing enthusiasm. In 1978 the spot market had covered only 5 per cent of the trade in oil; by 1986, 40 per cent of oil was changing hands through it, though this trade was based in Rotterdam. 'Futures contracts on the British Brent blend of North Sea oil,' Susan Strange commented in that year, 'are thought to add up to as much as eight times the total annual output of the Brent field.'[20]

After the catastrophe of 1979–81 there were, in other words, plenty of authoritative voices to tell the British people how well it was now doing, and why boats, no matter how leaky, should not be rocked.

Everything for Sale

Encountering the gloomy discourse of fact about manufacture meant that the Thatcher 'miracle' had to be other than economic. In its most ambitious definition it was a cultural revolution, and this boosting of individualism made it marketable – particularly to parts of the world which had not been affected by it. Expertly projected – the 1980s was the decade of the advertising agency, in which Saatchi and Saatchi nearly took over the Midland Bank – Mrs Thatcher became revered as an image of freedom in Eastern Europe, a triumph purchased through the substitution of a 'two-thirds society' of sovereign consumers for the notion of a

British 'commonwealth'. Its dissolution had gone so far that by 1990 the beneficiaries only halfheartedly tried to justify their gains in any social terms. Youngish ministers quit their careers to 'spend more time with their families', who often turned out to be warm and generous finance companies. Indeed, so internationalized had the rich become – Mrs Thatcher and her family being notable examples – that even her own post-ministerial career seemed largely organized from, and directed at, the wealthy of the American 'sunbelt'. In this, the sense of 'British' identity seemed steadily to be eroded. A Scottish Office defence of the Union in 1992 managed to mention 'Britain' only once in sixty pages.[21]

One of the principal vehicles for this denationalizing was the privatization of industry. This had not figured prominently in the Conservatives' election manifestos, and indeed only got into its stride after the victory of 1983. But, long before Sid was told, the sell-off of the government's fuel holdings took priority. Between 1980 and 1984, £2,509 millions-worth of assets were sold off, of which £1,972 million, or over three-quarters, were oil-related.[22]

This was not exactly music to the ears of Thatcher's first Energy minister, David Howell, aged only forty-three and a former head of the Conservative Political Centre in 1964–6. Hugo Young had him down as a Thatcherite true believer:

One of the gratifying certainties which beckoned was that the first Thatcher government would coincide with the swift escalation of production of North Sea oil, the greatest uncovenanted economic blessing the country had ever enjoyed. It was important to have a true believer at Energy, and Howell was now a man of the cloth in full monetarist orders.[23]

In fact the reality was more complex. Howell had been influenced by many of the themes of 'alternative' economics by E.F. Schumacher and James Robertson, he was conservation-minded (too much so for the majors), and he saw his mission at Energy as an assault on 'giantism'.[24] 'It is the micro-processor, the computer and the information revolution which break everything open,' he later wrote, 'cartels, state monopolies, bureaucratic domination and large-scale industrial organization and power.'[25]

This ambition had much in common with the ideas of the smaller North Sea independents – Howell was particularly struck by the successful venture of Thomson in the Piper field, though one suspects he knew relatively little about the company's complex Scottish background. The British Indigenous Technology Group – which included Dickson Mabon and Ian Wood – also generally backed the strategy which had been set out in the 'Stepping Stones' document favoured by the 'manufacturing' right within the Tory party.[26] After all, in no other sector of British industry had the unions been put so firmly in their place. Howell found, however, that his attempt to encourage smaller non-state bodies in oil, and meanwhile to retain BNOC's directive role, met with little encouragement from his Conservative colleagues, who saw privatization and competition as two quite different things. In August 1980 Kearton thought that he had persuaded Howell to preserve BNOC and its assets more or less intact. But Howell was defeated in a Cabinet committee chaired by the premier; BNOC retained for the moment its North Sea assets, but lost its information and advisory role.[27] By 1983 Howell was out of office, bemoaning the intellectual nullity of his party:

For the Conservatives . . . one major difficulty is that their thinking apparatus as a party, which was very highly tuned in both the 1960s period of opposition and in the 1970s, has been allowed to run down to a miserable level.[28]

Howell had, in the interim, been switched to Transport in 1982, leaving his successor Nigel Lawson to cope with a legacy of many tiny firms inserting themselves into the oil business, without any expertise and in search of quick profits, and the ambiguity, to say the least, of the City of London taking an interest in the North Sea. According to Martin Lovegrove, back in the City of London after his stint at BNOC, the result was 'an almost unmitigated disaster': over seventy seventh-round companies had either sold out or remained torpid.[29]

Such forebodings began to come true when the oil price started to sink in 1985, and the short attention-span of the City –

to anything other than immediate profit – was exposed. A politician obsessed with the creation of images, Mrs Thatcher had little time for a logic of truly competitive reform, a position shared by the former civil servants and nationalized industry executives who stood to benefit from monopoly capitalism. Adrian Hamilton, a critic of Labour government policy from the Institute of Economic Affairs position, commented emblematically in 1994 on British Gas: an attempt through privatization to introduce the disciplines of the market which seemed, for everyone else but management, to have become outrageously unstuck:

Whatever else privatization has done, it has done little for the customer, at least in the case of the electricity and resource industries. The City has done well out of the sales of shares. The users have been bribed with the offer of cut-price shares. The management has been bought off with huge pay rises and substantial share options. (The present chairman of British Gas earns as much in a year as his predecessor did in his entire career of building up the industry) . . . Privatization of British Gas has been a scandal. As a nationalized industry, it had converted the entire country to natural gas and revolutionized the energy scene. As a privatized company, it has done little more than sit back and reward itself and its advisers from the benefits of former investments and its dominant position.[30]

Niglet Fixes It

On 15 September 1981 Mrs Thatcher appointed Nigel Lawson to the Department of Energy. A bulky former financial journalist with the appearance of a Beardsley Roman emperor, he had earlier edited the *Spectator*, a magazine which figured much in Simon Raven's tales of political skulduggery. Like many a Raven character, Lawson was clever and unconcerned about who knew it. Unlike Howell, with his somewhat Prince of Wales-like concern with the environment and small-scale organization, 'Niglet' had no doubts about either large-scale organization or the making of profits. At a time when Mrs Thatcher sometimes felt it necessary to refer to her faith in democracy, albeit of the attenuated British sort, Lawson's hero was a nineteenth-century Chancellor, Robert Lowe, who had gone down in the last ditch opposing the Reform Bill of 1867, coldly contemptuous of the working class of the time.[31]

Lawson wasn't kidding. An *Observer* reporter, visiting his former constituency of Blaby, outside Leicester, in the course of a fairly sympathetic survey of the Conservative grass-roots, was appalled at the attitudes voiced, not in the bar of some Conservative Club, but by a well-heeled party élite: 'I begin to worry about the heart of Conservatism. If it has one, I mean.'[32] Judging by references to the Third World and the working class this was anything but Disraeli's 'One Nation' Toryism.

Lawson considered himself to be radical in the same sense that Lowe had been. As the latter's friend the great Benjamin Jowett had put it, Lowe was 'one of the quickest, the clearest, the ablest, and one of the most public-spirited men (really) whom I have ever known, but . . . he wants to do everything by force'.[33]

The difference was that while Lowe and his *laisser-faire* contemporaries could follow a regime favourable to international capital, they did so in the full knowledge that it was dominated by the City of London, which they represented. Lawson, as clever as Lowe in the role of an apologist in the metropolitan press, was confronted not with an international capital regime which represented the 'hard-and-fast' rules he claimed he was encouraging, but an oil regime which was frankly oligopolistic. And he represented a weak, de-industrialized economy.

Lawson pronounced himself agnostic about oil, and his detachment increased when in 1986 he became Chancellor. Was this the same man who had adapted Belloc,

> Whatever happens, we have got
> North Sea oil, and they have not.

in the *Spectator* of January 1978? And who went on: 'I am not of that austere school who believe that even this black manna will prove a curse in disguise.'[34]

It was not Lawson's intention to have intervention or, for that matter, an energy policy of any sort:

I do *not* see the Government's task as being to try and plan the future shape of energy production and consumption. It is not even primarily to try and balance UK demand and supply for energy. Our task is rather to set a framework which will ensure that the market operates in the energy sector with a minimum of distortion, and that energy is produced and consumed efficiently.[35]

One radical agenda was lying before him – Odell's proposals to Benn – but it did not engage his attention. He was as uninterested in downstream development as he was in offshore technology. In fact, he was generally hostile to manufacturing industry. There was some logic behind this: the notion that it might be possible to generate employment, and give the environmentalists a body-swerve, by de-industrializing. In 1978, at the time of the Sizewell inquiry, the Central Electricity Generating Board had accepted the proposition, on the basis of a scenario by Gerald Leach, that

The energy ratio . . . has been declining since well before the 1973 oil crisis . . . the fastest rate of decline would be associated with a buoyant, successful, service-led economy.[36]

Lawson was, however, sympathetic to the UK Offshore Operators Association. The Association was claiming that profits at the top end were now subject to over 90 per cent tax. Tax cuts were what they wanted, and in due course they got them in the Budget of spring 1983. In the words of an American commentator,

Britain . . . shifted from participatory intervention to regulatory intervention, not out of necessity, but out of political conviction, bolstered by the hounding of the oil companies and the cash-poor Treasury.[37]

But this was not all. Lawson ended British Gas's monopoly of the purchase of North Sea gas: 'the largest denationalization operation in British history'. In 1984 he went on to sell BNOC, for which he got between £1.5 and £2 billion, and then British Gas itself, which brought the Treasury more than £1 billion. William Keegan asked, purely rhetorically,

Was the Cabinet to abandon any pretence that the Public Sector Borrowing Requirement side of the Medium Term Financial Strategy was under control, and make a virtue of higher spending? Or was it to put the best face on things, and fudge the figures through a massive programme of asset sales?[38]

Lawson was to argue that he got out in time, while oil prices were high, before the slump of 1985–6. As Chancellor in 1986 he defended both his strategy of rapid exploitation and of government disengagement:

Meanwhile let me repeat that there is no question whatever, and never has been any question, of the United Kingdom cutting back its oil production in an attempt to secure a higher oil price. In the first place the whole outstanding success of the North Sea has been based on the fact that it is the freest oil province in the world, in which decisions on levels of output are a matter for the companies and not for the government. In the second place we are not only, or even principally, a major oil producer; we are also a major world producer and trader of many other goods and services, and a major oil consumer.

There is no overall United Kingdom interest in keeping oil prices high.[39]

Lawson took pride in the rise in overseas assets from £12 billion in 1979 to almost £90 billion in 1985. In due course, he announced, this would lead to major growth in the manufacturing contribution to the balance of payments. Instead he kept the price of sterling high while fostering domestic demand through lower interest rates, to produce the euphoria of the boom which captured for Mrs Thatcher her third election victory in June 1987, and soon afterwards ended in the slump of October of that year.

What was Lawson's motivation? Evidently, to use the collateral of the oil – still being pumped out at full speed – to bring the British petro-currency in line with the Deutschmark. This was logical enough: Germany was where most of Britain's foreign investment had gone, as well as, physically, much of the oil. Britain could become – with the financial services on offer in the City of London – the brains to Germany's industrial brawn. The goal was for Britain to join the Exchange Rate Mechanism which the Germans and French had set up in 1982. Did Mrs Thatcher share this view? Probably not, granted an economic expertise limited at the best of times, and a moralistic revulsion from the hedonistic acquisitiveness of the City. None the less she maintained support for Lawson's economic direction even after the collapse of share prices in the Western stock exchanges. Lawson attempted to compensate for this in his 'giveaway' Budget of 1988.

In the middle of a self-satisfied monologue his speech was interrupted by Alex Salmond, the newly elected SNP MP for Banff and Buchan, who protested about its gross inegalitarianism. Salmond was thrown out of the Chamber, much to Lawson's satisfaction. However, Salmond was the former head of the oil department in, ironically enough, the Conservative Party's bankers, the Royal Bank of Scotland. His presentiment was accurate: the Lawson boom was predicated on an overvalued currency and a fuel deficit. Within a year, Lawson's economic settlement would be falling apart, and Thatcher, aided by her arch-monetarist adviser Sir Alan Walters, would be trying to disengage from the Exchange Rate Mechanism. More immediately, it announced that the Scottish National Party was back in business. By November of that year Jim Sillars was back in the House as the MP for Govan, Salmond had settled himself into the Energy Select Committee as its oil expert, and the 'Scottish question' was again being asked.[40]

Dishing Labour

Why did Lawson get away with it? Sure, oil as an issue was never more than episodically interesting to the politicians. But there were also specific sequences of political events. There was, for a start, no consistent or effective critique of energy policy from the Labour Party throughout the 1980s. One has to look up the reference books to find out who the Labour spokesmen were; none had anything like the grasp of the issue that Benn had shown while in office.

The answer to this dysfunction may lie more in the tangled political situation of the early 1980s than in personalities. If energy in the 1970s had been 'mystified' by Scottish devolution, in the 1980s it was masked by the split in the Labour Party. To look up *Dod's Political Facts* means – for a start – to discover that the Labour Energy spokesman after May 1979 was Dr David Owen.

'Centrist' history asserts that Labour was doomed to internal crisis after its defeat in 1979. But the fortunes of Mrs Thatcher, far from being assured, rapidly hit bottom; between June 1979 and the spring of 1981, had a general election been forced on her, she would certainly have lost to Labour, even when led by the unenthusiastic Callaghan. And the dynamism within the Labour Party was represented by the former Energy minister, Tony Benn. Benn's exercise in *étatisme* had been successful; the oil majors reckoned him as formidable an opponent as his Norwegian or Middle Eastern counterparts. But the experience had driven Benn decisively to the left, into a type of British nationalist Jacobinism. Whether this was well judged was one question, but it reflected a widespread feeling, not just within the constituency parties and some trade unions, but also among the political activists who had been advisers to ministers in 1974–9. This is patent from publications such as *Manifesto: a Radical Strategy for Britain's Future*, produced by a group headed by what could be described as the 'Fabian left' in 1981, which essentially advocated a 'Norwegian' policy of withdrawal from Europe and the defence of the welfare state within a national framework; or John Eatwell's *Whatever Happened to Britain?*, produced in parallel with a Channel 4 critique of economic policy in 1983. The right was much more worried about Benn as a personality than Bennism as a policy. Funkhouser disliked Owen no less, but considered that what made Benn formidable was his organization, his charm, and his American connections.[41]

In areas where Labour still enjoyed substantial support, such as Scotland, 'Britain' was not the best of rallying calls. A substantial number of left-wing theorists had taken a pro-EEC line in 1975, and stuck to it; to them the Benn line was chauvinism and his adoption of Marxism implausible. But there was no significant way in which the policies of Benn and those associated with him went further than his Scandinavian or French contemporaries. The Norwegians had chosen unrestricted control over their oil in preference to joining the EC; in France, Mitterrand was just about to bring in a socialist and nationalist programme, involving sweeping extensions of state control. As Ken Livingstone was to demonstrate at the Greater London Council, such left-wing policies could command considerable support, when the government was in the depths prior to the Falklands.

It was at this point that the Labour Party split. The Social Democratic Party effectively removed about 10 percentage points from Labour's poll support in 1981, which led to the disastrous election result of 1983. Looking at this, it's possible to see a significant American, if not oil-related, pressure behind the secessionists.

First, there were the propagandists for the Labour right, such as the egregious Dr Stephen Haseler, Shirley Williams and David Owen, all of whom had American connections. Dr Colin Phipps was a major figure in the independent oil industry, so too was Dr Dickson Mabon, who had been Minister of State in the Energy Department, and had married the daughter of an oil magnate. Edmund Dell was an early, albeit largely inactive, member; and the party's first consultant on economic policy, Dr Christopher Smallwood, had been the opponent of the then nationalist-inclined Donald Mackay, while Smallwood was concerned with oil economics at the Scottish Office. Was there therefore an oil plot to split Labour?

In 1979–80 North Sea oil became more important, with the Iranian revolution and the unexpected doubling in the oil price. However ideologically reliable Mrs Thatcher was from the

American point of view, in 1981 she could not have stopped
Labour; the Social Democrats could. Moreover, they could get
assistance from that substantial section of the British press which
had oil interests: from Pearson Longman, which owned the
Financial Times and *Economist*, from Trafalgar House, which
owned the *Daily Express*, from Atlantic Richfield, which owned
the *Observer*, and from the Thomson Organisation, which owned
the *Scotsman*. All these organizations could use the precedent of
Scotland, where manipulation of party politics had been used to
create, contain, and ultimately chop down the SNP menace.

And yet . . . If North Sea oil figures scarcely at all in Mrs
Thatcher's memoirs, it was even more unobtrusive in the autobiog-
raphy and diaries of Lord Jenkins of Hillhead, than whom no
one, in the eyes of the metropolitan media and the 'chattering
classes', embodied the Keynesian virtues in a more civilized form.
No one had been a more circumspect Chancellor, no one had
pressed more enthusiastically for entry into Europe, than this son
of a South Wales miners' leader. Yet in a way there was no one
more capable of embodying what Thatcherism was against: despite his conviction that 'Britain was one of the worst-governed
countries in Western Europe', Jenkins personified, to left and
right, 'the orderly management of decline'.[42]

There was something to this. Arthur Jenkins had been the sort
of Europhile ILP socialist who set out to learn French and
German; his son represented the post-Godesberg abandonment
of Marxism for the mixed economy, liberal culture and civil
rights. He was much more at home in the 'agreeable' company
of dons and civil servants, British, German or French, than
with trade unionists or, for that matter, industrialists. He had
considered becoming editor of the *Economist* in 1962, but believed
he was neither competent nor committed enough. He was right.
'Roy wasn't really interested in economic policy,' recollected
David Marquand, his aide in Brussels and a co-founder of the
SDP.[43]

Tony Benn also came from a political family, but one moving
from Liberalism to Labour, transferring the 'fire and strength' of

its nonconformity to a Manichaean idea of politics as a struggle between good and evil: honest manufacture against the deceitful world of the service industries. In this he coincided more with the ostensible ideology of Mrs Thatcher than any ideas represented by Jenkins; the difference was twofold, however. A straight-forward appeal to the individual's liberation through consumerism counted more than appeals to accelerate the social revolution through a trade-union movement whose indiscipline and poor leadership had left it discredited. Thatcher and her advisers were clever enough to seize on the popular aspects of Bennism – the sense of people's empowerment, the fascination with new technology, the suspicion of Europe – and repackage these as Conservative propaganda points. Allied to the oil funds that Benn had nurtured, these served (even if they only just served) to destroy his trade-union allies in the confrontation with the miners in 1984–5.

It is possible to see the whole exercise as a manoeuvre which went off at half-cock. In the 1950s, when the left had threatened to take over policy-making in the Labour Party, the right had organized effectively at the grass-roots in the Campaign for Democratic Socialism. In the 1980s it decided to split the party, and was encouraged so to do by the media. Most political commentators were agreed that this was a gamble, but they felt that Thatcher was so unpopular that it had a fair chance of success. Otherwise, the balance of probabilities was that it would penalize the left far more than it would scare the right. Thatcher was not wholly convenient to the oil majors; her *petit-bourgeois*, Kiplingite aggressiveness boded little good to relationships with Europe, and implied a real threat that she would be brought down in full flight; but on balance she was preferable to a Labour government.

The modest talents of the 'Gang of Four' were over-hyped by the press; and the secessionists were too much an army of officers (and largely Oxbridge officers at that) without a rank-and-file, save in some of Labour's rotten boroughs. In Scotland only two MPs went over – Robert MacLennan in Caithness and Sutherland

and Dickson Mabon in Greenock. They had one success, with Roy Jenkins being elected for Glasgow Hillhead in March 1982, but the hopes of the SDP were, it turned out, as illusory as those of the Labour left. Like the SNP in the context of the Scottish central belt eight years earlier, they overestimated their chances in the Labour heartlands and assumed that by-election behaviour would persist into a general election. They might have got at least to a break-even position, where they could have interdicted a Benn ministry in the 1983 election and kept Thatcher from office. But events at the other edge of the world – a gamble by a failing South American dictator – prevented that.

Hutton

Companies had different policies for naming their fields. Some went in for seabirds (Auk or Fulmar), some remembered wives, others like Occidental went Scots-patriotic at Piper. The Conoco naming policy was based on Scots geologists: Sir Roderick Murchison, followed by William Hutton, and the tragic Hugh Miller. Hutton it was who fathered the modern profession, so it was fitting that the Hutton field provided the most important innovation in the history of the province.[44]

Hutton had been discovered in 1973 and had 200 million barrels of reserves, but the field was not developed until the second boom of 1980. When it opened at the end of 1984, in the middle of the miners' strike, it introduced a revolutionary type of platform, the 'tension-leg'. The principle of this was like that of a child pulling a balloon down under the surface of the bathwater. The platform, standing in 485 feet of water, was held steady by tethers, four bearing on each corner, attached to templates 'bolted' to the sea-bed strata. The principle had been known since the war, but only in the 1970s was a one-third-size prototype tested in the Caribbean. The project was expensive, as the tension required constant monitoring and adjustment by a complex computer system. It needed about twice the planning manpower of a conventional design, and, at £1 billion, cost 15 per cent more than a conventional platform. Neither was it easy for the two UK contractors, Brown and Root, who built the hull at Nigg, and MacDermott, who built the deck at Ardersier. The difficulty was faulty welding, which delayed the project by eight months.

However, the completion of the assembly of the platform was far faster than would have been the case with a conventional or concrete one. The hull was floated out into the Moray Firth on 10 May and partly submerged, sinking into the Firth like some dead six-legged elephant. Tugs towed the deck over it on a barge, and then the hull was de-ballasted and, as it rose, smoothly locked the deck into position. Eight weeks later it was towed into position over its templates, ninety miles north-east of Shetland, where it was almost immediately linked up to them. Three weeks later, the first oil started to flow. A conventional platform would have taken a year to have completed this stage. The gain which Conoco hoped for was a type of platform which, once the field was exhausted, could simply break its tethering tubes and float free – avoiding the costs of abandoning a fixed platform; and one which could operate in depths of over 2,000 feet, where a fixed tower would be technically impossible. The Hutton operation could be counted a qualified success for British technology – which had supplied 70 per cent of the inputs – particularly for the tethering system devised by Vickers.

But it was the only tension-leg platform to be built in Britain. By 1992 the Norwegians had captured this technology for their concrete yards, and Ardersier was in mothballs. In 1986 Conoco passed from American to French hands. And in 1985 BNOC had ceased to exist.

I I

The Glass is Falling

When the price of a barrel of crude is less than the price of a
bottle of good Scotch, then the North Sea oil industry's in
trouble.

North Sea proverb

A Rig Too Far

In 1949 I remember seeing the Bennie Railplane. It stood in a
field outside Milngavie, north-west of Glasgow, and we spotted
it in the gloaming as my grandfather drove us back from what
had been our first car trip, to Aberfoyle. It was a construction
rather like the Forth Bridge, a big red gantry about half a mile in
length, along which a silver cigar-shaped carriage, suspended on
castor-like wheels, would be propelled by an airscrew. George
Bennie, who otherwise built lifts, intended it to run from Glasgow
to Edinburgh. But he erected his prototype just before the 1929
slump, and there it stayed, a touching monument to technical
precocity and economic folly, until someone cut it up in the early
1950s.

Ocean Alliance, the Britoil rig at Scott Lithgow's, loomed up
nearly forty years later while I was filming a documentary on
Scottish politics, and inspired similar feelings. Towering over
Greenock, it was vast, more like a production platform than a
rig, weighing over 30,000 tons. A semi-submersible of advanced
design, costed at £88 million, BNOC had intended to use it to
explore the West Shetland field, out in the wild Atlantic, over

309

1,000 feet down to the sea-bed. It had been ordered in 1981 for delivery in 1984: a good turn to a state-owned tanker-building yard with no other orders on the books. But this was late 1986, £200 million had been spent, and it was still there. There had been strikes, but these were reactive and minor: the management of the contract had, with design mistakes, policy changes and total cock-ups, completely collapsed. Scott Lithgow had tackled drill-ships, quite successfully; they had built the elaborate catamaran support-and-rescue vessel *Iolar*; but they had never built a rig, and it showed. By the time *Ocean Alliance* was ready, in 1988, there was no future for the Greenock yard. Nothing has since been built there. And there was little for the rig to do.[1]

In 1984 the *Ocean Alliance* was still strewn in bits across the Scott Lithgow yard, which the government had sold to a consortium of Trafalgar House and Howard–Doris. The year was otherwise charged with Orwellian foreboding. But in the North Sea it looked like being prosperous. In 1982 analysts in Houston had been talking in terms of the hundred-dollar barrel by A.D. 2000, and 1983's results seemed to bear this out.[2] They had been good: output at 2.36 million barrels a day, up 11 per cent on 1982. In September the Magnus field had commenced pumping its oil to Sullom Voe; the Norwegians had turned their technology on the Trench, and were for the first time laying a pipeline from the Statfjord to Karsto on the mainland.[3] In 1983 the gross value of production to the UK was £18.8 billion, trebling the £6.3 billion registered in 1979. This was an increase from 2.3 to 5.3 per cent of total British GNP. It yielded nearly £9 billion in tax, enough to undertake several Falkland campaigns at £1 billion a throw. 'The people don't want social reform,' Lord Salisbury had growled sometime in the 1890s. 'Give them a circus.' Not surprisingly, his posthumous reputation advanced in Mrs Thatcher's party.

Mrs Thatcher had switched the Magnus field on from BP headquarters in London, frustrating attempts by the Post Office Workers' Union to stop her. Symbolic enough. It looked to Nigel Lawson, now Chancellor, as if there would be lots more money around for circuses. Expectations had received a major boost with an upward revision showing an extra 25 per cent of possible reserves. Oil companies which had been disputing the figures of Professor Odell now shuffled their feet and said, Ah well, there might be something in them. Was this due to the fact that they no longer had government as a competitor, with its ingrained suspicion that they were downplaying their own calculations? Perish the thought.[4]

Since 1974, 4.3 billion barrels had been lifted. The bottom edge of the new calculations showed 10.6 billion remaining; the top had risen from 30 to almost 40 billion. This might extend the life of the field to over forty years at current rates of production.

With price per barrel nudging $40, and the government determined to settle accounts with the National Union of Mineworkers – 'the enemy within' at the other end of the energy menu – further exploitation was encouraged. Removing royalty payments on fields developed after April 1982 took drilling to a record level of 126 wells; the previous best had been 116 in 1975. It had cost $20,000 a day to hire a drilling-rig in 1978; after the Iranian-induced price doubling, the going rate soared to a crazy $90,000 in 1981, which probably choked off more activity than it encouraged. Since then, panic had ebbed away and trouble in the Gulf had induced more rigs to come into the field. The cost had come down to a more reasonable $30,000.[5]

Lawson's successor as Energy minister, Peter Walker, took little interest in oil affairs: the prospective confrontation with the miners was already throwing its shadow. The responsible junior minister, the liberal Scots Tory Alick Buchanan-Smith was, helpfully, MP for the 'oil constituency' of Kincardine and Deeside; he tried both to encourage the development of medium-sized fields and, like Howell, to encourage the smaller British independents. But the latter remained a pious hope rather than a policy, despite the stock market's enthusiastic but less than well-informed interest. More than 90 per cent of the business lay with the majors, who could afford the £60 million now required to commission even a medium-sized field. Still, the overall signs seemed good, and the numbers employed offshore climbed from 21,500 in 1982 to 28,700 in 1983. On- and offshore, the British province employed 70,000 directly and another 20,000 indirectly, and the development of smaller oilfields was expected to lead to new platform orders: sixteen were contemplated for 1985, fifteen for 1986.[6]

In 1984, Britain's North Sea oil income stood at over £20 billion, but the price was beginning to decline. It was now around $27 a barrel, $13 down from its 1981 level. Even this situation was already being undermined − not least by the fact that the Iranian-provoked price rise had shocked most European countries into curbing their energy consumption, using technology developed since the first crisis of 1973−4. Global demand had peaked in 1979 at 6.93 billion tons of coal equivalent; in 1980 this fell to 6.88 billion. Between 1975 and 1980 the demand for oil of the biggest European economy, West Germany, went down from 53 per cent of consumption to 44.6 per cent.[7] In my 1960s flat in Tübingen the landlord got a *Land* grant to install new double-glazed windows and insulate the whole building with a three-inch polyurethane skin. Had this white, almost lighter-than-air stuff, at some stage of its career, passed through the tubes and retorts of Moss Morran? Quite possibly. But this particular oil derivative enabled the Harvie family to dispense with six of the flat's eight radiators and still stay warm. Throughout Europe the appalling inefficiencies of energy production and consumption were being probed in ways which subverted the whole basis of traditional energy politics: large-scale generators which wasted two-thirds of the heat they used, national grid transmission lines. And, last but not least, the whole notion of energy being, in principle, cheap.

OPEC Down and BNOC Out

At the end of 1984 a crisis, not utterly unwelcome to Mrs Thatcher, began to grip the British National Oil Co., which in a rump form, with a staff of only 140, had continued to stabilize prices by buying its 51 per cent at quarterly fixed prices. Indeed, under Walker and Buchanan-Smith, it had become, like that other legion of the lost, the Northern Ireland Office, a last redoubt of Conservative 'wets'. For most of 1984 these prices – expressed as 'Brent crude' – had been fixed at $30 a barrel, and the government had held to its determination to carry on doing this.[8] But in July 1984 the resolution of OPEC was crumbling fast, and quiet pressure from the companies to abandon fixed prices grew. Thatcher's government – and Thatcher herself – held to quarterly prices, hoping in this way to keep OPEC prices high. By the autumn BNOC had to drop its buying price to $ 28.65. This was not enough; it was still having to sell on the spot market at a couple of dollars less.

At this point noises from Downing Street indicated that a policy change was in sight. The government would go with the market and ditch BNOC's intervention. Was there an alternative – to co-operate with Norway and become what Lawson called a 'country member' of OPEC? Perhaps, but the Norwegian Conservative government, promoting its own financial boom, was irresolute; and the Saudis were preparing to frighten and, so they hoped, discipline the rest of OPEC by increasing their own production, regardless of the immediate consequences. Moreover, cheap oil would not be unwelcome to a British government faced, in the middle of the miners' strike, with dwindling supplies of coal. The oil industry's assault was four-pronged: BNOC's prices were encouraging 'spinning' (sales and purchases made for tax-avoidance reasons) by private companies and speculators, and thus destabilizing the market; BNOC 'participation' ought to be reduced; it should be deprived of its informational role, seen as inquisitorial; and of the last of its 'insider' activities.[9]

In the *Financial Times* Dominic Lawson, the son of the former Energy minister, was sceptical of BNOC's pretensions to be 'to the Department of Energy on oil prices what the Bank of England is to the Treasury in foreign exchange management'. Nevertheless, he could see a logic to this:

BNOC (and on stated intentions so far the government) wants to be able to interfere in the oil market, to prevent prices falling too sharply if it can, at a time of chronic world oversupply. Its new policy is not to avoid intervention, it is *to appear* to avoid intervention. There is little doubt that if, in a year's time, BNOC thought market conditions would permit it to return to a less flexible system of official prices and longer contract periods it would do so. BNOC is retreating, not retiring.[10]

Neither of the Lawsons wanted *that*. And circumstances were to wipe out the last traces of BNOC faster than even they believed possible.

The seat of the problem was in the Middle East, where OPEC was dissolving fast. A basic desideratum of any cartel is the solidarity of producers: difficulties emerge when two of its major members are dedicated to slaughtering each other's citizens, as had been the case with Iran and Iraq since 21 September 1980. OPEC's physical reserves of oil had grown from 66 per cent of the world total in 1980 towards the 77 per cent they would reach in 1992, but its actual output was steadily declining. The Gulf warriors went over-quota in order to bankroll their arms purchases; the Saudis kept their price up, and fewer and fewer bought their oil. Saudi production was falling, from 10 million barrels a day in 1981 to 2 million in June 1985.[11]

In June 1985 they gave up. Economic disruption plus Islamic militancy – an unavoidable contamination, pouring off every jumbo touching down at Jiddah Airport – was too terrifying a prospect. But with the Saudis' desertion, the quota system on which OPEC's control had been based collapsed completely. Production shot up by nearly 38 per cent, there was no reduction of non-OPEC output, and the price per barrel started to sink, from $30 a barrel in November 1985 to $10 in April 1986.

On 13 March 1985 Britain gave up its own attempt to manage prices. It had still supported the BNOC mechanism in the summer of 1984, but now Buchanan-Smith announced to Parliament,

There has ... now been a major change in the market away from term

314

contracts and towards spot and similar short-term transactions. This trend is unlikely to be reversed in the near future. In these circumstances BNOC could avoid the risk of losses only by linking its prices for participation oil closely and continuously to movements in the spot market. Such a system would mean that BNOC could no longer contribute to stability in the market. The government have concluded that this shifts the balance of advantage decisively against the retention of BNOC in its present form.[12]

The option of participation was to be retained; also the payment of royalties in kind and the management of pipelines; but the effective end of the national/cartelized oil regime meant that the prospect of Britain becoming a 'country member' of OPEC had come to an end.

T. Boone Pickens Makes a Killing

The oil price slump and the extinction of BNOC had two main consequences. In 1983 the City interests which had gone into oil had already shown signs of 'consolidation' – Cityspeak for panic-driven retrenchment. As OPEC's ability to control oil prices wavered, City institutions decided to cash in their stakes before they sustained losses. Especially threatened were the little guinea-pig companies David Howell had backed in 1979–81. The government now hoped that the larger independents would be sensible and amalgamate: much was made of a possible merger between Charterhouse Oil and Saxon Oil, each valued at about £130 million. Was Charterhouse's boss, Tony Craven-Walker, not the chairman-designate of Brindex, the Association of British Independent Oil Companies, and 'the voice of the independent North Sea explorers', who had sharply criticized the midget North Sea ventures of 'biscuit makers'? But the formerly state-owned concerns Britoil and Enterprise Oil were now in the stream, snapping up the plumper minnows. Throughout 1985 the takeovers accelerated: at first, modest buys in the £10 million range. But by

September Enterprise Oil had swallowed Saxon Oil and in December the Belgian firm Petrofina took over Charterhouse, only hours before Craven-Walker was due to take the Brindex chair.

Dominic Lawson interviewed an oil company chief executive in the *Financial Times*, who was grimly realistic:

The City has put a lot of money into us, but without entirely understanding what they were doing with the money. They did not realize that the oil price could go down as well as up. They did not realize what a long-term business this is. It takes ten years to turn an oil find into cash flow in the North Sea.[13]

'Long-term' was rarely a phrase that sprang to mind when the City was mentioned, and all this was happening while the price of oil still stood at around $27 a barrel. Yet overall, Lawson was optimistic. 'Most expect,' he wrote, 'that this year could see the price drop down to no more than $20.' That was in mid-January 1985, before Yamani did his Samson act. By September it stood, or rather lay, at $8. The price subsequently recovered from this horrendous deep, well under the North Sea 'floor', but only to half its 1984 level.

A second influence on the oil scene was symbolized by a *Times* edition in 1982 which announced the abandonment of the gas-gathering pipeline, and the consolidation of the London oil futures market, which had started trading on 6 April.[14] The abolition of BNOC encouraged speculation on an impressive and, for oil, unprecedented scale. Frank Frazer wrote in the *Scotsman* about the victory of a kind of transaction deeply foreign to the sort of economic world he had been surveying for twenty years:

. . . the amount of oil changing hands in paper deals on trading floors in London, New York, Chicago and other financial centres each day can equal at least one-and-a-half times the combined volume of all the world's oil wells . . .

Since BNOC's demise, the way has been cleared for a cargo of crude from a field in the East Shetland basin to change hands perhaps 100 times as it is shipped across the Atlantic.[15]

Always eager to see a kenspeckle face, the *Glasgow Herald* homed in a year later on the New York Mercantile Exchange (NYMERX), organized under the presidency of one Rosemary McFadden, born in Port Glasgow but raised since infancy in the United States. Ms McFadden's operation reflected the expansion in the futures market from a mere 1,962 contracts when it began in 1983 to 33,254 contracts in 1986, equal to 70 per cent of Free World output. Trading on the spot market was now old hat; what mattered was dealing in futures, contracts to buy oil at a fixed price in so many months: originally an attempt by firms to plan their requirements, then an attempt at second-guessing the market, and finally, and very rapidly, straightforward gambling. The *Herald*'s guide to the wonderful world of futures trading was Thomas McHale of the New York firm of Drexel Burnham Lambert, shortly to win notoriety in another, but not wholly separate, context.[16]

The NYMERX's previous business had been potato futures. This was now dumped. Energy ruled. Oil was touted, bought and sold by frenetic youths in blazers, Paul Gascoigne lookalikes 'earning fucking millions for England' (or whoever), who transferred the nuances of roustabout life to the dealing floors of the City in the year of the Big Bang. North Sea oil had helped in this, of course.

You will remember T. Boone Pickens, who happened on the Cromarty Firth at the end of the Ludwig saga, whose Beatrice field was sold, after some very hard bargaining, to BNOC. Pickens did not repine. He subsequently discovered, in 1983, that by speculating in oil futures he could make as much money in a week as in years of laborious drilling, testing, platform-building and pipeline laying. In 1985/6 he sold 3 million barrels when the price was at $26.50 a barrel, and then bought the same quantity as futures for $16.50, netting $30 million. Commodity speculation, something which along with currency speculation had grown as a result of the end of fixed exchange rates, was a rough business, with a lot of bluffing and double-bluffing involved, and deliberate defaults and future lawsuits written into the game. Futures and leveraged buyouts, in association with Michael Milkin and Ivan Boesky, were to make Pickens very rich.

Pickens, a gung-ho Reaganite Republican, proclaimed his mission as the overthrow of the conspiracy of the CEOs – the Chief Executive Officers who ran the oil giants – on behalf of the 'little guys', which could be translated as the minor millionaires, the beneficiaries of the Texan boom who felt snubbed by the corporate patriciate. He found he did not even have to take over a company to succeed, but needed only to buy into its share stock while it rose under the threat of takeover, and then sell at the top of the market. In 1987 he bid for Gulf Oil, driving it into the arms of the 'white knight' Chevron.[17] The Seven Sisters were reduced to six. By then the activities of Pickens's associate Boesky had helped to remove Distillers, the 'jewel in the crown' of Scottish capitalism, from Scottish control.

All businesses tend to pass from a competitive, chaotic phase to one of corporate organization and integration with civic goals, and a buzz phrase of the 1980s, which would snugly fit the Pickens view of life, was 'creative chaos'. The phrase had been culled from the writings of the long-dead Austrian economist Joseph Schumpeter. In the 1940s, seeing where creative chaos had got continental Europe, Schumpeter turned up in Britain, and lauded the ideological and social solidity of the British élite, its capacity gradually to transform itself from an aristocratic interest to the patron of social democracy and the incorporation of trade union power. But this solidity – in its financial aspect – was being rapidly sapped by the collective assault of fluctuating exchange rates, Third World debt and global real-time communications. Into this, oil was drawn. In 1978 the spot market handled only 5 per cent of the trade in oil; in 1986 this had risen, in dealings in Rotterdam, to 40 per cent. 'Financial services' no longer meant the means of facilitating manufacturing investment – a small part of City business – but had acquired a life of its own, bankrolled by the payoffs on gambling on commodity and currency flows.[18]

Six years later little had changed, despite attempts at legislation in 1987. Tax 'spinning' still reigned, and companies kept their rigs and pipelines going for purposes other than producing fuel. Companies were taxed on 83 per cent of North Sea profits, but only on 33 per cent of the profits made by *trading* oil. As the *Economist*, not usually a friend to regulation of any sort, wrote:

For tax purposes, oil companies declare any sales made when the oil price is low to be unprofitable sales of equity crude; whereas all sales made when the price is high are declared as highly profitable traded cargoes. All this is done after the event, when the companies report to the tax collectors.

It calculated that as many as 90 per cent of oil trading deals were made for tax-dodging purpose.[19] Somehow, as an MP who could remember the Public Accounts Committee of 1972 might comment, we seemed to have been here before.

Too Little for Too Much

In 1986 income from British North Sea oil production fell from nearly £20 billion to under £10 billion. Drilling fell by 40 per cent, as companies abandoned projects like the discovery of new fields in favour of the limited expansion of existing ones. Rigs lay idle off Cromarty and Burntisland, as tankers had done in the seventies and cargo steamers in the thirties. The majors could ride this one out: petrol pump prices had a curious reluctance to descend when the international price of oil tumbled into the cellar. But the effect on supply and exploration companies was more deadly. The Royal Bank of Scotland calculated that sums of £60 billion in future North Sea investment, 1985–90, would have to be revised downwards by at least 50 per cent.[20]

For the suppliers, even a fall in demand for their services of more than a third was near-catastrophic. Sir John Howard

Engineering, of Loch Kishorn, went bankrupt, as did the fabricators ITM, which had shown profits of £5 million only a year earlier. But the worst-hit were the infant supply companies that Scots entrepreneurs had laboured to build up. These had prospered in the 1980–82 period, but such was the competition that margins were tight and reserves non-existent. Most of these were soon in the hands of their wealthier American competitors.[21] The survivors would come from among the subsidiaries of the big players, from those independents 'with either strong balance sheets or low overheads' (the Wood Group was an impressive but rare example), from suppliers to established fields or from the 'high-technology applied to cost-cutting' business. Most of these areas had been neglected by the relatively primitive UK entrepreneurs: even the unique expertise that the best of them had – working in deep and difficult waters – was at the very margin of development, which would be the first to be cut back.

But the damage went further. The British economy had contracted its industrial base drastically in the previous five years. The diversion of investment to oil-related activity had certainly inhibited investment in manufacturing in the 1970s, which attained only 19.3 per cent of GDP between 1974 and 1979, the lowest figure of any of the European states. But between 1980 and 1984 it fell even further, to 16.8 per cent, overtaking only Denmark.[22] This withdrawal of investment was accompanied by the collapse of many of the firms which had supplied electrics and pipework and entire modules, those anonymous metal-bashing factories found around the docks and railway-sidings of the Mersey, the Tyne, the Tees and the Wear, whose fate it was to figure neither in the economic historians' accounts nor in the oil story itself. Fifty years before, such places were known as 'derelict areas'; then, through the athletic use of euphemism, they graduated through 'depressed regions' and 'special areas' to 'development areas'. In 1987 Mrs Thatcher was photographed in the latest manifestation, the 'enterprise zone', finger wagging, handbag at the ready. Around her, rubble, and rust, and weeds.

This collapse had been partially masked by the trade in oil. In deficit by £685 million in 1979, it had risen to a positive, and record, level of £8,772 million *net* in 1985. In 1986 it fell back to £3,970 million, and only covered a deficit of £5,701 million in manufactures thanks to a surplus of £5,631 million in services. In only one more year – 1987 – would this work, yet such prospects did not shadow the Polyanna optimism of Mrs Thatcher, addressing the Conservative Central Council at Felixstowe:

What is it that now gives us such optimism for the future? First, oil. Only a year ago a single barrel of oil cost around $25 to buy. Today it costs about $13. To read some reports you'd think we all ought to go into mourning to mark the death of expensive oil. Yes, of course it will lose us some revenue and some exports. But all those who thought the oil price explosion of the 1970s did harm to our industry and slowed our growth rate were right. Falling oil prices are, on the whole, good news. There's more money to spend on other things . . .[23]

In 1987 the final accounts remained in balance; in 1988 they were in deficit by nearly £9 billion.[24]

Dynamite or Fairylight?

At the end of 1985 oil prices were heading towards single figures, in real terms what they had been in the early 1970s. Bigger fields such as Brent could live on $3–4 a barrel; smaller and more complex fields could not. The majors cut their budgets by 30 to 40 per cent. Divers operating from the Aberdeen base of Wharton Williams were down from 1,000 to 500. Seaforth Marine had to lay up two of their sixteen supply vessels. Their profit on a turnover of over £45 million was only £85,000. Firms complained that the 'disaster market' in offshore supply had waited two years to be officially recognized, while the competition of their Norwegian rivals received a heavy state subsidy.[25] The government did little, so the managements took it out on the labour force:

The contractors have become flesh pedlars and the companies who hire us have been having a field day. We work 15 days on and 15 days off, but men don't get paid for the time off any longer. The 12-hour shifts have been lengthened to 15-hour shifts and that is the norm now, with never a day off in the fifteen days. We go home exhausted.[26]

1986 saw 22,000 jobs lost in the industry. The fall in demand for platforms and modules left the yards in the north of Scotland operating at 36 per cent of capacity, and forecasts were made of this falling to 19 per cent in 1987. Could things possibly get worse? They could.

The declining profitability of the North Sea brought a new prospect into view, melancholy and very expensive. What was to be done with the production platforms when the oil wasn't worth removing? Were they to be dismantled and sold for scrap, or toppled over into the lower depths, or cut off forty-five metres below the surface? At any rate this would come expensive, and at the taxpayer's expense. Sums of £6 billion were talked about – rather more than the government made out of oil taxation in 1986. BP estimated that it would cost £2.2 billion for the partial removal of its platforms, £1.7 billion to topple their upper structures; a pipeline would cost £85 million to 'clean and flood', £1.4 billion to remove completely; onshore removal of pipes would cost £790 million.[27] The reek of the 'try-on' hovered over this, with government and companies arm-wrestling about who was going to pay; if it was to be the companies, they would require a tax rebate to offset this cost. If they didn't get the rebate, they would prematurely cease production. A formidable threat, and not one that government, having divested itself of its oil expertise, was in any position to query. Both sides probably wanted the least-cost or 'fairylight' solution, in which the platforms would be festooned with warning lights and left where they were, which (translated) meant until they fell apart.[28]

There were low-tech and hi-tech variants on this fate. The low-tech one was that the proven capability of the platforms and the equipment and junk around them to attract fish would give them a future as artificial reefs conserving the fish stocks of a sea which was otherwise being severely over-fished.[29] Exactly how fishermen were going to extract the shoals from around these huge wrecks was never made quite plain.[30] The hi-tech response was to devise forms of deviated drilling and sub-sea production units which could double the range of such wells from 15 to over 30 kilometres from a fixed platform. The creation of remotely controlled multi-phase pumps which could separate water, oil and gas on the sea-bed had been thought impossible in 1984. After 1987 it was reckoned practicable.[31]

There was another intriguing high-tech variant, first explored by German technologists in the 1970s, which might still ease this particular problem: the conversion of platforms into power stations. New types of gas turbines could be powered by both oil and gas on the fields, and re-inject into them the carbon dioxide they produced, thus getting rid of one greenhouse gas for a century or so, and depleting a much greater percentage of each field's oil. In the early 1990s Hamish Paton was advocating this to the SNP's think tank as a means of Scotland recapturing its energy dominance. And who was 'Hamish Paton' but Donald Bain, once the SNP's energy expert, and now doing the same thing for EURATOM?[32]

'Aw a muddle' was the phrase that Charles Dickens put into the mouth of his bewildered working man, Stephen Blackpool, in *Hard Times*, before dropping him down a mineshaft, an early victim of redundant energy investment. This would have been a charitable judgement on British energy practice – it could not be dignified by the term policy – in the 1980s and 1990s. The nuclear industry was still directly owned by the state, no one being willing to bear the costs of decommissioning its reactors. It managed to destroy research into wave power, pioneered at Edinburgh University by Professor Stephen Salter; but it proceeded with its own risky and uneconomic THORP reprocessing project at Sellafield, commenced in the 1960s and not commissioned until 1994. Privatization of electricity meant cuts in the energy research budget, and in 1993 the destruction of most of the British coal industry, in circumstances of political chicanery, which even the hardened observer could only view with disgust. The gas industry we have already encountered; I cannot add to Adrian Hamilton's comments. A lot of money had been made, by consultants, advertisers, the stock market, company executives, but no approach had been evolved which would restrict the amount of energy produced and see that it was employed in the most efficient way. For this triumph to be commemorated by huge metal towers serving as the world's most expensive fish farms, decked with coloured lights, seemed somehow appropriate.

The Norwegian Way

In 1986, evidently moved by sentiments similar to the foregoing, the dramatist Trevor Griffiths devised a four-part television film, *The Last Place on Earth*, about the race between the Englishman Scott and the Norwegian Amundsen to reach the South Pole. In this the English, hitherto regarded as tragic heroes, were depicted as arrogant incompetents, who would face death, in the bravest possible way, rather than compromise their class-ridden customs. The Norwegians were solemnly egalitarian and democratic, and survived. Plainly the North Sea hovered about in the background of this essay in comparative national character.

For the British, however, cross-sea comparisons were mildly consoling. The understated competence demonstrated, infuriatingly, by the Norwegians in the 1970s was not maintained. The 1980s were distinctly turbulent. The Labour Party and the social democratic ethos had been dominant in Norway since the 1930s, and received the unwonted congratulations of the carnivorously free-market *Economist*: 'Modern Norway is essentially the creation of social democracy, which is being rewarded for its recognized competence.'[33] This ensured that when revenues started to come on stream after 1976 they were channelled into public expenditure projects and intervention on the side of the work-force in industrial disputes.

In February 1980 a White Paper, the first for five years, attempted to assess the overall oil situation. It saw oil and gas production reaching 70 to 90 million tons in 1985 and staying at this level for a decade, providing 20 to 25 per cent of the country's gross national product and 40 to 45 per cent of total exports. Spending would be in the region of 13 to 21 million kroner annually, equivalent to between $2.6 and $4.2 billion. This would be recouped by production at 100 to 125 billion kroner, giving annual revenues to the state of between 45 and 60 billion kroner, and enabling the paying-off of the large foreign debt of 100 billion kroner in 1980. But this assumed a constant price of $30 a barrel.[34]

Such plans were doubtful, as Norway experienced on a larger scale what the north-east of Scotland had gone through. Labour became scarce in the areas close to major onshore installations; the country's shipyards found their costs being pushed up and the demand for tankers declining. This figured: far fewer were needed when the oilfields were a couple of hundred, not ten thousand, miles away. Many yards closed down. Employment in agriculture fell by nearly two-thirds, to 6 per cent between 1960 and 1990; in industry it declined from 26 per cent to 17 per cent. A country withdrawn from the rest of Europe, let alone the Third World, found its guest-worker population increasing, servicing the offshore activities with low-paid manual jobs; for the first time racialism became a political issue. The taxation derived from the oil meant at the same time that the public sector service industries, 13.1 per cent of employment in 1960, rose in thirty years to 34.4 per cent. Taxation levels rose, as higher wages brought more manual workers into the net.

Norway was discovering, as did the other West European welfare states, that the tendencies within modern technology and social development towards a retreat from society, towards 'cocooning' and self-regarding individualism, were not checked by

growing affluence and social expenditure, and were barely constrained by a social-democratic tradition. As in Denmark and
Sweden, affluence (and the absence of affluence: the protests of
the losers) led to the rise of a populist anti-tax, anti-immigrant
party. In 1981 these disquiets cut into the Labour Party vote. In
the election of 1981 a Conservative government under Kaare
Willoch, with a workable majority, took power.

Willoch lasted in office until 1986. He was slow to introduce
neo-liberal economic policies, which of course looked pretty
unappetizing in Britain until Thatcher had, for quite different
reasons, won the 1983 election. Then he rapidly liberalized the
banking and share-dealing market. Because of the low valuation
of the krone and a cheap money policy, share prices went up by
70 per cent between 1981 and 1983.[35] Oil revenues were switched
from public expenditure to financing tax cuts, and exchange
controls were eased in 1984. This resulted in private consumption
increasing by 16 per cent between 1984 and 1986, and Norwegian
stock market transactions soaring from 2 billion to 32 billion
kroner between 1981 and 1985. Between 1983 and 1986 the
financial services sector increased by 40 per cent, performing as
dramatically as London and much better than Scotland. But
although stock market transactions might go up by a factor of
fifteen, the value of new shares only doubled. The shift was, as in
London (with 90 per cent of its business in currencies and
commodities), away from capital supply and towards speculation
pur sang. As the economist Arne Fagerberg complained,

. . . the major achievement of these years . . . was the rise of a speculation
economy in which it became far more profitable to engage in asset-
stripping, or in home-ownership changes, than to create new real assets in
the industrial sector. There was no improvement in cost-competitiveness in
spite of several devaluations and only slow growth in manufacturing
output. The share of manufacturing in total output continued to decline.
Full employment was attained in 1986, but with a large deficit on the
current account.[36]

But the Norwegian government held on to Statoil. Why?

The reason was that the culture of the Norwegian civil service had been firmly moulded by more than two generations of social democracy. The role of the state was unquestioned as the reforming institution of first resort; there was no regional movement demanding withdrawal from the national consensus.[37] Even here, however, the oil brought its stresses. The public sector proved an effective instrument of exporting capital, keeping the value of the krone down while accumulating overseas assets. Yet the risk was always there that they could become over-mighty subjects, as was proved by the Mongstad affair in 1985, when Statoil was detected developing its own caucus of MPs in the Storting, in order to build an oil refinery in a region in which there was considerable opposition on environmental grounds.

By then, however, the country's dependence on oil, and *de facto* alignment with OPEC, made it dependent on that cartel's shaky and ultimately fruitless diplomacy. When OPEC lost control, this rapidly led Willoch to reduce prices, which triggered the collapse from $27 to (ultimately) $10 a barrel in 1985–6. Norwegian income from tax and royalties plummeted from 52 billion kroner in 1985 to only 15 billion in 1986, with the prospect of only 6–8 billion thereafter.[38]

Willoch's coalition ran into difficulties. In April 1986 the Labour Organization was involved in the biggest lock-out the country had seen since the 1930s. The budget deficit ran at 15 per cent and the stock exchange had 20 per cent knocked off its values. In May the Willoch government fell, and was replaced by a minority Labour administration under Gro Harlem Bruntlandt – Willoch hoping that Labour would take on the unpleasant business of reconstruction, while he bided his time. Never someone to dodge a challenge, Mrs Bruntlandt captured a few headlines by forming a Cabinet with seven women out of seventeen, an intriguing contrast with Mrs Thatcher's male harem.

The Bruntlandt government lasted until September 1989, and was in no way gentle. It devalued the krone by 12 per cent, brought in a regime of fixed exchange rates and austerity, including a wages policy agreed with the Labour Organization, whose authority had been sapped by the growth in the oil business.[39] The gradual recovery of the oil price, and the substantial reserves still available — in 1990 Norway had still 8,800 billion barrels, compared with Britain's 4,143 billion barrels — overall trade moved back into balance in 1989 and into surplus in 1990—91.

In reaction to Labour's austerities, and a rise in unemployment levels to an unheard-of (in Norway) level of 5 per cent in 1989 and 8 per cent in 1992, the Conservatives came back as part of a coalition, but they were incapable of coping with the crisis in the financial services area and resigned in November 1990, leaving Labour to impose what amounted to a comprehensive programme of bank nationalization.

Norway had, on the face of it, made the mistake that the *Economist* had cautioned against in 1974. It had operated a depletion policy, and saved up the oil that it could have sold at a high price in the early 1980s to sell at a lower price in the later 1980s. Assessing the balance in 1992, the *per capita* income of the Norwegians had gone up from $13,790 to $23,120 since 1984; Britain's had grown from $8,510 to $16,070.[40] Norwegian growth was thus 69 per cent, while British growth was 88 per cent. But the British growth was from, and to, a much lower level, and deviations from that norm, that is, the very poor and the very rich, were much greater than in Norway.

By 1992 Norway was the world's largest net exporter of oil outside OPEC, and the fourth largest exporter of natural gas.[41] There were fears that the economy was much more dependent on oil than it ought to be. Oil now accounted for 50 per cent of Norwegian exports, double what it had been in the early 1980s. Yet in 1993 Finn Kristensen, the Minister for Industry and Energy in the second Brundtlandt government, regarded the outlook as favourable:

That Norwegian oil policy has displayed a high degree of continuity and predictability is one of the reasons why it is attractive for oil companies from all over the world to invest in Norway.[42]

The role of the Norwegian state in the oil business was set to decline after the Act of 1991, but this would be used to facilitate Norway's entry into the European Community, and the export into other offshore oil provinces of the formidable technology that the land had developed.

Death by Fire

Late in the evening of 6 July 1988 fire broke out in the south-eastern quadrant of C Module of the Piper Alpha platform. A maintenance team had not properly replaced a valve removed from one of the pumps and the riser pipe which brought the gas under pressure from the sea-bed was leaking. A low-lying cloud of gas condensate caught alight. The fire surged through the structure, boosted by a series of explosions, enveloping the platform in twenty minutes. Those of the crew who could move fast got down the jacket stairways to the surface, but most of them were trapped in the accommodation module when a series of explosions blew thousands of tons of metal apart. The flames, pipes and tangled steel swept rescue vessels to destruction.

The rig safety vessel *Tharos*, its paint scorched off by the heat, played millions of gallons of water on to the platform, while the rescue trawler *Sirius* picked up survivors and sought rescue helicopters. On the morning of the 7th nothing remained on the surface of the grey sea save a couple of metal legs, supporting, in a tragic joke, the flaring booms for Piper Alpha's waste gas.[43]

Ed Punchard, a young diver, was fortunate to be working on one of the lower levels of the platform. He managed to scramble down the ladders to sea level and swim out to the old trawler. In the following hours the trawler picked up over sixty men, but it was only a small vessel, and unfitted for the sort of rescue it had to carry out; its crew seem to have been as deeply in shock as the men it recovered. It was over six hours before they were flown to hospital in Aberdeen.[44]

Sixty-five men survived the explosion, the fire on the

installation, and the blazing sea. The rest of the crew of over 250 were missing. Occidental's ancient chairman, Armand Hammer, hastened to Aberdeen, followed by the Queen, Mrs Thatcher, and Cecil Parkinson and Malcolm Rifkind, the Energy and Scottish Secretaries. In storm-force winds, Red Adair went into action to try to plug the blowout, and when the wind had dropped succeeded in doing so on 13 July.

A strange funeral was held in St Machar's Cathedral, Aberdeen, on 20 July. Only twenty bodies were there to be buried by bewildered families; it took weeks for the remaining 145 to be recovered from the wreckage of the accommodation module. Twenty were never found. The politicians mourned, and departed. A relief fund was set up, and reached £3.85 million by the 20th (including £1 million from the government, £1 million from Occidental, £560,000 from the European Community, £500,000 from Thomson). Dr Armand Hammer promised £100,000 to each of the families of his thirty-one dead employees, plus life pensions, and departed for Tel Aviv to inaugurate offshore drilling there. A public inquiry was set up, under Lord Cullen, Senator of the College of Justice in Edinburgh.

On the 7th of July, a Hammer assistant attributed the blast to a faulty underwater module. Occidental's UK manager John Brading claimed that, 'The forthcoming public inquiry into the explosion would show Occidental had the highest standards of safety in the industry.'[45]

This claim did not last long; and Hammer's apparent generosity seemed somewhat qualified by the fact that (a) this settlement was no more than standard practice; and (b) he claimed, somewhat insensitively, that production might be restarted using the one module which survived.[46] Even before the departmental and public inquiries into the tragedy had convened, the true state of affairs on the platform was becoming disturbingly clear. The accommodation module was made of wood, and highly combustible (one had actually burned down while under construction in Houston); the gas compression chamber ought to have been fitted with steel blast walls after the fire of 1986. In the opinion of a former Occidental safety manager, such inadequacies were aggravated by the government's safety regime: 'The system is not set up to make sure that the standards are enforced by the certifying authorities.'[47]

Piper Alpha had pumped more than 120,000 barrels a day, well above its original capacity. Its weight had risen to 34,000 tons, making it top-heavy. Complaints about the structure 'falling apart', voiced ten years before, had resumed. A former government inspector calculated that the platform was now too small for its load:

A number of facilities were added over the years and the additional equipment it required increased the weight capacity. Fractures and weaknesses were discovered in the supporting legs in the early 1980s.[48]

The work-force remembered attempts to get men to work at night, lit only by the flare stack, something which could be fatal if anyone fell overboard. The spray system, according to an engineer, Robert Buchanan, rarely worked anyway, and not at all on 6 July: 'Nothing like that happened, not even in the accommodation area. I was in the accommodation module for twenty minutes.'[49] Yet by the time the accommodation module with its tragic freight was raised from the sea-bed by one of the crane barges in November, other news – the Scottish Constitutional Convention, the threat to Ravenscraig steelworks, the decision to close the Dounreay reactor in 1997 (that would-be 'fast breeder' in which another energy interest had placed such faith) – was flooding in. Even the circumstances of the tragedy were occluded by the arrival of flash Texas lawyers promising the bereaved astronomical levels of damages.

Dundee District Council found that it had still in its coffers £6,000 that had been subscribed for the survivors of the Tay Bridge disaster 109 years before. It sent this to the fund. This had a grim symbolism, as the first Tay Bridge had been a horror of bad design and faulty construction. Its designer, Sir Thomas Bouch, never recovered from the inquiry. Something similar was on its way, but this time there was no Bouch to scapegoat.

Two and a half years passed. Lord Cullen took evidence, interviewing 260 witnesses over thirteen months. The counsel for Fife Regional Council at the Moss Morran inquiry, he reflected an awkward tendency among the judiciary to make themselves well informed and not disposed to pull punches.[50] Out at sea more fatalities occurred. In June 1990 the rig *Ocean Odyssey* exploded and sank. The radio operator stayed at his post and drowned. On 24 July 1990 a helicopter crashed into the Brent Spar loading platform; six were killed. In August, demanding better contracts and working conditions, thousands of bears struck work or occupied their rigs. Forty installations were out, co-ordinated by an umbrella organization, the Offshore Industry Liaison Committee, set up the previous summer, and benefiting from a heatwave, the beginning of the Kuwait crisis, and an articulate leader, Ronnie MacDonald.[51]

BP refused to meet a strikers' delegation in Glasgow, but the action became more widespread. After an attempt to force workers ashore, 1,500 Shell workers joined in. MacDonald condemned the 'thuggery' of BP and Shell, in hiring 850 Malaysian strikebreakers at £12 a week. The companies condemned OILC's 'despicable methods', although the Americans – Amoco, Conoco and Chevron – were more conciliatory. Possibly with reason; the Aberdeen oil expert Alex Kemp said that the strike would have 'little or no impact' on day to day production. The main unions, aggrieved at the direct action taken by MacDonald and OILC, moved in to try to regain the bargaining position they had been losing for years. Between 25 and 29 August a compromise was reached in which longer-term contracts would give better labour protection, something which Ian Wood, for the contractors, and Tommy Lafferty, for the AEU, could accept.[52] They knew that Lord Cullen would shortly be reporting to the government. On 19 October Cullen reported; on 12 November his report was published.

What Lord Cullen found was this: the initial fire broke out because a safety-valve had been removed from one of the pumps in the course of maintenance and the 'blind flange' on the pipe which replaced it was leaking:

The lack of awareness of the removal of the valve resulted from failures in the communication of information at shift handover earlier in the evening and failure in the operation of the permit to work system in connection with the work which had entailed its removal.[53]

It was in fact rather like a railway signalman failing to hand over the token which a driver requires to proceed on to a single-line section of track, and the results were what can be imagined. As soon as the new crew opened the second valve they were hit by the full force of the condensate, bursting through the leak. Ignited, it was like a vast blowlamp playing on a structure swimming in oil. The fire was intensified by the failure of the other platforms in the oil and gas network – Tartan and Claymore – to shut down fast enough. They continued to feed Piper Alpha with oil and gas. They were, Cullen found, 'ill-prepared for an emergency on another platform with which their own platform was connected'.[54] The water–spray system went out of action as soon as the flames reached the power station and the control-room. The stand-by diesel fire pumps were on manual control, and no one could reach them. For the men in the accommodation, twenty minutes remained. Observers noted 'confusion but not panic' among them. But they had no chance. The consequences were appalling, even when conveyed in Cullen's judicial terms:

The system for control in the event of a major emergency was rendered almost entirely inoperative . . . 61 persons from Piper survived. 39 had been on night-shift and 22 had been off duty. At no stage was there a systematic attempt to lead men to escape from the accommodation. To remain in the accommodation meant certain death.[55]

Cullen found that the key cause of the explosion, 'the failure in the operation of the permit to work system', was 'not an isolated mistake . . . there were a number of respects in which the laid-down procedure was not adhered to and unsafe practices were followed'.

The diesel fire pumps were – uniquely in the field – manually operated; three of the water–distributors were blocked with scale.

This was the result of the fact that over the years statutory inspection of the production platforms had been cursory in the extreme:

Evidence as to training for emergencies . . . showed that the induction was cursory and, in regard to demonstrating lifeboats and liferafts, not consistently given. Muster drills and the training of persons with special duties in an emergency did not take place with the frequency laid down in Occidental's procedures. The OIMs and platform management did not show the necessary determination to ensure that regularity was achieved.[56]

Occidental management 'adopted a superficial attitude to the assessment of the risk of major hazard'. In this they were more or less seconded by the Department of Energy. There had been inspections in June 1987 and June 1988, but

The findings of these inspections were in striking contrast to what was revealed in evidence at the Inquiry. Even after making allowance for the fact that the inspections were based on sampling it was clear to me that they were superficial to the point of being of little use as a test of safety on the platform. They did not reveal a number of clear-cut and easily ascertainable deficiencies.[57]

It was difficult to avoid the conclusion that the Department of Energy's inspectorate, unlike the Mines inspectorate, which surveyed pits *every two weeks*, was in the pockets of the offshore operators. Getting the oil out and selling it had taken precedence over the maintenance of safety standards – something that became apparent in the requirements for the generation of platforms constructed after the disaster and in the wake of the Cullen recommendations: platform reconstruction, efficient rescue equipment and procedures, bilaterally agreed between management and workers, and the inspection of rigs and platforms by the Health and Safety Executive.

The new platforms, with accommodation separated from production, would cost 50–60 per cent more than their predecessors. The companies claimed that they were already committed to an extra £750 million expenditure after Piper Alpha, but Piper

Bravo, the successor platform, alone was estimated at £1.3 billion.[58] Britain and Scotland took momentary notice, but the attention span of both was short. 'Well, they get good wages for working there' seemed an almost universal response. But after 1986 this was no longer the case. With crude down from $40 to $14 a barrel, the cost of hiring a rig dropped from $60,000 to between $15 and $20,000, and drastic economies had been made. A Scottish Tory candidate, Ross Leckie, remembered how as a student in the late 1970s he had earned £1,286 for a fortnight. When he did a further stint in 1987–8 he found that there was less shoving about and shouting; he was 'a name, not an obscenity', but his net income was down to £768 a month 'and economy was everywhere'. Companies' catering expenditure – the usual way in which they were assessed by their employees – was down from £5 to £2.10 per head:

... the real losers are the men who work offshore. After 18 months on the dole, most were willing to come back on any terms, even to a basic hourly rate of £2.96, to short-term contracts, to the abolition of travelling allowances and fringe benefits.[59]

The Cullen Report would be acted on, but politically it was an explosive charge which did not go off. It was as damning as the Tay Bridge inquiry. Those it arraigned suddenly vanished. Armand Hammer died only weeks after the report came out, and Occidental sold out its North Sea interests to the French state-owned oil company Elf Aquitaine in 1991. Most ironic of all, the report was immediately followed by Michael Heseltine's challenge to Margaret Thatcher, and then by her fall from power on 22 November. This, the only instance of the dispatch of a ruling prime minister by a governing party, meant that the premier never had to face indictment on an issue which went to the heart of the style of government which she had popularized.

As far as oil was concerned, luck – or perhaps the feckless organization of her opponents – was always on Mrs Thatcher's side. In 1975 the Burmah business might have finished her leadership of the Conservatives almost before it had begun. A week or so longer in office in 1990, and Piper Alpha might have stained her demission. She was never called on to account for the inadequacies which claimed the equivalent of two-thirds of the British dead in the Falklands War; and the victims of Piper Alpha did not figure anywhere in *The Downing Street Years*.

In contrast to the sabotage of the Pan-American jumbo jet over Lockerbie later in 1988, in which 270 died, and in which (despite imperfect and contradictory evidence) the finger was promptly pointed at Colonel Ghadafi's Libyan regime, there was no alacrity to pin the blame for Piper Alpha, even after the Cullen Report. In 1992 the Scottish Lord Advocate, Lord Fraser of Tullybelton, called off attempts to get a criminal prosecution of Occidental in the courts. Civil proceedings continued (and, in 1994, still continue); the Engineering Union official Tommy Lafferty, treasurer of a fund to support the victims' families, apparently distraught after irregularities were found in it, committed suicide in the summer of 1993. Although the disaster was a contributory factor in the downward spiral of Lloyd's, the London insurance market, full compensation has yet to be paid.

Not everyone lost. In July 1988 oil prices rose by $1.25 to $15.70 a barrel, bringing windfall gains to City speculators in the oil commodity market.

12

The Muezzin at Kyle

No King will heed our warnings,
  No Court will pay our claims –
Our King and Court for their disport
  Do sell the very Thames!
For, now De Ruyter's topsails
  Off naked Chatham show,
We dare not meet them with our fleet –
  And this the Dutchmen know!

Rudyard Kipling, 'The Dutch in the Medway (1664–1672)'[1]

Whatever Happened to . . .?

At Kyle of Lochalsh the voice of the muezzin echoed across the narrows of the Little Minch. The crew of the Saudi gunboat *Al Sabra* prostrated themselves towards Mecca, roughly in the direction of Balmacara. They were there for diving practice in a school built to serve the needs of the rigs; all that remained of the industrial hectic of sixteen years before, when Captain Gray's seven tugs had hauled Ninian Central into the Sound of Raasay. Eighteen miles south of Kyle, Sir Iain Noble sipped his own whisky in Eilean Arnain house, by his whitewashed inn, which would have seemed welcoming to Johnson and Boswell 220 years ago. Seaforth Marine had been a venture undertaken for Scotland, just like the Gaelic College which he had helped set up at Ostaig, seven miles south. But Seaforth, a victim of the oil price collapse after 1985, had only survived as a subsidiary of an American contracting firm. Noble continued as a

337

merchant banker, but his real enthusiasm was the struggle to save the Gaelic language and the economy of Skye. Against the odds, both were making progress. The population of Skye and Lochalsh was the highest it had been for fifty years. Most of the incomers were young, and many were sending their kids to Gaelic-speaking playgroups, an initiative which had gone out from Sabal Mor Ostaig, which was preparing Highlanders to tackle high-technology and business studies in their native tongue. The waves slapped at the pier, the yellow fronds of seaweed shifted in the clear water; the engines of the *Al Sabra* coming down the Little Minch sounded remarkably loud.

Noble came from the family which had once controlled Armstrong-Whitworth's Elswick arsenal at Newcastle, and sold the Japanese the guns which had blown the Russian Baltic Fleet apart at Tsu-Shima. He had remained obdurate in his nationalism, but regretted the absence of a Scottish party which appealed to a patriotic business class. The SNP had moved too far and too fast to the left.[2] A line which was central in the ideology of middle-class nationalism in Alberta or Catalunya seemed somewhat eccentric in Scotland. This was not because of anything in Noble's argumentation, but because a Scottish business class existed which, far from favouring greater autonomy, was steadily moving into the ambit of the City of London.

This didn't accord at all with the analysis of Eric Hobsbawm, the magus of orthodox British Marxism:

The triumph of the SNP, a classic petty-bourgeois nationalist party of the provincial right, can only be achieved on the ruins of the Labour party . . . Anyone who thinks that the SNP would readily let itself be transformed into something like a socialist party is whistling in the dark. What the Scottish Tories or Liberals might do is anybody's guess. The safest prophecy is that Scottish politics would be complex and unpredictable, and might be rather savage if the hope of universal prosperity as the Kuwait of the north . . . proves unreal. What is pretty certain is that it will be nothing like another Norway.[3]

The SNP defied Hobsbawm and moved firmly to the left of Labour, but it was a troublesome process. The oil issue had proved a two-edged sword, and the team which had used it so successfully ended by falling on it. In 1979 the SNP dropped from eleven MPs to two, Donald Stewart and Gordon Wilson; both were rather conservative figures, and once in opposition, Labour's Scottish vote obstinately refused to crumble in anyone's direction. A 'national left' emerged – Stephen Maxwell, Alex Salmond and the unruly new recruit, Jim Sillars – out of the people who had been mobilized in the 1970s, in and out of Sillars's Scottish Labour Party. Their initiative, called the '79 Group, aimed at the creation of a socialist, republican Scotland, believed to be attractive to the masses of Strathclyde. It proved no more so than the old Tartan Toryism, but caused a split which weakened the SNP and led to a poor result of 11 per cent and two MPs in the 1983 election. Politics had lost the magnetism of the 1970s. Margo MacDonald married Sillars, but left for the media; George Reid and Donald Bain found prestigious niches in the Red Cross and Euratom, the European higher bureaucracy.

From the Labour front bench Bruce Millan followed them in 1988, to become Regional Commissioner in Brussels: a position in which this modest and competent man did well. The vacancy he left at Glasgow Govan was shortly filled by Sillars, his peace made with the Common Market, his eye on a further fuel crisis, which he predicted for the mid-1990s, preaching an independent Scotland in a united Europe.[4] With polls showing a substantial minority of Labour voters favouring independence, little enough separated him from many Labourites – beyond the razor-wire of party rhetoric. But *that* was enough to ensure that the division was unbridgeable. Led by Gordon Wilson, egged on by Sillars, the SNP rejected the attempts of the Labour and Liberal dominated Scottish Constitutional Convention in 1989 and 1990 to gain an agreed measure of home rule. The Convention was ignored but the government remained unloved. People left the Scottish political parties – all of them – in their thousands.

Other political enthusiasts from 1970s Scotland turned to literature or gardening or drink, got married, had children and mortgages. 'Every man has his price': Bernard Shaw's dictum was true of several *ci-devant* home-rulers who, faced with the suspension of their ideal for the foreseeable future, decided to cut their losses. Rifkind was not alone. Professor Gavin Kennedy, *animateur* of the SNP's *Radical Approach* manifesto in 1976, became a sharp, slangy high priest of the theory of negotiating and deal-making; not the first or the last ex-Trotskyist to end up as a management guru. Professor Donald Mackay left full-time academe for his industrial consultancy PIEDA, and various directorships; maintaining his hostility to devolution, and keeping quiet about his former secessionist tendencies, he became an energetic if not always convincing cheer-leader for Mrs Thatcher. He was rewarded in 1992 with the chairmanship of Scottish Enterprise – the business-led successor to the Scottish Development Agency. One or two businessmen once thought sympathetic to home rule – Angus Grossart, Sir Norman Macfarlane – aligned themselves with the Conservatives and unionism. Their conviction in this role was limited, given their failure to protect the autonomy of Scottish capitalism. Between 1984 and 1986, at the climax of the City's takeover binge, two-thirds of Scottish industrial capital was transferred south.[5] Various actors from the oil episode figured here, particularly in the climax: the takeover by Guinness of Distillers. Charles Fraser, now Sir Charles, and Sir Thomas Risk were the main contact men for 'Deadly Ernest' and the Guinness board in Scotland; T. Boone Pickens's one-time associate Ivan Boesky, it later turned out, played as important a role in the infamous share support operation in New York.[6]

As Secretary of State after 1986 Rifkind became enthusiastically authoritarian, and drew preposterous parallels with the Enlightenment of the eighteenth century. With measures such as the Poll Tax he provoked a national resistance. This *chutzpah* paid off, for a time. Mrs Thatcher described him, proprietorially, as 'the greatest Secretary of State Scotland has ever had' – and then, when he dissented, tried to remove him. Rifkind had the last word, on 22 November 1990.[7] Alick Buchanan-Smith won plaudits as oil minister, but maintained his independence of view and an essentially *étatiste* policy until BNOC was abolished in 1986. Subsequently he was fiercely critical of Thatcher's policy towards Scotland. He was therefore dropped from the government in 1987. He died young, of cancer, in 1991. The Liberals won his former seat in November, creating the expectation that the Scottish Conservatives would be wiped out at the impending general election.

They were not. But the Labour generation which had sparred with the SNP in the 1970s – John Smith, Gordon Brown, Robin Cook – later dominated Westminster. Yet, despite their intelligence, they were non-ideologists, making links with such 'liberal' constitutional reformers as Charter 88, trying to re-create a 'British' ideology on the rubble of Tony Benn's state socialism, backing measures of devolution far more ambitious than those defeated in 1979: Cook, the former unionist, going further than most. But despite this their international profile was low, and the potential for a conserving 'British' reform had deteriorated. Consul Funkhouser, in Washington in March 1994, had lost track of John Smith; the salience of UK politics elsewhere in the world was now almost imperceptible.

Scots furnished almost a third of the Labour front bench; even on the Tory side, John Major had initially no fewer than five Scots in his Cabinet – Rifkind, Lang, Lord MacKay, Lamont and MacGregor: remarkable for a country which returned only eleven Tory MPs, and where more Scots Tories sat for English than for Scottish seats. Arguably this Scots over-representation on both sides of the House, something which hadn't happened since 1914, was an indirect consequence of the oil factor. The fact that Scots politics between 1974 and 1979 were exciting and ideological meant that talent was attracted to them – and had to make something of the situation when the tide set against devolution. This created the paradox of a Scoto-British élite, at a time when fewer Scots thought of themselves *as* British.

On the other hand, the SNP got little further along its own line. 'Scotland's Oil' had seemed a powerful argument for un-compromising nationalism, but it could only make this sort of sweeping impact in a society more homogeneous, less class- and region-divided, than that of Scotland, and one in which the SNP was already a significant force. The historian Christopher Smout – an Englishman but also active in the magazine *Scottish International* and in environmentalist groups – noted in one of the many symposia of the 1970s that the Scots lacked the Scandinavian habit of 'resignation' in the face of state action – even when the state was a *Scottish* state.[8]

There was in the 1970s no consensus over whether or what that Scottish state ought to be. In *The National Movement in Scotland*, Jack Brand saw 'modernizing' ideology as fundamental to the SNP. Borrowing from the American sociologist Neil Smelser, he talked of an incremental approach: 'at every stage of the explanation, the conditions of the development of the social movement are specified more precisely'.[9] In terms of the long-term migration of nationalist ideology from the SNP into the general Scottish political culture this was certainly true. Polls taken in the 1990s showed a much more proprietorial attitude to Scots natural resources. But only very gradually did this work in favour of the SNP, which was, as the 1992 election showed, badly penalized by the 'first-past-the-post' system.

In the 1970s, 'Rich Scots or Poor British' was a less successful slogan than the SNP had imagined. 'British' consciousness, com-municated through the Labour Party and the trade unions, re-mained strong – as opinion polls indicated. And an 'ethical view of the world', perhaps a bequest from the Liberal past, provoked the accusation that the SNP slogan appealed to a primitive acquisitiveness.[10] Devolution bought off most of the pressures making for nationalism, but went beyond Labour's capacity to satisfy it. In 1979 this could withstand neither the Conservatives' apparent promise, through the trusted figure of Lord Home, of 'something better', nor the energetic anti-devolution campaigning of many Labour activists, nor the industrial anarchy loosed by trade-union leaders ignorant of the delicate Scottish political situation. But if 'British' politicians in Scotland secured the defeat of the SNP by modifying their policies and strategy to blunt the impact of the oil issue, and deflect the thrust of the SNP's drive to independence, the result of this was that in Scotland during the 1980s 'British' politics – in the sense of a range of issues broadly similar throughout the country – ceased to exist.[11]

Mr Benn's Map

Tony Benn had a map of Britain in his Department of Trade and Industry office calculated to convince not just the visiting reptiles of Fleet Street that the man was off his chump. It was upside down, with Cornwall kicking the ceiling and Shetland next to the carpet. It was Benn's way of hinting that the way of the London world might not meet with general agreement. In 1975 this could be laughed off; fifteen years later matters were not so straight-forward.

In December 1990 the British economy was at the end of Nigel Lawson's boom. The trade figures for November – a 'good' month – were in deficit by £970 million. In the same month, it was disclosed that Britain's fuel trade, which had been in annual surplus of £6,132 million in 1985, was now down to a projected surplus for 1990 of only £310 million. North Sea oil was no longer the saviour. Privatization and the fall in demand for oil meant that the government share also dwindled. In 1984–5 it had taken £12 billion from sales of nearly £22 billion, or about 55 per cent. By 1992 it was taking £2.2 billion from £11.73 billion, or just under 19 per cent. In May 1990 was announced the closure of the first of several sections of Ravenscraig steelworks at Motherwell, the putative beneficiary of a Scottish heavy industry revived by oil-related contracts. Opened only in 1961, Ravenscraig was likely to be dismantled and shipped to Indonesia. Various replacement industries were canvassed, but in

1992, when the steelworks finally closed, the only one to make an impact was the Motherwell Food Park, which gained a reputation for meringues. Motherwell seemed strangely emblematic of that dystopic Britain which Bernard Shaw had sketched out in 1936 in *The Apple Cart*: a country whose destinies were determined by a huge multinational called Breakages Limited, while its manufacturing was limited to chocolate creams.

It would have been only too easy for the community to despair, and indeed, in comparison with Norway, there was much to prompt total gloom. Ravenscraig exemplified a traditional manufacturing sector in accelerated decline. From 27 per cent of Scottish GDP, and 29 per cent of the labour force in 1976, it had fallen to 22 per cent and 21 per cent by 1990. In metals it contributed only 4.2 per cent of British exports, and in metal goods 5.2 per cent: the heavy engineering staples were now falling beneath the British average. Outside of oil, in fact,

Scotland's superior aggregate export performance depends very heavily on the exceptionally good performances of just two out of 21 industries examined: namely office machinery and data processing equipment, and food, drink and tobacco.

Office machinery – Silicon Glen – contributed 46.6 per cent of UK exports in its class; food and (especially) drink, 30.2 per cent.[12] Salmon-farming – with an output worth £30 million in Shetland alone – was earning more than shipbuilding.

Far from transforming Scottish prospects, oil-related work, after peaking in 1984 at about 90,000 jobs, contracted to 50,000 jobs by 1990, although this rose a little as firms, drawing in their horns, moved more offices from London to Aberdeen. The Scott field commissioned in 1993, appeared to be the last project of real size, particularly after the abolition of Petroleum Revenue Tax on existing fields in the 1992 budget, which switched incentives away from exploration to the more intensive exploitation of existing fields. The price of oil continued to fluctuate gently downwards; $20 a barrel in 1988, it fell to $15 in 1990 and after a Kuwait-war-triggered revival, to $13 in 1994, costing no more in real terms than it had been in 1973, before the Arab policy took full effect.[13] (Troubles in Nigeria and Russia, however, pushed it back to $19 by the summer of 1994.) The Scots were immune from Falklands fever, but by and large approved of the Kuwait war, not least because so many of them, trained in the North Sea province, were now working in the Gulf.

And yet, and yet . . . When Tebbit Senior had pulled himself together and got on his bike, he had set off south. And this seemed to be the extent of his son's advice to subsequent generations, in spurning a 'positive' regional policy for the 'free play of market forces'. But market forces no longer worked in favour of the metropolis. The diseconomies of the over-congested south-east finally took their toll, in terms of planning chaos, traffic congestion, rising house prices and rocketing crime, and the Scottish cities registered on a cost-benefit basis as very attractive places in which to live. Aberdeen's high-technology repertoire at last began to take off, but would this be enough to combat the magnetism of London?

In his study of the British regional problem, David Smith of the *Sunday Times* thought not; London's domination of the air routes would still mean that executives jetting in from Texas or the Gulf would prefer to stay there and 'take in a show' rather than proceed north.[14] This pessimism was borne out by Glasgow's attempt to enter the oil business, which foundered with the privatization of BNOC and the subsequent takeover of Britoil by BP in 1988.[15] Yet the city itself underwent a commercial revival not least because of the bounty of Scotland's maritime past. In 1957 Sir William Burrell died. A tight-fisted shipping contractor, Burrell had cannily bought up freighters at the bottom of cyclical depressions and sold them off, equally astutely, at the top of booms. With the profits, he bought works of art. Burrell was a son of that progressive epoch in Glasgow's history when trade went hand-in-hand with art patronage, and his purchases were as shrewd as his marine dealings. A town councillor in the city's 'municipal socialism' period, in the early 1950s he donated the lot to the Corporation. It was then valued at £7 million. By

1985 this had risen to Monopoly-money figures, and was at last fittingly displayed in a superb museum in the Pollok estate, south of the city and set against the backdrop of the southern Highlands.

The Burrell Collection – housing it cost as much as a medium-sized oilfield – became the motor for the reconstruction of Glasgow as 'City of Culture': a project essentially carried through by the city's new Catholic middle class. The Merchant City; one of Europe's biggest transport museums; an entire Rennie Mackintosh flat reconstructed: suddenly Glasgow began to take on almost Florentine pretensions – not least because the place was also culturally alive. Many of the liveliest artistic performers – Gray, Kelman, Lochhead – took a baleful attitude to the business of selling it, but still benefited from the publicity it generated.[16]

Even in the financial area Scotland did well, while the City of London fell on its face. Scottish firms managed £50 billion in funds in 1986, £100 billion in 1992 and £211 billion in 1994. Finance and services were 15 per cent of Scottish GDP in 1992; their workforce of 165,000 in 1987 rose to 220,000, or 11 per cent, in 1992, and they were the business of eleven out of the twenty top Scottish companies. When the City was running into a downturn after 1991, losing 81,000 jobs in 1992 in England, it put on 17,000 jobs in Scotland.[17] Perhaps, as Funkhouser's own ambitions for Scotland indicated, the enduring impact of the oil was not as an industrial sector but as part of a new business culture in which the information revolution gave a new utility to the country's endowment of golf courses and salmon rivers, arts festivals and universities:

Is not the United Kingdom ideally situated to represent the fulcrum between East and West, North and South, third and fourth worlds, between the EEC and EFTA, between Scandinavia and the Continent, where the British and the Scots have such an extensive experience? What should the Scottish Council Research Institute do to further these changes? Should SCRI recommend special programmes to attract Arabs to Scotland in universities, hospitals, business, finance?[18]

Douglas Crawford's idea of a northern Switzerland was not so *outré*, after all.

Glasgow and Edinburgh were not utopias of social solidarity. There were yuppies north of Carlisle, glitzy temples devoted to shopping and guzzling, and on the far fringe of town – at Castlemilk or Ferguslie Park or Wester Hailes or Pilton – housing schemes which made Eastern Europe look like Shangri-La. In the countryside there were 'white settlers', a minority of whom, wealthy and noisy, were alternately arrogant and apprehensive in their relationships with the natives. But there was none of the 'savagery' which Hobsbawm had prophesied. As the example of Skye showed, many of the incomers were anxious to exchange the metropolis and the philistinism of Thatcherism for a more communitarian existence. At the same time this tolerance, and indeed positive approval for the idea of a 'mongrel nation', was not accompanied by any reconciliation to the Union or enthusiasm for the Conservative Party. As the British economy, apparently unresponsive either to fiscal or monetary controls, lurched into the 1990–93 recession, the opinion-poll fortunes of nationalism changed. In 1974 only about 20 per cent of the Scottish electorate favoured the SNP's goal of independence, a percentage which actually fell as the party's vote increased. By 1993 not only was Scotland more socialist, more republican, more Europe-minded than the rest of Britain; support for independence was around 35 per cent and rising.

Studies of the Scottish economy in the later 1980s showed the high value placed by incoming firms on environment, quality of life, cultural and educational facilities.[19] The fall in the oil price weakened the economic case for Scottish secessionism, but other cultural factors encouraged it. Oil's very unobtrusiveness meant that its contraction did not impede a cultural renaissance within Scots society, which made the place livelier to be in than at any time for the better part of a century.

Instead, Hobsbawm's 'savagery' happened in the south, in semi-derelict housing schemes and declining inner cities. The motor-car – with the out-of-town shopping mall, the second home, and the dispersed semi-suburb – continued to be an implement for the individuation of society among the haves, and a means of vengeance, when stolen or joy-ridden, by the have-nots. The Conservative government used its additional oil supplies to equivocate on transport policy. Mrs Thatcher was never seen on or near a train; but the rail system remained intact and even grew a little. But the Ministry of Transport continued to foist elaborate road schemes on an increasingly unwilling public. In 1994, however, a confrontation seemed to be unavoidable, with the dogmatic privatization of British Rail and the £23 billion road programme provoking resistance, right and left.

Offshore and at Sea

The tenth Offshore Europe Exhibition and Conference took place from 7–10 September 1993 in the Aberdeen Exhibition and Conference Centre, on a bleak industrial estate dominated by the offices and storage sheds of oil and construction companies. There were 30,000 visitors and 1,800 exhibitors from eighteen countries. Two decades earlier the first such show, held at the university in 1973, had had only 7,000 visitors and 160 exhibitors. The discourse among the 'men in suits' disgorging from slab-like hotels (only one or two stetsons were visible, and hardly anyone answering to the description of roustabout or roughneck) was determinedly positive. The theme, 'Managing Change in a New Era', was upbeat, its 'can do' rhetoric that of half-a-dozen other conferences disgorging similar squads of men in suits in other British, European or American towns.

But translated, this meant that the future would be austere, salvaging more production from existing fields with a labour force reduced by as much as two-thirds, while coping with oil prices which remained at best static. What the construction companies wanted – more exploration and development – worried the surviving majors. The more production, the lower the price. The horror that continually recurred was the prospect that Saddam Hussein would rejoin the human race and that Iraqi production would resume; or that the resources of the Commonwealth of Independent States would be unloosed and swamp the West. The hope was that, if there was going to be such expansion, the North Sea professionals could sell the new fields their technology before lower prices overwhelmed them.

It was evident that the expertise of the American multinationals, which had in the first generation of North Sea fields drawn on its experience in the Gulf of Mexico, had its limits, and was now being overtaken. Exploration had increasingly drawn on satellite communications and new information technology techniques; three-dimensional seismography had not just enabled the mapping of the sea-bed and the geology beneath it, but the determining of exact routes to oil reservoirs for new types of self-propelling horizontal drills. Satellite communications and computer databases could now plot the positioning of equipment within a few centimetres – crucially important in a sea-bed criss-crossed by pipes and cables. In the Gulf of Mexico the recovery of oil had averaged only 30 per cent in the 1960s; now in the North Sea it was 45 per cent. Efforts to increase this to 60 or 70 per cent, by cutting the flaring-off of gas, re-injecting drilling-waste into earlier drillings to keep the pressure up, detecting hitherto unprofitable minor fields: these had all been products of the North Sea experience. They had, *inter alia*, underlain that spectacular but brief boom in the early eighties which had made Texas the jewel of 'sunbelt' individualism, and done wonders for the career of ex-oilman George Bush.

But oil enterprise was operating under increasing constraints from governments and environmental pressure groups, worried about safety and marine pollution, not to speak of global warming. The atmosphere in Aberdeen was overall not one of gung ho exploitation so much as maintaining an industrial interest in difficult times. It was possible to see some international specialisms: the dominance of the Norwegians – Aker and Kvaerner – in deep-sea technologies, developing new styles of re-usable

349

production platforms; the rapid advance of giant European construction and marine service conglomerates, such as the Swedish–Swiss Asea-Brown Boveri and the Dutch Smit Tak groups.

The Dutch disease seemed to have retreated into the irrecoverable past. Had it even been plausible that Holland's gas wealth would have caused Europe's greatest entrepôt to de-industrialize? Sailing to Rotterdam, the ferry passed the supertankers waiting for their pilots, the huge rigs building on the banks of the ship canal, the lights blazing on the Heerrema crane barges, the flares of Europe's greatest oil refinery – and everywhere the barges and push-tows of the Rhine. Sober, consensual social-democratic and Christian Democratic policies, including a cross-party planning body and that thing unthinkable in Britain, a wages policy keeping earnings under the rate of inflation, had ministered to the ills of the Dutch economy in 1982. Since then, growth had been among the most rapid in Europe, from an index of 100 in 1987 to 115 in 1993, compared with a UK growth of 100 to 105; while the budget deficit had fallen from 6 per cent of GDP to 4 per cent, the British equivalent had risen from 2 per cent to 8 per cent.[20]

Where did the British fit into this? Privatization had aided the development of groups like ABB and Kvaerner. The first had swallowed British Rail Engineering, the second Govan Shipbuilders, the last civil yard on the Clyde. The adaptation of defence electronics was more positive in the positioning, surveying and assessment branches. But here too this was essentially only realizable in terms of non-national organization. In the financial institutions of Britain the values that mattered were those of the quick profit, values which could, as in the case of Ferranti, lead to catastrophic acquisitions. Of the ten leading companies which conferred in 1976 under the aegis of the Scottish Council: Development and Industry to discuss the impact of North Sea oil, three had fallen under London control by 1985, and the careers of all of these – House of Fraser, Distillers and Ferranti – were to be marked by accusations, and the actuality, of fraud.

The rot went further. Piper Alpha was one of a series of disasters which befell the insurance market of Lloyd's of London, where the very wealthy – and many Conservative MPs – had been in the habit of underwriting risks. Theoretically a form of unlimited liability, this drew to it many of the winners of the Thatcher years, attracted by what seemed a painless form of accumulating more wealth. Lloyd's itself shifted in 1988 into a remarkable building by Richard Rogers in Bishopsgate, which looked like a Rolls-Royce of oil-rigs clambering out of the chrysalis of the old neo-classical insurance building. In the early eighties outgoings were well covered by policies. When things changed, the new generation of underwriters found that they had in many cases been organized in syndicates shunned by the professionals and the Council of Lloyd's itself, which were heavily exposed to risks. With an effect as deadly as Getty's endowment, Lloyd's sucked wealth, new and old, out of the country.

Fin de siècle, fin du monde?

Richard Funkhouser had written his War College thesis on the importance of the frontier between Russia and Persia. This still seemed to underlie his notion of strategy in the 1970s: accounting for his suspicion of the Camp David Agreement and his 'dooms-day scenario' of a United States overcommitted to Israel and perilously dependent on the conservative Arab states.[21] This awoke echoes from way back. A few years before the discovery of oil in Iran Halford Mackinder, geographer, principal of Reading University College and sometime MP for Glasgow St Rollox, postulated the importance of the 'Heartland', the territory between the Carpathians and the Caucasus. Control of this territory was the key to world power. Momentarily influential on Hitler and his adviser Albrecht Haushofer in the 1930s, this doctrine, or a variant on it, obsessed the Soviet Union in the 1970s.[22] Corrupt and inefficient, Brezhnev's Russia had now come, as much as the United States, to fear radical Islam. This fear provoked it to invade Afghanistan in 1979, as fruitless and wasting an imbroglio as several earlier attempts by Britain in that particular 'great game'. The consequences of this débâcle gave Ronald Reagan and Margaret Thatcher their chance against the 'evil empire': to subject Russia to an armaments race which the latter could not hope to win, and thus destroy her economy.

Meanwhile the USA and the UK had since 1974 been intervening without scruple to supply the Middle Eastern powers, radical or conservative, with all the weaponry that they could sell them. The tanks and supersonic fighters and missiles had been produced through the military-industrial complex, and were unaffected by market forces; they could be used against the Russians, which was good, or by the Middle Eastern powers against each other. Beneath the intrigue and obscurity which marked the policy of the West towards the combatants in the Iran–Iraq war was the supposition that such disruption was at least helpful in keeping the price of oil up.[23]

In this context the collapse of oil prices in 1985–6 had a crucial diplomatic importance. After 1971 oil became the major source of foreign income for the Soviet Union, rising from one-sixth to half of all exports. In 1984 oil and gas exports totalled $16.7 billion. But the price collapse – a decline in oil income of about $8 billion – turned the Russian balance of payments into deficit.[24] Combined with the United States' embargo on high-technology equipment for COMECON countries, which boosted the growth of Japan's protégés, the 'little tigers' of the Pacific rim, and hit the exports of East Germany and Czechoslovakia, this led at first to the acceleration, and then to the self-destruction, of Mikhail Gorbachev's attempts at *perestroika*. Frustrated as an exporter to the West, Russia demanded payment for its oil in dollars from COMECON, and forced her satellites into greater and greater debt. Afghanistan made the Soviet Army unreliable; so there was little prospect of squashing dissent, once it surfaced.

In all of this, Britain's role ought to have been marginal. It was not. In the years 1987–8, no Western leader enjoyed such a high profile, in the West and East, as Mrs Margaret Thatcher, the 'reconstructor' of the British economy, the victor of the Falklands, the living embodiment of those market forces which would, if left to themselves, bring wealth to the crumbling streets of central Moscow, to the drab flats at the end of the tramlines, the forgotten kolkhoz in the steppes. In 1975, when she captured the Conservative leadership, Mrs Thatcher's proximity to the Burmah catastrophe had escaped political notice; she was equally fortunate that Mr Gorbachev's preoccupations diverted his attention from the impact that the oil price fall was having on her 'economic miracle'.

Market forces and 'shock therapy' – the wiser Western advisers counselled – were not enough. The shift to a mixed economy had to be carefully undertaken, with the creation as a priority of a compensatory social net which would care for and retrain those laid off from overmanned state industries.[25] But here was the living and articulate proof that shock therapy worked; that the mixed economy and social policies were a mirage. Market forces, however, had never worked in the business which had, until 1988, kept Mrs Thatcher's Britain in balance, and had piled up enough reserves to keep the country above water for a few years yet. For their own reasons OPEC and the American majors had given the North Sea its bounty in 1973, and taken it away in 1986. And for their own reasons they were modest about it.

Motown to Notown

The two executives on the Washington metro were discussing churches: a conversation mainly concerned with mortgages, multi-function halls and car parking. One was a Catholic, the other evidently not, as his daughter had just been ordained. Disclosure of something which was causing fear and loathing on the current English religious scene did not affect ecumenism; the two were still chatting away, as they set off up the escalator at Vienna, about church property. Vienna was about eight miles away from Consul Funkhouser's house in Georgetown. It was a station in the middle of a ten-lane freeway, surrounded by a car park so big that a shuttle bus carried commuters to their cars.

Vienna exemplified the great car economy which Mrs Thatcher had preached to an East Europe to which, bluntly, cars mattered much more than democracy or freedom of expression as the image of progress. Or did it? The cars had changed. The road was no longer open or free. It was a concrete-sided trench; the maximum speed was fifty-five miles an hour. The underground, built after 1971 at vast expense, was the condition of the capital's survival, its monumental stations eerily similar to those the Soviet Union had bequeathed to Prague and Budapest. Still, American gasoline was 85 cents a gallon, or about 60 pence, compared with roughly the same price *per litre* in Europe, and President Clinton's attempt to raise it by 50 cents had got nowhere, thanks to a counter-attack by the oil companies.

Motorized society still dominated America, but it survived through compromises with public transport and public finance: the undergrounds of the northern cities; the huge publicly financed airports; the survival of a half-decent train service in the Washington–Boston corridor. Even so, the compromise was by no means stable: speeds were slow; the airlines were congested; the roads themselves were deteriorating to East European levels. Suburbanization was already drawing investment out of the city centres when industry, decimated by the fuel crisis of the 1970s, retreated as well; unemployment, drugs and guns completed the job. Henry Ford's Detroit was perhaps the worst: when OECD finance ministers conferred there in March 1994 on unemployment they found a city which had gone, so to speak, from Motown to Notown.

Parts of Britain, remote from the suburban leisure centres and shopping malls, plagued by endemic unemployment now stretching into the third generation (Pilton in Edinburgh, Ely in Cardiff, Ferguslie Park in Paisley), were beginning to evolve this way, into Britain's dangerous places. And near all too many of these were the rusting sheds and sidings of those works whose North Sea service had been their last: the wasted windfalls lay round the stricken trees.

Now Dance!

How should we sum up the whole episode? Very early on, the journalist and novelist Mervyn Jones was sensibly circumspect:

Since I came back from Scotland, I've often been asked whether the North Sea venture is going to be a success. To answer this question one would have to be a geologist, a production engineer and an economist rolled into one, and even then one could be wrong. Besides, statements about what's happening and likely to happen are generally made by oil companies, or by writers and journalists using information provided by oil companies. It is wise to receive such statements – which themselves influence events and are in themselves actions, or moves in the game – as we receive statements by politicians, rather than as the dispassionate judgements of 'experts'.[26]

Such ambiguities were more important for a failing industrial power like Britain than they were for a small state like Norway, to whom the oil appeared as an unprecedented resource which could be exploited by the expertise available within Norwegian society – the seafaring and shipbuilding tradition, the competence of a social-democratic bureaucracy – but was not bound up with preserving a particular political and social hierarchy.

At the start, Britain had to cope with the consequences of the rapidity of block allocations in the mid-1960s, and the slowness of technological adaptation in the same decade. There was no risk of mis-investment, or over-extension in an unknown technology, involved here, as the success of gas exploitation had already been demonstrated. The British government and British manufacturers had five or six years to appraise the market and work out alternative scenarios, in terms of differing rates of exploitation. And they did nothing about it until the emergency was upon them.

Two factors seem to have been important here. Gas was seen as a national resource, to be produced as cheaply as possible in order to benefit the domestic economy. This fitted into the old notion of the 'national interest' and, for that matter Fabian 'gas-and-water' socialism; but it wasn't seen as a technological regenerator, or as a factor in international trade. Peter Odell, as a young geography lecturer, sketched out a utopian east coast in a *New Society* article, but this was unique. The second factor was the fateful prior investment made, through Britain's own military-industrial complex, in the nuclear industry, which must count as Britain's most catastrophic miscalculation: something as distorting and wasteful of trained personnel as the commitment to mass bombing in the Second World War. But inevitable, given Britain's great power pretensions.

When the pressure for exploitation became real, the British government's room for manoeuvre was limited. The general evolution of the economy in the 1960s was away from the production of the sort of capital goods which the oil industry required. Keynesian demand-management favoured consumer goods and the control of their supply, and not the lumpy business of capital goods production – of ships, specialized steels, high-technology manufactures – whose use depended on international economic decisions. Thus Britain lost out to those economies which had consciously developed a specialized high-technology resource – the Dutch and Norwegians, the Germans and French – or to the American economy, which was simply big enough to develop such resources as one among several options.

Exploiting the oil to benefit the British manufacturing economy required organization of a 'war socialism' sort: centralized, specialized, committed to long-term planning and the integration of the trade unions into the decision-making process. This sort of planning was patent in Norway. But it was ruled out in Britain by two things. In 1970–73, 'Selsdon Park' Heath moved sharply away from planning and towards a free market. This resulted in both a destructive, speculative boom, and in confrontation with the unions; a confrontation in which the two British oil majors were committed to common action with the rest of the producers' cartel. By the time 'social-democrat' Heath had reversed his position in 1973, another factor had come on the scene: Scottish nationalism.

Was the nationalist menace real? Not in the sense that the SNP could generate real enthusiasm for a Scottish, oil-powered break-away. The emotions of the country were still fundamentally 'British'. The critical issue was the cohesion of the Labour Party, which was torn between the centralized 'war socialism' position, and an attitude to Scottish affairs which was partly neo-nationalist and partly reflected the 'basis democracy' ideas of the New Left. If Scottish Labour had split in the middle of 1974, then the possibility of a majority of SNP MPs was real; and with it the likelihood of an autonomous Scottish 'Dail' in Edinburgh, backed by international oil interests. In the 1980s there would be a general tendency towards a Scottish 'national left', but this came too late. The SNP of the 1970s wasn't sophisticated enough to detach Labour devolutionists; instead, it tended to accept their terms, at the cost of ditching the oil weapon.

Labour rode out this crisis in 1974; but at a cost. Thereafter policy had always to be carried out with regard to a Scottish dimension, a factor which reduced the necessary co-ordination of planning and consultation. As a result the government was strug-gling to keep up with centralized and efficient oil majors. The other sapping factor was Britain's accession to the Common Market; this both divided the Labour Party and created a drive, within the centre left, as opposed to the socialist left, to trade the oil off against the costs of integration. This crisis was made particularly acute by the exposed position of Tony Benn at the Department of Energy. It continued to dog Labour after it fell from power in 1979. To the 'Lib–Lab' moderates, the protection of the European idea became more important than the survival of the Labour Party itself. By the time they realized that the Social Democrat–Liberal Alliance could not displace Labour it was too late. Almost incredibly, Thatcher had managed to blow the oil bounty: to land on the right musical chair, and nearly fall off it. But by 1983 she was quite secure.

Finally, there was the economy itself, which was increasingly divided between a sophisticated financial sector and a flawed manufacturing sector. The City of London had always been slow to sustain manufacturing industry. Under the pressure of oil an alignment developed between finance and the majors, but was not extended to the development of the areas where real value-added manufacturing developments were possible. This could only be remedied by government, which was under sustained pressure by international bankers to reduce its expenditure.

Ultimately, as the memoirs and biographies of the personalities involved reveal – or even more significantly – do not reveal, the responsibility lay with a small, self-satisfied and fundamentally incompetent British élite. The almost total failure of the oil issue to surface in the historiography of Britain in the 1960s and 1970s testifies to the self-preoccupation of a small group of metropolitan Labour politicians whose intellectual reference and expertise was constrained by what they imagined the purposes of British politics to be. Managing the impact of something on the scale of North Sea oil was simply beyond them. The politicians who anticipated oil's impact – Balogh, Dell, Gordon Wilson, Benn – were distinguished by being marginal or hostile to the élite tradition.

In the 1980s the personnel of the élite and its chosen implements had changed, but its frame of reference was little different. The importance of markets and the money supply was boosted, but the multinational framework of the majors, OPEC and the Common Market still had to be navigated. There was no monolithic policy direction, as projected by Thatcher's hagiographers, but instead a series of opportunistic lurches, often contradictory, masked by the personality and power of the leader. The damage was done early on. Mrs Thatcher's personal handling of the economy in 1979–81, adding a dear money policy to the peril of a rising petro-pound in the pursuit of monetarist dogma, was catastrophic. She was stopped short of party suicide because of the positive balance of payments donated by the oil. But this episode destroyed a fifth of manufacturing capacity, and with it the possibility of turning the expertise painfully acquired in the 1970s into marketable enterprise.

Thereafter the apparent confidence of the premier, assured by the willingness of the Labour Party (with some help from outside interests?) to tear itself apart, masked a fundamental chaos in political direction. Was the oil to be used as collateral for EC membership and an economy based on financial and communications services? Geoffrey Howe and Nigel Lawson took this line. Was the oil to fund a more national industrial policy, based on the 'stepping stones' strategy of weakening the unions through a high pound, and then attracting foreign-owned plants? Tebbit and Thatcher inclined in this direction. What essentially counted was the *political* imperative of maintaining a coalition of satisfied voters through tax cuts and rising real wages directed at the booming south-east. And this service-based economy was by definition inefficient. 'Stepping stones' required investment in the manufacturing regions of the north and west once the unions had been sorted out, and productivity increased; but the voters in these areas were unlikely to vote Tory. The south-east would vote Tory, but it had little manufacturing and low productivity.

If the government was, in this way, locked into stasis, this was reinforced by the very fact of North Sea oil being about energy production. And the whole concept of energy altered in its evaluation over the two decades, as its ecological implications became apparent. In the context of global warming and pollution, cheap energy stopped being a benefit and became instead a hidden environmental cost. For many in Britain the mobile, high-energy-consuming society became anathema; the solution to its problems a low-energy-consumption/high-energy-cost economy. Even Mrs Thatcher, latterly seeking immortality as 'the woman who saved the planet', began to be captured by an environmentalist agenda.

The flight out of this stasis was supplied by the brilliant extemporization of 'popular capitalism': the creation of private monopolies by abandoning the state's stake in the economy, and allowing the speculative input into it to balloon. The values of the City of London were thus extended to energy and the infrastructure. The premier's international mission, another triumph of presentation, reached its most splendid point in 1986–8, just as the oil boom collapsed and Britain's ancient enemy, the balance of payments, roused itself for a redoubled assault.

In La Fontaine's fable, the grasshopper and the ant went through the summer with the gorgeous grasshopper dancing around and the dull ant burrowing away to furnish its winter quarters. When autumn and winter came on, the grasshopper became tired and cold, while the ant was ensconced in its snug ant-hill. To the grasshopper's complaints, the response of the ant was brief: '*Dansez maintenant!*'

As with insects, so too with nations.

In the autumn of 1993 the Rt Hon. Peter Lilley, the son of a BBC executive, who had made his pile as an oil analyst in a merchant bank in the 1970s – 'He was always a big stock man; he favoured the major oil companies, the Shells and BPs of this world' – and was an architect of the 'stepping stones' strategy against the unions, called at the Conservative Party Conference for a campaign against those who took advantage of the welfare state. His 'little list' speech attacking foreigners and claimants was greeted with rapture by the delegates, though perhaps with less enthusiasm from the Prime Minister.

John Major's defence of his position awoke the admiration of Andrew Neil, former *Economist* correspondent in Scotland, one-time supporter of Scots independence, now editor of the *Sunday Times*. His editorial of 2 January 1994 appeared under the headline 'Major 1, Turkeys 0'. Mr Major, however, failed to sustain his recovery. Neil's next editorial ran 'Time for Major to Go'. In May, Neil left for New York to organize a TV chat show.

On 7 January 1994 the MP for Rutland, Andrew Duncan, a former president of the Oxford Union, admitted lending a council tenant £50,000 to buy his own house, on condition that he re-sold it to Duncan, who could dispose of it at the market rate, pocketing the profit. Duncan, 'a capitalist since my balls dropped', claimed to have made £1 million speculating on oil prices at the time of the Kuwait war.

On 3 May 1994 the new platform Piper Bravo suffered several explosions and ninety-eight offshore workers had to be lifted off by helicopter.

On the 13 January 1994 the Norwegian foreign minister, Johan Jörgen Holst, died after securing a peace agreement between the state of Israel and the Palestine Liberation Organization. The negotiations had been lengthy and secretive, but the outcome seemed fitting. The issue which had in 1973 brought such unimaginable, if temporary, wealth to the North Sea had been settled (as far as human reason and goodwill could settle it) by the small country which had used the bounty of its mineral resources to increase its commitment to human rights and ecological reason, throughout the world. The settlement in the Gaza Strip and Jericho would be guaranteed by a sum of $32 million, $8 from every inhabitant of Norway. Norway's commitment to foreign aid was 1.14 per cent of gross national product.

Britain's was 0.33 per cent, and scheduled to fall.

Appendix

Table 1 Value of Sales 1977–1992

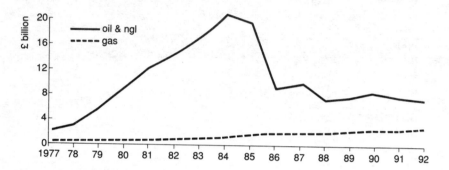

APPENDIX

Table 2 Production and Demand 1977–1990

Year	Production		Demand	
	Crude and NGLs (million tonnes)	Natural Gas (million tonnes oil equivalent)	Oil (million tonnes)	Natural Gas (million tonnes oil equivalent)
1977	38.3	35.4	92.8	36.9
1978	54.0	33.9	94.0	38.3
1979	77.9	34.2	94.0	41.8
1980	80.5	32.0	80.8	41.8
1981	89.5	32.4	74.8	42.4
1982	103.2	33.0	75.5	42.2
1983	114.9	34.0	72.4	44.0
1984	125.1	33.2	89.9	45.0
1985	127.0	37.1	78.3	48.4
1986	127.0	39.0	77.7	49.2
1987	123.4	40.8	75.4	50.5
1988	114.5	39.3	80.1	47.9
1989	91.7	38.3	81.7	47.3
1990	91.6	42.2	82.6	48.8

Source: *Brown Book*, 1992, p. 4.

Table 3 Oil Exports: United Kingdom and Norway

Year	Percentage of world exports		Quantity (mT)		Value ($ bn)	
	UK	Norway	UK	Norway	UK	Norway
1980	3.6	2.0	38.4	23	9.8	6
1985	9.8	3.6	79.0	32	16.7	6
1990	6.25	8.0	53.8	68	9.4	11

Source: United Nations, *International Trade Statistics Yearbook*, New York, 1976–1992, pp. 950 and 982.

Table 4 Rounds at which blocks of the North Sea were allocated for development under the Petroleum Production Act of 1934 and the Continental Shelf Act of 1964*

Round	Year	Blocks on Offer	Bids for	Blocks Awarded
First	1964	960	394	348
Second	1965	1102	127	127
Third	1970	157	117	106
Fourth	1971/72	421/15 for tender	271/15	282
Fifth	1976/7	71	51	44
Sixth	1978/9	46	46	42
Seventh	1980/1	Northern North Sea Area and 80 elsewhere	97	90

* Subsequent rounds, dealing usually with wider areas than the North Sea, occurred in (8) 1982/3, (9) 1984/5, (10) 1986/7, (11) 1988/9, (12 and 13) 1990/1, (14) 1992/3.

Source: *Brown Book*, 1992, pp. 92–3.

Maps

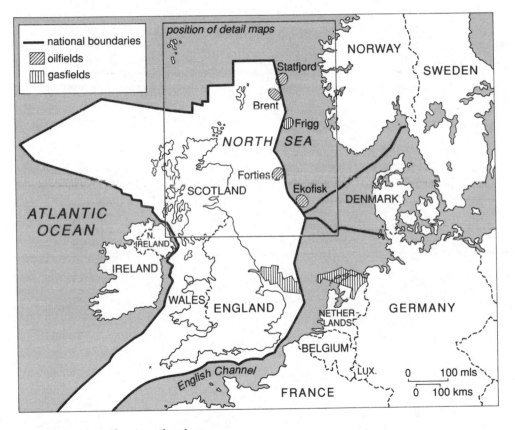

Map 1 Location of major oil and gas areas

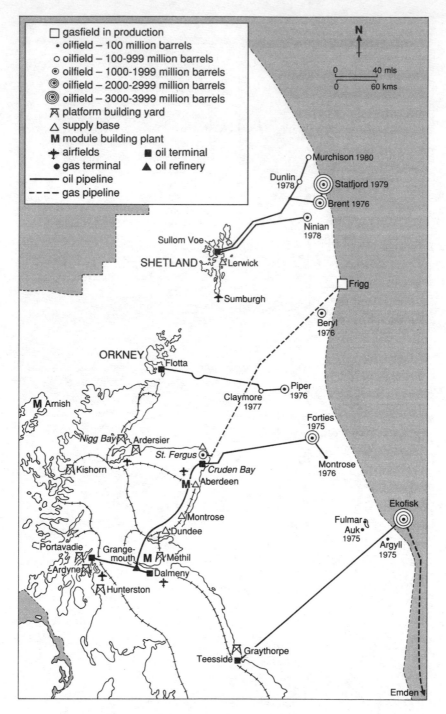

Map 2 The Northern North Sea in 1980

Map 3 The Northern North Sea in 1993

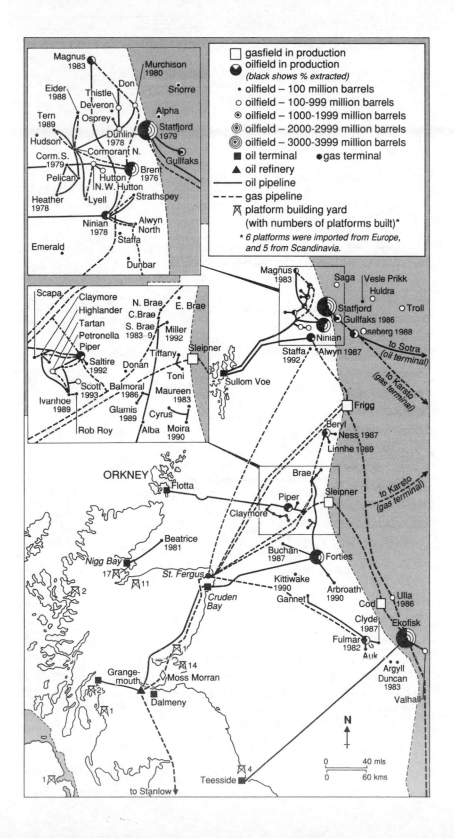

Legend:

- ☐ gasfield in production
- ⬤ oilfield in production *(black shows % extracted)*
- • oilfield – 100 million barrels
- ○ oilfield – 100-999 million barrels
- ◉ oilfield – 1000-1999 million barrels
- ◎ oilfield – 2000-2999 million barrels
- ◉ oilfield – 3000-3999 million barrels
- ■ oil terminal   ● gas terminal
- ▲ oil refinery
- —— oil pipeline
- - - - gas pipeline
- ⋈ platform building yard
  (with numbers of platforms built)*

** 6 platforms were imported from Europe,
and 5 from Scandinavia.*

Magnus 1983, Murchison 1980, Don, Snorre, Eider 1988, Thistle, Deveron, Alpha, Osprey, Tern 1989, Dunlin 1978, Statfjord 1979, Hudson, Cormorant N., Corm.S. 1979, Pelican, Hutton, N.W. Hutton, Brent 1976, Gullfaks, Heather 1978, Lyell, Strathspey, Ninian 1978, Alwyn North, Staffa, Emerald, Dunbar

Scapa, Claymore, Highlander, Tartan, Petronella, Piper, Saltire 1992, Ivanhoe 1989, Scott 1993, Balmoral 1986, Glamis 1989, Rob Roy, N. Brae, C.Brae, S. Brae 1983 9, E. Brae, Miller 1992, Tiffany, Donan, Toni, Maureen 1983, Cyrus, Alba, Moira 1990, Sleipner, Sullom Voe

Magnus 1983, Saga, Vesle Prikk, Huldra, Statfjord, Troll, Gullfaks 1986, Oseberg 1988, Ninian, Alwyn 1987, Staffa 1992, to Sotra (oil terminal), to Karsto (gas terminal)

Frigg, Beryl, Ness 1987, Linnhe 1989, to Karsto (gas terminal)

ORKNEY, Flotta, Brae, Piper, Sleipner, Claymore

Beatrice 1981, Buchan 1987, Forties, Nigg Bay, 17 ⋈, ⋈ 11, St. Fergus, Kittiwake 1990, Arbroath 1990, Ulla 1986, ⋈ 2, Cruden Bay, Gannet, Cod, Clyde 1987, Fulmar 1982, Auk, Ekofisk, Grange-mouth, ⋈ 1, ⋈ 14, Moss Morran, Argyll, Duncan 1983, Valhall, ⋈ 25, Dalmeny, ⋈ 1, 1 ⋈

N

0 ___ 40 mls
0 ___ 60 kms

Teesside, ⋈ 4, to Stanlow →

Notes

INTRODUCTION (pp. 1–12)

1. *Scotsman*, Offshore Oil Supplement, 3 September 1979, p. iv.
2. Speech at the Forties field, September 1977.
3. Grampian Regional Council, *Oil and Gas Prospects: 1993 Update* (Aberdeen: Grampian Regional Council, 1993), p. 18.
4. Statistics from *Development of the Oil and Gas Resources of the United Kingdom, The Brown Book* (London: Department of Energy to 1992, Department of Trade and Industry subsequently). Supplemented by *Inland Revenue Statistics* (annual) and *Economic Trends* (monthly) (London: HMSO).
5. Joint Trade and Industry, Treasury and Foreign Office memorandum, 1984, cited in William Keegan, *Mr Lawson's Gamble* (London: Hodder & Stoughton, 1989), p. 110.
6. Will this last, one wonders? Haynes Johnson's elegant dissection of 1980s America, *Sleepwalking through History* (New York: Norton, 1991), fails to mention Mrs Thatcher once.
7. Matthew Arnold, *Culture and Anarchy* (London: Macmillan, 1868).
8. Ben Pimlott, *Harold Wilson* (London: HarperCollins, 1992); Austen Morgan, *Harold Wilson* (London: Pluto Press, 1993); Philip Ziegler, *Harold Wilson* (London: Weidenfeld & Nicolson, 1993).
9. North Sea oil has four mentions in Margaret Thatcher, *The Downing Street Years* (London: HarperCollins, 1993).
10. Noel Annan, *Our Age* (1990; London: Fontana, 1991).
11. Guy Arnold, *Britain's Oil* (London: Hamish Hamilton), 1978, pp. 299–300.
12. W.L. Guttmann, *The British Political Elite* (London: Weidenfeld & Nicolson, 1967).

CHAPTER I   PRELUDE ON THE RED CLYDE (pp. 13–44)

1. Christopher Harvie, *Scotland and Nationalism: Scottish Society and Politics, 1707–1977* (London: George Allen & Unwin, 1977), pp. 239–41.
2. Lothar and Cordula Ulsamer, *Schottland: das Nordseeöl und die britische Wirtschaft* (Schondorf: Kriegel, 1991), p. 246.

3. See Ian Jack, 'The Meccano Man', in *Before the Oil Ran Out* (London: Constable, 1986); Frank Frazer remembers a plastic oil-rig kit, but thinks it might have been a trade giveaway. Offshore oil, to be fair, seems no more of a draw in European toyshops.

4. Tony Benn, typescript diaries, entry for 4 April 1978.

5. Andrew Neil, 'Make or Break', *Economist*, 26 July 1975, Survey, p. 18.

6. William L. Miller, *The End of British Politics* (Oxford: Clarendon Press, 1981).

7. Christopher Harvie, *No Gods and Precious Few Heroes: Scotland Since 1914* (1981; Edinburgh: Edinburgh University Press, 1993), p. 56.

8. Alasdair Buchan, *The Right to Work* (London: Calder & Boyars, 1972), 24.

9. Sir William Lithgow, conversation, 11 October 1988.

10. Buchan, op. cit., p. 25.

11. Jack MacGill, *Crisis on the Clyde* (London: Davis-Poynter, 1973), Chapter 7.

12. ibid., p. 118.

13. ibid., p. 125.

14. 'James Hamilton Muir' (James and Muirhead Bone), *Glasgow in 1901* (Glasgow: Hodge, 1901), p. 188.

15. George Blake, *The Shipbuilders* (London: Faber, 1935); filmed by John Baxter in 1943.

16. Gordon Brown, 'Inequality and the Occupational Structure', in Gordon Brown and Robin Cook, *Scotland, the Real Divide* (Edinburgh: Mainstream, 1982), Chapter 3.

17. John Firn, 'External Control and the Scottish Economy', in Gordon Brown (ed.), *The Red Paper on Scotland* (Edinburgh: Student Publications Board, 1975), pp. 153–69.

18. See Christopher Harvie, *No Gods and Precious Few Heroes*.

19. Walter Scott, *Rob Roy* (1817).

20. 'On a Raised Beach', in *Stony Limits* (1934), reprinted in Michael Grieve and Alexander Scott (eds.), *The Hugh MacDiarmid Anthology* (London: Routledge, 1972), pp. 166–76.

21. See Chalmers M. Clapperton, *Scotland: a New Study* (Newton Abbott: David & Charles, 1983), pp. 15–27.

22. T.C. Smout, *A History of the Scottish People* (London: Collins, 1969), pp. 168–70.

23. Brian Cooper and T.F. Gaskell, *North Sea Oil: the Great Gamble* (London: Heinemann, 1966, reprinted 1967), pp. 15–30.

24. Guy Arnold, *Britain's Oil* (London: Hamish Hamilton, 1978), p. 95.

25. Robert Louis Stevenson, 'Records of a Family of Engineers' (1893), in *The Works of Robert Louis Stevenson* (London: Chatto & Windus, 1912), p. 38.

26. D.I. Mackay and G.A. Mackay, *The Political Economy of North Sea Oil* (London: Martin Robertson, 1975), p. 50.

27. *Economist*, 14 July 1973, p. 25.

28. Walter Galenson, *A Welfare State Strikes Oil: the Norwegian Experience* (New York: University Press of America, 1986).

29. *OTV Magazine*, No. 1, January 1985, pp. 3–6.
30. Ulsamer, op. cit., p. 55.
31. Department of the Environment, *Our Common Future* (London: HMSO, 1988), p. 37.
32. Vicky Hutchings, 'The North Sea', *New Statesman*, 2 September 1988, 32.
33. Edmund Dell, 'The Origins of the Petroleum Revenue Tax', *Contemporary Britain*, Autumn 1993, p. 246.
34. Fernand Braudel, *The Mediterranean* (1949; London: Collins, 1979 and 1985); George K. Young, *Merchant Banking* (London: Weidenfeld & Nicolson, 1971), pp. 10–13; and see Christopher Harvie, *The Rise of Regional Europe* (London: Routledge, 1994), pp. 6, 22.
35. Alan Milward, *The European Rescue of the Nation State* (London: Routledge, 1992).
36. Llewellyn Woodward, *Short Journey* (London: Faber, 1942), p. 17.
37. 'England vor dem Stillstand', *Der Spiegel*, 14 January 1974, pp. 61–8.
38. Sidney Pollard, *The Development of the British Economy, 1900–1990* (London: Edward Arnold, 1992), p. 248–9.
39. John Williams, *Why are the British Bad at Manufacturing?* (London: Allen & Unwin, 1985), pp. 49–50.
40. *Der Spiegel*, art. cit., p. 67.
41. Tom Wilkie, *British Science and Politics since 1945* (Oxford: Blackwell, 1991), pp. 68ff.
42. C.P. Snow, *Science and Government* (Cambridge: Cambridge University Press, 1961).
43. Anthony Crosland, *The Future of Socialism* (London: Cape, 1956), pp. 13–14.
44. Thomas Balogh, 'The Apotheosis of the Dilettante: the Establishment of Mandarins', in Hugh Thomas (ed.), *The Establishment* (London: Anthony Blond, 1959), p. 111.
45. ibid., p. 135.
46. Marcia Falkender, *Downing Street in Perspective* (London: Weidenfeld & Nicolson, 1983), p. 69.
47. Harold Wilson, *The Labour Government, 1964–70: A Personal Record* (London: Michael Joseph, 1971); Wilfred Beckerman (ed.), *The Labour Government's Economic Record* (London: Duckworth, 1972).
48. Thomas Balogh in the *Sunday Times*, February 1972.
49. Alastair Dunnett, *Among Friends* (London: Century, 1985), p. 162.
50. 'Der Grosse Zeit der Gasmänner', *Der Spiegel*, 10 October 1979, pp. 79–93.
51. Peter R. Odell, 'What Will Gas Do to the East Coast?', *New Society*, 5 May 1966.
52. See George T. Murray, *Scotland: The New Future* (Glasgow: Blackie and STV, 1973), pp. 85–106.
53. Andrew Hargrave, 'Economy and Industry', in Duncan Glen, *Whither Scotland?* (Gollancz, 1971), p. 35.

CHAPTER 2   THE HIGH-ENERGY SOCIETY (pp. 45–65)

1. See Christopher Harvie, 'The Motorway Interest', *New Statesman*, 16 November 1973, pp. 274–5.
2. *Scotsman*, 7 December 1993.
3. Günter Haaf, 'Von der Freiheit des Fahrens', in *Geo: Verkehr und Mobilität* (Hamburg: Gruner & Jahr, 1991), pp. 24–7.
4. Christopher Schrader, 'Ein Monster schnappt nach Luft', in *Geo: Verkehr und Mobilität* (Hamburg: Gruner & Jahr, 1991), pp. 45–9.
5. 'Hamish Paton' (Donald Bain), *Scotland's Second Chance: Energy Opportunity Post–1993* (Scottish Centre for Economic Research, 1992), pp. 1–4.
6. Aaron David Miller, *Search for Security: Saudi Arabian Oil and American Foreign Policy, 1939–1949* (Chapel Hill: University of North Carolina Press, 1980), pp. ix–xiii.
7. D.I. Mackay and G.A. Mackay, *The Political Economy of North Sea Oil* (London: Martin Robertson, 1975), pp. 1–7.
8. Walter C. Patterson, *The Energy Alternative* (London: Boxtree, 1990), p. 40.
9. George Rosie, *The Ludwig Initiative: A Cautionary Tale of North Sea Oil* (Edinburgh: Mainstream Publishing, 1978), pp. 19–25.
10. Anthony Sampson, *The Seven Sisters: the Great Oil Companies and the World They Made* (London: Hodder & Stoughton, 1975), p. 191.
11. Conversation with Richard Funkhouser, 21 March 1994.
12. Patterson, op. cit., p. 61.
13. Roger Williams, *The Nuclear Power Decisions: British Policies, 1953–1978* (London: Croom Helm, 1980), p. 328.
14. ibid., p.63.
15. Clive Ponting, *Breach of Promise: Labour in Power, 1964–1970* (London: Hamish Hamilton, 1989), pp. 238–56.
16. Donald Cameron Watt, 'Britain and North Sea Oil: Policies Past and Present', in *Political Quarterly*, Vol. 47, 1976, pp. 377–97.
17. Haynes Johnson, *Sleepwalking Through History: America Through the Reagan Years* (New York: Norton, 1991) pp. 127ff.
18. Anthony Sampson, *The Arms Bazaar* (London: Sphere, 1979), p. 125.
19. R.W. Johnson, 'The Great Debt Explosion' and 'Oil, Credit and Crisis', in *The Politics of Recession* (London: Macmillan, 1985), pp. 62–72.
20. ibid., p. 69.
21. Table from *The Seven Sisters*, p. 202.
22. ibid., p. 174.
23. George W. Stocking, *Middle East Oil: a Study in Political and Economic Control* (New York: Vanderbilt University Press, 1970), p. vii.
24. Sampson, *The Seven Sisters*, pp. 160–64.
25. See Simon Bromley, *American Hegemony and World Oil: The Industry, the State System and the World Economy* (Cambridge: Polity, 1991), Chapter 4.

26. Janet Morgan (ed.), *The Backbench Diaries of Richard Crossman* (London: Hamilton and Cape, 1981), p. 751. (Entry for 5 June 1959.)
27. Paul F. Kennedy, *The Rise and Fall of the Great Powers* (1988; London: Fontana, 1989).
28. Anthony Sampson, *The New Europeans* (London: Hodder & Stoughton, 1968), pp. 80–82.
29. Bromley, op. cit.

CHAPTER 3   THE CAPTURE OF THE PROVINCE (pp. 66–96)

1. Robert Louis Stevenson, 'Records of a Family of Engineers', (1893), in *The Works of Robert Louis Stevenson* (London: Chatto & Windus, 1912), p. 58.
2. Robert Orrell, *Blow-Out* (London: Robert Hale, 1989), p. 66.
3. Hans Jürgen Witthoft, *Energie aus der Nordsee* (Herford: Koehler Verlag, 1979), p. 16.
4. *Shetland's Oil Era* (Lerwick: Shetland Islands Council, 1981), p. 32.
5. Witthoft, op. cit., p. 18.
6. George T. Murray, *Scotland: The New Future* (Glasgow: Blackie and STV, 1973), p. 94.
7. John Browne (managing director, BP), speech at Offshore Europe Conference, Aberdeen, 7 September 1993; Gerry Corti and Frank Frazer, *The Nation's Oil: A Story of Control* (London: Graham & Trotman, 1983), pp. 27–30.
8. Witthoft, op. cit., p. 40.
9. Brian Cooper and T.F. Gaskell, *North Sea Oil: the Great Gamble* (London: Heinemann, 1966, reprinted 1967), pp. 62–70.
10. Orrell, op. cit., p. 53.
11. Lothar and Cordula Ulsamer, *Schottland: das Nordseeöl und die britische Wirtschaft* (Schondorf: Kriegel, 1991), pp. 176ff.
12. T.A.B. Corley, *A History of Burmah Oil, 1924–1966* (London: Heinemann, 1988), p. 377.
13. Orrell, op. cit., pp. 95–100.
14. ibid., p. 69.
15. *International Petroleum Encyclopaedia* (Tulsa: Petroleum Publishing Co., 1974), pp. 264–7.
16. Guy Arnold, *Britain's Oil* (London: Hamish Hamilton, 1978).
17. *Euroil*, April 1993, p. 50.
18. *Observer*, 5 January 1975.
19. Arnold, op. cit., pp. 95–6.
20. *Observer*, 5 January 1975.
21. *Economist*, 25 December 1971, p. 72.
22. *Brown Book* (London: HMSO, 1992), p. 92.
23. *Economist*, 18 March 1972, p. 89.

24. Jonathan Wills, *A Place in the Sun: Shetland and Oil – Myths and Realities* (St John's, Newfoundland: Social and Economic Studies No. 41, Institute of Social and Economic Research, Memorial University of Newfoundland, 1990), p. 6.
25. George T. Murray, *Scotland: the New Future* (Glasgow: Blackie and STV, 1973), p. 87.
26. John Fernie, 'The Development of North Sea Oil and Gas Resources', *Scottish Geographical Magazine*, Vol. 93, No. 1, April 1977, p. 21.
27. ibid., p. 24.
28. *Economist*, 20 November 1972, p. 92.
29. *Economist*, 20 November 1971, p. 92.
30. W.J. Pike, 'The Oil Price Crisis and its Impact on Scottish North Sea Development, 1986–1988', in *Scottish Economic and Social History*, Vol. 13, 1993, pp. 56–71.
31. *Economist*, 29 January 1972, p. 70.
32. Andrew Neil, 'Make or Break: a Survey of North Sea Oil', *Economist*, 26 July 1975, p. 41.
33. Keith Chapman, *North Sea Oil and Gas: a Geographical Perspective* (Newton Abbot: David & Charles, 1976), p. 102.
34. Witthoft, op. cit., p. 79.
35. D. Buckman, 'The Netherlands: Europe's Major Gas Supplier', in *European Offshore Oil and Gas Yearbook, 1975–6*, cited in John Fernie, 'The Development of North Sea Oil and Gas Resources', *Scottish Geographical Magazine*, Vol. 93, No. 1, April 1977, p. 27.
36. Arnold, op. cit., p. 38.
37. Fernie, art. cit., p. 30.
38. ibid., p. 80.
39. Witthoft, op. cit., p. 80.
40. *Economist*, 18 March 1972, p. 89.
41. *Economist*, 25 December 1971, p. 20; 29 January 1972, p. 70.
42. Cited in *Economist*, 30 January 1973, p. 38.
43. D.I. Mackay and G.A. Mackay, *The Political Economy of North Sea Oil* (London: Martin Robertson, 1975), p. 75.
44. Richard Marsh, *Off the Rails* (London: Weidenfeld & Nicolson, 1978), p. 105.
45. ibid., p. 106.
46. ibid., p. 107.
47. Aubrey Jones, *Oil, the Missed Opportunity* (London: Deutsch, 1981), p. 152.
48. Colin Robinson and Jon Morgan, *North Sea Oil in the Future: Economic Analysis and Government Policy* (London: Macmillan/Trade Policy Centre, 1978), p. 26.
49. *Financial Times*, 8 December 1972.
50. Peter Wybrow, 'The Scottish Labour Movement and the Offshore Oil Industry', in Tony Dickson (ed.), *Capital and Class in Scotland* (Edinburgh: John Donald, 1984), pp. 251–77.

51. Conversation with Richard Funkhouser, 21 March 1994.
52. Chapman, op. cit., p. 73.
53. Chapman, op. cit., p. 124.
54. Arnold, op. cit., p. 42.
55. ibid., p. 180.
56. Harold Wilson, *The Labour Government, 1964–70: a Personal Record* (London: Weidenfeld & Nicolson; 1983), p. 522.
57. Peter Hennessy, *Whitehall* (London: Secker & Warburg, 1989), p. 445.
58. Jones, op. cit., p. 156.
59. Mackay, art. cit., p. 328.
60. Abstract of report in *Economist*, 30 January 1973, p. 38.
61. Committee of Public Accounts (First Report), *North Sea Oil and Gas* (London: HMSO, 1973), pp. 110ff; abstracted in *Economist*, 3 March 1973, p. 66.
62. *Economist*, 10 March 1973, p. 77.
63. Interview with Tony Benn, September 1993.
64. *Observer*, 10 June 1973.
65. Richard Funkhouser, Planning and Co-ordination Staff, Department of State, report to Secretary of State, 22 May 1973.
66. Richard Funkhouser, 'The Consulate in Edinburgh': report to State Department, 28 August 1974.
67. Richard Funkhouser, cable to State Department, 27 December 1974.
68. Anthony Sampson, op. cit., p. 169.
69. Benjamin Disraeli, *Tancred* (1847; London: Longmans Green, 1900), p. 222.

CHAPTER 4   ON STREAM (pp. 97–131)

1. Edith Penrose, 'The Structure of the International Oil Industry: Multinationals, Governments, and OPEC', in Judith Rees and Peter Odell, *The International Oil Industry: An Interdisciplinary Perspective* (London: Macmillan, 1987), p. 12.
2. Richard Funkhouser to State Department, 27 December 1974.
3. *Economist*, 6 April 1974, p. 17.
4. T. Boone Pickens, Jnr, *Boone* (London: Hodder & Stoughton, 1987), p. 136.
5. Barry Rubin, 'Multi-million Dollar Graft to Rig the Crisis', *Spectator*, 9 March 1974, p. 288.
6. Richard Funkhouser to State Department, 27 December 1974.
7. *Economist*, 4 May 1974; Guy Arnold, *Britain's Oil* (London: Hamish Hamilton, 1978), p. 67.
8. Peter R. Odell, *Optimal Development of the North Sea's Oil Fields* (London: Kogan Page, 1976); and see Peter R. Odell, *Oil and World Power* (Harmondsworth: Pelican, eighth edition, 1986), pp. 131–2; and the speech of John Browne (managing director, BP), Exploration to the Offshore, 1993 Conference, Aberdeen, 11 September 1993.

9. Pickens, op. cit., p. 112.
10. *Economist*, 6 April 1974, p. 17.
11. *Economist*, 17 July 1976, p. 96.
12. L.P. Tempest, 'The Financing of North Sea Oil, 1975–1980', *Bank of England Quarterly Bulletin*, No. 19, March 1979, pp. 31–4.
13. *Economist*, 6 April 1974.
14. Kathleen Burk and Sir Alec Cairncross, *Goodbye Great Britain: The 1976 IMF Crisis* (New Haven: Yale University Press, 1992), p. 178.
15. Denis Healey, *The Time of My Life* (1989; Harmondsworth: Penguin, 1990), p. 400.
16. State Department, *Report on Oil Supplies*, 9 March 1972, p. 65.
17. Tony Carty, 'Oil', in Tony Carty and Alexander McCall Smith (eds.), *Power and Manoeuvrability* (Edinburgh: Q Press, 1978), pp. 100–124.
18. *Shell UK Review, 1976*, cited in Carty, art, cit., p. 106.
19. Richard Funkhouser to State Department, 27 December 1974, p. 3.
20. John Scott and Michael Hughes, *The Anatomy of Scottish Capital* (London: Croom Helm, 1980), p. 249.
21. Arnold, op. cit., p. 185.
22. *Economist*, 23 September 1972, p. 39; Arnold, op. cit., p. 85.
23. Arnold, op. cit., p. 174.
24. Charles Munn, *Clydesdale Bank: The First One Hundred and Fifty Years* (London: Collins, 1988).
25. D.I. Mackay and G.A. MacKay, *The Political Economy of North Sea Oil* (London: Martin Robertson, 1975).
26. Pickens, op. cit., p. 118.
27. Jim Slater, *Return to Go* (London: Weidenfeld & Nicolson, 1977), pp. 60–65.
28. Sidney Pollard, *The Development of the British Economy, 1914–1990* (London: Edward Arnold, 1992), p. 394.
29. *Economist*, 2 February 1974, p. 80.
30. Hansard, Vol. 891, 1974–5, col. 534 (30 November 1974).
31. W. Turrentine Jackson, *The Enterprising Scot* (Edinburgh: Edinburgh University Press, 1966), p. 187.
32. Ray Burnett, 'Socialists and the SNP', in the *Red Paper*, pp. 108–24.
33. *Economist*, 2 February 1974, p. 80; interview with Hamish Morrison, September 1993.
34. *Investors' Review*, 6–19 September 1974.
35. ibid., p. 254.
36. ibid., p. 257.
37. *Private Eye*, 21 February 1975, p. 5.
38. Robert Orrell, *Blow-Out* (London: Robert Hale, 1989), p. 49.
39. ibid., pp. 74, 174.
40. Jack Webster, *Another Grain of Truth* (London: Collins, 1988), p. 67; Al Alvarez, *Offshore: A North Sea Journey* (London: Hodder & Stoughton, 1986), p. 129.

41. Interview with Hamish Morrison, Scottish Council: Development and Industry, September 1993.
42. *Economist*, 16 February 1974, p. 4.
43. Interview with Professor Gavin McCrone, September 1993.
44. Interview with Hamish Morrison, September 1993; George Rosie, *Cromarty: the Scramble for Oil* (Edinburgh: Canongate, 1974), p. 6.
45. Rosie, op. cit., p. 17.
46. ibid., p. 22.
47. ibid., p. 49.
48. *Private Eye*, 9 September 1974, p. 17.
49. George Rosie, *The Ludwig Initiative: A Cautionary Tale of North Sea Oil* (Edinburgh: Mainstream Publishing, 1978), p. 44.
50. ibid., p. 53.
51. ibid., p. 85.
52. ibid., p. 107.
53. ibid., p. 131.
54. Peter Wybrow, 'The Scottish Labour Movement and the Offshore Oil Industry', in Tony Dickson (ed.), *Capital and Class in Scotland* (Edinburgh: John Donald, 1982), pp. 251–61.
55. *Economist*, 9 March 1974.
56. Billy Wolfe, *Scotland Lives* (Reprographia, 1973), p. 157.
57. *Economist*, 9 February 1974, p. 22.
58. Wolfe, op. cit., p. 158. But for the intervention of a maverick ex-SNP candidate, Wilson might have – narrowly – won.
59. Mackay 1947, Porteous, op. cit., p. 41; *SNP and You* (1962) put the southward flow at £1,250 million over 1951–61.
60. See Christopher Harvie, *Scotland and Nationalism* (Allen & Unwin, 1977), p. 252.
61. *Economist*, 6 April 1974, p. 38.
62. Interview with Dr Gordon Wilson, 19 March 1994.
63. *Economist*, 9 March 1973, p. 78.
64. Michael Keating and David Bleiman, *Labour and Scottish Nationalism* (London: Macmillan, 1979), pp. 162–3.
65. See John Scott and Michael Hughes, 'Finance Capital and the Upper Classes', in *The Red Paper*, pp. 174, 186.
66. *Scotsman*, 15 June 1974.
67. *Economist*, 18 May 1974, p. 26.
68. Alastair Dunnett, *Among Friends* (London: Century, 1986), pp. 162–79.
69. *Economist*, 12 January 1974, p. 104; 13 April 1974; p. 6.
70. *Economist*, 1 June 1974, p. 53.
71. *Economist*, 12 October 1974, p. 69.
72. Philip Larkin, *Collected Poems* (London: Marvell Press and Faber, 1988), p. 157.
73. *Economist*, 5 January 1974, p. 79.

74. *Economist*, 12 January 1974, p. 83.
75. *Economist*, 23 February 1974, p. 13.
76. 'A Country of Nations', broadcast on BBC 2, 8 May 1976.
77. *Economist*, 23 February 1974, p. 18.
78. *Economist*, 13 April 1974, p. 6; 27 April 1974, p. 59.
79. *Economist*, 19 January 1974, p. 92.

CHAPTER 5   'THE BIGGEST MOVABLE THING ON EARTH' (pp. 132–74)

1. Tony Benn, *Against the Tide: Diaries 1973–76* (London: Hutchinson, 1989), entry for 3 November 1975, p. 453.
2. Kenneth Roy, *The Closing Headlines* (Ayr: Carrick Books, 1993), p. 28.
3. Andrew McBarnett, 'The North Sea Oil Story: Government, the Oil Industry and the Press', *Scottish Journal of Sociology*, Vol. 3, 1978–9, pp. 37–49.
4. *Research into the Social Impact of North Sea Oil Developments in Scotland* (London: Social Science Research Council, 1975).
5. John Fernie, 'The Development of North Sea Oil and Gas Resources', *Scottish Geographical Magazine*, Vol. 93, No. 1, April 1977, p. 25.
6. Tony Mackay, 'The Oil and Oil-Related Sector', in Neil Hood and Stephen Young, *Industry, Policy and the Scottish Economy* (Edinburgh: Edinburgh University Press, 1984), p. 326.
7. Sidney Pollard, *The Development of the British Economy, 1914–1990* (London: Edward Arnold, 1992), p. 241.
8. W.G. Carson, *The Other Price of Britain's Oil* (Oxford: Martin Robertson, 1982), p. 127.
9. *Euroil*, May 1993, p. 13.
10. Interview with Frank Frazer, 18 March 1994.
11. Robert Louis Stevenson, 'Random Memories: II. The Education of an Engineer', in *The Works of Robert Louis Stevenson* (London: Chatto & Windus, 1912), pp. 167–77.
12. Al Alvarez, *Offshore: A North Sea Journey* (London: Hodder & Stoughton, 1986), p. 169.
13. ibid., p. 175.
14. Carson, op. cit., p. 22; Ed Punchard, *Piper Alpha: a Survivor's Story* (London: W.H. Allen, 1989), p. 29.
15. John Browne (managing director, BP), address to International Offshore Conference, Aberdeen, 7 September 1993.
16. Guy Arnold, *Britain's Oil* (London: Hamish Hamilton, 1978), p. 94.
17. Dick Mutch in *International Herald Tribune*, 19 July 1984.
18. *Euroil*, April 1993, p. 55.
19. *Economist*, 17 September 1977, pp. 94–5.
20. *Financial Times*, 17 October 1984, pp. 13–20.

21. Arnold, op. cit., p. 114.
22. Ian Jack, 'Wigan, 1982', in *Before the Oil Ran Out* (London: Secker & Warburg, 1987), p. 133.
23. Richard Funkhouser, interview, 21 March 1994.
24. *Petroleum Economist: The North Sea*, London: August/September 1992, p. 6.
25. ibid., pp. 42–3.
26. Arnold, op. cit., p. 211.
27. 'The Gifthorse Gallops By', *Economist*, 26 July 1975, Survey, p. 21.
28. Arnold, op. cit., pp. 47–8.
29. ibid., p. 46.
30. Richard Funkhouser to State Department, cable of 27 December 1974, paragraph G.
31. Interview with Rev. Dr Andrew Ross, 9 September 1993.
32. See Frank Stephen, 'Backing the Oil Effort', *Financial Times*, 19 November 1975.
33. Fernie, art. cit., p. 27.
34. Alexander McKay, 'The Fear of Facing up to the Alpha Factor', *Scotsman*, 27 July 1988.
35. Odd H. Hellesoy, *Work Environment: Statfjord Field: Work Environment, Health and Safety on a North Sea Oil Platform* (Bergen: Universitetsforlaget, 1985).
36. Benn, op. cit., entry for 1 August 1975, p. 426.
37. Interview, 9 October 1993.
38. Mackay, art. cit., p. 352.
39. Sir Iain Noble, interview, 9 October 1993.
40. Benn, op. cit., entry for 16 July 1976, p. 419.
41. Mervyn Jones, 'The Men on the Rigs', *New Statesman*, 23 January 1976, pp. 92–4.
42. Peter Frost, 'The Work on a Rig', *New Society*, 19 June 1975, p. 701.
43. Dan Shapiro, 'The Industrial Relations of Oil', *Scottish Journal of Sociology*, 3, 1978–9, pp. 1–20.
44. ibid., p. 19.
45. Mark Hollingsworth and Charles Tremayne, *The Economic League: The Silent McCarthyism* (London: National Council for Civil Liberties, 1989), pp. 43, 67.
46. Robert Orrell, *Blow-Out* (London: Robert Hale, 1989), p. 28.
47. ibid., p. 278.
48. ibid., p. 295.
49. Jones, art, cit., p. 94.
50. Carson, op.cit., p. 113.
51. Anna Coote, 'Why Are Women Banned from Britain's Oilrigs?', *New Statesman*, 16 February 1979, p. 206.
52. Hellesoy, op. cit., p. 40.
53. Stewart Hennessy and Sarah Villiers, 'Oceans Apart', *Scotland on Sunday*, 17 February 1991.
54. Morris, Taylor, Clark and MacCann in *British Journal of Psychiatry*, 1985, cited in art. cit.

55. Alvarez, op. cit., p. 113.
56. Hellesoy, op. cit., p. 340.
57. J. Graeme Robertson, *The Environmental Impact of North Sea Oil-Related Developments on Scotland* (Portree: Habitat Scotland, 1984), pp. 36–7.
58. George Rosie, *Cromarty: the Scramble for Oil* (Edinburgh: Canongate, 1974), p. 22.
59. Mervyn Jones, 'Life at the Big Hole', *New Statesman*, 6 February 1976, pp. 152–4.
60. Lothar and Cordula Ulsamer, *Schottland: das Nordseeöl und die britische Wirtschaft* (Schondorf: Kriegel, 1990), pp. 406–412.
61. Karlhans Muller, *Jagd nach Energie: Kohle, Öl und Schnelle Bruter* (Reutlingen: Ensslin & Laiblin, 1979), pp. 13–31.
62. Professor Gavin MacCrone, interview, 9 October 1993.
63. Professor Gavin McCrone, interview, 10 October 1993.
64. Jack Webster, *Another Grain of Truth* (London: Collins, 1988), p. 125.
65. Sir Iain Noble, interview, 9 October 1993.
66. Deirdre Hunt, 'The Sociology of Development: its Relevance to Aberdeen', *Scottish Journal of Sociology*, No. 1, 1976–7, pp. 137–54.
67. Hamish Morrison, interview, September 1993.
68. Robert Moore, *The Social Impact of Oil: the Case of Peterhead* (London: Routledge, 1982), pp. 167–72.
69. Ray Hudson, 'Trying to Revive an Infant Hercules: the Rise and Fall of Local Authority Modernisation Policies on Teesside', in Michael Harloe, Chris Pickvance and John Urry, *Place, Policy and Politics* (London: Unwin Hyman, 1990), pp. 64–80.
70. Reginald Byron, 'Buying a Share: State Institutions and Local Communities on the Periphery – A Case from Shetland', R.D. Grillo (ed.), *'Nation' and 'State' in Europe: Anthropological Perspectives'* (London: Academic Press, 1980), pp. 137–49.
71. *Economist*, 20 January 1973, pp. 37–8.
72. *Shetland's Oil Era*, compiled by Elizabeth Marshall (Lerwick: Shetland Islands Council, 1981), pp. 60ff.
73. Sir Iain Noble, interview, 9 October 1993.
74. *Economist*, 26 July 1975, p. 46.
75. ibid., p. 20.
76. Anthony P. Cohen, 'Oil and the Cultural Account: Reflections on a Shetland Community', *Scottish Journal of Sociology*, No. 79, 1978, pp. 129–41.
77. Mark Meredith, 'Islanders Turn the Screw on Sullom Voe', *Financial Times*, 4 March 1986, p. 6.
78. Richard Funkhouser to State Department, 30 June 1975, cited by Wills, in *A Place in the Sun*, p. 1.
79. Wills, op. cit., p. 155.
80. *Economist*, 20 August 1977; Nevis Institute, *The Shetland Report* (Edinburgh: Nevis Institute, March 1978).

81. Robertson, art. cit., p. 12.
82. ibid., p. 30.

CHAPTER 6   BENN AND THE DEFENCE OF BRITAIN (pp. 175–215)

1. Tony Benn, *Conflicts of Interest: Diaries 1977–80* (London: Hutchinson, 1990), entry for 11 January 1977, p. 3.
2. H.G. Wells, *Tono-Bungay* (1908; New York: Scribners, 1925), p. 522.
3. Dunnett, interview, September 1993.
4. Edith Penrose, 'The Structure of the International Oil Industry: Multinationals, Governments, and OPEC', in Judith Rees and Peter Odell, *The International Oil Industry: An Interdisciplinary Perspective* (London: Macmillan, 1987), p. 15.
5. Francis Boyd, *British Politics in Transition* (London: 1960); James Margach, *The Anatomy of Power: An Enquiry into the Personality of Leadership* (London: W.H. Allen, 1979).
6. Anthony Sampson, *Anatomy of Britain Today* (1965; New York: Harper, 1966), pp. 480–89.
7. David Butler and Jenny Freeman (eds.), *British Political Facts 1900–1985* (London: Macmillan, 1987), pp. 261–2.
8. Guy Arnold, *Britain's Oil* (London: Hamish Hamilton, 1978), p. 78.
9. Richard Funkhouser, interview, 21 March 1994.
10. William L. Miller, *The End of British Politics: Scottish and English Political Behaviour in the Seventies* (Oxford: Oxford University Press, 1981), pp. 62–5; interview with Sir Iain Noble, 5 October 1993.
11. John Francis and Norman Swan, *Scotland in Turmoil* (Edinburgh: St Andrew Press, 1973).
12. Naomi Mitchison, *Oil for the Highlands: Fabian Research Series No. 315* (London: Fabian Society, June 1974), p. 28.
13. Gerry Corti and Frank Frazer, *The Nation's Oil: A Story of Control* (London: Graham & Trotman, 1983), p. 64.
14. Edmund Dell, 'The Origins of the Petroleum Revenue Tax', *Contemporary British History*, Autumn 1993, pp. 215–53.
15. Committee of Public Accounts, *First Report: North Sea Oil and Gas*, Cmnd. XIX, London: HMSO, 14 February 1973).
16. ibid., pp. 102ff.
17. Dick Douglas, *A Way for Oil. North Sea Oil: Its Prospects and Problems* (London: Cooperative Party, February 1973).
18. Dell, art. cit., p. 221.
19. Report from the Select Committee on Science and Technology: Offshore Engineering, Session 25 July 1974, in *Reports*, etc. (1974), Vol. XV (London: HMSO), pp. 1057–1110.
20. *Daily Telegraph*, 8 October 1986.

21. For Scottish politics at this and subsequent junctures, see James Kellas, *The Scottish Political System* (Cambridge: Cambridge University Press, 1973).

22. *Devolution within the United Kingdom: Some Alternatives for Discussion* (London: HMSO, 1974).

23. See Frances Wood, 'Scottish Labour in Government and Opposition, 1964–79', in Ian Donnachie, Christopher Harvie and Ian S. Wood (eds.), *Forward! Labour Politics in Scotland, 1888–1988* (Edinburgh: Polygon, 1989), pp. 107ff.

24. Henry Drucker and Gordon Brown, *The Politics of Nationalism and Devolution* (London: Longman, 1980), p. 93.

25. Edmund Dell, *A Hard Pounding: Politics and Economic Crisis, 1974–77* (Oxford: Oxford University Press, 1991), pp. 51, 61.

26. *Democracy and Devolution*, Cmnd. 5732 (London: HMSO, 17 September 1974).

27. Michael Keating and David Bleiman, *Labour and Scottish Nationalism* (London: Macmillan, 1979), pp. 164–75.

28. Bernard Donoghue, *Prime Minister: the Conduct of Policy under Harold Wilson and James Callaghan* (London: Cape, 1987), p. 40.

29. *Financial Times*, 15 February 1974.

30. Corti and Frazer, op. cit., p. 85.

31. Dell, art. cit., p. 223.

32. Cited by Eric Varley, in Second Reading debate on 30 April 1975, in *Hansard*, Vol. 891, 1974–5, col. 482.

33. *United Kingdom Offshore and Gas Policy*, Cmnd. 5696 (London: HMSO, 1974).

34. Article in *Financial Times*, cited in op. cit., p. 104.

35. Dell, art. cit., p. 229.

36. ibid., p. 234.

37. ibid., p. 240.

38. ibid., p. 110; and see Andy McSmith, *John Smith: Playing the Long Game* (London: Verso, 1993), pp. 48ff.

39. Richard Funkhouser, interview, 21 March 1994.

40. *Hansard*, Vol. 891, 1974–5, col. 499.

41. Corti and Frazer, opus cit., pp. 91–2.

42. ibid., col. 528.

43. Details from Andrew Roth, *The Business Background of MPs* (London: Parliamentary Profiles, 1972); and *The Times Guide to the House of Commons, October 1974* (London: Times Publications, 1974).

44. John Smith and Patrick Jenkin, cited in Corti and Frazer, op. cit., p. 111.

45. ibid., pp. 111–12.

46. *Hansard*, Vol. 891, 1974–5, col. 598.

47. ibid., col. 580.

48. ibid., col. 541.

49. *Hansard*, Vol. 891, 1974–5, col. 534 (debate of 30 April 1975).

50. *Hansard*, col. 551.
51. *Hansard*, Vol. 896, cols. 1303ff., especially contributions of Norman Buchan and Alex Wilson.
52. Richard Funkhouser to State Department, 30 June 1975.
53. ibid., p. 118; and see John G. Liverman, 'Without Precedent: the Development of North Sea Oil Policy', *Public Administration*, Vol. 60, Winter 1982.
54. Funkhouser, p. 106; Funkhouser, as Consul, arranged for Conally to tour Scotland and Norway; interview, 20 March 1994.
55. ibid., p. 119.
56. MacSmith, op. cit., p. 52.
57. Frank Frazer, interview, 19 March 1994.
58. Bernard Ingham, *Kill the Messenger* (London: HarperCollins, 1991), pp. 142ff.
59. Corti and Frazer, op. cit., p. 142.
60. John Davis: 'Burmah: a Suitable Case for Treatment', *Observer*, 19 November 1972, p. 13.
61. Sir Iain Noble, interview, 9 October 1993.
62. John Davis, 'Burmah Oil's Troubled Waters', *Observer*, 5 January 1975, p. 11.
63. ibid., p. 11.
64. Dell, art. cit., p. 223.
65. Dell, *A Hard Pounding,* op. cit., p. 119.
66. Margaret Thatcher, *The Downing Street Years* (London: HarperCollins, 1993), p. 23.
67. Penny Junor, *Margaret Thatcher: Wife, Mother, Politician* (London: Sidgwick & Jackson, 1983), pp. 78, 104.
68. See, for example, Hugo Young, *One of Us* (1989; London: Pan, 1990), p. 37.
69. ibid., p. 132.
70. ibid., p. 133.
71. Arnold, op. cit., pp. 154–65.
72. ibid., p. 151.
73. ibid., p. 166.
74. T. Boone Pickens, Jnr, *Boone* (London: Hodder & Stoughton, 1987), pp. 119–21.
75. *Economist*, 22 April 1978, p. 119.
76. Richard Funkhouser, interview, 21 March 1994.
77. *Economist*, 14 February 1981, p. 97.
78. Tony Benn, *Against the Tide: Diaries 1973–76* (London: Hutchinson, 1989), p. 403.
79. ibid., entry for 15 July, p. 417.
80. ibid., p. 429.
81. ibid., p. 450.
82. Ingham, op. cit., p. 141; Tony Benn, interview, September 1993.
83. Richard Funkhouser, interview, 21 March 1994.

84. Benn, op. cit., entry for 5 November 1975, p. 455.
85. ibid., entries for 9 and 31 December 1975, pp. 477, 485.
86. ibid., entry for 25 January 1976, p. 507.
87. ibid., entry for 25 January, p. 505.
88. ibid., entry for 2 February, pp. 513–14.
89. ibid., entry for 17 September, p. 610.
90. Tony Benn, *Conflicts of Interest: Diaries 1977–80* (London: Hutchinson, 1990), entry for 11 January 1977, p. 1.
91. Armand Hammer, with Neil Lydon, *Hammer: Witness to History* (London: Simon & Schuster, 1987), p. 395.
92. Benn, *Conflicts of Interest*, op. cit., entries of 9 and 16 February 1977, pp. 276, 280–81.
93. *The Challenge of North Sea Oil* (London: HMSO, 23 March 1978), Cmnd. 7143, p. 13.
94. Benn, *Conflicts of Interest*, op. cit., entry for 6 July 1977, p. 322.
95. ibid., entry for 4 October 1978, p. 617.
96. ibid., entry for 24 October 1977, p. 234.
97. ibid., entry for 24 June 1978, pp. 174–5.
98. ibid., entry for 7 July 1978, p. 322.
99. *Financial Times North Sea Letter*, 9 May 1979, No. 191, p. 7.
100. Richard Funkhouser, interview, 21 March 1994.
101. Oystein Noreng, *Oil Politics in the 1980s: Patterns of International Collaboration* (New York: McGraw Hill, 1978), pp. 137–8.
102. Benn, *Conflicts of Interest*, op. cit., entry for 28 February 1979, p. 470.
103. ibid., entry for 9 January 1980, p. 226.
104. ibid., entry for 6 March 1976, p. 527.
105. Dell, *A Hard Pounding*, op. cit., p. 140.
106. Richard Funkhouser, interview, 21 March 1994.
107. Sir Ian Gilmour, *Dancing with Dogma* (London: Simon & Schuster, 1992), p. 58.

CHAPTER 7   THE MATURE PROVINCE (pp. 216–240)

1. Seamus Heaney, 'Sybil', from *Field Work*, 1979, in *New Collected Poems* (London: Faber, 1992), p. 95.
2. *Blue Book* (1992), pp. 3–5.
3. Reiner de Man, 'United Kingdom Energy Policy and Forecasting: Technocratic Conflict Resolution', in Thomas Baumgartner and Atle Midttun, *The Politics of Energy Forecasting* (Oxford: Clarendon Press, 1987), pp. 110–32.
4. Richard Funkhouser, conversation, 21 March 1994.
5. Tony Benn, typescript diaries, entry for 22 January 1979; *Conflicts of Interest: Diaries 1977–80* (London: Hutchinson, 1990), entry for 20 June 1978, p. 171.

6. Guy Arnold, *Britain's Oil* (London: Hamish Hamilton, 1978), pp. 17–22.
7. Neil Robertson, 'Oil and the Non-Oil Economy in Scotland', in *The Scottish Government Yearbook, 1984* (Edinburgh: Unit for the Study of Government in Scotland, 1984).
8. *The UK Refining Industry* (London: Institute of Petroleum Information Service, 1993), p. 2.
9. *Scotsman*, 13 September 1986.
10. *Scotsman*, 6 June 1986.
11. *Scotsman*, 3 January 1990.
12. *Scotsman*, 13 June 1990.
13. *The UK Refining Industry*, op. cit., p. 2.
14. ibid., p. 97.
15. *Financial Times North Sea Letter*, 5 March 1980 (No. 234), p. 1.
16. Andrew Neil, 'Make or Break: A Survey of North Sea Oil', *Economist*, 26 July 1975, pp. 26–38.
17. Richard Funkhouser, conversation, 20 March 1994.
18. Bernie and Mason, 'Oil and Gas: the International Regime', in C.M. Mason (ed.), *The Effective Management of Resources* (London: Pinter, 1979), pp. 26–7.
19. *Economist*, 23 February 1974, p. 98.
20. Thomas Lind and G.A. Mackay, *Norwegian Oil Policies* (London: C. Hurst, 1980), p. 145.
21. *Economist*, 30 November 1974, p. 4; 26 July 1975, p. 37.
22. *Economist*, 23 February 1974, p. 85.
23. Lind and Mackay, op. cit., p. 142.
24. Richard Funkhouser to State Department, cable of 27 December 1974.
25. Tony Benn, interview, September 1993.
26. Jonathan Wills, *A Place in the Sun: Shetland and Oil – Myths and Realities* (St John's, Newfoundland: Social and Economic Studies No. 41, Institute of Social and Economic Research, Memorial University of Newfoundland, 1990), pp. 79–91.
27. ibid., p. 167.
28. Jonathan Wills and Karen Warner, *Innocent Passage: the Wreck of the Tanker Braer* (Edinburgh: Mainstream, 1993), p. 143.
29. ibid., p. 160.
30. Malcolm MacGarvin, *The North Sea* (London: Greenpeace: Collins & Brown, 1990), pp. 104–8.
31. ibid., p. 105.
32. Interview with Rob Edwards, 29 April 1994.
33. ibid., p. 106.
34. ibid. p. 80.
35. Red Adair, cited in Arnold, op. cit., p. 22.
36. W.G. Carson, *The Other Price of Britain's Oil: Safety and Control in the North Sea* (Oxford: Martin Robertson, 1982), p. 21.
37. *Scotsman*, 8 July 1988.

38. ibid., p. 31.
39. Carson, op. cit., Chapter 6.
40. Arnold, op. cit., p. 153.
41. J.H. Burgoyne, *Offshore Safety: Report of the Committee*, Cmnd. 7366 (London: HMSO, 1980).
42. Foster, annotated comments on précis of the Burgoyne Report.
43. Roger Lyons of ASTMS and John Miller of TGWU, cited in *North Sea Newsletter*, 12 March 1980, p. 255.
44. Odd H. Hellesoy, *Work Environment: Statfjord Field: Work Environment, Health and Safety on a North Sea Oil Platform* (Bergen: Universitetsforlaget, 1985), p. 15.
45. ibid., p. 160.
46. Dr Sem-Jacobsen to Polytechnical Society, Oslo, and Stein B. Jensen, Technological University of Trondheim, reported in *Financial Times North Sea Letter*, 16 May 1979, p. 10.
47. ibid., p. 37.
48. ibid., p. 89.
49. Hans Jürgen Witthoft, *Energie aus der Nordsee* (Herford: Koehler Verlag, 1979), p. 84.
50. Donald Cameron Watt, 'Offshore Britain: Today and Tomorrow', *International Affairs*, Vol. 56, No. 2, April 1980, pp. 225–41, 237.
51. Robert L. Trillo (ed.), *Jane's Ocean Technology, 1979–80* (London: Jane's Yearbooks, 1979), pp. 310–31.
52. Richard Funkhouser to State Department, cable of 27 December 1975.
53. *Scotsman*, 19 July 1988.
54. Hellesoy, op. cit., p. 92.
55. *Survey of Current Affairs*, Vol. 8, No. 5 (London: HMSO, May 1988), p. 170.
56. Peter Wybrow, 'The Scottish Labour Movement and the Offshore Oil Industry', in Tony Dickson (ed.), *Capital and Class in Scotland* (Edinburgh: John Donald, 1984), pp. 251–77; Ed Punchard, *Piper Alpha: A Survivor's Story* (London: W.H. Allen, 1989), pp. 52 ff.
57. Wybrow, op. cit., p. 256.
58. Burgoyne, *Offshore Safety: Report of the Committee*, p. 62.
59. Robert Taylor, *The Fifth Estate* (London: Routledge, 1958), p. 90.
60. Tony Benn, *Against the Tide: Diaries 1973–76* (London: Hutchinson, 1989), p. 443, entry for 1 October 1975.
61. Carson, op. cit., p. 198.

CHAPTER 8   IT'S NOT SCOTLAND'S OIL AFTER ALL (pp. 241–58)

1. Paul Johnson, 'The Road to 1984–3': 'Land of Hope and – What?', in *New Statesman*, 28 June 1974, pp. 907–8.
2. Donald Mackay, *Scotland 1980: the Economics of Self-Government* (Edinburgh: Q Press, 1977).
3. See Tony Carty and Alexander McCall Smith (eds.), *Power and Manoeuvrability* (Edinburgh: Q Press, 1978), J.P. Grant (ed.), *Independence and Devolution: the Legal Implications for Scotland* (Green, 1976); and Clive Archer and John Main (eds.), *Scotland's Voice in International Affairs* (Royal Institute of International Affairs, 1980).
4. Harvie's personal bag was a book for Allen and Unwin, *Scotland and Nationalism*, in 1977, British Council lecture tours in Finland in 1977 and 1978, and trips to the Sorbonne and Ecole National d'Administration in Paris in early 1979.
5. George Rosie, *Cromarty: the Scramble for Oil* (Edinburgh: Canongate, 1979).
6. See Andrew Neil, 'Make or Break? A Survey of North Sea Oil', *Economist*, 26 July 1975; Ruth Dudley Edwards, *The Pursuit of Reason: The Economist, 1843– 1993* (London: Hamish Hamilton, 1993), pp. 851–2.
7. Richard Funkhouser, conversation of 21 March 1994.
8. David Gow, 'Devolution and Democracy', in *The Red Paper*, p. 65; Neal Ascherson, *Devolution Diary*, p. 49, entry for 8 June 1977.
9. Raymond Chandler, *The Long Goodbye* (London: Hamish Hamilton, 1953), p. 235.
10. Jonathan Wills, *A Place in the Sun: Shetland and Oil – Myths and Realities*, St John's, Newfoundland: Social and Economic Studies No. 41 (Memorial University of Newfoundland, Institute of Social and Economic Research, 1990).
11. Gordon Brown (ed.), *The Red Paper on Scotland* (Edinburgh: Edinburgh Student's Publication Board, 1975).
12. Tom Nairn, 'The Three Dreams of Scottish Nationalism', in Karl Miller (ed.), *Memoirs of a Modern Scotland* (London: Faber, 1970), p. 54.
13. Peter Smith, 'The Political Economy of "Scotland's Oil"', in *The Red Paper*.
14. Douglas Hurd and Andrew Osmond, *Scotch on the Rocks* (London: Collins, 1969).
15. *SNP Manifesto*, February 1974, p. 4.
16. Cf. the judgement of the English political scientist Keith Webb, in *The Growth of Scottish Nationalism*.
17. Henry Drucker and Gordon Brown, *Nationalism and Devolution* (draft, 1976), p. IV. 5.
18. See Charlotte Lythe and Madhavi Majmudar, *The Renaissance of the Scottish Economy* (Allen and Unwin, 1982), p. 144, and Arnold, op.cit., p. 212.
19. Raymond Levy, *The SNP at the Crossroads* (Edinburgh: Scottish Academic Press, 1989), pp. 47ff.

20. *The Economist*, 1 June 1974, p. 78.
21. Harvie recalls a conversation with Neal Ascherson on 1 January 1976, in which Ascherson reported that the SNP was disappointed at the level of support given by its business backers.
22. William Wolfe, chairman's address of 30 May 1975, p. 7.
23. *Scotsman*, 29 May 1975.
24. Donald Stewart, leader's address, 31 May 1975, p. 3.
25. C.R. Smallwood and D.I. Mackay, 'The Economics of Independence', reprinted from the *Scotsman*, 1976, in Clarke and Drucker, coll. cit., pp. 98–107.
26. Arnold, op.cit., p. 81.
27. Henry Drucker, *Breakaway: The Scottish Labour Party* (Edinburgh, EUSPB, 1978).
28. See *The Shetland Report* (Edinburgh: The Nevis Institute, 1978).
29. See Chris Allen's 'Bibliography' in M.G. Clarke and Henry Drucker (eds.), *Our Changing Scotland* (EUSPB, 1976–80).
30. Address of Dr Robert McIntyre, 27 May, William Wolfe, 28 May, and Donald Stewart MP, 29 May 1976.
31. Margo MacDonald, speech of 29 May 1976, especially p. 3.
32. In coll. cit., pp. 60–64.
33. See W. Miller, J. Brand and M. Jordan, *Oil and the Scottish Voter, 1974–79*, North Sea Oil Panel Occasional Paper No. 2 (SSRC, 1980).
34. Tony Benn, *Against the Tide: Diaries 1973–76* (London: Hutchinson, 1989), entry for 18 November 1975, p. 462.
35. Michael Keating and David Bleiman, *Labour and Scottish Nationalism* (London: Macmillan, 1979), pp. 150–88; Raymond Levy, *Scottish Nationalism at the Crossroads* (Scottish Academic Press, 1989), chs. 4, 5; John Bochel, David Denver and Allan Macartney, *The Referendum Experience* (Aberdeen: Aberdeen University Press, 1981).

CHAPTER 9   OIL CULTURE (pp. 259–85)

1. Alasdair Gray, *Lanark* (Edinburgh: Canongate, 1982), p. 243.
2. Louis MacNeice, 'An Eclogue for Christmas' (1934).
3. Al Alvarez, *Offshore: A North Sea Journey* (London: Hodder & Stoughton, 1986), pp. 187–8.
4. See Christopher Harvie, *The Centre of Things: Political Fiction in Britain from Disraeli to the Present* (London: Unwin Hyman, 1991), particularly Chapter 9.
5. *Halliwell's Film Guide* (London: HarperCollins, 1993).
6. Philip Larkin, 'Going, Going', in *High Windows* (London: Faber, 1991), reprinted in *Collected Poems* (London: Faber, 1988), p. 189.
7. G. Tomasi de Lampedusa, *The Leopard* (London: Collins, 1957), pp. 145–7.

8. Martin Wiener, *English Culture and the Decline of the Industrial Spirit, 1850–1980* (Cambridge: Cambridge University Press, 1981), pp. 154–66.

9. Armand Hammer with Neil Lydon, *Hammer: Witness to History* (London: Simon & Schuster, 1987), p. 382.

10. Linda Christmas, *Chopping Down the Cherry Trees* (Harmondsworth: Penguin, 1991), p. 58.

11. Paul Theroux, *The Kingdom by the Sea* (Harmondsworth; Penguin, 1987), pp. 295–6.

12. Jack Webster, *Another Grain of Truth* (London: Collins, 1988), pp. 140–48.

13. Jonathan Raban, *Coasting* (London: Collins Harvill, 1986), p. 150.

14. ibid., p. 166.

15. ibid., p. 286.

16. Jonathan Raban, *Soft City* (London: Hamish Hamilton, 1974), p. 160.

17. J.U. Nef, *War and Human Progress* (New York: Russell and Russell, 1951), pp. 383ff.

18. See Harvie, op. cit., particularly Chapters 2 and 10.

19. See Lessing's Introduction to *The Golden Notebook* (London: Panther, 1973), pp. 1–21.

20. Tony Benn, *Conflicts of Interest: Diaries 1977–80* (London: Hutchinson, 1990), p. 276, entry for 8 February 1978.

21. For the literary background, see Cairns Craig (ed.), *The Twentieth Century*, Volume 4 of *The History of Scottish Literature* (Aberdeen: Aberdeen University Press, 1988).

22. See William Donaldson, *Popular Literature in Victorian Scotland* (Aberdeen: Aberdeen University Press, 1986); and Christopher Harvie, 'Gnawing the Mammoth: History, Class and Politics in the Modern Scottish and Welsh Novel', in Gavin Wallace (ed.), *The Scottish Novel, 1970–1991* (Edinburgh: Polygon, 1993).

23. Alasdair Gray, *1982 Janine* (Harmondsworth: Penguin, 1985), p.185.

24. D.I. Mackay and G.A. Mackay, *The Political Economy of North Sea Oil* (London: Martin Robertson, 1975), p. 42.

25. John McGrath, *The Cheviot, the Stag and the Black, Black Oil* (Breakish: West Highland Publishing Co., 1974), pp. 27–8.

26. John McGrath, Introduction to *The Cheviot, the Stag and the Black, Black Oil* (London: Methuen, 1983), pp. v–xiv; and see Laurence Gourievidis, 'The Image of the Clearances in Scottish History', unpublished Ph.D. thesis, St Andrews University, 1993.

27. *Scots Independent*, August 1973.

28. Alan Massie, *One Night in Winter* (London: Jonathan Cape, 1984), p. 112.

29. In 'Devolution Diary', *Cencrastus*, No. 22, 1986, p. 10.

30. James Campbell in conversation with the author, 1983.

31. James Campbell, *Invisible Country: A Journey through Scotland* (London: Weidenfeld & Nicolson, 1984), p. 57.

32. Cairns Craig, 'Scotland Ten Years On', *Radical Scotland*, February/March

1989, p. 9. Kenneth O. Morgan, *The People's Peace* (Oxford: Oxford University Press, 1990) regards the devolution issue as merely an 'essay in survival' by the Labour government (p. 371).

33. Gray, *Lanark*, op. cit, pp. 492–3.
34. Liz Lochhead, from 'Quelques Fleurs (A Tale of Two Sisters)', in *Bagpipe Muzak* (Harmondsworth: Penguin, 1991), pp. 45–6.
35. George Mackay Brown, *Greenvoe* (Harmondsworth: Penguin, 1976), p. 249.
36. Stuart C. Aitken, 'A Transactional Geography of the Image-Event: the Films of the Scottish director Bill Forsyth', in *Transactions of the Institute of British Geographers*, New Series, Volume 16, No. 1 (1991), pp. 105–18.
37. Cited in S. L. Malcolmson, 'Modernism Comes to the Cabbage-Patch', *Film Quarterly*, 38, 1985, pp. 16–21.
38. Alastair Dunnett, *Among Friends* (London: Quartet, 1985), p. 179.

CHAPTER 10   OIL AND MRS THATCHER (pp. 286–308)

1. Sidney Pollard, *The Development of the British Economy: 1914–1990*, fourth edition (London: Edward Arnold, 1992), p. 278.
2. Bernard Donoughue, *Prime Minister: The Conduct of Policy under Harold Wilson and James Callaghan* (London: Cape, 1987), p. 191.
3. Michael Artis and David Cobham (eds.), *Labour's Economic Policies, 1974–1979* (Manchester: Manchester University Press, 1991), p. 302.
4. *Britain* (London: HMSO, 1993), p. 376.
5. J. Graeme Robertson, *The Environmental Impact of North Sea Oil-Related Developments on Scotland* (Portree: Habitat Scotland, 1984), pp. 83–8.
6. Neil Robertson, 'Oil and the Non-Oil Economy in Scotland', in *The Scottish Government Yearbook, 1984* (Edinburgh: Unit for the Study of Government in Scotland, 1984), p. 100.
7. Alexander Kemp, 'North Sea Oil Policies: an Assessment', in *The Scottish Government Yearbook, 1984* (Edinburgh: Unit for the Study of Government in Scotland, 1984), p. 68.
8. Margaret Thatcher, *The Downing Street Years* (London: HarperCollins, 1993), pp. 595–7.
9. Denis Healey, *The Time of My Life* (1989; Harmondsworth: Penguin, 1990), p. 401.
10. Nigel Lawson, *The View from Number Eleven* (London: Bantam, 1992), pp. 220, 372.
11. *Observer*, 16 February 1975, p. 13.
12. Richard Funkhouser, interview, 21 March 1994.
13. Sidney Pollard, *The Wasting of the British Economy* (London: Croom Helm, 1982), pp. 2–3.
14. ibid., p. 379.

15. Sir Iain Gilmour, *Dancing with Dogma* (London: Simon & Schuster, 1982), p. 46.

16. D. Harvey and K. J. Thomson, 'Costs, Benefits and the Future of the Common Agricultural Policy', *Journal of Common Market Studies*, Vol. XXIV, No. 1, September 1985.

17. C. J. Harbury and Richard G. Lipsey, *An Introduction to the United Kingdom Economy* (London: Pitman, 1986), p. 119.

18. R.E. Rowthorn and J.R. Wells, *Deindustrialisation and Foreign Trade* (Cambridge: Cambridge University Press,) pp. 180ff.

19. Kenneth O. Morgan, *The People's Peace, 1945–1990* (Oxford: Oxford University Press, 1992), pp. 446ff.

20. Susan Strange, *Casino Capitalism* (Oxford: Basil Blackwell, 1986), pp. 18–20.

21. The *Guardian* estimated Mark Thatcher's wealth at around £20 million (2 October 1993); *Business Age* estimated his mother's wealth at anything up to £100 million (September 1993).

22. *Keesing's Contemporary Archives* (London: Longmans, April 1986), col. 34319.

23. Hugo Young, *One of Us* (London: Macmillan, 1991), p. 144.

24. David Howell, *Blind Victory: a Study in Income, Wealth and Power* (London: Hamish Hamilton, 1986), p. 24.

25. ibid., p. 185.

26. Interview with Professor John Foster, October 1993.

27. Richard Funkhouser, conversation, 21 March 1994.

28. Howell, op. cit., p. 186.

29. Dominic Lawson, 'The Recession Strands the North Sea Minnows', *Financial Times*, 17 January 1986.

30. Adrian Hamilton, 'Curse of the Nationalised Jobsworth Lives On', *Observer*, 2 January 1994.

31. Nigel Lawson, 'The Moral Dimension', in Arthur Seldon (ed), *The Coming Confrontation* (London: Institute of Economic Affairs, 1978), pp. 190–92.

32. Andrew Billen, 'Tory Party Blues', *Observer Magazine*, 26 September 1993, p. 28.

33. Quoted in Evelyn Abbott and Lewis Campbell, *The Life and Letters of Benjamin Jowett*, Vol. I (London: John Murray, 1897), p. 241.

34. Cited in William Keegan, *Mr Lawson's Gamble* (London: Hodder & Stoughton, 1989), p. 44.

35. Quoted in Reiner de Man, 'United Kingdom Energy Policy and Forecasting: Technocratic Conflict Resolution', in Thomas Baumgartner and Atle Midttun, *The Politics of Energy Forecasting* (Oxford: Clarendon Press, 1987), p. 135.

36. ibid., p. 124.

37. Brent F. Nelsen, *The State Offshore: Petroleum, Politics and State Intervention on the British and Norwegian Continental Shelves* (New York: Praeger, 1991), p. 189.

38. Keegan, op. cit., p. 94.

39. Speech of 18 March 1986, cited in *Keesing's Contemporary Archives* (London: Longmans, April 1986), col. 34384.

40. Alex Salmond, interview, 19 March 1994.
41. Richard Funkhouser, interview, 21 March 1994.
42. Roy Jenkins, *A Life at the Centre* (London: Macmillan, 1992), p. 444ff.
43. David Marquand, interview, September 1993.
44. *Financial Times*, 11 December 1984, pp. 11–13.

CHAPTER II   THE GLASS IS FALLING (pp. 309–36)

1. *Financial Times*, 18 April 1984; *Scotsman*, 31 January 1987.
2. *Scotsman*, 20 August 1986.
3. *Scotsman*, 20 June 1983, 14 September 1983.
4. *Economist*, 12 May 1984, p. 81.
5. Lucy Kellaway, 'UK Oil Supply Industry: the Worst is yet to Come', *Financial Times*, 7 November 1986.
6. *Scotsman*, 2 May 1984.
7. *Der Spiegel*, No. 14, April 1982, p. 123.
8. Ian Hargreaves and Dominic Lawson, 'Crisis at BNOC: Retreating, not Retiring', *Financial Times*, 11 December 1984, p. 18.
9. *Financial Times*, 11 December 1984.
10. *Financial Times*, 11 December 1984.
11. *Der Spiegel*, No. 19, May 1986, p. 151.
12. *Hansard*, Vol. 75, 1984–5, cols. 304–5 (13 March 1985).
13. Dominic Lawson, 'The Recession Tide Strands the North Sea Minnows', *Financial Times*, 17 January 1986.
14. *The Times*, 11 September 1982.
15. Frank Frazer, 'Dealers Turn Present Oil Crisis into Future Profits', *Scotsman*, 18 July 1986.
16. Robert S. Martin, 'North Sea Oil's New York Connection', *Glasgow Herald*, 4 May 1987.
17. Anthony Sampson, *The Seven Sisters*, third edition (London: Coronet, 1988), pp. 346–8.
18. Susan Strange, *Casino Capitalism* (Oxford: Basil Blackwell, 1986), p. 20.
19. *Economist*, 13 February 1993, p. 72.
20. Alex Salmond and J. Walker, 'The Oil Price Collapse: Some Effects on the Scottish Economy', Fraser of Allander Institute, *Quarterly Economic Commentary*, Vol. 12, No. 2, November 1986, pp. 63–9.
21. W.J. Pike, 'The Oil Price Crisis and its Impact on Scottish North Sea Development, 1986 1988', in *Scottish Economic and Social History*, Vol. 13 (1993), pp. 56–71.
22. Gordon Brown, *Where There is Greed* . . . (Edinburgh: Mainstream, 1989), p. 37.
23. Margaret Thatcher, speech of 15 March 1986, in *The Revival of Britain:*

Speeches on Home and European Affairs, 1975–1988, compiled by Alistair B. Cooke (London: Aurum Press, 1989), p. 202.

24. Gordon Brown, *Where There Is Greed*, p. 26.
25. *Scotsman*, 10 April 1986.
26. Jean Stead, 'Lean Times Ahead for Oil Capital', *Guardian*, 6 May 1986.
27. House of Commons, Session 1990–1991: Energy Committee, Fourth Report, *Decommissioning of Oil and Gas Fields* (London: HMSO, 20 March 1991), p. 110.
28. Max Wilkinson, 'A £6 Billion Demolition Job', *Financial Times*, 9 September 1986.
29. *Scotsman*, 19 August 1991 (interview with Dr Graham Picken, Aberdeen University).
30. Malcolm MacGarvin, *The North Sea* (London: Greenpeace: Collins & Brown, 1990), p. 108.
31. *Financial Times*, 17 March 1987.
32. 'Hamish Paton' (Donald Bain), *Energy: Scotland's Second Chance?* (Edinburgh: Scottish Centre for Economic and Social Research, 1991).
33. Cited in *Der Spiegel*, No. 21, May 1986, p. 142.
34. Abstracted in *Financial Times North Sea Letter*, 231, 13 February 1980, pp. 6–7.
35. Jan Fagerberg, Adne Cappelen and Lars Mjoset, 'Structural Change and Economic Policy: the Norwegian Model Under Pressure', *Norsk Geografisk Tidsskrift*, Vol. 46, 1992, pp. 95–107, 101.
36. ibid., p. 102.
37. Brent F. Nelsen, *The State Offshore: Petroleum, Politics and State Intervention on the British and Norwegian Continental Shelves* (New York: Praeger, 1991), p. 188.
38. 'Kein Silicon Valley', *Der Spiegel*, No. 21,. May 1986, pp. 142–4.
39. ibid., p. 103.
40. *Britannica Book of the Year* (1993).
41. *Special Report: the North Sea, Petroleum Economist*, August/September 1992, p. 12.
42. *Offshore Engineer,* September 1993, Norway Supplement, p. 5.
43. This account is taken from the *Scotsman*; Ed Punchard, *Piper Alpha: A Survivor's Story* (London: W.H. Allen, 1990); and *The Public Inquiry into the Piper Alpha Disaster*, by Lord Cullen, Department of Energy, Cmnd. 1310 (London: HMSO, November 1990).
44. Punchard, op. cit., pp. 146–59.
45. *Scotsman*, 11 July 1994.
46. *Scotsman*, 9 July 1994.
47. Interview with Jack Donaldson, *Scotsman*, 9 July 1988.
48. Alan Hutchison, 'The Patched-Up Platform', *Scotsman*, 22 July 1988.
49. Cited in Hutchison, art. cit.
50. *Scotsman*, 13 November 1990.
51. *Scotsman*, 3 August 1990 and following days.

52. *Scotsman*, 24–9 August 1990.
53. *The Cullen Report*, op. cit., p. 1.
54. ibid., p. 2.
55. ibid., p. 2.
56. ibid., p. 3.
57. ibid., p. 3.
58. *Scotsman*, 16 August 1990; *Petroleum Economist*, August/September 1992, p. 22.
59. Ross Leckie, 'Long Hours, Low Pay, and the Grimmest Job Around', *Scotsman*, 22 July 1988.

CHAPTER 12   THE MUEZZIN AT KYLE (pp. 337–55)

1. Rudyard Kipling, 'The Dutch in the Medway (1664–1672)'.
2. See Sir Iain Noble's Fletcher of Saltoun lecture, 1992 (Edinburgh: Saltire Society, 1992).
3. Eric Hobsbawm, *Politics for a Rational Left* (London: Verso, 1989).
4. See Jim Sillars, *Scotland: the Case for Optimism* (Edinburgh: Polygon, 1985).
5. George Rosie, *Losing the Heid* (Edinburgh: Scottish Centre for Economic and Social Research, 1990).
6. See Nick Kochan and Hugh Pym, *The Guinness Affair* (London: Christopher Helm, 1987).
7. See Christopher Harvie, *Scotland and Nationalism* (1977; London: Routledge, 1994), Chapter 7.
8. Christopher Smout, 'The Scottish Identity', in Robert Underwood (ed.), *The Future of Scotland* (London: Croom Helm, 1977), p. 19.
9. Jack Brand, *The National Movement in Scotland* (London: Routledge, 1978), p. 20.
10. Michael Fry, *Patronage and Principle: A Political History of Modern Scotland* (Aberdeen: Aberdeen University Press, 1987), p. 148; Levy, op. cit., p. 53.
11. William L. Miller, *The End of British Politics* (Oxford: Clarendon Press, 1981).
12. Mark Cox, 'Scotland's Export Performance: a Closer Look', Fraser of Allander Institute, *Quarterly Economic Commentary*, Vol. 12, No. 4, May 1987, pp. 64–6.
13. Grampian Regional Council, *Oil and Gas Prospects: 1993 Update* (Aberdeen: Grampian Regional Council, 1993), p. 7.
14. David Smith, *North and South: Britain's Economic, Social and Political Divide* (Harmondsworth: Penguin, 1989), p. 251.
15. John Scouller, 'The BP bid for Britoil: Should Scotland take it lying down?', Fraser of Allander Institute, *Quarterly Economic Commentary*, Vol. 13, No. 3, March 1988.
16. See Michael Keating, *Glasgow: the City that Refused to Die* (Aberdeen: Aberdeen University Press); Ian Spring, *Phantom Village* (Edinburgh: Polygon, 1989).
17. James Scott, 'The Role of the Scottish Financial Sector', Fraser of Allander

Institute, *Quarterly Economic Commentary*, Vol. 18, No. 4, June 1993, pp. 52–5; Chris Baur, 'Finance Organisation in Search of a Role', *Scotland on Sunday*, 6 March 1994.

18. Richard Funkhouser to Craig Campbell, Scottish Council Research Institute, 10 July 1979.

19. Scottish Development Agency, *120*, No. 1, 1988, p. 9.

20. *Economist*, 20 March 1993.

21. Richard Funkhouser, conversation, 22 March 1993.

22. Halford Mackinder, *Democratic Ideas and Reality* (London: Constable, 1919).

23. Anthony Sampson, *The Arms Bazaar* (London: Sphere, 1979).

24. 'Die Zeit der goldenen Quellen geht zu Ende', *Der Spiegel*, No. 16, 14 April 1986, pp. 166–9.

25. See the essays in Paul B. Stares (ed.), *The New Germany and the New Europe* (Washington: Brookings Institution, 1992).

26. Mervyn Jones and Fay Godwin, *The Oil Rush* (London: Quartet, 1976), p. 24.

Index

INDEX